حادى الأرواح إلى بلاد الأفراح

DRIVING THE SOULS TO THE ABODES OF HAPPINESS

TRANSLATION OF ARABIC ORIGINAL TEXT TO ENGLISH

Explained by Ibn Qayyim al-Jawziyyah
Translated by Abdul Ali Hamid

www.darussalam.com

Darussalam International Publications Limited

Office : 0208 539 4885
Fax: 020 8181 6544
Web : www.darussalam.com
Email : info@darussalam.com

FOREWORD

It is another valuable work of well-known scholar Ibn Qayyim al-Jawziyyah. It was written to create interest in the hearts of the Muslims to work in order to get entrance into Paradise. The book is written in Arabic and its title is حادى الأرواح إلى بلاد الأفراح, which literally means "Driving the souls to the abodes of happiness".

The author eloquently detailed the beauty and luxury of the Gardens, which Allah has prepared for those who sincerely believe in Him and do good deeds in accordance with what His Messenger, Allah's peace and blessing be upon him.

He started the book by asserting that Paradise and Hell are created and they are in existence. He did so because there were groups among the Muslims who believed that they are not present at the moment and that Allah will create them when the Day of Judgement comes. He refuted their claim and proved beyond doubt that both Paradise and Hell are in existence now. He quoted Abu 'l-Hasan al-'Ash'ari, the leader of the people of the Sunnah, who cited the beliefs of the followers of the Qur'an and the Sunnah, which included belief in the existence of Paradise and Hell and their being created. He also asserted that both Paradise and Hell will remain forever. He repeated at the end of the book the beliefs of the followers of the Qur'an and the Sunnah from the 'Masa'il' of Harb, one of the disciples and followers of Imam Ahmad.

He dealt with another issue which was debated among the Muslim scholars which is about the Garden where Adam was lodged after being created and expelled from it: was it on earth or was it the same Garden which the believers will enter?

He presented the arguments of both groups and was inclined to support the view that it was on earth.

He then goes to describe the gates, numbers, levels, names, wideness and keepers of Paradise, and all that Allah has prepared in it for His successful and devoted worshippers. He, the Glorious, has declared in a Divine Hadith:
"I have prepared for my righteous servants that which no eye has seen, no ear has

heard of and no heart has imagined."

He goes in detail to describe the luxurious materials of Paradise, decoration of the palaces and apartments and their furniture. He mentions the beauty and charm of the virgin dark-eyed women whom Allah has created for His friends. He mentioned at the end of the book the categories of the people who are going to enjoy these pleasures and delights.

He based his discussion on the Qur'anic verses and authentic sayings of the Prophet, ﷺ. However, it is noted that he quoted reports that are not very genuine. It would have been better if he had avoided citing them. His main sources in this are the books of al-Hakim, al-Bayhaqi, Ibn Abi al-Dunya and Abu N'aym al-Isfahani. They are not very reliable, and record in their books Traditions the chains of which are not authentic. The author indicated the weakness of some of the reports and left others to the discretion of the readers.

The book was written in Arabic as many other books of the author. I decided to translate it in English because some brothers who did not know Arabic were keen to know what is in it. I had to drop some parts because they were related with discussions of grammatical points or some reports that were repeated. I also did not translate a long poem (48 lines) by the author, which he put in his introduction.

I acknowledge those who helped post translation to bring the manuscript to publishing readiness especially Robert Farooq, the Project Co-Coordinator of al-Naṣr Centre, who took the trouble of going through the manuscript and correcting English. May Allah the Almighty reward them for their support!

I hope that Allah Almighty will make it beneficial to the readers. I pray to Allah, the Most Powerful and Mighty, to include us among the people who will achieve His pleasure and be among those who will enjoy the bounties and graces of Allah, the Exalted.

Abdul Ali Hamid
Slough, Berks. U.K.
SL1 3PP
e-mail: dr.aahamid@gmail.com

GLOSSARY

The following is the explanation of terms used in the book to denote theological groups:

Al-Mu'attilah: Another name given to the followers of Jahm ibn Safwan. It means those who deny Allah's names and attributes. They believe that human acts are predestined upon him.

Batiniyah: (Arabic) Meaning internal or inner, a term used by Muslim theologians to refer to groups and sects who interpreted religious texts exclusively on the basis of their hidden or inner meanings (Arabic: batin) rather than their literal meanings (zahir). Chief among them are the Ismaili Shi'is, the Druz and the Alawite of Syria. Some Sufi orders were labelled as Batiniyah as well.

Jahmiyyah: Followers of Jahm ibn Safawan (killed in 746). According to Jahm only a few attributes can be predicated to Allah, such as creation, divine power and action whilst others such as speech cannot. Therefore, he believed that it was wrong to talk about the eternal word of the Qur'an, since Allah (according to Jahm) is not a speaker in the first place.

Khawarij: (Arabic: who went out, English: Kharijites).The name is given to a number of groups who rebelled against the Fourth Caliph Ali ibn Abi Talib during his struggle with Mu'awiyah ibn Abi Sufyan, the governor of Damascus at that time. When Alı ibn Abı Talib accepted the offer made by Muawiyah at the battle of Siffin in 657, a group from Alı's army defected, saying that judgment belonged only to Allah and not to a human conference.

Majus: (Arabic: Zoroastrian) The Majus is a term originally applied to Persian priests but later was applied by the Arabs more generally to anyone who was a Zoroastrian.

Mujassimah: (Arabic), Anthromorphists (English). They are those who believe that Allah has a jism (body) but not like the (created) bodies, rather [with] a jism that befits Him. They were of many of sects, though they differed between them on the shape of Allah. The great theologian Abu al-Hassan al-'Asha'ri presented 16 different views on this matter.

Mushabihah: Another form of Anthropomorphism. It is concerned with the question as to whether Allah resembles human beings in his features (attributes), actions, and emotions. The issue was raised in debates about statements in the Qur'an and Hadith as well as in efforts made by early Muslims to distinguish their religious beliefs from non-Islamic ones, especially those of the ancient Near Eastern cultures, the Greeks and Christians. Political conflicts within the Muslim community in the eighth century may have intensified the debate.

Mu'tazilah: (Arabic: Those Who Withdraw, or Stand Apart, English Mutazilites). This theological school is traced back to Wasil ibn 'Ata' (699-749), a student of al-Hasan al-Basri, who by stating that a grave sinner (fasiq) could be classed neither as believer nor unbeliever but was in an intermediate position (*al-manzilah bayna manzilatayn*), withdrew (*i'tazala,* hence the name Mu'tazilah) from his teacher's circle. They called themselves the "People of Justice and Unity" ('*Ahl al-'Adl wa al-Tawhid*) holding that Allah is Just and Unitary. Their doctrine is based on five principles: Unity, Justice, the intermediate stance, promise and punishment and commanding the good and prohibiting the bad. Their most famous doctrine held was that the Qur'an was created. They argued in favour of it to prevent a plurality of eternals. This doctrine was used in the *mihnah* (ordeal) of the early Abbasids Dynasty. Their speculative theology influenced all later theological movements in Islam and is being revived in some circles today.

Qadariyah (or Qadariya): A name given to a group who adheres to the doctrine of free will. The word Qadar is derived from *qadr* (power or rights). It was one of the earliest theological schools of thought in Islam, its adherent hold the view that humans have free will and are not limited by Qadar or predestination.

Qaramitah, or **Qarmatı:** (Arabic. English: The Carmathians, also spelled Karmathians). An offshoot of early Ismaili. The group is a revolutionary one and is founded by Hamdan al-Qarmati (disappeared c. 286/899). Their doctrine was a mixture of extreme Shi'i thought, Gnosticism and other philosophical ideas. They captured the Black Stone from the Ka'bah in 317/929, which they kept for over twenty years. With the rise of the Fatimids dynasty in Egypt, the group lost its momentum and later absorbed into the main Ismaili Shi'is.

Sabi'ah: (Arabic), Sabaeans, or Sabeans (English) A group of people mentioned in the Qur'an three times, regarded as ahl al-kitab (people of scripture), entitled to special privileges under Islamic rule. Scholars have identified the group with either the residents of the kingdom of Saba', or Sheba, in South Arabia, or a group of star worshipers in northern Syria in the area of Harran. Remnants of Sabean still reside in modern Iraq. They follow the teachings of John the Baptists. They are known as the Mandaeans or Sabean Mandaeans.

Barzakh: The period between the death and resurrection

CONTENTS

INTRODUCTION

Praise belongs to Allah Who made Paradise a resting place for His believing slaves. He made easy for them to reach it by doing good deeds and they dedicated themselves to strive for them. He facilitated for them the path leading to it. He created it for them before He created them and put them up in it before He brought them into existence. He made the path to it filled with unpleasant deeds to human beings. The Almighty then brought them to this world to test which of them does good deeds. He fixed the time of entrance to it the day when they will come to Him, and appointed the period of the vanishing life a date for them. The Most Beneficent deposited in it what no eye has ever seen, no ear has ever heard of and its thought has not passed in any mind. He revealed it to them so they were able to see it by the eye of insight, which is sharper than the physical eye. He gave them good tiding of what He has prepared for them through His best Messenger and completed the good news by saying that they would abide there forever and would not desire leaving.

Praise be to Allah, Creator of the heavens and earth Who made the angels messengers. He sent messengers bearing good news and warning, so that mankind would have no excuse before Allah, after receiving the messengers. He did not create them in vain and did not leave them uselessly. He did not leave them neglected but has created them for a great matter and prepared them for an important work. He established two abodes for them, one for those who responded to the caller and did not look for any one in replacement of their Honourable Lord; and the second one for those who did not pay attention to the call, turned a deaf ear to it and did not set any hope on it.

Praise is for Allah Who was pleased with little deeds from His slaves and relinquished many of their shortcomings, bestowed upon them His favour. He took upon Himself to be merciful and set down in the Book He wrote before He created the heavens and earth that His mercy dominated His wrath. He called His worshippers to the Home of Peace and included everyone in His call to remove the excuse and maintain the justice. He chose those He selected for help and guidance as a favour and bounty from Him. This is how He acted with justice and wisdom. He is the Almighty and Wise. It is His bounty He grants it to whoever He wills. Allah is possessor of immense bounty.

I bear witness that there is no being worthy of worship but Allah, alone having no partner with Him. It is the witness of His slave, the son of His slave and the son of His maiden. He cannot do without His favour and mercy for one moment, and he has no hope in being successful to attain Paradise and get rid of Hell without His pardon and forgiveness. I also bear witness that Muhammad is His slave and Messenger and His trusty on His Revelation. He is the best of His creatures, He sent him as the mercy for the whole worlds, a model for the working people, an example for the spiritual people and a proof for all the believers. Almighty sent him as a caller to the faith inviting the mankind to the Home of Peace. He came as the guide for the people, reciting His Book, striving to achieve His pleasure, commanding what is good and forbidding what is bad. Allah, the Most Wise, sent him after a break of sequence of the Messengers, and guided the people by him to the straight path and clear way. He made obedience to him compulsory, and commanded them to love him, support him and fulfil their duties to him. He closed all the entrances to Paradise except through following his way. If the people come from all directions and try every door He will not open it unless they come through him and had followed his teachings and his ways.

Glory is to Him Who opened His Messenger's breast, removed his burden, raised his reputation high and placed humiliation and disgrace on those who violated his command. He embarked on calling to Allah and His Paradise openly and secretly and announced it among the people day and night. His call resulted in the appearance of the dawn of Islam, and the sun of the faith rose bright. The word of the Most Merciful went high, the call of Satan vanished. The light of his message illuminated the earth after it was darkened, and the hearts were brought together after their differences. The face of the time shone in beauty, the darkness turned into light and every confused person got the right path. When Allah, the Most High, perfected His religion through him and completed His blessing, spread His mercy over the creature, and the Messenger passed His message with sincerity to the people, and strove in the cause of Allah faithfully; Allah gave him choice between staying in the world and meeting with Him. Having desire of meeting with Allah and because of his love for Him, he chose to depart from this world. Allah moved him to the High Companion and the noble place. He left after he set the community on bright path and clear way. His Companions and followers followed his footsteps to the Gardens of pleasure and those who did not pay attention to his call went to the ways of Hell.

"So that who were to die might die after seeing a clear proof, and those who were to live might live after seeing a clear proof. Allah is, surely, All-Hearing, All-Seeing." *(8:42)*

May Allah, His angels, His Prophets and Messengers and all His believing slaves send blessing to him, as he singled out Allah for worship, gave us knowledge of Him and called the people to Him!

Allah, the Exalted, did not create the creatures in vain and leave them alone. He rather created them for a great matter and important assignment. This great assignment was offered to the heavens, the earth and the mountains but they refused to undertake it and were afraid of it. They said: 'Our Lord, if You command us, we will listen and obey, and if You give us option, we will choose to be released of it, and will not exchange it for anything else.' However, mankind despite his weakness and incapability of carrying it out undertook it, and being ignorant and unjust took it upon himself to fulfil it. Many people could not carry it out because of its heaviness and gravity, and they passed their life in this world like grazing animals. They paid no attention to recognize their Lord and His right upon them. They never thought about the purpose of their creation and settlement in this world, which is only a passage and crossing to the permanent home. They paid no attention to the fact that their stay in this vanishing world is only for a short period and soon they will move to the Hereafter. The sensual matters controlled them and their reasoning power slipped away. Negligence dominated them and vain desires and false deceptions misled them. Long hope deceived them and their hearts were covered by bad deeds. Their interest rested only in the pleasure they found. When some worldly fortune appears to them against the pleasure of the Hereafter, they rush to it in groups and alone, and when some benefits of the world come to them they do not mind sacrificing the reward and pleasure of Allah for it.

"They know outer surface of the worldly life, and they are unaware of the life to come." *(30: 7)*

"They forgot Allah, so He made them forget themselves. They are the rebellious ones." *(59: 19)*

It is a matter of great surprise from the heedlessness of a man that every moment of his life is counted, every breath he takes is not going to return to him. The mounts of day and night are speeding with him, but he never pays attention where he is being taken. He is moved faster than the mail but he is not aware to which of the two homes he is being moved. When death comes to him, his worries increase because of the devastation of his soul and disappearance of his pleasure. It is not due to what he sent forward of the crimes and shortcomings as he did not send anything ahead for his life. During his lifetime anytime the thought of what he has been created for came to his mind, he dismissed it for relying on pardon of Allah, and said that we have been told that He is the Most forgiving, Most Merciful, as though he was never told that His punishment is the most painful one.

When the guided people realised the purpose of their creation and the objective of coming to this world, they raised their heads and saw the banner of Paradise raised for them. They hurried to it and realised that its straight path has been made clear to them. They stood fast on it and saw what no eyes had ever seen, no ear had ever heard of and no mind had ever thought about it. They became aware that selling this valuable and eternal commodity with little comfort of this world is like confusing dreams, or the fantasy that appeared in sleep. They understood that this life is full of worries and distress. If it makes one laugh for a while, it makes him cry for long. It brings happiness for a day and causes anguish for months. Its pains are more than its pleasures. Its suffering is greater than its delight. Its beginning is full of fears and its end is destruction. How strange it is that a stupid person in the form of a smart one, and a crazy one in the shape of reasonable one, prefers the vanishing contemptible matter over a lasting, precious one. He sells the Garden as wide as the heavens and the earth for a narrow prison among the people of diseases and suffering. He exchanges the pleasant residence in Paradise below which the rivers flow with dirty and narrow places the end of which is ruin and perdition. He chooses filthy and disgusting women of evil characters, adulteresses and secret lovers in place of virgins loving and of matching age like rubies and brilliant pearls. He goes for despicable whores instead of dark-eyed and sheltered maidens. He abandons the rivers of wine, a delight for its drinkers, and goes for a filthy drink that spoils the reason and destroys the world and religion. He forsakes the pleasure of looking at the Face of the Mighty and Merciful for looking at the horrible repulsive face. Instead of listening to the address of the Most Merciful he listens to music and songs. He prefers sitting in the company of the disobedient Devil, to sitting on the cushions of pearls and rubies. He does not pay attention to the call of the caller: 'O people of Paradise! Lead a comfortable and care free life without being distressed, live without suffering death and remain young without the fear of being old.' Instead the song of the singers absorbed him:

'Your love made me standstill where you are, now I cannot go ahead or back. I find blame for your love delightful, let the accusers reproach me.'

The clear deceit of the sale will be exposed of the Day of Resurrection and the stupidity of the seller will result in the regret and grief. On that Day the righteous will be gathered as an honoured company before the Lord of Mercy, and the sinful will be driven like a thirsty herd into Hell. A caller will call for the entire world to see: 'Let the people of gathering know who deserves more honour among the slaves.' If the person who stayed behind those lucky companions thinks about the honour which Allah bestows on His dedicated slaves, and the bounty and favour He has preserved for them, and the reward He kept secret for them, which no eye has ever seen, no ear has ever heard of and no imagination has ever thought of, he will realize what a valuable commodity he has lost. He will understand that his life has no value and he is counted among the scraps. On the other hand the fortunate ones will find out that they have attained a great opulence, which is not going to be affected by calamities and is not going to end. They have succeeded in getting the permanent delight near the Great, the Exalted. They will be leading a life of ease and comfort in the meadows of Paradise, leaning on beautiful cushions and reclining on the beds whose linings are of silk brocade. They will enjoy the company of large eyed fair women, and relish the variety of fruits.

"Everlasting youths will go round among them with glasses, flagons, and, cups from a flowing spring. They will not suffer from headache, nor will they be intoxicated. (They will have) fruits of what they select, and the meat of any bird they like from whatever they desire. (And for them) are fair women with large beautiful eyes, like pearls well protected pearls, as reward for what they used to do." (56: 17-24)

"Dishes and goblets of gold will be passed around them with all that their souls desire, and their eyes delight in, and you will abide there forever." (44: 71)

It was announced in the market of recession, and only a few people responded. How strange is that its seeker was asleep and its suitor did not take interest in its dower! How life was pleasant after listening to the news of it, and how the lover found rest without embracing its virgins! How the souls of the believers had patience, and how most hearts of the people turned away and what replacement they had! (There is a long poem about 48 lines in the description of Paradise that has not been translated).

This is a book I have struggled in its composition, arrangement, classification and division into chapters. It is a source of comfort for the distressed, and unveiling of those brides for an aspiring man. It is stimulating the hearts to a desired goal, and driving the souls to meet Allah, the Holy, the King. The reader will enjoy it and the one who looks through it will be thrilled. A companion will not be fed up with it and a friendly person will not feel bored by it. It contains the unique lessons and incomparable information. A man who is interested in search may not find such information in any other book. It is based on number of Prophetic sayings and the statements of the Companions and the Followers. The secrets of many verses of the Qur'an are revealed. There are amazing anecdotes in it. It solves many difficult problems and clarifies the fundamental questions about the Divine Names and Attributes. When a man reads it he will increase in his faith and the Paradise will be presented to him as though he sees it openly. It is stimulating the desires to the meadows of the Gardens and arouses the noble ambitions towards peaceful life in those lofty dwellings. I named it

حادى الأرواح إلى بلاد الأفراح

'Driving the souls to the abodes of happiness'.

It is a name that matches its contents, and a word that denotes its meaning. Allah knows well my intention and objective for its composition and writing. He, the Exalted, is with the tongue and heart of every slave and aware of his intention and work. My aim is to give good tiding to the followers of the Sunnah about what Allah, the Most Gracious, has prepared for them in Paradise. It is they who deserve to have good news in the world and the Hereafter, are entitled for the secret and open bounties of Allah, as they are the friends and allies of the Messenger; and those who neglect his way are his enemy and opponents. These devoted people do not care for the reproach of anyone in the support of the Prophet's way and do not abandon what has been proved of it for the saying of anyone. The Sunnah is greater in their hearts than any juristic opinion, disputed discussion, Sufi imagination, theological inconsistency, philosophical analogy or political judgement. If someone puts any of the above before the Sunnah of the Prophet, the door of the right is closed for him and the way of guidance is shut before him.

O reader, you have the benefit of it and the author will bear its loss. You have the pure part of it and the author will have the filth of it. This is his little merchandise offered to you and the result of his thought presented to you. If it finds a capable and kind person, he will keep or release it in right manner, otherwise only Allah can help. What is correct in the book comes from the One Who is Gracious, and what is wrong; it comes from Satan and me. Allah and His Messenger are free from it.

I have divided the book into the following seventy chapters:

Chapter 1: The declaration that Paradise exists now

Chapter 2: Dispute among the scholars whether Paradise in which Adam was lodged was this eternal one or another one on earth.

Chapter 3: The arguments of those who say that it was the eternal Paradise

Chapter 4: The arguments of those who say that it was on earth

Chapter 5: Reply of these people to those who oppose them

Chapter 6: Refutation by those who claim that it is the eternal Heaven to the arguments of their opponents

Chapter 7: Illustration of the doubts of those who claim that Paradise has not been created

Chapter 8: Refutation of their doubts

Chapter 9: The number of the gates of Paradise

Chapter 10: Illustration of their width

Chapter 11: Description of these gates

Chapter 12: The distance between one gate and another

Chapter 13: The location of the Heavens

them before

I pray to Allah, the Exalted, to make it purely for His sake, and bring its author, its reader and its copyist close to Paradise of pleasure. May Almighty make it a proof for its author and not against him, and benefit by it anyone who reads it. He is the best one to be asked, the noblest one to be hoped for. He is Sufficient for us and He is the best Protector.

CHAPTER 1:
DECLARATION THAT PARADISE IS IN EXISTENCE NOW

The Companions of the Messenger of Allah ﷺ, their followers and their followers and the people of the Sunnah and the Hadith as well as the jurists, the Sufis hold the belief that Paradise is created and exists now. They support their view by the texts of the Qur'an and the Sunnah and the fact that all the Messengers, from the first to the last, have affirmed it. They called their communities to believe in it. This was the situation until the misguided group of the Qadariyyah and Mu'tazilah appeared and denied its existence. They claimed that Allah will create it on the Day of Resurrection. They base their view on their false rule concerning the acts of Allah. They suggest to Allah what He should do and what He should not do. They compare Almighty with His creation in acts. After that they reached the point of denying the Attributes of Allah saying that creation of Paradise before accounting is vain, as it will remain neglected for a long period without having anyone inside it.

They argued that it is known that if a king prepared a house and arranged all types of food and facilities in it and kept it neglected without allowing people to enter it for prolonged period, his work would be considered unwise, and the reasonable people would find it open for criticism. They declared the Lord Almighty incompetent by their corrupt reasoning and false thinking. They compared His work with the works of the people and rejected the texts that did not comply with their faulty principles concerning Allah, the Exalted, or distorted their meaning. They declared those who oppose them as misguided or innovators, and stuck to the principles which cause the reasonable people laugh. To refute these beliefs the early scholars asserted in their belief system that the Heavens and Hell are created. Those who wrote about this asserted that it was the view of all the followers of the Sunnah and the Hadith without there being any dispute about it.

Abu al-Hasan al-'Ash'ari wrote in his book, *The Statement of the Muslims and*

Dispute of the Believers, "The total belief of the people of Hadith and the Sunnah is to have faith in Allah, His angels, His Books, His Messengers and whatsoever has come down from Allah and reported by the reliable sources from the Messenger of Allah ﷺ. They do not reject any of them. They also believe that Allah is the only Deity, One, Single, Eternal; He has no spouse or son, that Muhammad is His slave and His Messenger, and Paradise is truth, and Hell is truth, the Hour is definitely coming and Allah will raise those who are in the graves. Allah is on His Throne as He has said:

"The Lord of mercy established on the Throne." *(20: 5)*

He has two hands, which cannot be described as He said:
"I created him (i.e. Adam) by My Hands." *(38: 75)*
"His Hands are open wide." *(5: 64)*

He has two eyes indescribable, as He said:
"It (i.e. the ark of Noah) floated under Our watchful eyes." *(54: 14)*

The Almighty has a face as He confirmed:
"The Face of your Lord, full of majesty, bestowing honour, will remain." *(55: 27)*

It is not appropriate to say the Names of Allah are apart from Him as the Mu'tazilah and the Khawarij have said. The followers of the Sunnah affirm that Allah possesses knowledge as He stated:
"He sent it down with His full knowledge." *(4: 166)*
"No female conceives or gives birth without His knowledge." *(35: 11)*

They asserted that Allah has hearing and seeing and did not deny it from Him as the Mu'tazilah did. They also asserted the power for Allah as He has said:
"Did they not realize that Allah, who created them, was stronger than them?" *(41: 15)*

They also said that no good or bad takes place on earth without the will of Allah, and everything is found with His permission. He stated:
"You do not will except that which Allah wills." *(76: 30)*

Or as the Muslims say: 'What Allah willed was done, and what He did not, was not done.'

They also believe that no one can do anything before Allah wills it, nobody can get out of the knowledge of Allah and no one can do something which Allah knows that he will not do it. They assert that there is no creator beside Allah. It is He who creates the acts of the people and they have no power to create anything. Allah guided the believers to His obedience and deserted the unbelievers. Almighty showed kindness to the believers, put their affairs right and showed them right path, but He did not show mercy to the unbelievers and deprived them from His guidance. If He had decreed for them good luck, they would have been put on the right path; and had He guided them, they would have been rightly guided. Allah has power to amend the affairs of unbelievers and be kind to them to become believers. But He willed them to remain unbelievers, left them in lurch and sealed their hearts. All good and bad are by the decree and will of Allah.

They believe in the fate and the Divine Decree whether good or bad, sweet or bitter. They also believe that they are not able to bring any good or bad to themselves except what Allah wills. They refer their affairs to Allah and assert their poverty and need to Allah in all the matters. They believe that the Qur'an is the word of Allah uncreated. The pronunciation of the Qur'an is neither created nor uncreated. They also believe that Allah, the Glorious, will be seen by physical eyes on the Day of Judgment as the full moon is seen. Only the believers will see Him, the unbelievers will not be able to see Him; they will be screened off their Lord. Allah said:
"Indeed from their Lord they will be kept veiled." *(83: 15)*

They also say that Musa, peace be upon him, asked Allah, the Glorious, to see Him in the world, but when He revealed Himself to the mountain, He made it crumble. The Almighty thus told Musa that he cannot see Him in the world, but will see Him in the Hereafter. The followers of the Sunnah do not declare any Muslim as unbeliever for committing a grave sin like adultery, theft and so on. Such a person remains believer even after committing a grave sin. The belief according to them is to believe in Allah, His angels, His Books, His Messengers and in fate whether good or bad, sweet or bitter. They also believe anything that missed them was destined not to reach them, and what they received was not to miss them. Islam to them is to witness that there is no god but Allah, and Muhammad is the Messenger of Allah, and Islam is different from Iman (belief).

They declare that it is Allah who turns the hearts. They also believe in the intercession of the Messenger of Allah ﷺ, and that is for those of his followers who committed grave sins. They also have faith in the punishment of the grave, and that the pool is true, the bridge is true and the resurrection after death is true, Allah's calling His slaves for accounting is true and standing before Allah for reckoning is true. They also believe that faith is combination of statement and deed, which increases and decreases. They also hold that the Names of Allah Almighty are Himself. They do not declare any of the believers who committed grave sins to be among the people of Hell, or any of the believers to be among the people of Paradise; it is to Allah, the Exalted, to place them where He wishes. However, they hold that Allah, the Most High, will take a group of true believers from Hell as the reports from the Messenger of Allah ﷺ, have stated. They refuse to get involved in dispute about religion and arguments about fate. They avoid debate in those matters, which the people of controversy discuss. They accept what has been reported by reliable narrators from the Messenger of Allah ﷺ. They do not ask why and how, they consider this question as innovation.

They also maintain that Allah, the Exalted, does not command evil, but rather prohibits it and commands good deeds. He did not accept association of other being with Him though it is under His power of will. They recognize the rights of the ancestors who were chosen by Allah Almighty for the company of His Messenger ﷺ. They acknowledge their merits and refrain from discussing what happened among them. They put Abu Bakr ahead of others then 'Umar, then 'Uthman then 'Ali and believe that they were the rightly guided Caliphs, and the best persons after the Messenger of Allah ﷺ. They also accept the reports of the Messenger of Allah ﷺ, concerning the descending of Allah Almighty to the lowest heaven and asking people: 'Is there anyone who is asking for forgiveness' and so on.[1]

They refer every matter to the Book and the Sunnah according to the commandment of Allah:
"If you are in dispute over any matter, refer it to Allah and the Messenger."
(4: 59).

They consider following the early religious scholars as commendable, and avoid taking the way which Allah has not permitted. They believe that Allah, the Most High, will appear on the Day of Judgement as He said:

----
1. Bukhari (1145), Muslim (758)

"And your Lord comes with the angels, row after row." *(89: 22).*

They confirm that Allah, the Exalted, comes close to His creature as He wishes: "We are closer to him than his jugular vein." *(50: 16).*

They consider performing two 'Id prayers, Friday prayer and congressional prayer valid behind every righteous or evil person. They consider wiping over the socks Sunnah at home and while travelling. They regard struggle against the unbelievers as obligatory since the time Allah sent His Messenger to the last group who will fight *Dajjal* (ant-Christ). In the meantime they desire to pray for the leaders of the Muslims to be on the right course and not to fight them in situation of sedition. They believe in appearance of *Dajjal* and that Jesus, the son of Mary, will kill him. They also have faith in *Munakar* and *Nakir*, the ascension of the Prophet (*mi'raj*) and dream in sleep. They also assert that prayer for the Muslims and giving charity after their death brings benefit to them. They affirm the existence of sorcerers and consider them unbeliever as Allah has stated. [2]

They approve of funeral prayer over every dead person of the believers whether righteous or evildoer. They assert that Paradise and Hell are created, and anyone who dies, dies at his appointed time and anyone who is killed, is killed at his appointed time. The provision comes from Allah Almighty, which He gives to His creatures whether lawful or unlawful. Satan whispers to mankind and creates confusion and doubt in their minds. The righteous people may be chosen by Allah for some particular signs to be shown by them. The Sunnah cannot be abrogated by the Qur'an. The fate of children is in the hand of Allah; if He wishes, He may punish them or do whatever He wishes. Allah is aware of what the people do; He has decreed it because everything is in the hand of Allah.

They consider patience on the command of Allah right, and regard following what He has commanded and refraining from what He has prohibited as the duty of believers. They are commanded to make their acts purely for the sake of Allah, and to be helpful to the Muslims. They consider as obligatory to worship Allah alone and show sympathy to the community of the Muslims, and to avoid grave sins like adultery, telling lies, disobedience, arrogance, haughtiness, conceit and to defame people. They believe in keeping away from anyone who calls to innovation, and recommend people to engage in reading the Qur'an, writing

2. Cf the Qur'an (2: 102)

and reporting the narrations and studying the *fiqh* with humility, and lowliness, and good behaviour, show magnanimity and avoid hurting people, backbiting, slandering and investigation of other people's food and drink.

The above are the total of what the followers of the Sunnah promote and abide by. We follow all that they believe in and act upon them. Our support comes from Allah alone. He is Sufficient for us and He is excellent supporter. We seek His help and put our trust in Him, and to Him is the return.

This long passage was quoted here to show that all the followers of the Sunnah and Hadith believe that Paradise and Hell are created. We quoted the statement of Al-Ash'ari so that this book is based on recognizing those who deserve the above mentioned good tiding, and that they are the people who believe in what is mentioned. The guidance comes only from Allah.

The matter of Paradise being created is indicated in the Qur'an, when Allah said: **"He (the Prophet) saw him (i.e. Gabriel) by the lot tree beyond which none may pass near the Garden of Restfulness."** *(53: 13-15)*

The Prophet ﷺ, saw the lot tree and saw the Garden of Restfulness near it as reported in the two authentic records of Hadith[3] on the authority of Anas who related the story of nocturnal journey by the Prophet ﷺ. At the end of it says: "Then Gabriel took me until he reached the lot tree which was covered by colours which I cannot describe." He further said: "Then I entered Paradise and it had domes of pearl and its ground was of musk."

It is also recorded in two Sahihs[4] on that authority of Abdullah ibn 'Umar that the Messenger of Allah ﷺ, said: "When one of you dies, his place is shown to him in the morning and evening. If he is from the people of Paradise, his place in it is shown to him; and if he is from the residents of Hell, his place in it is shown to him. He is told that it is your place of living till Allah, the Most High, raises you."

In the Musnad of Imam Ahmad, the Sahih of Hakim and Ibn Hibban and others al-Bara'ibn 'Azib's narration is cited as follows: 'We went out in the funeral of a man from the helpers.'

---

3. *See Bukhari (349), Muslim (163)*
4. *Bukhari (1378), Muslim (2866)*

Then he narrated the story at length and related that the Prophet ﷺ, said: "Then a caller calls from the heaven: My servant has spoken the truth, so prepare a spread for him from Paradise and provide him with dress from Paradise, and open for him a door to Paradise. Then he receives its fragrance and sweet odour." [5]

The following report is in two Sahihs[6] on the authority of Anas that the Messenger of Allah ﷺ, said: "When a slave is put in his grave and the people turned away from him, he listens to the sound of their shoes; then two angels come to him, seat him and ask him: 'What do you say about this man?'

The believer will say: I bear witness that he is the slave of Allah and His Messenger. They will say to him: Look at your place in Hell, Allah has replaced it with a place in Paradise. He will see them both."

Al-Bara' narrated a long report from the Prophet ﷺ, about the taking of the soul, it included the following part:

"Then a gate from Paradise and another from Hell are opened for him and said to him: 'This was your place if you had disobeyed Allah Almighty, but now it has been changed for this.' When he would look what is in Paradise, he would say: 'O Allah, bring the Hour quickly so that I can return to my family and wealth.' He will be told to rest." [7]

Abu Sa'id related: 'We attended a funeral with the Messenger of Allah ﷺ, and he said: "People, this community are tested in their graves. When a person is buried and his companions turn away from him, an angel holding a hammer comes to him. He seats him and says: 'what do you say about this man i.e. Muhammad?' If he is a believer, he will reply: 'I bear witness that there is no god but Allah, and Muhammad is His slave and Messenger.' They will say: You told truth. Then a door from Hell will be opened for him and they will say: 'this was your place if you had disbelieved in your Lord. But since you are a believer this is your place, and a door

from Paradise will be opened for him. He will try to stand to go to it, but they will tell him to rest." [8]

---

5. Ahmad (18559), Hakim (1: 37) See also Abu Dawud (4753)
6. Bukhari (1338), Muslim (2870)
7. Abu Dawud (4754)
8. Ahmad (3/ 11000), al-Bazzar (872)

'A'ishah narrated: 'The sun was eclipsed during the lifetime of the Messenger of Allah, ﷺ. Then she related the story and said: 'The Messenger, may the peace and blessings of Allah be upon him, stood and spoke to the people. He praised Allah with what He deserves then said: "The sun and the moon are the signs of Allah, the Exalted, they do not eclipse for the death or birth of anyone. When you see it, take resort to prayer."

He further said: "I saw in this situation all that you have been promised. I wanted to pick a bunch of fruit from Paradise when you saw me advancing. I also saw Hell where some of its people were crushing others when you saw me retreating." [9]

Abdullah ibn Abbas reported: 'The sun eclipsed during the period of the Allah's Messenger, blessing and peace of Allah be upon him.' Then he cited the story and said that the Prophet spoke on the occasion and said: "The sun and the moon are the signs of Allah, the Exalted. They do not eclipse for the death or birth of someone. When you see it, engage in remembrance of Allah."

The Companions said: 'Messenger of Allah, we noticed that you were trying to pluck something then you retreated?' He said: "I saw Paradise and plucked a bunch of grape, if I kept it, you would have eaten from it till the end of the world. I also saw Hell and I did not see more horrible scene than today. I noticed that women make up the majority of the people of Hell."

The Companions asked: 'why is it so, Messenger of Allah?

He replied that it was because of their ungratefulness.

They asked: 'It was because they deny Allah?'

He replied: "They show ungratefulness to their husbands and deny their kind acts. If you act nicely to one of them throughout your life and she notices something wrong from you, she will see: 'I never saw anything good from you.'" [10]

Asma' bint Abu Bakr narrated the Prophet ﷺ saying in the above story. "Paradise came close to me. Had I had courage I would have picked some fruits from it. Hell

9 Muslim (901), see also Bukhari (1040, 1063, 1463)
10. Bukhari (1052), Muslim (Kusuf: 902)

also came close to me till I said: My Lord! Am I one of its people? I saw a woman being mauled by a cat. I asked: What is the case with her? I was told that she tied it till it died of hunger. She did not feed it nor leave it to find its food." [11]

Jabir related similar story. It included in it that the Messenger ﷺ, said: "Everything you are going to see was presented to me. Paradise was shown to me and I intended to pick a bunch of fruit from it but my hand did not reach it, and the Hell was shown to me and I saw a woman from the children of Israel being punished concerning a cat."

He said further: "Nothing of what you have been promised but were presented to me in this prayer of me, Hell was brought to me. When you saw me coming back that was because I was scared of being touched by its flame. I saw the man of the hook dragging his guts in Hell. He used to steal the pilgrims by his hook. When someone noticed him, he would say that it stuck to my hook, and when he did not notice he went away with it. I also saw the owner of the cat who fastened it and did not feed it nor released it to find vermin to eat until it died of hunger. Then Paradise was presented to me and there you saw me advancing and rest in my place. I extended my hand to pick its fruit so that you see it, then it occurred to me not to do it. All things you are promised I saw in this prayer." [12]

The same story was related by Abdullah ibn Amr in which the Prophet ﷺ said: "By the One in whose hand Muhammad's soul is, Paradise was brought near me to the extent that if I had extended my hand, I would have plucked its fruits. Hell was brought so near to me that I feared that it may touch me." [13]

Anas ibn Malik narrated that while the Messenger of Allah ﷺ stood for the prayer, he said: "People I am your Imam, so do not go before me to ruku' or sujud and do not raise your head before me because I see you from front and behind of me. By the One in whose hand my soul is if you were to see what I have seen, you would laugh little and cry much."

The companions asked: 'what did you see, Messenger of Allah?'

11. Bukhari (745)
12. Muslim (Kusuf: 904)
13. Abu Dawud (1194), al-Nisa'i (1481)

He replied: "I saw Paradise and Hell." [14]

Ka'b ibn Malik reported that the Messenger of Allah ﷺ be upon him, said: "The souls of the believers are birds hanging on a tree of Paradise till Allah returns them to their bodies on the Day of Resurrection." [15]

The above Hadith makes it clear that the souls of the martyrs will enter Paradise before the Day of Resurrection. It has been made clear in a report of Tirmidhi [16] that the souls of the martyrs are in the craws of green birds hanging on the tree of Paradise. The full text of the report will be cited at the end of the book.

Abu Hurayrah reported that the Messenger of Allah, blessings and peace of Allah be upon him, said: "When Allah Almighty created Paradise and Hell, He sent Gabriel to Paradise and said to him; 'Go and look at it and see what I have prepared for its people.' He went and watched what Allah had prepared for its residents. After returning he said to Allah: 'By Your might, no one will hear about it but will enter it.' So Almighty filled the way to it with discomfort. He asked Gabriel again to go and watch it. He came back and said: 'I am afraid that no one will be able to enter it.'

Then Allah, the Exalted, sent him to Hell to see what has been prepared for its people. He went and saw that its residents crushing one another. He came back and said: 'By Your might and honour, no one who hears about it will enter it.' Allah then filled it with desires and sent Gabriel again to see what is there. He came back and said: 'I am afraid that no one will be able to avoid it." [17]

Abu Sa'id al- Khudri related that the Prophet ﷺ, said: "Paradise and Hell argued and Hell said: 'My Lord! Why is that the only weak and lowly people enter it (i.e. Paradise)?' Paradise said: 'My Lord! Why only arrogant and haughty people enter it?' Almighty said to Paradise: You are my mercy, I will show it to whomever I wish; and said to Hell: 'you are my punishment I afflict with it whoever I wish. Each of you will get its full." [18]

---

14. Muslim (112, 113)
15. Al-Nisa'i (2072), Tirmidhi (1641), Ibn Majah (1412), Ahmad (6493)
16. (1641), See Ahmad (27233)
17. Tirmidhi (2560), Abu Dawud (4744), Ahmad (8406)
18. Muslim (2847), Tirmidhi (2561)

Ibn 'Umar narrated that the Prophet ﷺ, said: "Hell complained to its Lord and said: 'My Lord, some of my people crush others.' So Almighty allowed it to have two breathes, one in the winter and the other in summer." [19]

Abd al-Malik ibn Bisher reported from the Prophet ﷺ, that he said: "No day passes but Paradise and Hell ask Allah Almighty; Paradise says: Lord, my fruits are ripe and my rivers are full and I am desirous to my friends, so make them come to me quickly. Hell says: 'my heat had become intense, my depth has gone deeper and my flames are great, so bring my people quickly to me." [20]

Anas reported the Prophet ﷺ, as saying: "While I was walking in Paradise I passed by a river the parts of which were of domes of hollow pearls. I asked: what is this Gabriel? He replied: This is the Kawthar that Allah has given you. The angel touched it by his hand and found that its ground was of highly flavoured musk." [21]

Jabir related that he heard the Messenger of Allah, blessing and peace of Allah be upon him, saying: "I entered Paradise and I saw a palace in it. I asked for whom did it belong? I was told that it was for a man from Quraysh. I hoped to be the one. Then it was said to me that it belonged to 'Umar. If it were not for your sense of honour, Abu Hafs, I would have entered it. Hearing this 'Umar cried and said: 'I would feel jealous concerning you, Messenger of Allah?" [22]

The report of Bilal to whom the Messenger ﷺ, said: "I entered Paradise and heard your slipper's sound in front of me", will come later, if Allah wills.

Anas related: 'The Prophet ﷺ, performed the dawn prayer one day and extended his hand then withdrew it. When he completed the prayer it was said to him: 'Messenger of Allah, you did something in your prayer that you did not do in any prayer? He said:

"I saw Paradise and noticed an espalier with clustered fruit within his reach; its size was like cucumber. I intended to pick it but I was told to keep back. I saw Hell very close till I saw my shadow and yours. I made gesture to you to keep away. Then Allah revealed to me that let them because if you and they accepted Islam,

---

19. Bukhari (3260), Muslim (617)
20. Abu Nu'aym in his book "The description of Paradise" (85). It is a weak report
21. Bukhari (6581)
22. Muslim (Merits of the Companions: (2394)

30

you migrated and they migrated, and you struggled and they struggled you will be saved from it. I did not see any advantage for me over you except only by prophethood. [23]

If you ask what stopped you from arguing for the existence of Paradise by the story of Adam and his being lodged in Paradise and then being driven away from it after eating from the forbidden tree? Argument by it was very clear.

The reply will be that though argument by it is very clear to the common people, it is very complicated. The scholars are not agreed whether Paradise in which Adam was lodged was the eternal Paradise that the believers will enter on the Day of Resurrection or a garden on earth that was honoured. We will mention the views of both groups and their arguments concerning it, by the power and support of Allah.

23. Abu Nu'aym (85)

CHAPTER 2
THE LOCATION OF GARDEN IN WHICH ADAM WAS LODGED

The Scholars are in disagreement concerning the Garden in which Adam was lodged and expelled from it. Was it the Garden of Eternity or another Garden in a high place of the earth?

Mundhir ibn Sa'id wrote the following in his *Tafsir*: 'Allah said to Adam: "Live with your wife in the Garden." *(2: 35)*

A group of scholars said that Allah settled Adam in the Garden of Eternity, which the believer will enter on the Day of Resurrection. Others believe that it was another garden which Allah created for him and settled him in it and it was not the Garden of Eternity. This is an opinion for which there are many evidences.'

Abu al-Hasan al-Mawardi said in his commentary:'People are in disagreement about the garden in which Allah settled Adam. There are two views: One that it was the Garden of Eternity; second that Allah prepared a Garden for them and made it a place of test for them. It is not the Garden of Eternity, which has been made the place of recompense.

The ones who held the second opinion also differed among themselves. One group said that it was in the heavens because they were asked to go down of it. This is the view of Hasan.

The other group said that it was on the earth. They justify their view on the pretext that Allah put them to test in it by prohibiting them from eating a particular fruit with exclusion of other fruits. This is the view of Ibn Bahr. Allah knows the correct view.'

Ibn al-Khateeb (i.e. al-Razi) said in his renowned commentary: 'The people have disputed about the garden mentioned in the verse: was it on the earth or in the heavens? If it was in the heavens then was it the garden of reward and eternity or another garden? Abu 'l-Qasim al-Balkhi and Abu Muslim al-Isfahani said this garden was on earth. They explained 'going down' by moving from one place to another. The statement of Allah supports it:

"Go to any town." *(2:61)*

2. The second view is that it was in the seventh heaven; it is the opinion of al-Jubba'i.

3. The third opinion held by majority of our people is that it was the Garden of recompense. Abu -l Qasim al-Raghib said in his commentary: 'There is difference of opinion concerning the garden in which Adam was lodged. Some theologians are of the opinion that it was a garden which Allah made a place of examination; it was not the home of refuge (i. e. Paradise').

He cited some evidences for both views.

Among the people who mentioned the differences of the opinions is Abu 'Isa al-Rummani, who went to the view that it was the Garden of Eternity. He said that the view chosen by us is the one which is adopted by Hasan, 'Amr, Wasil and many of our fellows. Abu Ali and our teacher Abu Bakr also adopt it. It is chosen by the commentators of the Qur'an. However, Ibn al-Khatib preferred to be silent in the case, which is the fourth opinion.

4. Everything is possible and the evidences are conflicting. It is better to keep silent and not to give a definite answer. Mundhir ibn Sa'id said that it was a garden on earth and not the Garden of Eternity. It was the opinion of Abu Hanifah and his followers. He said: 'I noticed that some people embarked on our opposition concerning the garden of Adam and supported their view without any evidence except the claims and wishful thinking. They could not produce any evidence from the Book or the Sunnah or report from the Companions or their followers or their followers. We told them that the learned scholar of law from Iraq and his colleagues had said that Adam's garden was not the Garden of Eternity. These books are full of their knowledge and they were not isolated people but the leaders of the opposition. I said this to tell that I was not supporting the view of Abu Hanifah, but follow what has been proved to me by the Qur'an and the Sunnah.

This is Ibn Zayd al-Maliki who said in his commentary: 'I asked Ibn Nafi' about the Garden whether it was created? He replied: 'Keeping silent about this matter is better.'

Ibn Uyaynah commented on the following verse, saying that it applied to the earth: **"You will not go hungry in it or feel naked."** *(20: 118)*

Ibn Nafi' is an Imam and so is Ibn Uyaynah. The other group did not cite any authority like them.

Ibn Qutaybah said in his book *'al-Ma'arif.* 'After Allah created Adam and his wife, He left them saying to them: 'Bring about plenty children and fill the earth, get control over the fish of the seas, birds of the sky, cattle, the plants of the earth and its trees and fruits. So He told that Adam was created on the earth and it was there that He was ordered.

He further said that He set the Garden which included four rivers: Sayhun, Jayhun, Tigris and Euphrates.

He then spoke about the serpent and said that it was the biggest animal of the land. It said to the woman: 'if you eat from this tree you will never die.' Then he further said that Allah expelled him from the east of the Garden of Eden to the land from which he was taken. Then he quoted Wahab who said that Adam was brought to the east of the land of India. He further said that when Qabil killed his brother he carried his body until he reached a valley in the east of Eden where he buried it.

Mundhir ibn Sa'id said: 'Wahab ibn Minabbih relates that Adam was created on the earth and was settled in it. Allah set the Garden in Eden and four rivers emerged from its river, which was known as the Garden of Adam. These rivers remained on the earth, and there is no dispute about it among the people. Learn from this all of you with insight.

He also said that the serpent that spoke to Adam was the biggest beast of the land. He did not say the beast of the heaven. But these people say that the garden was not on the earth but in the seventh sky. He also said that Adam was taken out from the east of the Garden of Eden while in the Garden of Eternity there is no east or west because there is no sun.

He said that this news that Ibn Qutaybah mentioned speaks about the land of the Yemen and Eden. He also reported from Abu Hurayrah who said: 'Adam desired at the time of his death a bunch of the garden he was put in, and according to their claim it was in the seventh sky while Adam was on the earth. So, his children went in search of that bunch until the angels informed them of their father's death. Were the children of Adam crazy if what Ibn Qutaybah is saying true? We did not say anything other than what these scholars said. If it was the Garden of Eternity, Adam would have lived in it forever. We forwarded evidences from the Qur'an but our opponents claimed something for which there is no evidence.

These are some of the statements of those people who mentioned dispute in this matter, and we will cite the evidences of both groups and make our judgement.

CHAPTER 3
THE EVIDENCES OF THOSE WHO SAID THAT IT WAS THE ETERNAL GARDEN WHICH THE PEOPLE WILL ENTER ON THE DAY OF RESURRECTION

They claimed that their view is to be the one which Allah Almighty put in the instinct of the people, young and old. No other thought passed in their hearts, and most of them do not know any dispute about it.

They said Abu Hurayrah and Hudhayfah narrated that the Messenger of Allah ﷺ, said: "Allah, the Exalted, will gather the people. The believers will stand when Paradise will be brought near them, and go to Adam and ask him: 'Father, get the door of Paradise open for us.' He will say: 'It was the sin of your father which brought you out of Paradise.'" [24]

He cited the rest if the report. They said that it shows that the Garden from which Adam was expelled was the same which his children will ask him to get it opened.

The report about the argument of Musa and Adam mentions that Musa will say to Adam that you're the one who got yourself and us out of the Garden.[25]

If it were on the earth, it would have meant that they were taken out of gardens and not Paradise. The reply of Adam to the believers that it was the sin of their father that brought them out of Paradise proves it because his sin did not bring them out of a garden of the world.

They further argued that Allah, the Most High, said:
"We said, 'Adam, live you and your wife in the Garden. Both of you eat freely

24. Muslim (Iman: 195)
25. Bukhari (6614) Muslim (2652)

there as you will, but do not go near this tree, or you both will be wrongdoers.' But Satan made them slip, and removed them from the state they were in. We said, 'Go down all of you! You are each other's enemy. On earth you will have a place to stay and a livelihood for a time.'" *(2: 35-36)*

This shows that their going down was from Paradise to the earth for two reasons: Firstly the words 'go down' indicate moving downwards from a higher distance. Secondly, Allah's saying, "you have a place to stay" after saying "go down" shows that they were not on the earth before that. The Almighty affirmed this by saying in Chapter 7:
"In it you will live and in it you will die and from it you will be brought forth." *(7: 25)*

If the garden were in the earth, their living in it would have been before being expelled and after it.

They further argued that Allah, the Glorious, described the garden of Adam with specific qualities that are found only in the Garden of Eternity. He said: **"In it you will never go hungry, feel naked, be thirsty, or suffer the heat of the sun."** *(20: 119-120)*

It is not possible in the world because even if a man is in the most pleasant home, he will be subject to those things. Almighty put hunger and thirst opposite nakedness and heat of the sun. This was because the hunger is the disgrace of the inner side, nakedness is the disgrace of outside; thirst is the heat of inner side and the heat of the sun is the heat of outside. In this way He negated from the people of the Garden the disgrace of outside and inner side, and the heat of outside and the inner side. It is the best arrangement of opposites between hunger, thirst, nakedness and heat. All these are for the residents of the Garden of Eternity.

They also argued that if the garden were to be in the world, Adam would have noted the lie of Iblis in his statement: **"Shall I show you the tree of immortality and power that never decays?"**
(20: 120)

Adam knew that the world was going to end and its power would decay.

They went further to say that the story as cited in Chapter 2 shows clearly that the Garden from which Adam was expelled was above the heaven. Read it:

"When We told the angels, 'Bow down before Adam', they all bowed, but not Iblis, who refused and was arrogant: he was disbeliever. We said, 'Adam, live you and your wife in this Garden. Both of you are free to eat as you wish, but do not go near this tree, or you will both become wrongdoers.' But Satan made them slip, and removed them from the state they were in. We said, 'Get out, all of you! You are each other's enemy. On earth you will have a place to stay and livelihood for a time.' Then Adam received some words from his Lord and He accepted his repentance. He is Ever Relenting, the Most Merciful." *(34-37)*

These verses speak about bringing Adam, Eve and Iblis out of the Garden. For this reason the plural was used. It is said that the reference was to Adam and Eve and the serpent, but it is very weak view. There is no mention of serpent in the story of Adam, nor is there any indication of it in the context.

It is said that the address was for Adam and Eve, and the plural pronoun was used as it was done in Almighty's statement: "We witnessed their judgement" (21: 78) wile the case was for David and Solomon. All these explanations are weak. It is then proved that Iblis was included in the address and he was among those who were ordered to get down. Now the Almighty spoke of the second bringing down. He said: **"We said, 'Get out, all of you! But when guidance comes to you from Me, as it certainly will, there will be no fear for those who follow My guidance nor will they grieve.'"** *(2: 38)*

It is clear that this second bringing down is other than the first one. The latter refers to bringing down from the heavens to the earth and the first from the Garden. This shows that the Garden from which Adam was brought down is above the heavens. Al-Zamakhshari claimed that Allah's address: "Get out, all of you!" is particularly for Adam and Eve. The plural was used to include their progeny. It is proved by Divine order: "Get out both of you, all being enemy for one another." *(20: 123)*

He said that it is shown by the following statement:

"Whoever follow My guidance will have no fear nor will they grieve. But those who disbelieve and deny Our messages shall be the inhabitants of the Fire, and there they will remain forever." *(2: 39)*

This is a general rule for all the people.

The meaning of Allah's saying: "You are enemy of one another" refers to what the people are in enmity, injustice and misguiding of one another. What al-Zanakhshari has chosen is the weakest explanation of the verse. The enmity mentioned by Allah Almighty is the enmity between Adam and Iblis and their progeny. Allah said:
"Satan is your enemy, so treat him as enemy." *(35: 6)*

Allah, the Exalted, has affirmed the point of enmity between Satan and mankind repeatedly in the Qur'an because of its necessity for mankind to take care against their enemy. As for Adam and his wife He informed in His Book that Almighty created her so that Adam finds tranquillity in her, and He put love and compassion between them. Love and compassion are between a man and his wife while enmity is between Satan and mankind. Earlier Adam, his wife and Iblis are mentioned - who are just three - then why are they referred to as 'some'? It is incompatible with the sequence. In fact al-Zamakhshari failed to explain the verse.

As for the saying of Allah Almighty: "He said, 'Get down from it both of you, you are one another's enemy'", it addressed to Adam and Eve. The Almighty made them enemy of one another. The pronoun in 'Get down both of you' is referring to Adam and his wife or Adam and Iblis. Adam's wife is not mentioned because she is subordinate to him. In this case the enmity is for those who were ordered to get down and they are Adam and Iblis. It is obvious. So the verse contains two things: First Allah's order for Adam and his wife to get down. Second is information of enmity between Adam and his wife and Iblis. The Almighty told them clearly: "Surely, he is enemy for you and your wife". *(20: 117)*

He also warned his progeny:
"Satan is your enemy, so treat him as enemy." *(35: 6)*

Consider how all the places where enmity is mentioned, plural pronoun is used, as for order of getting down is concerned, it is mentioned in plural, dual and singular forms. The example of singular use is in the following verses: "Get down from it." *(7: 13, 38: 76)* This order was for Iblis only. Where the order occurred in dual form it either refers to Adam and his wife as they were who ate from the tree and committed the disobedience, or to Adam and Iblis because they are the fathers of the humans and jinn. He mentioned them in order for their progeny to learn a lesson. What supports this opinion that the pronoun in His statement: "Get down both of you from it" refers to Adam and Iblis, is that when Almighty mentioned the sin, He mentioned Adam alone not his wife. The example is:

"Adam disobeyed his Lord and was led astray. Later his Lord chose him, accepted his repentance and guided him. He said, Get out of it all of you." *(20: 121-123)*

This shows that the order of getting down was for Adam and the one who seduced him to disobey, the wife was included as subordinate.

Allah intended to tell humans and jinn about the calamity brought to them by their parents who disobeyed the order of Allah. To mention both of them was more effective in this matter than to mention only the parents of mankind. Almighty informed that the wife ate with Adam and he was expelled from the garden for this eating. It follows that the wife was treated in the same way, and her fate was similar to Adam's.

The statement "Get out, you are enemy of one another" refers to the group. It is not appropriate to refer to the two where it occurred in dual form.

The supporters of the view that the garden was the Eternal one further said that it is to be noted that the Garden was mentioned with definitive article in all the places. There is no garden known to the people except the Eternal one which Allah, the Beneficent, has promised His slaves, which is not seen. This word has become a name for it because of its regular use like al-Madinah (the city) al-Najm (the star), al-Bayt (The House of Allah) and al-Kitab (the Book) and other words. Anywhere the word al-Jannah is mentioned in definitive form, it will refer to the well-known Garden, which the believers know. If any other garden is meant it is cited in indefinite form or in genitive construction or the context will indicate it. The examples are:

"Two gardens of grape." *(18: 32)*

"Why did you not say when you entered your garden"? *(18:39)*

"We tried them as We tried the owners of the garden." *(68; 17)*

They further argued that Adam's Garden was the Eternal one is supported by the following statement of Abu Musa al-Ash'ari: 'When Allah Almighty expelled Adam from the Garden, he supplied him with the fruits of the Garden and taught him the skill of everything. This fruit you eat comes from Paradise except that it gets rotten and that does not rot.

They also said that Allah, the most Merciful, promised Adam that if he repented and turned to Him, He would return him to it. It is borne out by the commentary of Ibn Abbas on the following verse:

"Adam received some word from his Lord, and He accepted his repentance."
(2:37)

Ibn Abbas said: 'Adam said to Allah: My Lord didn't You create me with Your hand? He replied: 'Yes.' He said: 'Didn't You blow in me from Your spirit?' Almighty replied: 'Yes.' 'Didn't You settle me in Your Garden?' Adam asked.

Allah replied, "Yes." Adam said, "Does not Your Mercy dominate Your wrath?" The Almighty replied, "Yes." Adam said, "If I turn to You in repentance and mend my way, are You going to return me to the Garden?" He replied, "Yes."

This commentary has been reported through various chains. One of them goes as follows:

'Adam said to his Lord after he committed the mistake: "My Lord what will happen if I repented and did good deeds?" The Lord said. "I will return you to the Garden." These are the arguments of those who claim that the Garden of Adam was the Eternal one. Now we move to the claim of their opponents.

CHAPTER 4

THE CLAIM THAT THE GARDEN OF ADAM WAS ON THE EARTH AND IT WAS NOT THE ETERNAL ONE

The scholars who hold this view claim that there are many evidences to prove that the Garden of Adam was not the Garden of Eternity but it was a garden on earth. Here are some of them:

Allah, the Most Glorious, stated on the tongues of all His Messengers that admission into the Garden of Eternity will be on the Day of Resurrection. Its time has not yet come. Allah, the Exalted, has given many descriptions of it. It is impossible that Allah Almighty describes a thing with particular character and it is not according to it. For instance He described the Garden which is prepared for the righteous people as being the place of staying forever. Anyone who enters it stays there forever, and Adam did not stay there forever. He described it as the Garden of Eternity, but Adam did not live in it eternally. Almighty also stated that it was the home of reward and recompense and not the place of commandments and prohibitions. He also said that it was the place of complete safety and not the place of test and trial, but Adam was put in great trial in it. He spoke about it saying that it was a place where Allah will not be disobeyed, but Adam disobeyed Allah in the garden he was lodged. Almighty also said that it was not the home of fear and sorrow, but the parents suffered from great fear and sorrow because of what occurred. He described it as the abode of safety,[26] but the parents were not safe there from trial. He described it as the home of permanent settlement,[27] but they did not stay there forever. He said about the people in it that they were not to get out of it,[28] but the parents were driven out of it. Almighty said that the people in it will not suffer from worries,[29] but Adam ran and started covering himself from the leaves of its trees; this is exactly the worries. Allah stated that

---

26. See the Qur'an (6; 127)
27. Ibid (40; 39)
28. Ibid (15; 48)
29. Ibid (15; 48)

there will be no idle talk or sin,[30] but Adam faced the lie of Iblis.

Allah named it 'seat of truth', while Iblis told lie in it. Allah Almighty said to the angels: "I am putting a successor on earth." He did not say: "I am putting a successor in the Garden of Restfulness." The angels said: "Are You going to put in it someone who will cause corruption and shed blood?" (2: 30)

It is unthinkable that it should take place in the Garden of Eternity. Allah told us that Iblis said to Adam: "Should I show you the tree of immortality and power that will not decay?" If Allah Almighty had put Adam in the Garden of Eternity and unending power, why didn't he reply to Iblis: How can you show me something which I have already got? Allah Almighty did not tell Adam when He put him in the Garden that he was going to be immortal. If Adam knew that it was the Garden of Eternity, he would have not listened to Iblis or accepted his advice. Since He was not in the place of eternity, the Devil deceived him of eternal stay.

They further argued that if Adam was lodged in the Eternal Garden, which was the abode of sacredness where only clean and pure people can live, how then the dirty, filthy, condemned and banished Iblis got access to it? Not only did he enter it but was able to seduce Adam and whisper him. This whispering was either in his heart or his ear. In either case how was the outcast Satan able to enter the home of the righteous people? After being told to get out and warned that he was not allowed to show arrogance there, how would he be given chance to go up in the Garden of Restfulness on the seventh sky? Does this suit the statement of Allah: "It is not suitable for you to be arrogant in it"? (7: 13)

If his talk to Adam and his swearing to him is not arrogance, then what is the arrogance? If you say that his whispering reached the parents in the Heaven from his place in the earth, it is unreasonable from the point of language, sense and custom. If you claim that he entered the belly of the serpent and was able to whisper to them, it is more worthless. How can he ascend after being ordered to get down, and enter the Garden even in the belly of the serpent? If you say that he entered in their hearts and put his whispering, the question still remains. In addition, Allah related his talk to them, which they heard: "He said, Your Lord did not prohibit you from this tree." (7: 20) It indicates that he saw them and the tree.

---

30. Ibid (52: 23)

43

When Adam was out of the Garden, the Lord said to him and his wife: "Didn't I forbid you to approach that tree?" *(7: 22)*

Since Satan enticed them in the power and immortality, he referred to it by 'this', and Allah decided to take them out of it He used the word 'that' to indicate that they had no right to be in the Garden not even to see the tree they were asked to keep away. Allah said: "To Him rise good words." *(35: 10)*

The whispering of the accursed was the dirtiest words, which cannot rise to the holy lace.

Mundhir reported the Prophet ﷺ saying: "Adam fell asleep in the Garden."

There is no sleep in the Eternal Garden on the basis of the text and consensus of the Muslims. The Messenger of Allah, blessing and peace of Allah be upon him, was asked: 'Will the people of the Garden sleep?'
He replied: "No, sleep is similar to death, sleeping is death." [31]

The Qur'an has confirmed the similarity. [32]

Death is the change of condition and the Home of Peace is safe from change of conditions; the sleeping person is dead or like dead.

I say that the report referred to is a saying of Mujahid who said that Eve was created from the ribs of Adam when he was asleep.

Al-Suddi said: 'Adam was lodged in the Garden. He felt lonely not having a mate to find peace in her. Then he slept, when he woke up he found a woman sitting at his side. Allah created her from his rib. He asked her: 'Who are you?'
She replied: 'A woman.'
He asked: 'why are you created?
She replied: 'To provide peace to you.'

Ibn Abbas said: 'Allah caused Adam to sleep, and then He took a rib from the left side and filled with flesh. Adam was asleep and Allah created from that rib of him

---

31. *Reported by al-Bayhaqi in Shu'ab al-Iman*
32. *Q. (39: 42)*

his wife Eve in order to provide him with a source of tranquillity. When Adam woke up, he saw her beside him and said: 'My flesh, my blood and my soul.' He found tranquillity in her.'

The supporters of the claim that the Garden of Adam was on earth put forward the following argument:

There is no dispute that Allah, the Exalted, created Adam on the earth, and He never said that He moved him to the Heaven after that. If He had done so, it was worthy of mention because it was a great sign and great favour to him. It would have meant the ascension of his body and soul from the earth to the heavens. They said how will He move him and lodge him above in the heavens when He said to the angels that He was going to create a successor on the earth? How would He lodge him in the Eternal House from which no one comes out after entering it. The only point is that Allah, the Glorious, brought Iblis down from the heaven when he refused to bow down before Adam. But this is what He decided and it had to happen. After that He admitted Adam in to the Garden. Order of bowing down was immediately after the creation. If the Garden were above in the heavens, Iblis would have not got a chance to ascend to it after he was sent down from it. All those explanations forwarded by you are pretentions. For instance some people said that it is possible that Iblis ascended temporarily and not permanently. Others said that the serpent took him in; some said that he entered its belly. Some others said that his whispering may have reached from the earth to Adam and his wife in the Heaven. All this is arbitrariness and great pretention unlike what we have said that when Allah Almighty brought Satan down from the heavens because of his refusal to bow to Adam, the Devil was imbued with the enmity of Adam. When Allah lodged him in His Garden, his enemy felt jealous and began to plot by his scheme and deception to get him out of it. And Allah knows best.

They further said:
Another proof that the Garden of Adam was not the Eternal one, which the righteous slaves are promised is that when Allah, the Most Powerful, created Adam, He made him aware that there is an end for his life. He has not been created to remain forever. It indicated in the following report of Abu Hurayrah that the Messenger of Allah ﷺ said, "When Allah created Adam and blew spirit in him, he sneezed and said: 'Praise is to Allah'. He praised Allah by His permission.

His Lord responded by saying: 'May Allah show mercy on you.' Adam, go to those angels who were sitting. He went and said: 'Peace be on you', and they replied: 'And on you be peace'.

Then he returned to his Lord who said to him that it was the greeting for you and for your children among them. Allah then said while His hands were folded: 'Choose the one you wish.' He said: 'I choose the right hand of my Lord. Both hands of the Lord are blessed right. Allah then opened it and there were in it Adam and his progeny. Adam asked: 'Who are they, my Lord?' He, the Most Blessed, replied: 'They are your progeny.' Every person's age was written between his eyes. There was a man who was very bright. Adam asked: 'Who is he, my Lord?' Almighty replied: 'He is your son David, I have written forty years for his age.' Adam said: 'My Lord, increase in his life span.' Allah said: This is what I have written.' Adam said: 'My Lord, I give sixty years of my life to him.' Almighty said: 'Well, it is for you.'
Adam was lodged in the Garden as long as Almighty willed, afterwards he was brought down. He was counting his days of life. When the angel of death came to him, he said: 'You came early, my age is written to be one thousand years.' He said: 'Yes, but you gave sixty years of it to your son David.' Adam denied, and his progeny deny, he forgot and his progeny forget. From that day it was commanded to be written and witnessed."

This report shows clearly that Adam was not created in the home of Eternity, where once a person enters he does not die. But he was created in this vanishing world where Allah has fixed a known period for its residents, and it was there that he settled. If it is said that if Adam knew that he had a fixed time for his life, and that death would approach him one day and he was not to stay forever, how he did not realise the lie of Iblis when he said to him, **"Should I show you the tree of eternity?"** *(20:120)*

"Your Lord forbade you (to eat) so that you do not become immortal." *(7: 20)*

The answer is from two sides:
One that *Khuld* (immortality) does not necessarily indicate permanence and eternity, but it means long stay.

Second, When Iblis swore and deceived him and lured him and persuaded him for immortality, he forgot his age which was written for him.

They further contested that it is well known and undisputed fact among the Muslims that Allah, the Exalted, created Adam from the dust of this earth. He told us that He created him from an extract of clay, and from an altered dark mud. It has been explained as clattering because of dryness, or the one whose smell has changed. All these are the conditions of the dust, which was the beginning of him. The Almighty informed about the stages of the creation of his progeny as He said: **"From sperm-drop, then from a clinging clot, and then from a lump of flesh"** *(23: 5)*

He, glory be to Him, did not tell that He raised Adam from the earth to the heavens neither before creation nor after that. Where is then the evidence for taking his essence to the heavens, or raising him after his creation? You have no evidence and it is not indicated in the information of Allah Almighty.

They also said that it is well known that the Heaven is not a place for the dust, whose smell has changed. Its place is the earth, where all the rotten and spoiled matters are found. What is above in the heavens is not affected by change, evil smell or decay. It is a matter about which the reasonable people do not have any doubt.

They argued further that Allah, the Most High, said:
"As for those who have been blessed, they will be in Paradise, there to remain as long as the heavens and earth endure, unless your Lord wills otherwise- an unceasing gift." *(11: 108)*

Here The Almighty declared that the gift of the Garden of Eternity was not going to cease.

They contended that when we gather all that Allah, the Most Glorious, has said about Adam that He created him from earth, made him successor, and Iblis whispered to him in the place where he settled after being brought down from the Heavens, and Iblis refused to bow down to him and as a punishment was expelled.

Allah Almighty informed the angels that He was going to create a successor on earth. He also declared that the Eternal Garden was the place of recompense and reward for what the people had done. There will not be idle talk, sin or lie. Whoever enters it will not get out, and he will not be subject of despair, grief, fear or sleep. Allah has forbidden it for the disbelievers, whose head is Iblis. When all this information is put together, and a just man who has been raised above imitation pays attention to them, the correct idea will be clear for him. Only Allah can give help.

They said that if there was no other evidence apart from the fact that there was no commandment in the Garden, it would have been enough. Here the parents were commanded not to eat from the tree, which shows that it was a place of commandment not a place of recompense and eternity.

These are some of the arguments of the people who hold that the Garden of Adam was on earth and not in the heavens.

Allah knows the best.

CHAPTER 5
THE REFUTATION OF THE EVIDENCES OF THE FIRST GROUP BY THE SECOND

They said that we have declared that it is something which Allah has created in the nature of the people, and they are not aware of anything else. This is a traditional matter, which could be known only by the information of the Messengers. Now we and you have not received any information from the Qur'an, or logic or the natural disposition. What the Qur'an and the Sunnah of the Prophet indicate is to be followed. We challenge you to produce one Companion or a Follower, or an authentic report that the place where Adam was lodged was the Eternal Garden which Allah, the Exalted, has prepared for the believers. You will not find a way to do it. We have quoted the statements of the early scholars against what you claim. Since the word 'Garden' appeared in general in this story and it matched the Garden which Allah Almighty has prepared for His believing people, many people thought it to be that very Garden. If you mean by natural disposition that much, it is not going to help you at all. But if you claim that Allah created the people on it as He created them on considering the justice as good and injustice as bad and other natural dispositions, your claim is false. When we go to our instinct, we do not find this knowledge, as we know the obligation of binding matters and the impossibility of the absurd matters.

As for argument by the report of Abu Huraryrah in which Adam says: 'It is your father's mistake that brought you out of Paradise' it indicates Adam's delay in recognising in the world the mistake which he committed, which caused his expulsion from the Garden. He said in another version: 'I was forbidden to eat from the tree but I ate.' Where is any indication in this statement that it took place in the Garden of Restfulness? The same applies to the statement of Musa to Adam: 'You got yourself and us out from the Garden'. He did not say that you brought us from the Garden of Eternity.

Your claim that they were taken out to gardens similar to the garden on earth, the word 'garden' is used for them, but the difference between them and the

Garden of Adam is known only to Allah. Those gardens are like a prison compared with the Garden of Adam. Using the same word does not negate the difference between them.

Your argument by the statement of Allah: "We said: Get down" after their expulsion from the Garden does not imply descending from the heaven to the earth. It only means to move from a high place to a lower one. It is acceptable because it was a garden on the high ground and they were moved to a lower place. We have said that the command was for Adam and his wife and their enemy. If the Garden was in the heaven, their enemy would not have an opportunity to reach it after he was expelled because of refusing to bow down before Adam. The verse is clear evidence against your claim and various interpretations and vain explanations are not going to help you.

As for His statement: "You have a place of stay on earth and livelihood for a time", it does not indicate that they were not on earth before. The earth is a generic noun and they were on its higher and most pleasant place where they did not feel hunger, nakedness, thirst or sun, then they were moved to a place where they were subject to all these. Here is their life, their death and their resurrection from the graves. The Garden they were settled earlier was not a place of worry, fatigue, pain and other hateful matters. The land where they ended up was the place of fatigue, suffering pain and unpleasant matters.

Your statement that Allah has described the Garden with qualities that are not available in the world, its response is that how do you know that those qualities which were in the Garden Adam lived are not found in this world where he were taken? As for your saying that Adam knew that the world is going to end, if the Garden was to be on earth, he would have known the lie of Iblis, its response is by two ways:

First, the world 'Khuld' means long stay, and every thing's long stay is according to it. When a person lives long, he is called mukhallad. The Arabs called tripods khawalid because they remained for a long time after the disappearance of the ruins.

The second is that the knowledge of end of the world and coming of the Hereafter is acquired by the revelation. Adam was not yet appointed as a prophet to know it. He was made prophet and received revelation after he was brought down to the earth. The following statement of Allah Almighty attests it:

"Get out of the Garden as each other's enemy. If there comes to you guidance from Me - then whoever follows My guidance will neither go astray nor suffer" *(20: 123)*

Your statement that the word *'aljannah'* (garden) was cited in definitive form to indicate the Garden of Eternity, the response is that the word has been used in this form in many places in the Qur'an to mean a garden without any reference to the Garden of Eternity. *(See 68: 17)*

Your argument on the quote of Abu Musa that Allah took Adam from the Garden and gave him the provision from the fruits of Paradise; it indicates nothing more that Allah gave him provision. It does not show that it was from the Garden of Eternity.

As for your claim that this is subject to change and that is not, where do you get the information that the fruits of the Garden Adam was lodged in were subject to change as the fruits of this world are? The Messenger of Allah said: "If the children of Israel were not there, the meat would have not spoiled." [33] i. e. would have rotten.

Allah Almighty kept the food and drink of Ezra for a hundred years without change.

Your statement that Allah guaranteed Adam to bring him back to Paradise if he repented is true, but it is not necessary that he would be returned to the same Garden. The expression 'return' does not necessarily mean to return to the same condition and place. It is as Shu'ayb said to his people: "If we were to return to your religion after Allah has saved us from it, we would be inventing lies about Allah. There is no way we could return to it unless Allah, our Lord so wills." *(7: 89)*

These are the arguments of the group to their opponents.

---

33. Bukhari (3330)

CHAPTER 6
THE ARGUMENTS OF THOSE WHO CLAIM THAT THE GARDEN OF ADAM WAS THE ETERNAL GARDEN

Your claim that Allah, the Exalted, has stated that the people will enter the Garden of Eternity on the Day of Resurrection, which has not yet come, is true, but this is the general entrance for staying permanently there. Entry for brief period can take place before that Day. The Messenger of Allah, blessing and peace of Allah be upon him, entered it on the night of his ascension. The spirits of the believers and the martyrs are in Barzakh in Paradise. This is not the entrance of which Allah Almighty has spoken. That will happen on the Day of Resurrection. How can you deny that general entrance will not be in the world? It demolishes your claim that it is the place of stay and eternity.

Your arguments that there is no nakedness, worry, grief idle talk, lie, etc. in the Garden of Adam are true, we do not deny it nor does any follower of Islam deny it. However, this will happen when the believers will enter It on the Day of Judgement, as the context of the verses indicates. This does not discard that what Allah Almighty has told about the parents of man and jinn had taken place there. When the believers enter it the condition will be as Allah, the Most High, has stated.

To say that the Garden is the place of recompense and reward and not the home of commandment, while Allah, the Most Glorious, had commanded Adam not to eat from the tree; it is a clear sign that the Garden was the place of commandment. Its refutation is from two points:

First, it will cease to be the home of commandment when the believers enter it on the Day of Resurrection. There the commandment will come to an end. As for the commandment in the world there is no evidence that it is not possible. The Prophet 鸞 is reported to have said:

"I entered Paradise last night and saw a woman performing ablution beside a palace. I asked her: To whom do you belong?"[34]

It is not impossible that there be one who carries out the command of Allah and worships Him enters the Garden before the Day of Resurrection. This is what is happening because there are people in it who carry out the commands of their Lord exactly as He ordered whether you call it duties or something else.

The second point is the duties there are not the types of those which the people are commanded to carry out like fasting, performing prayer, taking part in jihad and so on. Adam and his wife were ordered not to approach a tree only, whether a specific or a kind. This type of order is not impossible to happen in the Garden of Eternity. It is like the order that no one should approach the wife of another person in it. Now if you claim that it is not a home where nothing of this sort will take place at any time, then there is no evidence for it. If you say that the duties of the world will come to end in It, then it is true but it does not prove your claim.

Your argument by the sleep of Adam in it and that the people of the Garden do not sleep, if this is proved by the reports; it will indicate that the people will not sleep when they enter it for staying permanently in it. There they will not die, but there is no evidence that before that it will not happen.

Your argument on the basis of the whispering of Iblis to Adam after he was taken out of the Garden is the strongest argument. But the arbitrary statement about the Devil's entrance in the Garden and going up to the Heaven after Allah expelled him from it is not acceptable to any fair-minded person. However, It is possible that he was given a chance to go up for deceiving and cheating Adam, which Allah had decided and decreed. Allah Almighty tells us that the devils used to sit in places to listen before the coming of our Prophet, ﷺ. It was a temporary ascension, which does not contradict the order of getting down. Allah knows best.

The claim that Allah, the Exalted, informed Adam about his age, it does not contradict His permission to let him enter the Garden and stay there for a while. It is on the Day of Resurrection that those who enter it will not die and will not be taken out.

---

34. Bukhari (3679), Muslim (2395)

Your claim that Adam was created from dust is very true, but how can you prove that his creation was completed on earth. There is a report which says that Allah left him at the gate of Paradise for forty days and Iblis went round him and said: 'For some big mission you have been created.' When he noticed that he was hollow, he realized that it is an unstable creature. He said: 'If I was given power over him, I will destroy him, and if he was given power over me, I will defy him.'[35] The following statement shows that he was with them in the Heaven, Allah said, **"He taught Adam all the names (of things), then He showed them the angels and said, 'Tell me the names of these if you are truthful.' They said, 'May You be glorified! We have knowledge only of what You have taught us. You are All-Knowing, All-Wise.' Then He said: 'Adam, tell them the names of these.' When he told them their names, Allah said, 'did I not tell you that I know what is hidden in the heavens and the earth?"** *(2: 31-33)*

It is unthinkable that all of them came down to earth to listen it. If Adam's creation was completed on the earth, it is not impossible that Allah, glory be to Him, took him to the heavens for reasons He designed and then brought him down to the earth. He did it with the Christ, took him to the heavens and before the Day of Resurrection He will bring him to the earth. He took the Messenger ﷺ with his body and soul to the heavens.

This is the refutation of those who claim that the Garden of Adam was the Eternal one. Allah knows best.

---

35. Muslim (2611)

CHAPTER 7
THE ARGUMENTS OF THOSE WHO CLAIM THAT PARADISE IS NOT YET CREATED

Their arguments are as follows:
• If Paradise were in existence now, it must be destroyed on the Day of Resurrection and all its residents must perish and die. Allah, the Exalted, has said, **"Everything will perish except His Face."** *(28: 88)*
"Every person will taste death." *(3: 185)*

So, the beautiful maiden and the serving boys will die while Allah almighty has stated that it was the home of permanent abode, and those who are in it will remain forever and will not die. This is what Almighty said and His statement cannot go wrong.

• Ibn Mas'ud reported that the Allah's Messenger ﷺ said: "I met Ibrahim the night I was taken to the heavens and he said to me: 'Muhammad, convey my greeting to your community and tell them that Paradise is of pure dust and sweet water, and its land is flat, treeless. Its seeds are to say: 'Glory be to Allah, praise is for Allah, there is no deity except Allah and Allah is greatest.'" [36]

It is also reported on the authority of Jabir that the Prophet ﷺ said: "Whoever says: 'Glory belongs to Allah and praise be to Him', a palm tree will be planted for him in Paradise." [37]

If Paradise was created and done, it would not be lowland, and the planting in it would make no sense.

*Allah, glory belongs to Him, stated about the wife of Pharaoh that she said:
"Build me a house near You in the Garden." *(66: 11)*

---

36. Tirmidhi (3462)
37. Ibid (3464)

It is impossible to say to someone who has prepared a dress or has built a house: 'Prepare me a dress and build me a house'. More clear is the statement of the Prophet ﷺ: "Whoever builds a mosque for the sake of Allah, Allah will build a house for him in Paradise."[38]

It is a conditional sentence, which requires fulfilment of the reward after the condition is found. It is a matter that is agreed among all the scholars of Arabic Language. The statement is reported by 'Uthman ibn 'Affan, Ali ibn Abu Talib, Jabir ibn Abdullah, Anas ibn Malik and 'Amr ibn 'Anbasah.

• There are Traditions stating that the angels plant the seed and build for the slave as long as he continues working. When he stops working, they stop as well.

• It is reported that the Messenger of Allah ﷺ said: "When Allah, the Glorious, makes the son of a slave to die, He asks the angel of death: 'did you take away the son of My slave? Did you take away the comfort of his eye and the fruit of his heart?' He replies: Yes. Almighty then asks him: "What did he say?" He replies that he praised You and said that we are for Allah and to Him we are going to return.' Almighty says: 'Build a house for him in Paradise and name it 'the house of praise.'" [39]

It is also related that the Messenger of Allah ﷺ said: "Whoever performs twelve rak'ah of prayer in addition to the obligatory ones, Allah will build a house for him in Paradise." [40]

It is not the statement of the people of innovation like the Mu'tazilah, but is reported from Ibn Nafi' who was a scholar of the Sunnah, when he was asked whether Paradise was created? He replied to keep silent in this matter is better. Allah knows the best.

----
38. Bukhari (450), Muslim (523)
39. Ahmad (19756), Ibn Hibban (726) Tirmidhi (1021)
40.Ahmad (19729)

CHAPTER 8
THE REFUTATION OF THE ARGUMENTS OF THESE PEOPLE

We have cited the evidences of the existence of Paradise in Chapter One, which are enough. However, we ask you: 'what do you mean by saying that Paradise is not created? Do you want to say that it is at the moment non-existent, and is like blowing of the Horn and rising of the people from their graves?' It is utterly a false statement rejected by the clear Prophetic Traditions, which have been cited and some will be cited later. It is an opinion that has not been adopted by any scholar of the past or the member of the followers of the Sunnah. It is completely absurd. Or do you want to say that it was not created completely and what Allah has prepared for its residents are in process of being created? When the believers enter it, Almighty will produce new things, and then it is true. All evidences that you have forwarded indicate only that much. The above-cited reports of Ibn Mas'ud and Jabir are very explicit to show that its ground is created, and Allah will plant for the man involved in His remembrance plants. Houses are built for the people who are engaged in the said deeds. When the slave does more of the good deeds, his reward in Paradise is added. Whenever a slave does a good deed a seed is planted for him and a house is built, and other enjoyable matters will be produced for him. This does not indicate that Paradise has not been created yet. It is not proper to claim it.

Your quotation of the verse: "Everything will perish except His Face," (28: 88) it seems that you failed to understand the meaning of it. Your argument by it on the nonexistence of Paradise and Hell is like the argument of your colleagues on their destruction and death of their residents. You and your colleagues missed the meaning of these verses. It was only the early scholars and the leaders of the followers of the Sunnah who were guided to it. Now we will cite some their sayings concerning the verse.

Al-Bukhari said in his Sahih: 'Everything will perish except His Face', means 'His kingdom'. It is also said: 'Except that by which His pleasure is sought.'

Imam Ahmad said, "The heavens and the earth are exterminated because their residents will be moved either to Paradise or to Hell. The Throne will not be removed because it is the roof of Paradise and Allah Almighty is above it. Allah's saying, 'Everything will perish except His Face'" was said because when Allah, the Most High, revealed: "Everyone on it will perish", the angels said, the people of the earth perished while they were interested in remaining, so Allah, the Glorious, stated that all the residents of the heavens and the earth will perish and only His Face will remain. Allah is Ever-living; He will not die. Then the angels realized that they also will die."

Ahmad said that it was the view of the people of the knowledge, and the followers of the Sunnah, those who have grasped the firmest hold hand, the ones who are followed since the time of our Prophet ﷺ to this day. I have found the scholars of the Hejaz, Syria and others holding this view. Whoever opposed it or criticised those who hold this view is to be considered an innovator, and is out of the right group, away from the path of the Sunnah. He has deviated from the true path.

He went on: The Heaven and all that it contained has been created, and Hell and what it contained is also created. Allah Almighty created them and for them He created the people. They are not going to perish and what is in them will not vanish. If a heretic or innovator argues on the basis of the statement of Allah Almighty: "Everything will perish except His Face", or similar verses of the Qur'an, he will be reminded that it refers to everything for which Allah has written to perish. Paradise and Hell are created to remain and not for destruction. They are in the Hereafter not from this world. The beautiful maidens are not going to die at the time of coming of the Resurrection or at the time of blowing the Horn. They are not going to disappear ever because Allah, the Most Powerful, has created them to remain and not to be destroyed. Death is not going to come to them. Whoever says anything against it is an innovator, and has missed the right path.

Allah originated seven skies one above the other, seven earths one below the other. Between the highest level of the earth and the lowest sky there is a distance of five hundred years and between every sky and the other is a distance of five hundred years. Water is above the seventh sky, and the Throne of the Most Merciful is above the water. Allah is established on the Throne, and the Chair is near His feet. He knows what is in the heavens and the seven earths and what is between them and what is beneath the earth, and in the bottom of the sea. He has knowledge of the root of every hair, tree, plant and the place of falling any leaf. He is aware of every spoken word, the number of pebbles, the dust, the sand and the mountains. He knows the deeds of the slaves, what they leave behind, their speech and their breath. He is aware of everything, nothing is hidden from Him, and He is on the Throne above the seventh sky. Below Him are curtains of fire, light, darkness and things He only knows.

If an innovator or opponent argues quoting the word of Allah: "We are closer to him than his jugular vein" (50: 16) or "He is with you anywhere you are" (57: 4) or "but He is with them anywhere they are" (58: 7) or "There is in no private conversation three but that He is the fourth of them, nor are there five but that He is the sixth of them" (58: 7) and similar ambiguous verses, tell them what is meant is knowledge. Allah, the Most High, is on the Throne above the seventh heaven. He knows all that takes place while He is away from His creature. No place is away from His knowledge.

Al-Khallal, a very learned man of his time said: Imam Ahmad was known for his ideas. People asked him questions and accepted his views. He dictated a treatise to me, which had in it: 'Paradise and Hell are created as it is reported from the Prophet, ﷺ. He said: "I entered and saw a palace in it." [41]
"I saw Kawthar". [42]
"I peeped in Hell and noticed most of its people being so and so". [43]

After this if someone says that they are not created, he is denying the Messenger of Allah, blessing and peace of Allah be upon him, and the Qur'an. He is a disbeliever in Paradise and Hell. He will be asked to repent otherwise he will be killed.'

Consider these statements, the discussions and useful points, which you will not find in another book. We have summarised the discussion, if we were to speak in detail it would require a huge book. Allah's help is sought, on Him we put our trust, and it is He who guides to the right opinion.

---

41. Tirmidhi (3689)
42. Bukhari (4964)
43. Bukhari (3241), Muslim (2737)

CHAPTER 9
THE NUMBER OF THE GATES OF PARADISE

This chapter contained issues related to the Arabic grammar and language, which have been dropped.

Allah, the Exalted, said:
"Those who are mindful of their Lord will be led in throngs to the Garden. When they arrive, they will find its gates wide open, and the keepers will say to them, Peace be upon you. You have become pure. Enter it to abide in it eternally." *(39: 73)*

The Almighty said about the people of Hell:
"When they arrive, its gates will be open." *(39: 71)*

About the people of Paradise Allah stated with 'waw' and in the case of the people of Hell He spoke without it. The difference in style has been explained in the different ways:

A group said that this letter (i.e.waw) is for eight because the gates of Paradise are eight, and it was dropped because the gates of Hell are seven. This is a faulty statement which has no support from the scholars of Arabic language.

Another group said that 'waw' here is an extra. This is also ridiculous. To put 'waw' as extra is not known in the style of the Arabs. It is not appropriate for the Qur'an, being the most eloquent speech, to have any extra words without need.
A third group claimed that the answer of the sentence is dropped and the phrase "and its gates are open" is linked with "when they arrive". This is the view of abu Ubaydah, al-Mbarrad, al-Zajjaj and others.

There is difference in style while describing the conditions of the two groups. In both cases the conditional sentences are used but in the case of the people of Hell the result of the condition has been cited while in the case of the people of Paradise it is dropped. The picture as drawn by the Qur'an is as follows:

The angels will drive the people of Hell to it while its gates are closed. When they arrive, they will be opened all of a sudden and they will face the torment without any delay. Hell is the abode of humiliation and distress. They were not allowed to enter until its keepers are told to let them in.

As for the Heaven it is the abode of Allah's grace and His chosen people and friends. When they arrive, they will find its gates closed. They will express their desire to get them open to its keepers for them, and will approach the messengers of firm resolve for mediation, but they will refrain until the matter is referred to the best, the chief and leader of them (i.e. our Prophet Muhammad ﷺ) who will accept the task. He will say: I will do it. He will advance to the Throne and fall down in prostration beneath it. He will remain in that condition as long as Allah, the Exalted, wills. Then He will allow him to raise his head and ask for his need. The Messenger ﷺ will implore Him to open the gates of Paradise. Allah will grant his request and open them in order to manifest the status and the rank of His Messenger. Such a house, which is the house of the King of the kings and the Lord of the worlds, will be open for the believers after they have suffered great hardships and troubles in the world. Allah Almighty will permit the last and the leader of His prophets and messengers to intercede and will open it for his followers. This is most profound grace and achievement of happiness and delight to show that it was not like any ordinary house for anyone to enter. Allah's Paradise is high and dear and can be acquired after many dangers and hurdles. Anyone who lets himself follow its desire and indulged in hopes has no place in it. He should keep away from it and go to the place that he deserves and for which he has been created.

Pay attention to the word used for taking both groups to their abodes. The Qur'an says that they will be taken 'in groups' (*zumara*), being happy to be in company of their brothers. Every group walking together with happiness, their hearts full of joy as they were in the world together in doing good deeds. They will find delight in one another and feel happy with one another. On the other hand the group of the other house (i.e. Hell) will walk while cursing one another and feeling distressed with one another. This is more humiliating and disgraceful than to be taken one by one. So consider the beauty of the word *zumara* in the Qur'an.

The keepers of Paradise will welcome its residents with greeting, 'Peace be upon you.' They start with greeting of peace, which indicates safety from any unpleasant matter. They will say to them: You are saved and after today you will not face any loathsome matter. They will say to them; 'you were pure. Enter it to abide in it for ever.' It means that your safety and entrance were for your purity as Allah has forbidden it for those who are not pure. They were given good tiding of safety, purity, entrance and eternal stay.

As for the people of Hell when they reach it in the condition of distress, worries and grief, and its gates are open, they will be stopped there. They will receive in addition to their distress, the reproach and rebuke of its keepers, who will say to them: "Did there not come to you messengers from yourselves, reciting to you the verses of your Lord and warning you of the meeting of this Day of yours?" *(39: 71)*

They will confess and say: 'Yes.' The keepers will ask them to enter it and stay there eternally.

Pay attention to the statement of the keepers to the people of Paradise: "Enter it'" and the order of the keepers of Hell to its people: 'Enter the gates of Hell'; you will notice a graceful secret and amazing meaning. The home of torment and its gates were the most horrible thing, greatest in heat and biggest distress, those who will enter it will find more severe punishment, which will be close to the grief, humiliation, worry and suffering they had met at the entrance. For this reason it is said to them: 'Enter its gates' to show humiliation, disgrace and contemp. It is said further to them that it was not enough to enter these horrible gates, but you are going to live there forever. Since Paradise is the home of honour and the place which Allah, the Most Honourable, has prepared for His friends, they are giving from the beginning the good tiding of entrance and staying there forever.

Pay attention to the statement of the Almighty:
"Gardens of lasting bliss, whose doors will be opened for them. They will be comfortably reclining within them, and will call for abundant fruit and drink."
(38: 50-51)

Here you will notice a wonderful message and that is that when they enter Paradise, its gates will not be closed for them but will remain open. On the other hand when the people of Hell will enter it, its gates will be shut on them. Allah, the Exalted, said:

"It will be closed down on them, in extended columns". *(104: 8-9)*

The columns will be holding the gates from behind like a huge stone, which is placed behind the gate.

In the opening of the gates for the people of Paradise there is indication that they will have freedom of going and moving in Paradise wherever they wish. The angels will visit them every now and then with presents and bounties from their Lord. It also indicates that it is a place of safety; they do not need to close the gates as they used to do in the world.

Sahl ibn Sa'd related that the Messenger of Allah ﷺ said: "There are eight gates in Paradise one of them is called 'al-rayyan' (filled with drinks), which is reserved for the fasting people; no one else will enter from it." [44]

Abu Hurayrah narrated the Prophet ﷺ saying: "Whoever gives out a pair of anything in the cause of Allah, he will be called from the gates of Paradise: 'O slave of Allah, this is good.' If he is one of the people of prayer, he will be called from the gate of prayer, if he is one of the people of jihad, he will be called from the gate of jihad, if he is one of those who give out in charity, he will be called from the gate of charity and if he is one of the fasting people, he will be called from the gate of al-Rayyan."

Abu Bakr said: 'my father and mother be ransom to you, Messenger of Allah! There is no need for being called from all these gates. Nevertheless, is there anyone who will be called from all these gates?'

The Prophet ﷺ replied: "Yes, and I hope you will be one of them." [45]

'Umar ibn al-Khattab reported that the Prophet ﷺ said: "No one of you performs ablution and does it perfectly then says: 'I bear witness that there is no god beside Allah, alone, Who has no partner; and I bear witness that Muhammad is His slave and Messenger', but all the eight gates of paradise will be opened for him to choose which one to enter." [46]

---

44. Bukhari (3666), Muslim (1152)
45. Bukhari (3666), Muslim (zakat: (85)
46. Muslim (Taharah: 17)

In another version the following addition has been mentioned at the end of supplication: "O Allah, make me among the ones who return to You in repentance often and make me among those who try to keep pure." [47]

Anas reported the Prophet ﷺ saying: "Whoever performs ablution and does it properly and then says three times: 'I bear witness that there is no god except Allah alone. He has no partner, and I bear witness that Muhammad is His slave and Messenger,' all the eight gates of Paradise will be opened for him. He can choose any of them to enter." [48]

'Utbah ibn Abdullah al-Sulami said: 'I heard the Messenger of Allah ﷺ saying:

"Any Muslim who has lost three children, who had not reached the puberty, will be met by them at the eight gates of Paradise. Any of them he will enter." [49]

47. Tirmidhi (55)
48. Ahmad (13794)
49. Ibn Majah (1604)

CHAPTER 10
DESCRIPTION OF THE WIDENESS OF THE GATES OF PARADISE

Abu Hurayrah related: 'A dish of sopped bread and meat was placed before the Messenger of Allah, blessing and peace of Allah be upon him. He took the shoulder of the goat from it, which he liked most. He took a bite of it and said: "I am the chief of the people on the Day of Judgment."

He had another bite and said: "I am the chief of the people on the Day of Judgement."

When he noticed that his Companions do not ask him, he said: "You do not ask how?"

They spoke saying; 'How is it going to be, O Messenger of Allah?' He said, "The people will stand before the Lord of the worlds. They will listen to the caller and will all be seen."

The Prophet ﷺ cited the story of the intercession in full and said at the end of it: "I will walk and go beneath the Throne and fall in prostration before my Lord. The Lord of the worlds will ask me to raise my head. He will place me on a stage where nobody before me was placed, and nobody after me will be placed. I will say, 'My community, my community! Allah, the Most Excellent, will say to me: 'Muhammad, let those of your community who have no accounting enter from the right gate. They will share other gates with other people. By the One in Whose Hand Muhammad's soul is the distance between two sides of Paradise is like the distance between Makkah and Hajar."[50]

Khalid ibn 'Umayr al-'Adawi narrated: 'Utbah ibn Ghazawan delivered a sermon to us. He praised Allah and glorified Him then said: 'This world has announced its end and has turned away. Nothing is left of it but a little like the left over water in

---
50. Bukhari (4712), Muslim (194), Tirmidhi (2434)

a vessel. We are told that between two gateposts of Paradise is a distance of forty years, and there will come a time when that gate will be crowded with people.'[51]

Hakim ibn Mu'awiyah reported his father saying that the Messenger of Allah, blessing and peace of Allah be upon him, said: "You are to complete seventy communities and you will be the best and noblest to Allah. The distance between two gateposts of Paradise is the distance of forty years. A day will come when it will be crowded."[52]

In another version the distance is shown to be the distance of seven years.
The report of Abu Hurayrah, cited earlier, is more authentic. All other reports have problems.

51. Muslim (al-Zuhd; 2967)
52. Ahmad (20045)

CHAPTER 11
DESCRIPTION OF THE GATES OF PARADISE

Al-Hasan commented on the words of Allah, the Exalted: "(Its) gates will be open for them" *(38: 50)*, saying that the gates will be seen.

Qatadah said: 'the outsides of the gates of Paradise are seen from inside, and the inside is seen from outside. They will speak and understand what is said to them i.e. open, close etc.'

Abdullah ibn Ghayath al-Fazari said: 'Every believer will have four gates in Paradise. One of them for the angels to enter to visit them, the second one for the beautiful maidens, the third one is a gate closed between them and the people of Hell. He will open it when he wanted to look at the people of Hell and appreciate the bounty of Allah on him. The fourth gate is that which is between him and the Home of Peace through it he will enter to his Lord when he wished.'[53]

Anas ibn Malik reported that the Messenger of Allah ﷺ said: "I will be the first person to hold the chain of Paradise. I am saying it with no pride."[54]

Anas also reported the Prophet ﷺ saying: "I will hold the chain of the gate of Paradise and clatter it."[55]

This shows that the chain will be perceptible which will move and rattle.

Abu Hurayrah related that the Prophet ﷺ said: "I will hold the chain of the gate of Paradise and permission will be granted to me."[56]

Ali ibn Abu Talib said: "If a person says: 'There is no god but Allah, the True, the Evident' hundred times every day, it will be a safety from poverty and the

---

53. *Abu Nu'aym in Sifat al-Jannah (147)*
54. *Al-Darimi in his Sunan (47)*
55. *Tirmidhi (3148)*
56. *Abu Nu'aym (184)*

loneliness of the grave. It will bring him wealth and be source of rattling the gate of Paradise."[57]

As paradise has levels one above the others, its gates are also like that. The gate of the higher Paradise is above the one below it. As we go above, the levels become specious, and the width of the gate is in line with the width of Paradise. For this Community there will be a special gate reserved for them. Ibn 'Umar reported that the Messenger of Allah ﷺ said: "The gate from which my community will enter Paradise is as wide as the distance covered by a rider in three days. Yet they will be squeezed till their shoulders are about to dislocate."[58]

Abu Hurayrah reported that the Prophet ﷺ said: "Gabriel came to me, held my hand and showed me the gate through which my followers will enter Paradise."[59]

Ali Ibn Abu Talib said: "The gates of Paradise are one above the other then he recited: 'When they arrive and its gates are open.' (39: 73)"

The believers will be near it under a tree below which two springs are flowing. They will drink from one of them and it will remove all the dirt and filth from them. They will take bath from the other and it will cast on them the radiance of bliss. After that their heads will never be dishevelled and their bodies will never be changed. He recited: "You become pure, so enter it to stay forever."

A man will enter and he knows his place. He will be met by the children who will feel joy by looking at them as the family is rejoiced by the coming of its members after being away. Then he will go to his spouses, stand at the gate and enter it. He will recline on his bed and look at its foundation and notice that it has been erected on the pearls. He will see green, red and yellow. He then will raise his head to the roof of his house. Had he not been created for it his eye would be gleamed. He will say: "Praise be to Allah, Who guided us to this, we were not able to get access if He had not guided us."

Allah knows better.

57. Abu Nu'aym (185)
58. Tirmidhi (2548)
59. Abu Dawud (4652)

CHAPTER 12
DESCRIPTION OF THE DISTANCE BETWEEN ONE GATE AND THE OTHER

'Laqit ibn 'Amir went to the Messenger of Allah ﷺ and asked him: 'What is Paradise and Hell, O Messenger of Allah?'

He replied: "By your God, Hell has seven gates between two of them a rider will travel seventy years. Paradise has eight gates between two of them a rider will travel seventy years." [60]

He cited the rest of the Hadith.

---

60. Tabarani (19: 213), Abdullah in Zawa'id (16206) This report will be cited in full later

CHAPTER 13
THE PLACE AND LOCATION OF PARADISE

Allah, glory be to Him, said:

"He saw him a second time near the Lot Tree of the utmost boundary, near it is the Garden of Refuge." *(53: 13-15)*

It is established that the Lot Tree is above the heavens. This name is given to it because anything that comes from Allah Almighty ends there. He holds what He wishes and to Him ascends matters and He deals with them as He wills.

Allah, the Great, also said:

"In the sky is your sustenance and all that you are promised." *(51: 22)*

Mujahid stated that Paradise and Hell are in the sky. This needs explanation because Hell is in lowest part of the earth. Ibn Abbas said that good and evil come from the sky. In this case the meaning will be that the causes of Paradise and Hell are with Allah in the sky.

Abdullah ibn Salam is reported to say: "The noblest creature of Allah is Abu al-Qasim, and Paradise is in the sky."[61]

Ibn Abbas said: "Paradise is above the seventh sky, and Allah Almighty will place it on the Day of Judgement wherever He wishes. Hell is in the seventh level of the earth."[62]

Abdullah said: "Paradise is in the fourth sky. On the day of Judgement Allah will place it where He wished. Hell is in the seventh earth. On the Day of Judgment Allah will place it wherever He wishes."[63]

Mujahid said: "I asked Ibn Abbas: Where is Paradise? He replied: 'Above seventh

61. *Abu Nu'aym in Sifat al-Jannah (131)*
62. *Ibid (132)*
63. *Ibid (134)*

sky.' I said: Then where is Hell? He replied: 'Below seven folded seas.'" [64]

There is a report from Abdullah ibn 'Amr that Paradise is folded and hung with the horns of the sun. It is spread once every year, and the souls of the believers are in the birds' bodies, they know one another, and are provided from the fruits of Paradise.[65]

It means that Paradise which is hanging with the horns of the sun is what Allah Almighty produces once every year the types of fruits and plants by the sun, which remind the people of Paradise, as He has made the fire as a sign of Hell. Paradise is as wide as the skies and the earth and is not hanging with the horns of the sun. It is above the sun and much bigger than it.

It is established by the authentic tradition that the Messenger of Allah ﷺ said: "Paradise is hundred levels; the distance between every two levels is as the distance between the sky and the earth."[66]

This shows that it is at utmost height and loftiness. Allah knows better.

The above Hadith has two wordings; the one which is cited, and the other is: "There are hundred levels in Paradise between every two levels is the distance as the distance between the sky and the earth. Allah has prepared it for those who strive in the cause of Allah."

This last wording is preferred by our Shaykh (i.e. Ibn Taymiyyah). It does not dismiss that the grades of Paradise are more than that. It is like the statement of the Prophet ﷺ: "Allah has ninety-nine names. Whoever counts them will go to Paradise."[67]

It means that this much is part of His names. This interpretation is supported by the fact that the grade of our Prophet ﷺ is above all grades. One hundred grades mentioned are achieved by the members of his community, by jihad.

64. Ibid (135)
65. Ibid (133)
66. Bukhari (2790)
67. Bukhari (6410), Muslim (2677)

Paradise has domes. The highest, most specious and the best one is 'Firdaws'. On its roof is the Throne as said by the Messenger of Allah ﷺ in the following report: "When you ask Allah, ask Him for Firdaws. It is the middle of Paradise and the highest one. Above it is the Throne of the Merciful, and from it flow the rivers of Paradise."

If you say: Paradise all of it is below the Throne and the Throne is their roof. The Chair encompasses the skies and the earth and the Throne is bigger than it.

The answer will be that since the Throne is closer to Firdaws excluding other Paradise. There is no Paradise above it, so the Throne is its roof and not of the other Paradises. Because of the greatness and height of Paradise the ascension will be from the lowest to the highest slowly and by grades. It is attested by the saying of the Prophet ﷺ that it will be said to the reader of the Qur'an: "Read and go up. Your position will be at the last verse you recite."[68]

This has two meanings: that his station will be at the last part he remembered or the end of his recitation. Allah knows better.

68. Abu Dawud (1464), Tirmidhi (2914)

CHAPTER 14
THE KEYS OF PARADISE

Mu'adh ibn Jabal narrated the Messenger of Allah ﷺ saying:"The key of Paradise is the declaration that 'there is no god but Allah.'"[69]

It was said to Wahab ibn Munabbih: "Is the declaration that 'there is no god but Allah' not the key of Paradise?" He replied: "Yes, but every key needs teeth. If you bring a key with teeth, it will open for you, otherwise it will not open."[70]

Anas reported that a Bedouin asked the Messenger of Allah ﷺ: "What is the key to Paradise?" The Prophet replied: "(Saying): 'There is no god but Allah.'"[71]

Yazid ibn Sakhbarah said: "Swords are the keys of Paradise."

Mu'adh ibn Jabal related that the Messenger of Allah ﷺ said: "Should I not tell you a gate of Paradise?" I said: "Surely, tell me." He said: "(It is saying): 'There is no power, no strength except with Allah.'"[72]

Allah, the Glorious, has made for every desired matter a key to open it. He made the key of prayer purity. The Prophet ﷺ said: "The key of prayer is cleanliness."[73]

In the same way the key of the pilgrimage is ihram; the key of piety is telling truth; the key of Paradise is to believe in the oneness of Allah; the key of learning is good question and proper listening; the key of victory and success is patience; the key of getting more is being thankful; the key of friendship is love and remembrance; the key of success is consciousness of Allah; the key of getting help is the hope and fear; the key of response from Allah is to supplicate Him; the key of achieving desire in the Hereafter is to show indifference to the world. Also the Almighty made the key of belief to contemplate in what Allah has called

69. Ahmad (22163)
70. Bukhari
71. Abu Nu'aym in Sifat al-Jannah (190)
72. Ahmad (22176)
73. Tirmidhi (3), Abu Dawud (61), Ibn Majah (275)

His servants to contemplate; the key of entering to Allah is the submission of the heart and its sincerity for Him in love, hatred, doing and abandoning. The key of the heart's life is to contemplate in the Qur'an and implore Allah in the morning, and keeping away from the sins; the key of receiving mercy is to perform the acts of worship properly and to be kind to His slaves; the key of provision is to strive accompanied with seeking forgiveness and being mindful of Allah; the key of the power is obedience of Allah and His Messenger. The key of preparation for the Hereafter is to have short hope. The key to every good is to have desire of Allah and the Hereafter, and the key of every evil is the love of the world and lengthy hope.

It is a lengthy chapter and most beneficial of the gates of knowledge, which is embodied in knowing the keys of good and evil. It is not available except for those who are lucky and supported by Allah. Allah, the Exalted, has made for every good and bad a key and a door to enter it. He has made *shirk*, turning away from what Almighty has sent His Messenger with and paying no attention to His remembrance and not carrying out His duties a key to Hell. He made wine key to every sin, made affluence key to committing adultery. He made gazing at images key to search and affection; made laziness and comfort key to frustration and failure. He made disobedience key of disbelief, telling lies the key of hypocrisy, made avarice and greed key of niggardliness, severing the bond and taking money in unlawful ways. He made turning away from what the Messenger has brought key to every innovation and misguidance.

These matters are not understood except by those who have the right perception and a perfect reason to know themselves and the good and bad of the wlt is, therefore, very important to know these keys and the matters for which they are made. Allah's support will come to such a person. To Him belongs the sovereignty and praise, and He alone reserves favour and grace. He is not to be questioned but the people are going to be questioned.

CHAPTER 15
THE ORDINANCE OF PARADISE GIVEN TO ITS PEOPLE AT THE TIME OF THEIR DEATH AND AT THE TIME OF ENTRANCE INTO IT

Allah, the Glorious, said:

"But the record of the truly good is in *'Illiyyin'* - what will explain to you what *'Illiyyin'* is? - A clearly written record witnessed by those brought near."
(83: 18-21)

The Almighty stated that the record of the righteous people is written. He specially mentioned that their record is written and witnessed by those who are close to Him from among the angels, prophets and high-ranking believers. He did not say that the record of the wicked is witnessed. He did so in order to glorify the record of the righteous people and to show its importance among the close circles of His creature. It is as a king writes Ordinance for the commanders and the distinguished members of his kingdom to express the importance of them and celebrate their names. It is a sort of blessing of Allah, the Most High, and His angels for His slaves.

Al-Bara' ibn 'Azib narrated: "We went with the Messenger of Allah ﷺ in a funeral. He sat on a grave and we sat around him silently as if there are birds on our heads. The grave was being prepared for the dead person. The Messenger ﷺ said three times: "I seek refuge in Allah from the torment of the grave." Then he said: "When a believer is drawing near the Hereafter and is about to leave the world, the angels descend to him their faces shining like the sun. Each one of them holding embalms and shroud. They sit with him as far as he can see. Then the angel of death comes he sits near his head. He says, 'O pleasant soul, come out to the forgiveness and pleasure of Allah.' It comes out flowing like drop flows from the water skin. He holds it, and immediately the other angels take it from him and put it in that shroud and embalm. It diffuses the best smell of musk ever found on the earth. They take it up, and do not pass by any group of the angels but they ask: 'what is this pleasant soul? They reply, so and so, giving the best name he was called by in the world. They reach the lowest sky and ask it to be open. In every sky the noble angels accompany him until he reaches the sky where Allah Almighty is. He, the Most Honourable, will order: 'Write the record of My slave in 'Illiyyin', and take him back to the earth. I created them from it, in it they will return and from it I will raise them again.'

His soul will return to his body and two angels will come to him and make him sit. They will ask him: 'Who is your Lord?' He will reply: My Lord is Allah. They will ask: 'What is your religion?' He will reply: 'My religion is Islam.' Then they will ask him: 'Who is this man who was sent to you?' They will say; 'He is the Messenger of Allah, blessing and peace of Allah be upon him.' They will ask: How do you know it? He will say: 'I read the Book of Allah, believed it and testified it.'

A caller will call from the sky: My slave has spoken truth; spread for him from Paradise, provide him with dress form the Paradise, and open a gate for him to Paradise.

Its smell and fragrance will reach him, and his grave will be expanded as far as his eye can see. Then a man of beautiful face, beautiful dress and with pleasant scent will come to him and say: 'Get good news, which will make you happy. This is the day which you were promised.' He will ask: 'Who are you? Your face is a sign of good.' He will reply: 'I am your good deeds.' He will say: 'My Lord, establish the Hour. My Lord, establish the Hour so that I can return to my family and my wealth.'"

"When a disbeliever comes close to the Hereafter and the departure from this world, angels with black faces come to him. They will be holding coarse sheets, and sit near him as far as his eyes can see. Then the angel of death comes and sits near his head. He says: 'O wicked soul, come out to the wrath and anger of Allah.' It spreads in his body and he pulls it out as the skewer is pulled from wet wool. He takes it and the angels take it from him and put it in those sheets. It diffuses the most horrible smell found on the earth. They carry it to the sky and do not pass by any group of the angels but they say: 'What is this wicked soul?' They name him with the most abominable names he was called in the world. They carry him to the lowest sky and ask for its opening. But it is not opened. Then the Messenger ﷺ recited: **"The gates of Heaven will not be open for them and they will not enter the Garden until a thick rope pass through the eye of a needle."** (7; 40)

Allah, the Exalted, will say: 'Write his record in Sijjin in the lowest earth. His soul will be thrown and the Messenger ﷺ read: **"He who assign partners to Allah is like someone who has been hurled down from the skies and snatched up by the birds or flung to a distant place by wind. "** (22: 31)

His soul will be returned to his body. Two angels will come to him and make him sit. They will ask him: 'Who is your Lord?' 'Oh, oh! I do not know.' They will ask him: 'What is your religion?' He will say: 'Oh, oh! I do not know.' They will ask: Who is the man who was sent to you?' He will say: 'Oh, oh, I do not know.' Then a caller will call from the sky; 'My slave has lied, prepare for him a bed from the Fire, clothe him from the Fire and open a door for him from the Fire. Its heat and hot wind will reach him, and his grave will be constricted for him till his ribs interlock. Then a man with ugly face and bad smell will come to him, and say: receive the bad news. This is the day you have been promised. He will say to him: 'Who are you; your face is the one which shows evil. He will reply: 'I am your evil deeds.' He then will say: My lord, do not bring the Hour." [74]

The second ordinance is indicated in the following report by Salman al-Farsi who said: "The Messenger ﷺ said: 'No one will enter Paradise without a card which has 'in the name of Allah, the Most Beneficent, the Most Merciful, it is Allah's decree for so and so. Let him enter the lofty Paradise with clustered fruits in his reach.'"

In another report Salman said that the Prophet ﷺ said: "The believer will be given a card on the Bridge which says: 'in the name of Allah, the Most Beneficent, the Most Merciful, this is a statement from Allah Almighty, the Wise for so and so. Admit him in lofty Garden with clustered fruits within his reach."[75]

---

74. *Abu Dawud (4753), Ahmad (4: 287), al-Bayhaqi in Sh'ab al- iman (395)*
75. *Tabarani (6: 272)*

CHAPTER 16
THE SINGLE WAY OF PARADISE AND ASSERTION THAT THERE IS ONE WAY TO IT

This is a matter upon which all the Messengers, Allah's blessing and peace be upon them, from the first to the last one have agreed. On the other hand the ways to Hell are innumerable. For this reason Allah, the Most Blessed, cited the way of Paradise in His Book in singular form and the ways of Hell in plural. He said: **"This is My path, which is straight, so follow it, and do not follow other ways. They will lead you away from it."** *(6: 153)*

"To Allah is the direction of the right way, for some paths lead to the wrong way." *(16: 9)*

It means that there are paths which drift from the right direction, and that is the path of deviation.

The Almighty also said:
"It is a straight path to Me."

Ibn Mas'ud narrated that Allah's Messenger ﷺ drew a line and said, "This the path of Allah." Then he drew lines to its right and left and said, "These other paths on each of them Satan is sitting and calling people to it." Then he recited, "This is My path, which is straight, so follow it, and do not follow other paths." [76]

Jabir reported that some angels came to the Prophet ﷺ. Some of them said, "He is sleeping." The others said, "The eye is sleeping but the heart is awake." Then they said, "Your companion has an example, so present it for him." Then they said, "His example is like a man who built a house and arranged a banquet in it. He sent a caller, whoever responded to the caller, entered the house and ate from the banquet. Those who did not accept the call did not enter the house and did not eat from the banquet." Then they said, "Explain it for him so that he understands

---

76. *Ahmad (4142)*

it." Some of them said, "The eye is sleeping but the heart is awake. The house is Paradise, and the caller is Muhammad. Whoever obeys Muhammad, has obeyed Allah, and those who disobeyed Muhammad, have disobeyed Allah. Muhammad is the distinguisher between the people."[77]

It is also reported from Jabir in a different version, where he said, "The Messenger of Allah, blessing and peace of Allah be upon him, came out to us one day and said, 'I saw in dream as if Gabriel is by my head and Michael is by my leg. One of them spoke to his colleague: 'Present an example for him. He said: 'Listen, may your ear be able to listen. Understand, may your heart understand. Your example and your community's example is like a king who took a house then built in it a home. He arranged a banquet and sent a caller to invite the people to its meal. Some of them responded the caller while others refused him. The king is Allah, the house is Islam, the home is Paradise, and You, Muhammad, are the caller. Whoever accepted your call entered Islam, and he will enter Paradise. The one who enters Paradise will eat from it.'"[78]

Abdullah Ibn Mas'ud narrated, "The Messenger of Allah, blessing and peace of Allah be upon him, led us in 'Isha' prayer, then he returned and held my hand until he reached the Batha'of Makkah. He made me sit and drew a line, and said to me, 'Do not leave your line. There will come people to you; do not speak to them; they will not speak to you.'

He left and while I was sitting by my line some people came as if they are *zutt*. I could not see their private part nor could I notice human being. They came to me but did not cross the line and went to the Messenger of Allah, blessing and peace of Allah be upon him.

When the night passed, the Messenger of Allah, blessing and peace of Allah be upon him, returned to me and found me sitting. He said, 'I saw myself this night.' He entered in my line, reclined on my leg and slept. The Messenger used to snore when he slept. While I was sitting, the Messenger of Allah, blessing and peace of Allah be upon him, was sleeping putting his head on my thigh.

Some men with white dress, only Allah knew how beautiful they were, came to

---

77. Bukhari (7281)
78. Tirmidhi (2860)

me and some of them sat by the head of the Messenger, blessing and peace of Allah be upon him, and others by his leg. They said, 'We saw a man who was given like what this Prophet is given. His eyes are asleep but his heart is awake, present an example for him. His example is like a chief who built a palace and arranged a banquet. He invited people to his meal and drink. Those who accepted his invitation ate from his meal and enjoyed his drink. Those who did not respond to his call were punished.' Then they went up. When the Messenger of Allah ﷺ woke up, he asked me, 'Did you hear what they said? Do you know who they were?'

I said, 'Allah and His Messenger know best.' He said, 'They were angels. Do you know what example they presented?' I replied, 'Allah and His Messenger know better.' He said, 'The Most Merciful built Paradise and called His slaves to it. Those who accepted the call entered Paradise, and those who refused, He will punish them.'" [79]

---

79. Ibid (2861)

CHAPTER 17
THE GRADES OF PARADISE

Allah, the Exalted, said:

"Those believers, who stay at home, other than the disabled, are not equal to those who commit themselves and their possessions to striving in the way of Allah. Allah has raised such people who strive through their wealth and their lives to a rank above those who stay at home by degrees, although He has promised all believers a good reward. Those who strive are favoured with a tremendous reward above those who stay at home, high ranks conferred by Him, as well as forgiveness and mercy. Allah is Most Forgiving and Merciful." (4:95-96)

Ibn Muhayriz said, "Allah has raised the ranks of the people who strive in the cause of Allah by seventy grades, between every two grades is the distance of seventy years by a fast horse."

Al-Dahhak said, "Some of them will be better than others. Those who are placed in better position will realize their position. And those who are at lower grade will not feel that anyone else has been placed over them."

Allah Almighty also said:

"Can the man who pursues the pleasure of Allah be like the one who brings upon himself the anger of Allah and whose refuge is Hell? And wretched is the destination. They are at different degrees in the sight of Allah, and Allah sees of whatever they do." (3: 162-163)

The Almighty said:

"The true believers are those whose hearts tremble with awe when Allah is mentioned, whose faith increases when His revelations are recited to them, who put their trust in their Lord, who keep up the prayer and give to others out of what We have provided for them. They have high standing with their Lord, forgiveness and generous provision." (8; 2-4)

Abu Sa'id al-Khudri related that the Messenger of Allah ﷺ said, "The people of Paradise will see the people of the chambers above them as they see the bygone glittering star in the east or the west because of the big distance between them."

The Companions asked, "Messenger of Allah, these are the places of the prophets; no one else will reach them." He said, "No, by the One in Whose hand is my soul, it will be for those who believed in Allah and supported the messengers."[80]

Sahl ibn Sa'd reported the Messenger of Allah, blessing and peace of Allah be upon him, saying, "The people of Paradise will see the people of chambers as you see the stars in the remote part of the sky."[81]

Abu Hrayrah reported that the Messenger of Allah, blessing and peace of Allah be upon him, said, "The people of Paradise will see one another as you see the far away glittering star because of the difference of grades."

The Companions enquired, "Messenger of Allah, they are the prophets." He said, "Yes, and by the one who holds my soul in his hand, and those who believed in Allah and supported the messengers."[82]

Abu Hurayrah reported that the Prophet ﷺ said, "The people of Paradise will see one another in their chambers as the eastern or western star is seen in the horizon because of the difference of the levels."

The Companions remarked, "These are the prophets, Messenger of Allah?"
He said, "Yes, but by the One in whose hand is my soul, there will be those who have belief in Allah and supported the messengers."[83]

Abu Sa'id al-Khudri narrated that the Messenger of Allah ﷺ said, "The chambers of those who love one another for the sake of Allah will be seen in Paradise like the eastern or western rising star. It will be asked: Who are they? The answer will be that they are the ones who loved one another for the sake of Allah."[84]

---

80. Bukhari (3556), Muslim 92831)
81. Bukhari (6555), Muslim (2830)
82. Ahmad (8479)
83. Tirmidhi (2556)
84. Ahmad (11829)

Abu Sa'id also narrated that the Prophet ﷺ said, "Paradise had one hundred grades. If all the people of the world gather in one of them, it will be sufficient for them."[85]

The Prophet ﷺ said, "It will be said to the reader of the Qur'an when he enters the Heaven: Read and go up. He will climb up a degree by every verse until he reads the last verse with him."[86]

This report shows that Paradise has more than hundred levels.

The report of Abu Hurayrah cited earlier that Paradise has hundred grades that Allah has prepared for those who strive in the cause of Allah; the distance between every two grades is like the distance between the sky and the earth. When you ask Allah, ask Him for Firdaws. It is the middle of Paradise and highest grade of it. Above it is the Throne of the Most Merciful, and from it flow the rivers of Paradise. The hundred grades mentioned in it may be among the all the levels of Paradise or the levels end at hundred and in every grade there are grades.

The first meaning is supported by a report of Mu'adh ibn Jabal who said that the Messenger of Allah ﷺ said, "Whoever performs the five obligatory prayer, fasts the month of Ramadan, Allah will definitely forgive him whether he migrated or sat where his mother gave him birth."

I said, "Messenger of Allah, shouldn't I go and tell people about it?" He replied, "No, leave them act. Paradise has hundred grades between every two grades is like the distance of the sky and the earth. The highest of them is Firdaws. On it is the Throne and it is the best grade of Paradise. The rivers of Paradise flow from it. When you ask Allah, ask Him for Firdaws."[87]

There is no contradiction between the distance mentioned in some report to be hundred and in some five hundred. This is based on the speed of the traveller. The Prophet ﷺ cited it to make the people understand the distance.

85. Ibid (11236), Tirmidhi (2532)
86. Ahmad (11360), Ibn Majah (3780)
87. Tirmidhi (2530, 2531, 2529)

CHAPTER 18
THE HIGHEST LEVEL OF PARADISE AND ITS NAME

Amr ibn al-As narrated that he heard the Messenger of Allah, blessing and peace of Allah be upon him, say, "When you listen to the mu'adhdhin (caller to the prayer), say as he says. Then confer blessing on me because whoever blesses me once Allah will reward him ten times. Then ask al-wasilah for me. It is a stage in Paradise, which is reserved for only one person of the believers. I hope to be that person. Whoever asks Allah for al-Wasilah for me, my intercession will be due to him."[88]

Abu Hurayrah reported that the Messenger of Allah, blessing and peace of Allah be upon him, said, "When you perform prayer ask Allah to grant me al-wasilah."

He was asked, "What is al-wasilah, Messenger of Allah?" He replied, "It is the highest rank in Paradise, which only one person will achieve. I hope to be that person."[89]

Jabir reported that Allah's Messenger ﷺ said, "Anyone who says after listening the call of prayer: 'O Allah, the Lord of this perfect call and the prayer which is to start grant Muhammad al-Wasilah and al-Fadilah and the high rank, and raise him to the highly praised status which You have promised him.' My intercession will be due to that person."[90]

Abu Sa'id al-Khudri reported that the Prophet ﷺ said, "Al-wasilah is a rank with Allah Almighty, there is no rank above it. Ask Allah to grant me al-Wasilah."[91]

'A'ishah narrated, "A man went to the Messenger of Allah, blessing and peace of Allah be upon him, and said, 'Messenger of Allah, you are more beloved to me

---

88. Muslim (al-Salat :11), Tirmidhi (3614), Abu Dawud (523)
89. Ahmad (7601)
90. Bukhari (624, 4719), Abu Dawud (525), Tirmidhi (210), Ibn Majah (722)
91. Ahmad (11783)

than myself, you are more beloved to me than my family, you are more beloved to me than my children. Sometimes I am at home and remember you and cannot control myself until I come and look at you. When I remember my death and your death, I realise that when you enter Paradise you will be placed high with the prophets. I am afraid that if I entered Paradise, I will not be able to see you.' The Messenger did not say anything to him. Then Gabriel brought this verse:

Whoever obeys Allah and the Messenger will be among those He has blessed: the messengers, the steadfast affirmers of the truth, the martyrs and the righteous. They are excellent companions. *(4: 69)*"[92]

The status of the Prophet ﷺ was called al-wasilah because it is the nearest one to the Throne of the Most Merciful, and is the nearest to Allah Almighty. The word *al-wasilah* comes from *al-waslah,* meaning link. It is the best and noblest part of Paradise. It is the most brilliant. The word means nearness. Allah, the Exalted said: **"Those they invoke seek means of access to their Lord (striving as to) which of them would be nearest."** *(17: 57)*

The phrase "which of them would be nearest" is the explanation of *al-wasliah*, which the polytheists seek to reach near Allah. Our Prophet ﷺ was the most devoted person to his Lord and the most knowledgeable and most fearing and having greatest love, his status will be the nearest one to Allah. He will be granted the highest status in Paradise. He asked his community to pray to Allah, the Great, to grant him that. This supplication will bring them closer to Allah and their faith will increase. Allah, glory be to Him, has decided to grant that status to the Prophet for following reasons among them is the prayer of his community in appreciation of his guidance for them.

92. Tabarani in al-Awsat (480). See majam' al-zawa'id (10937)

CHAPTER 19
OFFERING OF ALLAH, THE EXALTED, HIS COMMODITY TO HIS SLAVES, THE PRICE HE DEMANDED AND THE CONTRACT THAT TOOK PLACE BETWEEN THE BELIEVERS AND THEIR LORD

Allah Almighty said:

"Allah has purchased from the believers their lives and their property in return for the Garden. They fight in Allah's way, so they kill and are killed. This is a true promise given by Him in the Torah, the Gospel, and the Qur'an. Who could be more faithful to his promise than Allah? So be happy with the transaction you have contracted. That is the supreme triumph." *(9: 111)*

Allah, the Most High, has made in this verse the Garden the price of the lives and properties of the believers, which if they sacrifice, they will deserve the price. He made this contract with them and confirmed it by the following various assurances:

1. He gave the information in affirmative style starting with the word inna.
2. The information is given in past tense to indicate that it has been done.
3. He ascribed this contract to Him stating that it was He who has purchased the commodity.
4. He has given the promise of paying the price, which He is not going to break or fail to fulfil.
5. He asserted that it is something which he has put upon Himself for His slaves.
6. He confirmed it by saying that is binding upon Him.
7. He said that this promise was given in His Books that were revealed from the heaven i.e. the Torah, the Gospel and the Qur'an.
8. His assertion that there is no one who is truer to his promise than Allah.
9. The Almighty commanded His faithful believers to rejoice this transaction and

pass the good news to one another. It is a transaction which is established and will not be cancelled.

10. He, the Glorious, told them that this transaction was the great attainment.

After that the Almighty stated that the people with whom the transaction was made are those who turn to Allah in repentance from what He dislikes; worship Him in the way He likes. They are those who praise Him in the conditions of facility and adversary and those who are travellers. This word sa'ihun has been explained by fasting, by going out in the search of knowledge, by jihad and by consistent obedience to Allah. The true meaning of the word is travelling of the heart in the remembrance of Allah, devotion to Him and having desire to meeting with Him. It is the cause of all those acts which are mentioned. For this reason Allah, the Supreme, described the women who will be given to the Prophet if he were to divorce his wives as sa'ihat (66: 5). Their travelling is not for taking part in jihad or for seeking knowledge or continuous fasting. It is the journey of their hearts in the love, fear, devotion and remembrance of Allah, the Exalted.

Consider how Allah, the all-Knowing, has combined repentance and devotion together: the former being abandoning what He dislikes and the latter doing what He likes. He also combined the praise and travelling: the former is to extol Him by His perfect attributes and the latter is to use the tongue in best remembrance of Him. It refers to the travelling of the heart in His love, remembrance and exalting Him. The Almighty also put devotion and travelling together in the description of the wives of the Prophet because the first is the devotion of the body and the second one is the devotion of the heart. He also combined Islam and Iman because the first one is outward and the second one connected with the heart. There is a statement of the Prophet ﷺ which says, "Islam is open and Iman is in the heart."[93]

He, the Supreme, combined devoutly obedience and repentance the first refers to what He loves and the second refers to what He hates. He also put the previously married and the virgins together, the fist is that who has experienced sexual intercourse and was satisfied, and the second is that who is like untraded meadow which has not been grazed. In the same way the Almighty combined bowing and prostrating together and enjoining good and forbidding bad together and here He put waw between the two to indicate that both are inseparable, and He linked

---

93. See Ahmad (12348)

them with observing the limits of Allah, the first is connected with the protection of the self of the person and the second is connected with enjoining others guard them. The verse expressed the importance, nobility and the eminence of the soul of human. It is meant to show that if one is not aware of the value of it, then let him look at the person who is purchasing it. It also draws attention to the price given for it and by whom the contract is made. The commodity is the soul, the buyer is Allah, the Exalted, and the price is the Gardens of bliss and the broker in this transaction is the best of the creature of Allah whom He put over the angels, the best and the noblest of mankind.

Abu Hurayrah reported that the Messenger of Allah, blessing and peace of Allah be upon him, said, "The one who fears sets out at nightfall. The one who sets out at nightfall reaches the destination. Remember the commodity of Allah is precious. Remember the commodity of Allah is precious." [94]

Anas reported that a Bedouin came to the Prophet ﷺ and asked, "What is the price of Paradise?" He replied, "There is no god but Allah." [95]

There are many Hadith to give this message.

Abu Hurayrah related that a Bedouin came to the Messenger of Allah, blessing and peace of Allah be upon him, and said, "Messenger of Allah, tell me an act which if I do I will go to Paradise."

The Prophet said, "Worship Allah alone and do not associate partner with Him, perform the obligatory prayer, give the obligatory charity, and fast the month of Ramadan."

He said, "By Allah, I will not add and reduce anything of it." When he turned to go, the Prophet ﷺ said, "If anyone wants to look at a man of the People of Paradise should look at him." [96]

Jabir narrated that Al-Nu'man ibn Qawqal came to the Messenger of Allah ﷺ and said, "Messenger of Allah, if I do the obligatory prayers, regard the unlawful as

94. Tirmidhi (2450)
95. Abu Nu'aym in siaft al-jannah (51)
96. Bukhari (6924), Muslim (iman: 14)

unlawful and consider the lawful as lawful, will I go to Paradise?" He replied, "Yes." [97]

'Uthman ibn 'Affan reported the Messenger of Allah, blessing and peace of Allah be upon him, as saying, "Whoever dies and he is sure that there is no god but Allah, will go to Paradise." [98]

Mu'adh ibn Jabal related that he heard the Messenger of Allah ﷺ say, "Anyone whose last words were 'there is no god but Allah' will be admitted to Paradise." [99]

Abu Dharr related, "The Messenger of Allah, blessing and peace of Allah be upon him, said, 'A person came to me from my Lord and gave me good tiding that whoever of your community dies while he did not commit *shirk*, will go to Paradise.' I asked, 'Even if he committed adultery and theft?' He said, 'Even if he committed adultery and theft.'" [100]

Ubadah ibn al-Samit narrated that the Prophet ﷺ said, "Whoever says, 'I bear witness that there is no god but Allah, alone; He has no partner; and that Muhammad is His slave and messenger, Isa (Jesus) is Allah's slave and His messenger and His Word directed to Mary, and that Paradise is truth, Hell is truth,' Allah will admit him from any of the eight gates of Paradise he chooses." [101]

Once the Prophet ﷺ gave his shoes to Abu Hurayrah and said to him, "Take these shoes of mine and anyone you meet behind the wall who witnesses that there is no god but Allah being certain in his heart, give him good tiding of Paradise." [102]

Al-Hasan said, "The price for Paradise is to say there is no god but Allah." [103]

Jabir said, "I heard the Messenger of Allah, blessing and peace of Allah be upon him, say, 'No one's deed will take him to Paradise nor can it save him from Hell, even I except the declaration of the oneness of Allah.'" [104]

97. Muslim (iman: 15)
98. Ibid (26)
99. Abu Dawud (3116)
100. Bukhari (1237), Muslim (iman; 94)
101. Bukhari (3435), Muslim (28)
102. Muslim (31)
103. Abu Nu'aym in Sifat al-jannah (50)
104. Ibid (52) See also Muslim (2817)

There is a matter to which attention is to be paid. That is any person will be able to enter Paradise by the mercy of Allah. His deeds alone will not take him to it though they are the cause of his entrance. Allah said in the Qur'an that the people will go to Paradise because of their deeds and in the above Tradition the Prophet ﷺ denied it. There is no contradiction between the two for the following reasons:

Some scholars said that redemption from Hell is because of the forgiveness of Allah and entrance in Paradise is due to His mercy. The fixing of the grades and ranks will be by deeds. It is supported by the report of Abu Hurayrah, which says that when the people of Paradise will enter it, they will be placed according to their deeds. [105]

The Qur'an made the deeds the cause of entering in Paradise though they are not the only cause. This has been explained in the saying of the Messenger ﷺ: "Keep on the right path, be moderate, have good tiding and know that none of you will be able to be saved by his deeds."

The Companions asked, "Even you, Messenger of Allah?" He replied, "Even I, unless Allah covers me with His mercy." [106]

Whoever knows Allah, the Exalted and realises His right upon him and his shortcoming and sins, sees these two by his heart, will surely be able to understand it.

Allah's help is sought. He is Glorious and Almighty.

105. Tirmidhi (2549)
106. Bukhari (39, 6463) Muslim (2818)

CHAPTER 20

THE PRAYER OF THE BELIEVERS FOR PARADISE, AND ITS SEARCH FOR THEM AND ITS INTERCESSION TO THE LORD ALMIGHTY

Allah Almighty tells us about the prayer of his believing slaves in which they said: "Our Lord, we heard a caller calling to faith (saying): 'Believe in your Lord' and we have believed. Our Lord, forgive us our sins, wipe out our bad deeds, and cause us die with the righteous. Our Lord, bestow upon us all that You have promised us through Your messengers. Do not humiliate us on the Day of Resurrection. You do not fail in Your promise." *(3: 193-194)*

The meaning is 'grant us what You have promised on the tongues of Your messengers for admission in Paradise'.

Some others said that the meaning is 'grant us what You have promised us to have faith in Your messengers'. But the first interpretation is more appropriate because it includes belief in the Messenger and his message.

Then they implored by their faith to grant them what He had promised through the messengers. They heard through the messengers the promise of Paradise. It also contains belief in the messengers that they have conveyed the promise of Allah and they believed in them.

There is another explanation which is that 'grant us the victory and success which You have promised through the messenger'. However, the first explanation is more accurate and perfect.

Consider how their belief in Him included belief in His commandment and prohibition, His Messengers, His promise and threat, His names and Attributes and His acts. It also included the truth of His promise and fear of His threat and that they responded to His command. With all this they became believers of their Lord, and they deserved to implore Him to grant them what He had promised and rescue them from the Fire.

Some people found it difficult to comprehend their request for the fulfilment of His promise when He is going to do it. They tried to remove the problem by saying that it was real devotion, like the following saying of the Prophet:

"My Lord, pass the true judgment" (21: 112), or the saying of the angels:
"Forgive those who repented and followed You path" (40: 7).

These people did not realise that the promise was linked with conditions including the desire for Him and asking Him to fulfil what He has promised. It is also connected with faith and being certain that nothing spoils it. When they prayed for the fulfilment of His promise it included request for giving them support, assurance and help on the causes which will make Him fulfil His promise. This prayer, therefore, is the more important, and more useful than many other supplications.

As for the request "My Lord, pass the true judgement", it means to request Allah Almighty to grant them victory over their enemies. In the same way the prayer of the angels for forgiveness of those who repent, it is one of the reasons which produce the forgiveness. Allah, the Most Eminent, designs causes for what He wants to do with His friends and enemies, and He makes them the means of carrying out what He wishes.

If it is still posing a problem to you, then look at the causes He created for His love and anger. He loves, is pleased, gets angry and unhappy through the causes He created and wanted. Everything comes from Him and is based on His will and wisdom. This is a great gate of Tawhid only available for those who have knowledge.

Another example for asking Him about His promise is His statement:
"Say, which is better, this or the lasting Garden that those who are mindful of Allah have been promised as their reward and destination? There they will find everything they wish for, and there they will stay eternally. This is a binding

promise from your Lord." *(25: 15-16)*

His sincere believers will ask Him for that and the angels will ask for it for them. Paradise will ask its Lord for its people, and its people will ask Him for it. The angels and the messengers will ask for it for them and their followers. On the Day of Judgement Allah, the Most High, will place them before Him; they will be pleading for His believing worshippers. It shows the perfectness of His kingdom, the exposition of His mercy, kindness, generosity and benevolence. He will give whatever He is asked for and this is the result of His names and attributes, which cannot fail. The Lord Almighty is Generous; all generosity is exclusively for Him. He loves to be asked, begged, and entreated. He created people who will ask Him and inspired them to entreat Him. He also created what they will ask for. So, He is the Creator of the petitioner, his request and the matter which he asks for. All this because He loves His worshippers to implore Him, show interest in Him and ask Him. He gets angry when he is not asked.

'Allah gets angry when He is not begged and the son of Adam gets angry when he is begged.'

The most beloved of His slaves is the one who asks Him much and puts his request in proper form. He loves those who insist on imploring. The more a person insists on asking Him, the more he comes close to Him and He loves him and gives him what he is asking. There is no god but Him. What a tragedy brought by false rules about faith, which put a barrier between the hearts and the knowledge of their Lord and His names and His perfect Attributes. Praise is to Allah Who guided us to this. We would have never found the way had not Allah showed us the path.

Anas ibn Malik related Allah's Messenger ﷺ saying, "No Muslim asks Allah for Paradise three times but it says: 'O Allah, admit him into Paradise.' Anyone who seeks refuge from Hell three times, Hell says: 'O Allah, give him refuge from Hell'. [107]

Abu Hurayrah reported that the Prophet ﷺ said, "No believer asks Allah for Paradise seven times a day but Paradise says: 'O Allah, Your slave so and so asks You to get entrance in Paradise, so get him inside me." [108]

---

107. *Tirmidhi (2572), Nisa'i (5536) Ibn Majah (4340)*
108. *Abu Nu'aym in Sifat al-Jannah (68)*

Abu Hurayrah also narrated that Messenger of Allah ﷺ said, "No one ask Allah to protect him from Hell seven times but Hell says: O Allah, Your slave seeks protection from me, so grant him protection. No one asks for entrance in Paradise seven times but Paradise says: 'O Allah, Your slave so and so asks to enter me so admit him in me." [109]

Abu Hurayrah also reported that the Messenger of Allah ﷺ said, "Ask Allah frequently for Paradise and protection from Hell because they will intercede and their intercession will be accepted. When a man asks Allah frequently for Paradise, it says: 'O Allah, Your slave so and so asks You to come to me, so accommodate him in me, and Hell says: 'O Allah, this slave of Yours is seeking refuge in You from me, so grant him that." [110]

A group of early Muslims did not ask Allah for Paradise and said: 'it is enough that Allah keeps us away from Hell.' Among them was Abu al-Sahba' Silah ibn Ashyam who performed prayer one night till dawn, then raised his hand and prayed: 'O Allah, give me refuge from Hell. Can a man like me dare to ask You for Paradise.' Another person was 'Ata' al-Sulami who did not ask Allah for Paradise then he was told that the Prophet ﷺ has said, "Allah, the Exalted, says: 'Look in the record of My servant, if you find him asking for Paradise, I will grant him that. Whoever seeks refuge in Me from Hell I will grant him refuge." [111]

Jabir reported the story of Mu'adh who made lengthy reciting in prayer and a person complained to The Messenger ﷺ. He said that the Prophet ﷺ asked the person, "What do you do, the son of my brother, when you do the prayer?"

He replied, "I read the opening chapter, and ask Allah for Paradise and seek His refuge from Hell. I do not know your humming or Mu'adh's humming."

The Prophet ﷺ said, "I and Mu'adh hum around it as well." [112]

We have already cited the report that every day Paradise and Hell speak to Allah. Paradise says, "My Lord, my fruits have ripened, my rivers are full and I am longing for my friends, so send my people quickly to me.'"

----
109. Ibid (69), Al-Bazzar 3175), Abu Ya'la (6192)
110. Abu Nu'aym ((70)
111. Al-Hilyah (6: 175)
112. Abu Dawud (793)

It shows that Paradise looks for its people and attracts them to it. Hell also does the same. That is why the Prophet 變 ordered us to remember them regularly and never forget them.

Abdullah ibn 'Umar reported the Messenger of Allah 變 said, "Do not forget two great things."

We asked, "What are they, Messenger of Allah?"
He replied, "Paradise and Hell."[113]

Kulayb ibn Harb narrated:
"I heard the Messenger of Allah, blessing and peace be upon him, say, 'Seek Paradise as much as you can, and run away from Hell as much as you can. The seeker of Paradise does not sleep and the fugitive of Hell does not feel exhausted. The Hereafter if surrounded with unpleasant matters and the world is full of pleasures and desires. It should not turn you away from the Hereafter.'"[114]

---

113. Abu Nu'aym in Sifat al-Jannah (66)
114. Tabarani (449), see Majma' al-zawa'id (10: 230)

CHAPTER 21
THE NAMES OF PARADISE AND THEIR MEANINGS

Paradise has different names indicating its qualities; all of them refer to the same entity. These names are synonymous, but they are different in denoting different aspects of it. It is like the names of the Lord, glory be to Him, and the names of His Books, His messengers, the name of the Last Day and the names of Hell. Below are the names of Paradise:

1. The first name is *Jannah*, the Garden. It is a general name, which includes that house and all the sources of pleasure, delight, joy, happiness and the coolness of the eyes. The word (*jannah*) means covering and hiding. From it comes *janin*, meaning foetus, because it is hidden in the belly of the mother. Jinn are given this name because they are hidden from our eyes. The crazy person is called *majnun* for the absence of his reasoning. The word is used for the Garden because it is covered and hidden by trees. The word is given to Gardens, which have plenty of trees of various kinds. *Junnah* is the shield and similar materials, which are used for cover. In this sense Allah used it when He said, "They used their oaths to cover up." *(58: 18)*

The verse is speaking about the hypocrites who tried to cover up and escape from the criticism of the believers. The word Jinnah also comes from it, which refers to Jinn. Allah used it in the Qur'an:
"From among the Jinn and mankind" *(114: 6)*

Some commentators said that the angels are called jinnah as in the statement of Allah:
"They have claimed between Him and the Jinnnah a lineage." *(37: 158)*

These commentators said that this lineage was forged by statement of the polytheists that the angels are daughters of Allah. They supported their view in two ways:

First, the lineage the polytheist claimed was between Allah and the angels and not between Him and the Jinn.

Secondly, Allah said:
"The jinn have already known that they will be brought before Him." *(37: 158)*

They claimed that it is not the jinn but the angels who knew that those who have said this are going to be brought before Him.

The correct view is opposite of what these commentators claim. Jinnah mentioned in the above verse are the jinn not the angels. There are two interpretations of that verse:
First is the explanation of Mujahid who said, "The unbelievers said that the angels were daughters of Allah. Abu Bakr asked them, 'Who are their mothers?' They replied that they were the ladies of Jinn."

Al-Kalbi said, "The unbelievers said that they intermarried with Jinn and the angels were born from them."

A second commentary is the one given by al-Hasan who said, "The disbelievers associated the Devils in the worship of Allah, so this is the lineage they created."

The correct explanation is that of Mujahid and his colleagues. What the scholars holding the first view had said does not prove their case. When the disbelievers claimed that the angels were daughters of Allah, they created link between Allah and Jinn because of it. The pronoun in the verse quoted by them refers to jinn and the meaning is that the Jinn know that they are going to be brought for reckoning. If there was a lineage between Allah and them, they would have not been brought for reckoning. Allah, the Exalted said:
"The Jews and the Christians say "We are the children of Allah and His beloved ones'. Say, 'Why does He punish you for your sins?" *(5: 18)*

In this verse Allah, glory be to Him, has made their punishment for their sins as a refutation of their false claim.

2. The second name of Paradise is *Dar al-Salam*, the home of peace. Allah, the Glorious, called it by this name. He said:

"For them is the Home of Peace with their Lord." *(6; 127)*
"Allah invites to the Home of peace". *(10; 25)*

It deserves this name because it is the place of safety from every tribulation, distress and affliction. It is the House of Allah linked with His name *al-Salam* (The Giver of safety). He has surrounded it and its residents with safety. Its residents will be greeted with peace.

The Almighty said:
"Their greeting will be, 'Peace.' *(10; 10)*
"The angels will go to them from every gate, 'Peace be with you, because you have remained steadfast.'" *(13; 23-240)*

The Lord Almighty will greet them from above as He said:
"They will have fruit and whatever they ask for. 'Peace' a word from the Lord of mercy." *(36; 57-58)*

Later the report of Jabir about the greeting of the Lord Almighty to them will be cited. Their talk will all be words of peace; it will be free of futile, indecent or nonsense talks. Allah, the Most Merciful, said:
"There they will hear only peaceful talk, nothing bad." *(19; 62)*

Also consider the following statement of Allah:
"If he is one of those on Right, (they will hear), 'Peace be on you,' from his companions on the Right." *(56; 90-91)*

It has been explained in various ways, which do not convey the real sense. The meaning, and Allah knows best, is, *Peace be on you, O traveller from the world while being among the people on the Right. Peace be on you who have been rescued from the world and its troubles and from Hell and its torment.* Here they are given good tiding at the time of their departure from the world and going to Allah, the Glorious. It is as the angels say when they take the soul of a believer: "Have good tiding of rest and ease and a Lord who is not angry." [115]

This is the first good news for the believer in the Hereafter.

---

115. Ibn Majah (4262)

3. The third name is *Dar al-Kuld*, the Home of Eternity. This name is given to Heaven because its people are not going to move from it, ever. Allah Almighty said:
"An unceasing bestowal" *(11: 108)*
"This is Our provision that will never end." *(38: 54)*
"Its food Is lasting as is its shade." *(13: 35)*
"They are not to be taken out of it." *(15: 48)*

The claim of the Jahmiyyah and Mu'tazilah that Paradise will end will be refuted later, if Allah wills.

4. The fourth name is *Dar al-Muqamah*, the Home of staying forever. Allah, the Exalted, told us about the people of Paradise who will say:
"Praise to Allah, who has removed from us all sorrow. Our Lord is, indeed, Most Forging, Most Appreciative. He settled us in the everlasting home out of His bounty where no toil or fatigue will touch us." *(35: 34-35)*

5. The fifth name is *Jannat al-Mawa* (the Garden of Restfulness).

Ibn Abbas said that this is the Garden in which Gabriel and other angels take rest. Muqatil and al-Kalbi said that it was the Garden to which the souls of the martyrs take refuge. 'A'ishah and Zirr ibn Hubaysh said that it was one of the Gardens. The correct meaning is that it is the name of the one of the Gardens. Allah said:
"For anyone who feared the meeting with his Lord and restrained himself from bad desires, Paradise will be his refuge" *(79: 40-41)*

He said about Hell:
"Hellfire will be the refuge." *(79: 39)*

He said about the hypocrites:
"Your refuge is the Fire." *(57: 15)*

6. The sixth name is *Jannat Adn*, the Gardens of Eden.

It is said that it is the name of one of the Gardens. The correct explanation is that it is the name of all the Gardens. Allah, the Most Supreme, said:
"They will enter the Gardens of lasting bliss (jannat Adn), which Allah, the Most merciful has promised His slaves in the unseen." *(19: 61)*

"For them are the Gardens of perpetual residence which they will enter. They will be adorned there with bracelets of gold and pearls, and their garment in it will be of silk." *(35: 33)*

"He will admit you in pleasant dwelling in the Gardens of Eternity." *(61: 12)*

The derivation of the word indicates that all Gardens are *Jannat Adn* because it means perpetual residing.

7. The seventh name is *Dar al-Hayawan*, the Home of perpetual life.

Allah, the Most High, said:
"The home of the Hereafter is the eternal life." *(29: 64)*

The commentators explained that it is the life after which there is no death. The verse can have two meanings:
1. The life of the Hereafter is free from trouble and ending. It will be free from all that the life of the world is affected.

2. The home of the Hereafter is not going to perish or destroyed as the living creature of the world experience.

8. Another name is *Al- Firdaws*. Allah Almighty said:
"These are the inheritors who will inherit al-Firdaws. They will abide there eternally." *(23: 10-11)*

"Those who believe and do good deeds will be given the Gardens of al-Firdaws as lodging; there they will live for ever." *(18: 107-108)*

The word *al-Firdaws* implies all the Gardens, and especially spoken for the best and highest of them, as though it is more deserving than others.

9. The ninth name is *al-Na'im*, meaning Bliss. Allah, the Exalted said:
"For those who believe and do righteous deeds, there will be Gardens of bliss." *(31: 8)*

It is also a comprehensive name for all Gardens as all of them have variety of food, drink, garments, pleasant fragrances, beautiful scenery and spacious homes and other open and secret pleasures.

10. The tenth name is *al-Maqam al-Amin*, safe place of staying. Allah, the Glorious, said:
"Those mindful of Allah will be in safe place." *(45:51)*

It signifies a place that is safe from destruction, end and all kinds of defects. Its people are protected from trouble, concern and expulsion. Makkah was called as the city of safety because its people were safe from those things, which caused fear in other people. Consider Allah's statement:
"Secure and contented, they will call for every kind of fruit." *(45:55)*

The Almighty combined the security of the place and the safety of food. They will not fear cessation of the fruit or expulsion from it, as they will not be afraid of death.

11. The eleventh name is *Maq'ad Sidq*, the seat of truth. Allah, the Magnificent, said:
"The righteous will be among gardens and rivers, in a seat of honour near an All-Powerful Sovereign." *(54:54-55)*

The Almighty called His Paradise *maq'ad sidq* because it will have all perfect and permanent pleasures. The word 'sidq' implies the established truth, which is sought against the false lie, which includes nothing beneath it.

In another place Allah said:
"Give good tiding to those who believe that they will have sure footing with their Lord." *(10:2)*

The word 'qadam sidq' (sure footing) has been explained as *Heaven*. It has also been interpreted as the *deeds*, which are the cause of going to Paradise. Another meaning given to the word is *reward*, which Allah has preceded for the believers as well as the Messenger who brought the Book and guided them to the right path.

The truth is that the word includes all of it. Allah has decreed the good reward for those deeds which He guided them to by His Messenger and stored their reward with Him for the Day of Resurrection.

Allah, the Glorious has spoken of *liasan sidq* (good name) *(19: 50; 26: 84)*, which means true praise for good deeds and nice behaviour. It is also an indication that the praise is based on reality and there is no doubt of falsehood in it.

The Almighty taught His Messenger to pray for *madkhal sidq wa makhraj sidq* (go in truthfully and come out truthfully) *(17: 80)*. It refers to in and out in which the person has protection and safety from Allah. This supplication is the most beneficial for the believer because he is always in move going and coming. If his going and coming are for Allah and by Allah, he is going truthfully and coming out truthfully.

Allah's help is sought.

CHAPTER 22
THE NUMBER OF THE GARDENS AND EXPOSITION THAT THERE ARE TWO KINDS OF GARDEN: TWO OF GOLD AND TWO OF SILVER

Jannah is a general word, which includes all the Gardens, homes and palaces, which are located in it. There are many Jannah (gardens). It is attested by the report of Anas ibn Malik that Umm al-Rabi' bint al-Bara', who is the mother of Harithah ibn Suraqah, went to the Messenger of Allah 鬖 and said, "Messenger of Allah, tell me about Harithah."
"He was killed in the battle of Badr by an unidentified arrow."
She said, "If he was in Paradise, I will be patient, otherwise I will exert in crying."
The Messenger 鬖 said, "Harithah's mother, there are many Gardens in Paradise and your son is in the highest Firdaws." [116]

Abu Musa al-Ash'ari narrated that the Messenger of Allah, blessing and peace of Allah be upon him, said, "There are two Gardens of gold, their utensils, jewellery and whatever is in them, and two Gardens of silver, their utensils, jewellery and whatever is in them. The only barrier between the believers and their looking at their Lord is the curtain of Majesty on His Face in the Garden of Eden." [117]

Allah, the Exalted, said:
"For he who fears standing before his Lord (for accounting) there are two Gardens." (55:46)

Then He further said:
"Below them are two Gardens." (55:62)

So, they are four. Now there is dispute concerning the meaning of "min dunihima"

---

116. Bukhari (2809, 3982, 6550, 6567)
117. Ibid (4878, 4880, 7444), Muslim (iman: 180)

(below or above), whether the last two are below the previous two or above them. There are two views in this regard:

First, that the last two are closer to the Throne. It means that they are above the first two.

Secondly, that they are below the first ones. It is supported by the use of the word dun in Arabic, which is used opposite of fawq (above).

The context indicates the superiority of the first two Gardens in ten ways:

1. Allah said, "With shading branches." *(55: 48)*

The word "afnan" has been interpreted in two ways.

First it is the plural of "fanan" which means the branch.

Second, it is the plural of "fann", which means kind. The meaning of the verse is that the two Gardens have different kinds of fruit and other materials. This is not mentioned in the last two Gardens.

2. Allah Almighty said about the first ones, "In them are two flowing springs." *(55: 50)*

He said about the second pair, "In them is pair of gushing springs." *(55: 66)*

The flowing ones are better than the gushing ones.

3. The Lord said about the first ones, "They have every kind of fruits in pairs." *(55: 52)*

He said about the second pair, "There are fruits, date palms and pomegranate." *(55: 68)*

Definitely the description of the first ones is more perfect.

Then there is disagreement about the two kinds of the fruits. Some people said that it refers to two kinds of fresh and dry, which will not be below the fresh in its taste and excellence. Others said that the reference is to two kinds, one known and the other unusual in shape. Some other people said that they are two kinds, and no more.

The obvious sense is, and Allah knows better, that the reference is to sweet and sour, white and red. The difference of the qualities of fruits is more admirable and tasty and pleasant to the eyes and the mouth.

4. The Lord said about the first group, "They will be reclining on bed whose linings are of silk brocade." *(55: 54)*

The Almighty spoke of the lining to show the superiority of its covers.

He described the others as "Reclining on green cushions and beautiful fine carpets." *(55: 76)*

He did not describe the materials of the last Paradises as He did with the first ones.

5. He said about the first Heavens, "The fruits of both Gardens will be within reach." *(55: 54)*

The fruits of these Gardens will be close and within the reach of their residents. They will take them as they like. He did not say this concerning the other two.

6. He said about the first pair of the Gardens, "There will maidens restraining their glances." *(55: 56)*

That is they will restrain their glances to their spouses and will not look at any other person due to their love and affection of their mates. It also indicates that their husbands will also restrict their gazes to their wives; their beauty will not let them look at others. The Almighty said about the other two Paradises, "Dark-eyed, sheltered in pavilions." **(55: 72)**

It is obvious that the one whose gaze is fixed to their spouse is better than the one who is kept in pavilion.

7. The Almighty described the maidens of the first pair of Heaven as being like "rubies and beautiful corals." *(55: 58)* in their beauty and brightness of their colour. He did not say this concerning the second pair of the Heaven.

8. The Merciful said about the first pair of the Gardens, "Is the reward of good other than good?" *(55: 60)*

It shows that the residents of these Gardens were engaged in absolute good deeds, and for that they deserved perfect reward.

9. The Lord Almighty started the description of the first pair of the Gardens by saying that they are the reward of those who fear standing before their Lord to indicate that it is the highest reward for those who had fear of Allah. As those who fear Allah are divided between those who are ahead and those who are on the right. He mentioned the Gardens of those ahead then mentioned the Gardens of those on the right.

10. Allah, the Exalted said, "Beyond them there are two Gardens." *(55: 62)* The context indicates that the later Gardens are below the first ones.

Now someone may ask: How these four Gardens are divided among those who fear standing before Allah? The answer will be that since these people are of two types as indicated earlier, the two high Gardens will be for those who are ahead and the other lower two for those on the right.

There may be another question here. Do all those people share the two Gardens or for everyone there will be two Gardens?

The Commentators have two views and the second view is that everyone will have two gardens. It is more correct for two reasons: from the report and from the meaning.

As for the report there is a report from the Messenger of Allah, blessing and peace be upon him, that there will be two Gardens in the meadows of Paradise.

As for the meaning it is to be noted that the first Garden is the reward of carrying out the duty and the second one for keeping away from forbidden matters.

CHAPTER 23
ALLAH ALMIGHTY CREATED SOME GARDENS BY HIS OWN HAND TO SHOW THEIR SUPERIORITY OVER OTHERS

The Lord Almighty chose from among the Gardens a Home for Himself. He made it close to His Throne and prepared it by His Hand. It is the chief of the Gardens. Allah, the Exalted, selects from every category the highest and the best one. He selected Gabriel from among the angels, and Muhammad ﷺ from among the mankind. He chose from the Heavens the uppermost one, from the cities He chose Makkah, from the month Muharram, from the nights the night of decree, from the days Friday, from the parts of the night its middle and from the times the times of the prayers and so on. He, glory be to Him, "creates what He wills and chooses (what He wills)." *(28: 68)*

Abu al-Darda' reported that the Messenger of Allah, blessing and peace of Allah be upon him, said, "Allah, the Most Beneficent, comes down in the last remaining three hours of the night. In the first hour He looks in the book which no one else can look in, He erases and retains what He wishes. In the second hour He looks at the Garden of Eden, which is His home where He lives. Only the prophets, martyrs and truly faithful join Him. It has materials that no eye has ever seen and its thought has not passed in any heart. Then on the last hour announces: 'is there anyone who seeks forgiveness so I forgive him? Is there anyone who asks for anything so that I give him? Is there anyone who supplicates so that I grant his request?' This continues until dawn. Allah, the Exalted, said, '(Recite) the Qur'an at dawn, dawn recitation is always witnessed.' *(17: 78)* Allah witnesses it as do His angels." [118]

Anas ibn Malik reported the Messenger of Allah, blessing and peace of Allah be upon him, saying, "Allah, the Glorious, created Firdaws by His Hand and forbade it on every polytheist and those addicted to wine and drink." [119]

---
118. Al-Bazzar (3516), Abu Nu'aym in Sifat al-Jannah (8) See Majm'a al-zawa'id (18719)
119. Al-Bayhaqi, Shu'ab (5590), al-Hilyah (4: 93)

Abdullah ibn al-Harith reported that the Prophet ﷺ said, "Allah, the Most Supreme, created three things by His Hand. He created Adam by His Hand, wrote the Torah by His Hand and originated Firdaws by His Hand. He said afterwards, By My power and Majesty, an addicted of wine and *dayyuth* (pimp) will not enter it.

The Companions asked, "Messenger of Allah, we know the addict of wine, but who is *dayyuth*?" He replied, "The one who allows evil deed in his house." [120]

I say that the report is *mawquf*, i.e. based on the statement of the Companions.

Abdullah ibn 'Umar said, "Allah created four things by His Hand: The Throne, the pen, Eden, and Adam. Then He said to the rest of the creatures, 'Be', and it was." [121]

Maysarah said, "Allah did not touch anything from His creature but three. He created Adam by His Hand, wrote the Torah by His Hand and originated the Garden of Eden by His Hand, then ordered it to speak. It said: 'The believers have succeeded.'"

Shimr ibn 'Atyyah said, "Allah, the Exalted, created the Garden of Firdaws by His Hand. He opens it five times every day and says: 'Be more pleasant for My friends, increase in beauty for My friends.'"

Mujahid said, "Allah, the Most Supreme, originated the Garden of Eden by His Hand. When it spoke it was closed and it is opened every morning. Allah looks at it and it says: 'The believers have succeeded.'"

Abu Sa'id reported that the Messenger of Allah ﷺ said, "Allah circled the walls of Paradise putting one brick of gold and one of silver. He framed its Throne by His Hand and then ordered it to speak. It said; 'the believers have succeeded'. Allah said to it, 'Blessed place are you as the abode of the kings.'" [122]

Anas reported that the Messenger of Allah ﷺ said, "Allah created the Garden of Eden by His Hand putting one brick of white pearl, another from red rubies and another of green chrysolite. Its floor is of musk, its ground is of pearl and

120. Sifat al-Jannah (23)
121. Hakim (2: 319)
122. Al-Bayhaqi in al-Ba'th wa- nushur (214)

its grass is of saffron. Then He ordered it to speak. It said: 'The believers have succeeded.' Allah, the Glorious, said, 'By My majesty and honour, no stingy will be My neighbour in you.'"

The Messenger ﷺ recited, "Those who are saved from their soul's greed are truly successful." *(59: 9)*

Pay attention to this care how Almighty made this Garden which He originated by His Hand for the one whom He created by His Hand and for the best of His progeny to show care and honour to him, and to expose the superiority of the one whom He created by His Hand and put him above the rest of the creature. The help lies with Allah. This Garden among the Gardens is like Adam among the rest of the living creatures.

Al-Mughirah ibn Shu'bah reported that the Prophet ﷺ said, "Moses, peace be on him, asked his Lord, 'Who has the lowest grade in the Garden?' Allah said, 'A man who will come after the people of the Garden have entered it. He will be told to enter. He will say: How can I go in when the people have taken their places and occupied them? It will be said to him, 'Would you agree to have what a king of the world has?' He will say, 'Yes, my Lord.' He will be told, 'You will have that and similar to that, another similar to that, another similar to that, another similar to that, and another similar to that.' He said, 'I agreed, my Lord.'

Then Moses asked, 'Who has the highest rank in Paradise, my Lord?' Allah will reply, 'They are the ones for whom I built the Gardens. I originated their honour by My hand and closed it. It has things which no eye has seen, no ear has heard of and no heart has ever imagined. Read its evidence in the Qur'an:
'No soul knows what joy is kept hidden is store for them.' *(32: 17)* "[123]

---

123. *Muslim (iman: 189)*

CHAPTER 24
THE KEEPERS OF THE GARDENS AND THE NAME OF THEIR FOREMAN AND THE LEADER

Allah, the Blessed, said:

"Those who were conscious of their Lord will be led in throng to the Heaven. When they reach it, its gates will be opened, and its keepers will say to them, 'Peace be upon you.'" *(39: 72)*

The keeper of anything is a person who has been entrusted to guard it.

Anas reported that the Messenger of Allah ﷺ said, "I will come to the gate of Paradise on the Day of Resurrection, and ask for it to be opened. The keeper will ask, 'Who are you?' I will reply, 'Muhammad.' He will say, 'Yes, I have been ordered not to open it for anyone before you.'"

The following report of Abu Hurayrah has already been cited in which the Prophet ﷺ said, "Whoever gives out a pair in the cause of Allah every keeper of the Paradise will call him 'so and so, come this way.'"

Abu Bakr said, "Messenger of Allah, this is a man who needs nothing more." The Prophet ﷺ said, "I hope you will be one of them."

In another version, Abu Bakr said, "Will anyone be called from all the gates?" The Prophet replied, "Yes, and I hope you will be one of them."

Since Siddiq's ambition was to achieve all the grades of faith and he wished to be invited from all the gates, he asked the Messenger ﷺ in order to struggle to do the deeds which can bring him that honour. The Prophet ﷺ told him about the deeds and gave him good tiding that he would be one of them. How high was the ambition of Siddiq and how great his desire!

Allah, the Great, gave the chief of the keepers the name 'Ridwan', which is derived from 'Rida', having the meaning of pleasure. On the other hand the keeper of Hell was named 'Malik' derived from 'mulk' meaning power and strength.

CHAPTER 25
THE FIRST MAN TO KNOCK AT THE GATE OF PARADISE

Anas reported that the Prophet ﷺ said, "The keeper of Paradise will say, 'I will not open it for anyone before you and will not stand for anyone after you."

The keeper will stand to him only to express his grade and superiority. For this reason he will not stand for anyone else. The other keepers will be in service of the chief who will be like the king to them, but Allah, the Exalted, has appointed him in the service of His slave and Messenger so that he walked to him and opened the gate for him.

Abu Hurayrah reported that the Messenger of Allah, blessing and peace of Allah be upon him, said, "I will be the first to open the gate of Paradise except that a woman will come before me and I ask her, 'Who are you?' She will reply, 'I am a woman who used to attend on orphans.'" [124]

Ibn Abbas reported:
"Some people sat waiting for the Prophet ﷺ. He came out and when he approached them he noticed that they were talking among themselves. Some of them said, 'It is amazing that Allah has a close friend from His creation; He chose Ibrahim as a close friend.' Another said, 'More amazing is that Allah spoke to Moses.' A third person said, 'Jesus is the word of Allah and His spirit.' Another person said, 'Allah chose Adam.' The Prophet ﷺ came to them and greeted them. He said, 'I heard your talk and your surprise that Ibrahim was the friend of Allah; it is correct. Allah selected Moses for His speech; he is such. Jesus is the spirit of Allah and His word; it is also true. Adam was chosen by Allah, it is true as well. I am the beloved of Allah, and I am not boasting. I will be the first person to intercede and my intercession will be accepted. I say it without boasting. I will be the bearer of the banner of praise on the Day of Resurrection and I am not boasting. I will be the first person to shake the chain of Paradise; it will be open for me and I will

---

124. Abu Ya'la (6651)

enter with the poor people of the believers. I am not boasting. I am the noblest of all the earlier and later people, and I am not boasting.'" [125]

Anas related the Messenger of Allah ﷺ saying, "I will be the first person to rise when the people will be raised, the first to speak when they will be silent, their leader when they come, their intercessor when they will be stopped and I will be the carrier of good tiding when they will be in despair. The Banner of praise will be in my hand. The keys of Paradise will be in my hand on that Day. I will be the noblest of the children of Adam to my Lord. I say it without boasting. A thousand servants will attend on me as they are preserved pearls." [126]

Anas also reported that the Prophet ﷺ said, "I will have more followers on the Day of Judgment, and I will be the first person to knock at the gate of Paradise." [127]

125. Tirmidhi (3616)
126. Ibid (3610), al-Bayhaqi in Dala'il (5: 484)
127. Muslim (Iman: 196)

CHAPTER 26
THE FIRST PEOPLE TO ENTER PARADISE

Abu Hurayrah narrated that the Messenger of Allah ﷺ said, "We are the first and ahead of others on the Day of Resurrection though they were given the Book before us and we were given it after them." [128]

Abu Hurayrah reported that the Prophet ﷺ said, "We are last but first on the Day of Judgment. We will be the first to enter Paradise though they were given the Book before us and we were given it after them. They differed and Allah guided us to the truth by His leave in what they had differed about." [129]

In another version Abu Hurayrah related the Prophet ﷺ saying, "We are the last but first on the Day of Judgment. We will be the first people to enter Paradise except that they were given the Book before us and we were given it after them." [130]

'Umar ibn al-Khattab reported that the Messenger ﷺ said, "Paradise will be forbidden for the prophets until I enter it. It will be forbidden to other communities until my follower enter it." [131]

The above narrations prove that this Community will be first in rising from the graves and ahead of others in reaching the highest position at the time of gathering. They will be first to arrive to the shade of the Throne, and the first to be judged and their cases determined. They will pass the bridge before others and will enter Paradise ahead of them. Paradise will be prohibited for the early prophets until Muhammad ﷺ enters it and it will be forbidden on other communities until the Community of the Prophet ﷺ enter it.

Abu Hurayrah reported that the Prophet ﷺ said, "Gabriel came to me and held my hand. He showed the gate of Paradise through which my followers will enter." Abu Bakr said, "Messenger of Allah, I wished I would have been with you to see it!"

---

128. Bukhari (876, 896), Muslim (al-Jum'ah: 855)
129. Muslim (855)
130. Bukhari Muslim
131. Darqutni, see al-da'ifah of al-Albani (2329)

The Prophet ﷺ said, "Abu Bakr, you will be the first among my followers to enter Paradise."[132]

Ubayy ibn Ka'b reported that the Messenger of Allah ﷺ said, "The first person to shake hand with Allah, the Truth, will be 'Umar. He will be the first to be greeted by Him. He will hold his hand and take him to Paradise."[133]

It is a strange report. One of its reporters Dawud ibn Ata' has been rejected by Imam Ahmad and Bukhari.

132. Abu Dawud (4652) It is a weak report, see al-Da'ifah (1745)
133. Ibn Majah (104)

CHAPTER 27
THOSE WHO WILL ENTER PARADISE FROM THIS COMMUNITY BEFORE OTHERS

Abu Hurayrah reported that Allah's Messenger ﷺ said, "The first group to enter Paradise will be like the moon on a full-moon night. They will neither spit nor relieve nature nor blow their noses. Their utensils and combs will be of gold and silver. They will use aloes wood in their censers, and their sweat will smell like musk. Every one of them will have two wives; the marrow of the bones of their legs will be seen through the flesh out of excessive beauty. They will neither have differences or hatred among themselves, their hearts will be as if one heart. They will be glorifying Allah in the morning and in the evening."[134]

Abu Hurayrah also reported that the Prophet ﷺ said, "The first batch of people who will enter Paradise will be like the moon on a full-moon night, and the batch next to them will be like the most brilliant star glittering in the sky. They will neither urinate, nor relieve nature, nor spit nor blow their noses. Their combs will be of gold, their sweat will smell like musk. The fuel of their censors will be the aloes wood. Their wives will be from among the dark-eyed beautiful maidens. Their feature will be the same in the image of their father Adam, sixty cubits tall."[135]

Ibn Abbas narrated that the Messenger ﷺ said, "The first people to be called to Paradise will be those who praise Allah in prosperity and adversity."[136]

Abu Hurayrah reported that the Messenger ﷺ said, "The first three people of my Community who will enter Paradise were presented to me as well as the first three who will go to Hell. Those three who will enter Paradise are the martyr, a slave who was not kept by his slavery from fulfilling his duty to his Lord and a poor decent man of family. The first three to enter Hell will be a tyrant ruler, a

---

134. Bukhari (3245), Muslim (2934)
135. Bukhari (3327) Muslim
136. Tabarani (228), See al-Da'ifah (2632)

man of wealth who did not pay the dues of Allah in his money and an arrogant poor." [137]

Abdullah ibn 'Umar related the Prophet ﷺ saying, "Do you know who will be the first to enter Paradise?"
The Companions said, 'Allah and His Messenger know best.'
He said, "It will be the poor emigrants by whom the mishaps are removed. One of them dies and his desire remains in his heart; he finds no way to fulfil it. The angels will say, 'Our Lord, we are Your angels and Your keepers and the residents of Your heavens, do not put them in Paradise before us. Allah will say, 'They are My servants, by them mishaps are averted. One of them dies and his desire remains in his heart; he finds no way to fulfil it.' After that the angels will go to them from every gate saying, 'Peace be with you, because you have remained steadfast. An excellent is the final home!'" [138]

Allah, the Glorious, mentioned the categories of the children of Adam and divided them into the fortunate and unfortunate ones. Then He divided the fortunate ones into two categories: the forerunners and the people on the right. He said, **"And the forerunners, the forerunners."** (56: 10)

This statement is explained in three ways:
First that it is to emphasise, and the predicate is His saying:
"They are brought near." (56: 11)

Second is that the first forerunners is subject and the second forerunners is predicate like saying: Zayd is Zayd meaning that Zayd about whom you heard is the very Zayd.

This is the explanation of Sibwayh.

Third is that the second forerunners is different from the first one. The meaning is that those who are forerunners to good deeds in the world are the forerunners on the Day of Resurrection to Paradise. Those who went ahead of others to belief are the first to go to Paradise. This is very clear.

---

137. Ahmad (9497), See Da'if al-Jami' al-saghir (3705)
138. Ahmad (6581)

Now you may ask, what about the report of Buraydah ibn al-Husayb who said, "The Messenger of Allah ﷺ sent for Bilal one morning and asked him, 'How did you go before me to Paradise? Any time I entered Paradise I heard the sound of clatter in front of me. I entered Paradise last night and heard your clatter in front of me. I passed by a splendid lofty gold palace and asked 'for whom is that palace? The answer was that it belonged to a follower of Muhammad. I said, 'I am Muhammad, but for whom is this palace? I was told it was for 'Umar ibn al-Khattab."

Bilal spoke saying, 'Messenger of Allah, any time I called for prayer I performed two *rak'ah*. Whenever I became impure I performed ablution and I thought that I have to perform two *rak'ah* prayers for Allah.'

The Messenger of Allah ﷺ said, 'This was because of that.'"[139]

We will answer that we accept this report and believe in it, but it does not show that anyone can go ahead of the Messenger of Allah, blessing and peace of Allah be upon him. As for the case of Bilal's being ahead of the Messenger ﷺ in Paradise, it is because Bilal used to call to the worship of Allah before the Prophet, Allah's blessing and peace be on him. Then the Prophet ﷺ used to appear in the mosque. He served as chamberlain and servant to the Prophet. It is reported that the Prophet ﷺ will be raised on the Day of Resurrection and Bilal will be in front of him calling the adhan. Bilal's being ahead of the Prophet ﷺ was an honour for the Messenger and an indication of the Prophet's eminence and nobility. Bilal's going ahead is like his being the first for entering the mosque and performing the ablution. Allah knows the best.

139. Tirmidhi (3689), Ahmad (23057)

CHAPTER 28
POOR WILL ENTER PARADISE BEFORE THE RICH

Abu Hurayrah narrated that the Prophet ﷺ said, "The poor Muslims will enter Paradise half a day before the rich ones. Half a day means five hundred years." [140]

Jabir ibn Abdullah reported that the Messenger ﷺ said, "The poor people of my Community will go ahead to Paradise before the rich ones by forty years." [141]

Abdullah ibn 'Amr reported that the Messenger of Allah ﷺ said, "The poor emigrants will go to Paradise before the rich by forty years." [142]

Ibn Abbas related that the Prophet ﷺ said, "Two believers met at the gate of Paradise, a rich one and a poor one, who were friends in the world. The poor was admitted to Paradise and the rich was detained as long as Allah willed. Then he was also admitted to Paradise. The poor met him and asked: 'my brother, what kept you? You were so late that I was worried about you.' The rich replied: 'My brother, I was detained after you left in a horrible and unpleasant situation, and I could reach you after I shed so much sweat that if a thousand camels were to drink after eating sour food, they would have been satisfied."' [143]

Abu Hurayrah reported that he heard the Messenger of Allah ﷺ saying, "The poor believers will enter Paradise half a day that is five hundred years before the rich ones." [144]

In the authentic report the period of forty years is mentioned. Now it may be the correct version or may be both are correct and the different period will be in line with the conditions of rich and poor. There will be some who will be ahead

140. Tirmidhi (2354), Ahmad (8529)
141. Tirmidhi (2355)
142. Muslim (al-Zuhd: 2979)
143. Ahmad (2771)
144. Tabarani , See Majma' al-zawajid (17894)

by forty years and others by five hundred years. The same can be said about the disobedient Muslims who will be kept in Hell according to their conditions. Allah knows best.

Here is an issue to be remembered and that is that going ahead in Paradise does not mean that their grades will be higher. It is very possible that the one who entered late is accommodated in a higher level. This is borne out by the fact that seventy thousand of the Muslims will enter Paradise without accounting. There may be some who faced accounting and are better than them. When a rich is brought for accounting and it was discovered that he engaged in thanking Allah and did many good deeds of kindness, charity and other good deeds, he will be placed in a higher level than a poor who does not have similar good acts. If the rich has shared the same good acts as those of the poor and did more than him then Allah will not cause his reward to suffer. There are two merits: merit of going ahead and merit of high status. They may be found together in some and may be different in others. So one may acquire both the superiority of going ahead and the high rank; one may be deprived of both; some may receive the superiority of rank and another merit of going ahead. It will depend on the condition of the people. Help rests with Allah.

CHAPTER 29
THE CATEGORIES FOR THE PEOPLE FOR WHOM PARADISE IS GUARANTEED

Allah, the Most Merciful, said:
"Hurry towards your Lord's forgiveness and a Garden as wide as the heavens and earth prepared for the righteous, who spend, both in prosperity and adversity, who restrain their anger and pardon people. Allah loves those who do good deeds. Those who when they commit an immorality or wrong themselves remember Allah and implore forgiveness for their sins, and who forgives sins except Allah? And who never knowingly persist in doing wrong. The reward for such is forgiveness from their Lord, and Gardens graced with flowing streams, where they will remain eternally. How excellent is the reward of those who work righteously!" *(3: 133-136)*

In these verses Allah Almighty stated that He has prepared the Garden for the righteous people not for others. Then He described the characteristics of the righteous people as follows:

They spend generously both in prosperity and adversity, ease and hardship against some people who spend in prosperity and ease but do not spend in adversity and hardship.

They restrain their harm from the people by withholding their anger and put away revenge for forgiveness.

The Almighty then described their situation with their Lord concerning their faults. When they commit sins they resort to remembrance of Allah, turning in repentance to Him and asking for forgiveness. They do not persist in the sins. This is their condition with Allah, and that is His treatment of them.

Allah also said:
"The first forerunners (in the faith) from among the emigrants and helpers

and those who followed them with good conduct, Allah is pleased with them and they are pleased with Him. He has prepared for them Gardens beneath which rivers flow. They will abide in them forever. This is the great attainment. *(9: 100)*

In the above verse Allah, the All-Knowing, told us that He has prepared the Gardens for the emigrants, the helpers and their faithful followers. There is no chance for anyone who goes out of his or her way.

Allah, the Exalted, said:
"True believers are those whose hearts tremble with awe when Allah is mentioned, whose faith increases when His revelations are recited to them, who put their trust in their Lord, who keep up the prayer and give to others out of what We have provided for them. Those are the ones who are true believers. They have high standing with their Lord, forgiveness and generous provision." *(8: 2-4)*

'Umar ibn al-Khattab reported, "On the occasion of Khaybar some Companions of the Prophet ﷺ went to him and said: so and so is martyr, so and so is martyr, so and so is martyr. They mentioned a man and said that he was a martyr. The Messenger of Allah, blessing and peace of Allah be on him, said, 'Never, I saw him in the Fire concerning a garment or a cloak which he dishonestly took from the battle gain.' Then he said, 'Son of al-Khattab, go and announce to the people that no one but the believers will go to Paradise.'
So, I went out and announced that no one except the believers will go to Paradise.'"[145]

Abu Hurayrah reported that the Prophet ﷺ ordered Bilal to announce to the people that only a Muslim will go to Paradise.[146]

'Iyad ibn Himar al-Mujashi'I related, "The Messenger of Allah, blessing and peace of Allah be upon him, said one day in his sermon, 'Behold! My Lord has commanded me to teach you that which you do not know of what He has taught me on this day. Any wealth that I have bestowed upon a slave (of Allah) is permissible. The Almighty said, 'I have created all My slaves Hunafa' (with inclination to worship

---

145. Muslim (iman: 114), see also Bukhari (3074)
146. Bukhari (4203), Muslim (man: 111).

Allah alone), but the Devils come to them and turn them away from their religion. They forbid to them that which I have permitted to them, and they tell them to associate others with Me for which I have not sent down any authority.' Allah looked at the people of earth and hated them, Arabs and non-Arabs alike, except the remnant of the people of the Book. He said, 'I have only sent you to trial, and put others to trial through you, and I have revealed to you a Book that cannot be washed away with water, which you will recite when sleeping and when awake.' Allah commanded me to severely strike Quraysh and I said, 'Lord, they will break my head like bread.' He said, 'Expel them as they expelled you, fight them and We will help you, spend and you will be spent upon, send out an army, and We will send five like it, fight with the help of those who obey you against those who disobey you.'"

The Prophet ﷺ further said, "The people of Paradise are of thee types: A man of authority who is fair and just - who gives charity and does good, a man who is compassionate and kind to every relative and Muslims, and a man who refrains from asking for help even though he has dependents. The people of the Fire are of five types: A weak man who lacks the wisdom, those who are your followers that do not have any care for family and wealth, one who is dishonest and is a miser even for a little, a man who will betray you morning and evening with regard to your family and your wealth." He also mentioned miserliness and lying and then went on and said, "and the one whose language is obscene. Allah has revealed to me that you be humble not to boast against one another and no one should oppress others."[147]

Harithah ibn Wahab reported that the Messenger of Allah ﷺ said, "Shall I not tell you about the people of Paradise? It is every weak person who is regarded as insignificant, but if he were to beseech Allah, He would respond to him. Shall I not tell you about the people of the Fire? It is every violent, haughty and arrogant person."[148]

Abdullah ibn 'Amr reported the Prophet ﷺ saying, "The people of the Fire are every arrogant, haughty, proud hoarder and stingy while the people of Paradise are the weak and helpless."[149]

---

147. Muslim (al-Jannah: 2865) The last of this Hadith is a separate one.
148. Bukhari (4918), Muslim (2853) See also Tirmidhi (2605)
149. Ahmad (6591)

Ibn Abbas narrated that the Prophet ﷺ said, "Shall I not tell you your men from among the people of Paradise? The prophet is in Paradise, the faithful true person is in Paradise, the martyr is in Paradise, and a man who visits his Muslim brother in a remote place only for the sake of Allah is in Paradise.

Your women among the people of Paradise are affectionate and fertile who when her husband gets angry or she gets angry comes to him and puts her hand in his hand and says 'I will not sleep until you are pleased.'" [150]

Ibn Abbas reported that The Messenger of Allah, blessing and peace of Allah be on him, said, "The people of Paradise are those who hear people praising him, and the people of the Fire are those who listen people speaking evil about them." [151]

Anas ibn Malik related that a funeral passed and the people praised him. The Prophet said, "It has become necessary, it has become necessary, it has become necessary." Then another funeral passed and bad things were said about him, the Prophet said, "It became necessary, it became necessary, it became necessary."
'Umar asked him why he said that. The Messenger of Allah ﷺ said, "The one who you praised, Paradise became necessary for him, and the one you spoke badly about him, the Fire became necessary for him. You are Allah's witness on earth." [152]

In another report the Prophet ﷺ said, "You could know the people of Paradise from the people of the Fire."
They asked, "How, O Messenger of Allah?"
He replied, "By good praise or bad comment." [153]

In short the people of Paradise are of four categories that are mentioned by Allah the Most High in the following verse:

"Whoever obeys Allah and the Messenger will be with the ones upon whom Allah has bestowed favour: the prophets, the steadfast affirmers of truth, the martyrs and the righteous. And excellent are those as companions." (4: 69)

We pray to Allah to include us among them by His grace and favour.

---

150. Tabarani (12467), see Majma' al-zawa'id (7664)
151. Ibn Majah (4224)
152. Bukhari (1367), Muslim (949)
153. Ibn Majah (4221)

CHAPTER 30
THE MAJORITY OF THE PEOPLE OF PARADISE WILL BE FROM THE COMMUNITY OF MUHAMMAD ﷺ

Abdullah ibn Mas'ud reported that the Messenger of Allah, Allah's blessing and peace be upon him, said once, "Would you not like to be a fourth of the people of Paradise?" We exclaimed glorification of Allah. Then he said, "Would you not like to be a third of the people of Paradise?" We exclaimed the glory of Allah. He said, "I hope you will be half of the people of Paradise. I tell you about it. The Muslims among the disbelievers are like white hair in a black ox or black hair in a white ox."[154]

Buraydah ibn al-Husayb related that the Prophet ﷺ said, "The People of Paradise will be one hundred rows and this Community is eighty rows out of them."[155]

Abdullah ibn Mas'ud reported that the Messenger of Allah, blessing and peace be upon him, said, "How would you be when the fourth of Paradise belongs to you, and the remaining three quarter for all other people?" They said, "Allah and His Messenger know best." He asked, "What about you being one third of Paradise?" They said: 'It is plenty.' He then said, "What would you feel when half of Paradise belongs to you?" They said, "It is more." The Messenger, Allah's blessing and peace be upon you, said, "The People of Paradise are one hundred and twenty rows and you will be among them eighty rows."[156]

There is no contradiction in these reports. Some of them have been passed down through authentic chains. The Prophet hoped his community to be half of the people of Paradise, so Allah granted him that then He added another sixth above it.

---

154. Bukhari (6528), Muslim (iman: 221)

155. Tirmidhi (2546), Ahmad (2300), Tabarani (10682)

156. Ahmad (4328, 3661) Al-Bazzar (3534), Abu Ya'la (5358), Tabarani in kabir (10350, 10398) It is a weak report.

Jabir reported that the Messenger ﷺ said, "I hope that those who follow me from my Community will be a quarter of the people of Paradise." Jabir said that we cried the glory of Allah. The Messenger said, "I hope you will be half of the population of Paradise." [157]

157. Ahmad (15116), Al-Bazzar (3533) see Majma' (18675)

CHAPTER 31
WOMEN WILL BE MORE IN NUMBER THAN MEN IN PARADISE

Muhammad ibn Sirin narrated, "The people discussed who will be more in number in Paradise: men or women. So, Abu Hurayrah said, "Didn't Abu al-Qasim, Allah's blessing and peace be on him say that the first batch that will enter Paradise will be glittering, like the moon on a full-moon night and those who will follow them will be like a brilliant star shining in the sky? Every one of them will have two wives, each of them will be so beautiful and transparent that the marrow of the bones of their legs will be seen through the flesh. There will be no bachelors in Paradise."[158]

If these women are from the women of the world then women in the world are more than men, and if they are from the beautiful dark-eyed women then the case is easier. Apparently they will be the fair large eyed beautiful hur, as it is reported from Abu Hurayrah that the Messenger of Allah, blessing and peace of Allah be upon him, said, "For every man in Paradise there will be two wives from fair women of large beautiful eyes. Each of them will be dressed with seventy robes still the marrow of their legs will be seen through their dress."[159]

If it is said that how then you would reconcile this Hadith with the Hadith of Jabir reported in two *Sahihs* in which he said, "I attended Eid prayer with the Messenger of Allah, blessing and peace of Allah be upon him. He performed the prayer without adhan and iqamah, then delivered a sermon after the prayer and exhorted people and warned them. Then he went to the women with Bilal and exhorted them and ordered them to give charity. A woman would take her ring, earring and other materials to give out. The Prophet ﷺ asked Bilal to collect them. He said to them, 'You are in small number in Paradise.'
A woman asked, 'Why is that O Messenger of Allah?'
He replied, 'You curse much and show ingratitude to your husbands.'[160]

---
158. Bukhari (3246), Muslim al-jannah: 2834)
159. Ahmad (8550)
160. Bukhari (978), Muslim (885)

In another Hadith the Prophet is reported to say, "The minority of the residents of Paradise is women."[161]

It is said that they together with the large eyed beautiful Hur will be most of the residents of Paradise. The women of the world will be less in Paradise and most of them will be in Hell.

Imran ibn Husayn reported that the Messenger of Allah ﷺ said, "I looked in Hell and saw the majority of its people being women and I looked in Paradise and found the majority of its people being the poor."[162]

A similar statement has been reported by Ibn Abbas,[163] Abu Hurayrah[164] and Abdullah ibn 'Umar.[165]

Abdullah ibn 'Umar narrated that the Messenger of Allah, blessing and peace be upon him, said, "Women, give in charity and seek much of forgiveness, for I have seen that you are the majority of the people of Hell."

A wise woman among them said, "Why is it so, O Messenger of Allah that we are the majority of the people of the Fire?"

He replied, "You curse a great deal and are ungrateful to your husbands. I have never seen anyone so deficient in intellect and religion more overwhelming to a man of wisdom and reason than you."

She said, "O Messenger of Allah, how are we deficient in intellect and religion?" The Prophet ﷺ said, "As for lacking in intellect, the testimony of two women is equivalent to the testimony of one man. This is deficiency in intelligence. A woman does not perform prayer for several days and she does not fast in Ramadan (during her menses), which is deficiency in religion."[166]

The case of women being less in Paradise is attested by the following report of

161. Muslim (dhikr: 2738), Ahmad (19858)
162. Bukhari (3241)
163. Muslim (dhikr: 2737)
164. Ahmad (7956)
165. Ibid 96622)
166. Muslim (iman: 79), Ibn Majah (4003)

Mutarrif ibn Abdullah, who said that he had two wives. Once he came from one of them, so the other one said, you are coming from so and so.

He said, "I am coming from Imran ibn Husayn who narrated to us from the Messenger of Allah, blessing and peace of Allah be upon him, that the women will be the minority in Paradise.

There is also the report of Abu Hurayrah to consider, who said that the Messenger of Allah, blessing and peace of Allah be upon him, said in the presence of a number of his Companions, "A man of Paradise will enter to seventy two wives whom Allah will create for him and two from the children of Adam. They will be superior because of their devotion to Allah in the world." [167]

This report has come through weak narrators who are unacceptable.

There is a point to be remembered here. When a Hadith contradicting the authentic ones is reported, no attention should be paid to it.

Umarah ibn Kuzaymah ibn Tahbit reported, "We were in the company of 'Amr ibn al-'As in a trip of pilgrimage or 'Umrah. When we reached Marr al-Zahran, he entered a valley and we followed him. He said, 'We were with the Messenger of Allah ﷺ in this place and we saw a big number of crows. Among them was a white-footed crow with red beak. The Messenger ﷺ said, 'The women will not go to Paradise except like this crow among the crows.'" [168]

The Prophet intended to say that very few women will be admitted into Paradise because this type of crows is few. In another report he said, "A righteous woman is like the white-footed crow."

He was asked to explain what this crow was and he answered that it is that which has one foot white.[169]

The Prophet also said, "'A'ishah is like white-footed crow among the crows."

167. Abu Ya'la
168. Ahmad (17785) see Majam' (7441)
169. Tabarani (7817) see Majma' (7440)

CHAPTER 32
DESCRIPTION OF THOSE WHO WILL GO TO PARADISE WITHOUT ACCOUNTING

Abu Hurayrah narrated, "I heard the messenger of Allah ﷺ saying, 'A group of my Community will enter Paradise; they will be seventy thousand and their faces will be shining like the moon on the moon-night.' Upon hearing this Ukashah ibn Mihsan al-Asadi stood up collecting a blanket on him and said, 'Messenger of Allah, pray to Allah to include me among them.' The Messenger ﷺ said, 'O Allah put him with them.' A man from the Helpers stood and said, 'Messenger of Allah, pray to Allah for me to be included among them.' The Prophet said, 'Ukashah has surpassed you to it.'"[170]

Sahl ibn Sa'd narrated that the Messenger of Allah, blessing and peace be upon him, said, "Definitely seventy thousand or seven hundred thousand of my Community will enter Paradise without accounting holding one another until they enter from the first to the last; their faces will shine like the moon on a full moon night."[171]

This is the first group to enter Paradise without reckoning.

It is attested by Khusayf ibn Abd al-Rahman who said, "I was with Sa'id ibn Jubayr and he asked, 'Who among you saw the shooting star last night?'
I said, 'I did'. Then I added, 'I was not praying but I was stung (by a scorpion).
He asked me, 'What did you do?'
I asked someone to recite ruqyah[172] for me,' I said.
He asked, 'What made you do that?'
I replied, 'A Hadith which al-Sha'bi related to us.'
He asked, 'What did al-Sha'bi relate to you?'
I said, 'He narrated to us that Buraydah ibn Husayb al-Aslami said that there is no ruqyah except for the evil eye or a sting.'

---

170. Bukhari (5811, 6542), Muslim (iman: 216)
171. Bukhari (3247, 6543), Muslim (219)
172. Ruqyah is a sort of charm or incantation used for the treatment of particular illness

He said, 'He who acts according to what he heard (from the Messenger) had done well.

Ibn Abbas narrated that the Prophet ﷺ said, "The nations were shown to me and I saw a Prophet with a group of men, a Prophet with one or two men, and a Prophet accompanied with no one. Then a huge crowd was shown to me, and I thought they were my Community, but it was said to me: 'This is Musa and his people, but look at the horizon.' I looked and there was a huge crowd. It was said to me, 'Look' and there was a huge crowd. Then it was said to me, 'Look at the other horizon' and there was another huge crowd. It was said to me, 'These are your Community and among them are seventy thousand who will enter Paradise without being called for accounting or being punished.'"

Then the Prophet ﷺ got up and went into his house. The people started discussing as to who would enter Paradise without being called to account or being punished. Some of them said, "Perhaps they are the ones who always attended to the Messenger of Allah ﷺ." Some said, "Perhaps they are those who were born in Islam and did not associate anything with Allah." They mentioned several ideas. Then the Messenger of Allah ﷺ came out and said, "What are discussing?" They told him and he said, "They are the ones who did not perform Ruqyah nor asked others to do so, and did not follow omens and upon their Lord did they rely." Ukashah ibn Mihsan stood up and said, "Pray to Allah to make me one of them." He said, "You will be one of them." Another man stood and said, "Pray to Allah to make me one of them." He said, "Ukashah has surpassed you."[173]

In Bukhari's report the word "do not perform ruqyah" does not appear. Our Shaykh (i.e. Ibn Taymiyyah) said it was correct. Some narrators inserted this and it was wrong. The Prophet ﷺ described the quality which will make them enter Paradise without accounting and that is acting in the manner of pure Unity of Allah. Those people do not ask others to do ruqyah for them and they do not follow omens and upon their Lord they rely. Following omens is a kind of association, which these people do not believe in, and they put their trust in Allah not anyone else. Their abandoning Ruqyah and omens is part of their trust in Allah. There is a Hadith saying that following omens is association.

Ibn Msa'ud said, "There is no one among us but he has followed omens, but Allah

173. Bukhari (5705), Muslim (220)

131

takes it away by trust in Him."[174]

It shows that following omens is against trust in Allah.

As for the Ruqyah of evil eye it is a good thing for a man who does it. Gabriel did ruqyah to the Prophet,[175] and the Prophet 器 allowed it and said, "There is no harm if it does not contain *shirk* (association)." [176]

His followers asked him permission to do it and he said, "Whoever of you is able to be useful to his brother, he should do so."[177]

It shows that it is good deed and useful matter, which Allah and His Messenger love. The one who performs Ruqyah is doing something good. But the one who asks anyone else to perform it expects to get benefit from him. It is against the trust in Allah.

If it is asked that how you will explain that 'A'ishah performed Ruqyah on the Prophet as did Gabriel, the answer will be that it is true but the Prophet 器 did ask them to do it. He condemned those who ask for performance of Ruqyah for them. He wanted to close the door of misuse because it is very possible that a man asks someone who is not qualified to do it for him. Allah knows better.

Imran ibn Husayn narrated that the Prophet 器 said, "Seventy thousand of my Community will enter without facing accounting." He was asked, "Who are they O Messenger of Allah?" He said, "They are the ones who did not use cauterization or ask others to perform ruqyah for them and they put their trust in Allah." [178]

Jabir ibn Abdullah reported that he heard the Messenger of Allah, blessing and peace of Allah be upon him, say, "The first group will be saved from the punishment, their faces shining like the moon on a full-moon night. They will be seventy thousand who will not be called for accounting. They will be followed by others whose faces will be like the brilliant star in the sky."[179]

174. Ahmad (3687), Abu Dawud (3910), Ibn Majah (3538)
175. Muslim (salam: 2185)
176. Ibid (2200), Abu Dawud (3886)
177. Muslim (2199)
178. Muslim (iman: 218)
179. Ibid (191)

Ibn Mas'ud related that the Messenger of Allah ﷺ said, "The nations were paraded to me in the season and I looked for my Community. I saw them and was amazed by their big number and their feature. They filled the low land and the mountain. It was said to me, 'Did you agree, Muhammad?' I said, 'Yes.' Then it was said, 'There are with them seventy thousand who will enter Paradise without reckoning. They are the ones who did not ask someone to perform ruqyah for them, did not cauterize and put their trust in Allah alone.'"

Ukashah ibn Mihsan stood up and said, "Messenger of Allah, pray to Allah to make me one of them." The Messenger said, "You are one of them." Then another man stood up and put the same request. The Prophet said, "Ukashah took it before you."[180]

180. Ahmad (3806, 3819, 3987), Abu Ya'la (5318, 5339), See Majma' (15665)

CHAPTER 33
THE HANDFUL OF THE LORD, THE GLORIFIED, WHO WILL BE ADMITTED TO PARADISE

Abu Umamah al-Bahili reported that he heard the Messenger of Allah ﷺ say, "My Lord has promised me to admit into Paradise seventy thousand of my Community without reckoning. With every thousand will be seventy thousand who will be exempted from accounting and punishment, and three handfuls from my Lord." [181]

Another report from Abu Umamah says that the Messenger of Allah, blessing and peace of Allah be upon him, said, "Allah has promised me to admit from my Community seventy thousand without accounting."

Yazid ibn al-Akhnas said to him, "Messenger of Allah, they are just like yellow fly among the flies."

He said, "He, the Exalted, promised me seventy thousand with every thousand seventy thousand and three handful." [182]

'Utbah ibn 'Abd al-Sulami reported that the Prophet ﷺ said, "My Lord, the Glorified, has promised me to admit into Paradise seventy thousand of my Community without accounting. Then every one thousand will intercede for another seventy thousand then my Lord will take by His hand three handful."

'Umar exclaimed the glory of Allah and said, "The first seventy thousand Allah will accept their intercession about their fathers, children, and family members. I hope that Allah will make me one of the last handful of groups." [183]

181. Tirmidhi (2437), Ibn Majah (4286), Ahmad (22366)
182. Tabarani (7665)
183. Tabarani in al-awasat (312)

Abdullah ibn Amir ibn Qays al-Kindi narrated that Abu Sa'id al-Anmari told him that the Messenger of Allah, blessing and peace of Allah be upon him, said, "My Lord, the Magnificent, promised me to admit from my Community seventy thousand without reckoning, and every one thousand will intercede for other seventy thousand. After that my Lord will take three handfuls from the remaining ones."

Abdullah ibn Amir asked Abu Sa'id, "Did you hear it from the Messenger of Allah, Allah's blessing and peace be on him?"
He said, "Yes, by my ear, and my heart retained it." Then he said that the Messenger of Allah, blessing and peace of Allah be upon him, said, "This, if Allah wills, will contain all emigrants of my Community. Allah will complete the rest from our nomads."

Abu Sa'id further said, "It was calculated to the Messenger of Allah 🕮 and reached a million and nine hundred thousand. It was then the Prophet said that it would contain the emigrants of my Community."[184]

Umayr reported that the Prophet 🕮 said, "Allah has promised me that He will admit three hundred thousand of my Community into Paradise."
Umayr said, "Messenger of Allah, increase for us."
The Prophet made a gesture by his hand. Umayr again said, "Add to it, Messenger of Allah."
At this point 'Umar said, "Enough, Umayr."
He said, "What is the matter with you, son of al-Khattab? What matters if Allah admits into Paradise?"
Umar said, "If Allah, the Mighty and Honourable, wished, He would admit into Paradise by one handful."
The Prophet 🕮 said, "'Umar spoke truth."[185]

Anas related that the Prophet 🕮 said, "My Lord, the Mighty and Powerful, has promised me to admit one hundred thousand of my Community into Paradise."
Abu Bakr said, "Messenger of Allah, increase it."
The Prophet made a gesture by his hand.
Abu Bakr said again, "Increase it for us, Messenger of Allah."

184. Tabarani in kabir (22: 304) an in al-awsat (406)
185. Tabarani (123)

'Umar said, "'Allah has power to enter all the people with one handful."
The Messenger of Allah, blessing and peace be upon him, said, "'Umar is right."[186]

Anas narrated that the Messenger ﷺ said, "Allah Almighty has promised me to admit into Paradise four hundred thousand of my Community."
Abu Bakr said, "Make it more, Messenger of Allah'"
He made a gesture by putting two hands together. Abu Bakr again said, "Increase it for us, Messenger of Allah."
'Umar interrupted and said, "Enough, Abu Bakr!"
Abu Bakr said, "Leave me, what will you lose if Allah admits all of us into Paradise?"
'Umar said, "If Allah wills, He will admit His creation into Paradise by one handful."
The Prophet ﷺ said: "'Umar is right." [187]

The people of these handfuls are the ones who will be in the first grip on the Day of two grips.

If someone asks the question here that how it is that they were one grip in the beginning then became three handfuls, the answer will be that Allah, the Exalted, brought out on the Day of two grips their bodies and it is reported that they were like ants. On the Day of the handful they will be with full bodies and complete statures. It was suitable to have numerous handfuls by both hands.

Allah knows better.

186. Abu Nu'aym in al-Hilyah (2: 344)
187. Tabarani in al-Saghir (342) There is another report to this effect reported by Abu Ya'la (3783)

CHAPTER 34
THE DUST, SOIL, GRAVEL AND THE STRUCTURE OF PARADISE

Abu Hurayrah reported, "We said, 'Messenger of Allah, when we see you our hearts become soft and we become among the people of the Hereafter. But when we depart from you, we get involved in the world and get busy with women and children.'

He said, 'If you remain on the same condition on which you are with me, the angels would shake hands with you and visit you in your houses. If you do not commit sins, Allah will replace you with others who will commit sins so that He can forgive them.'

We said, 'Tell us about Paradise and its structure.'

He said, 'Its structure is of one brick of gold and another brick of silver, its plaster is musk, its gravel is pearl and ruby and its soil is saffron. Whoever enters it will be pleased and will not grieve. He will abide in it forever and will not die. His dress will not get dirty and his youth will not go away. Three people's supplications are not turned down: the just ruler, the fasting person until he breaks his fast, and an oppressed person. His prayer is taken up by the clouds, the gates of the heavens are opened for it and the Lord Almighty says, 'By My might and majesty, I will definitely help you even after a while.'" [188]

Ibn 'Umar narrated that the Messenger of Allah ﷺ was asked about Paradise and he said, "Whoever enters Paradise will live there and will not die; he will enjoy and will never despair; his clothes will not decay and his youth will not end."

He was asked, "Messenger of Allah, how is its structure?"

He replied, "It will have a brick of gold and a brick of silver; its paint is aromatic musk; its gravel is pearl and ruby and its soil is saffron." [189]

Abu Hurayrah narrated that the Messenger ﷺ said, "Paradise is erected with a

---

188. Ahmad (8049)
189. Abu Nu'aym in Sifat al-jannah (96)

brick of gold and a brick of silver and its mud is saffron and its soil is musk."[190]

These reports state that the soil of Paradise is saffron but in authentic traditions it is said to be musk as Abu Dharr related from the Messenger of Allah, blessing and peace of Allah be upon him, that he said, "I entered Paradise and saw in it domes of pearl and its soil was of musk."[191]

Abu Sa'id al-Khudri reported that the Prophet ﷺ asked Ibn Sayyad about the soil of Paradise and he said, "It is white pure musk." The Prophet said, "He spoke truth."[192]

Jabir ibn Abdullah narrated that a man went to the Messenger of Allah ﷺ and said, "Muhammad, your followers were defeated today." He asked how they were defeated.
The man replied, "The Jews asked them about the number of the keepers of the Fire and they said, 'we do not know till we ask our Prophet.'"
The Messenger ﷺ said, "Will a people be defeated who were asked something which they did not know and said till we ask our Prophet? But the Jews are enemies of Allah. They demanded their Prophet to show them Allah overtly. Bring the enemies of Allah to me and I will ask them about the soil of Paradise."
They came and asked the Prophet, "Abu al-Qasim what is the number of the keepers of Hell?'"
He indicated with his hands that they were nineteen. Then the Messenger of Allah asked them, "What is the soil of Paradise?"
They looked at one another and said, "Loaf of bread."
The Prophet, blessing and peace of Allah be upon him, said, "Loaf from white pure flour."[193]

Now there three descriptions of the soil of Paradise, but there is no contradiction among them. Some early scholars said that its soil is mixed of both saffron and musk. It may have two meanings:

Firstly, that the soil was of saffron and when it was kneaded with water, it became musk. When its mud was pure and its water was clean and they were mixed

---

190. Al-Bazzar (3509) see Majma' (18637)
191. Bukhari in a long report about the story of the mi'raj (349), Muslim (iman: 163)
192. Muslim (fitan: 2928)
193. Tirmidhi (3327)

together it produced another smell like musk.

The second meaning is that its colour is saffron and smell is musk. This is the best thing. There is beauty and radiance, the colour is of saffron and the fragrance is of musk.

In the same way its illustration by clean bread whose colour is yellowish and it is soft and smooth.

Mujahid explained it saying, "The land of Paradise is of silver and its soil is musk." That is the colour is white like that of silver and fragrance is that of musk.

Abu Hurayrah reported the Prophet ﷺ saying, "The ground of Paradise is white, its courtyard is hills of camphor. Dunes of musk surround it. It has continuous flowing rivers, the people of Paradise - the entire first and the last - get together around them; they get introduced. Allah sends the breeze of mercy, which diffuses over them the fragrance of musk. One of them returns to his wife while his beauty and smell have increased, she says to him, 'when you left me I admired you, but now I am more delighted by you.'" [194]

Abu Sa'id reported that the Messenger of Allah ﷺ said, "Allah constructed the Gardens of Eden by His hand, its structure is from a brick of gold and a brick of silver, its paint is aromatic musk, its soil is of saffron and its gravel is pearl. Then the Almighty asked it to speak and it said, 'The believers have succeeded.' The angels said, 'Blessed are you as the home of the kings.'" [195]

194. Musannaf of Ibn Abi Shaybah (15802)
195. Sifat al-jannah (140)

CHAPTER 35
THE BRIGHTNESS AND WHITENESS OF PARADISE

Ibn Abbas narrated that the messenger of Allah ﷺ said, "Allah created Paradise white and the most beloved dress to Him white. Dress your living people in it and shroud the dead in it."

Then the Prophet ﷺ gathered the shepherds of the goats and said to them, "If anyone of you had black goats, he should mix them with white ones."

After that a woman came to him and said, "Messenger of Allah, I have taken black goats and I see that they are not growing."

He told her to take white ones.[196]

Ibn Abbas reported that the Messenger of Allah, blessing and peace of Allah be upon him, said, "Hold on to white because Allah has created Paradise white. Your living people should wear it and shroud your dead in it."[197]

Al-Sammak reported that he met Abdullah ibn Abbas in Madinah after he had become blind and asked him, "What is the ground of Paradise?"

He said, "It is white marble of silver as though it a mirror."

Al-Sammak asked, "What is its light?"

Abdullah ibn Abbas replied, "Didn't you see the light before the sunrise? Its light will be like that but there is no sun or cold."

Laqit ibn Amir related that the Prophet ﷺ said, "The sun and moon will be held back and the People of Paradise will not see them."

So Laqit ibn Amir asked, "How we are going to see then?"

The Prophet ﷺ replied, "As you see at this moment." The time was the sunrise when it appeared and faced by the mountains.[198]

---

196. Sifat al-jannah (129) It is very weak report.
197. Ibid (130)
198. Ahmad (16206)

Usamah ibn Zayd related that he heard the Prophet ﷺ say, "Is there anyone who is prepared for Paradise? Paradise is very magnificent. It is, by the Lord of the Ka'bah, glittering light, moving basil and lofty palace. It has continuously flowing river, tasty fruit and beautiful attractive wife and plenty of dress. There will be a permanent residence in safe home with plenty of fruit, greenery, delight and pleasure in a lofty brilliant place."

They said, "We are ready for it, O Messenger of Allah."

He said, "Say if Allah wills."

The people repeated, "If Allah wills."[199]

---

199. *Ibn Majah (4332), Ibn Hibban (2620)*

CHAPTER 36
THE CHAMBERS, PALACES AND COMPARTMENTS OF PARADISE

Allah, the Most High, said:

"For those who are conscious of their Lord there are apartments above which there are apartments built high." *(39: 20)*

The Almighty told us that there will be apartments above apartments and they are built to remove the impression that it is only an illustration and there are no buildings. It is only imagination, as though a person sees built apartments one above the other. The word 'built' qualifies both apartments to give the meaning that they will have high living quarters some being higher than others. Allah, the Most Gracious, also said:

"They will be rewarded with high apartments because of their endurance." *(25: 75)*

Consider how the Almighty gave the reward of high apartments, due to their statements, which contained expressions of humbleness and modesty and submissiveness to Allah. This they deserved, for their endurance of harsh addresses from the ignorant to them. Allah rewarded them for their endurance, greeting them from Himself and the angels.

Allah, the Exalted, said:

"Neither your wealth nor your children will bring you near Us, but those who believe and do good deeds will have multiple rewards for what they have done, and will live safely in lofty dwellings of Paradise." *(34: 37)*

"He will forgive your sins; admit you into the Gardens graced with flowing streams, into pleasant dwellings in the Gardens of Eternity." *(61: 12)*

Almighty told us about the wife of Pharaoh that she said:

"Lord, build me a house near You in the Garden." *(66: 11)*

Ali reported that the Messenger of Allah ﷺ said, "In Paradise there are apartments the inner sides of which can be seen from outside and their outside will be seen from inside."
A Bedouin asked, 'For whom are they, Messenger of Allah?"
He ﷺ replied, "For the one who speaks nice words, offers food, continuously fasts and performs prayer in the night when the people are sleeping."[200]

Abu Malik al-Ash'ari reported that the Messenger of Allah ﷺ said, "There are apartments in Paradise the inner of which is seen from outside and the outside from the inner side. Allah has prepared them for the one who offers food, keeps fast consistently and performs prayer in the night when the people are asleep."[201]

The authentic report of Abu Sa'id quotes the Prophet ﷺ saying as follows:
"The people of Paradise will see the residents of the apartments as you see the bygone star in the horizon."[202]

Abu Musa al-Ash'ari narrated that the Prophet ﷺ said, "A believer will have in Paradise a tent of one hollow pearl the length of which will be sixty miles. His family will reside in it. The believer will go round them, but one of them will not see the other."[203]

In another Hadith the Prophet ﷺ said, "Whoever builds a mosque for the sake of Allah, Allah will build for him a house in Paradise."

He also said, "Allah, the most Magnificent, says, 'Build a house for My servant and name it *the house of praise* for a believer who at the time of the death of his son praised Allah and said 'we belong to Allah and to Him we are to return.'"

Abdullah ibn Abu Awfa, Abu Hurayrah and 'A'ishah reported that Gabriel said to the prophet ﷺ, "This is Khdeejah, convey her greeting from her Lord and give her good tiding of a house of pearl in Paradise where there will be no noise or fatigue."[204]

200. Tirmidhi (1984)
201. Tabarani (3467)
202. Bukhari (3256), Muslim (al-jannah: 2831)
203. Bukhari (4879), Muslim (2838)
204. Bukhari (3819), Muslim (fada'il: 2432)

Abu Hurayrah narrated from the Prophet ﷺ who said, "There is a palace of pearl in Paradise which has no crack or weakness, Allah has prepared it for His friend Ibrahim."[205]

Anas reported that the Messenger of Allah ﷺ said, "I was taken to Paradise and I came across a palace of gold. I asked, 'To whom does it belong?' They said, 'It is for a man of Quraysh.' I thought that it was me, but I asked, 'Who is he?' They said, 'Umar ibn al-Khattab.'"[206]

Hasan said, "A palace of gold is only for a prophet, faithful true, martyr and a just ruler." He said it raising his voice.

Mughith ibn Sumayy said, "There are in Paradise palaces of gold and other of silver, pearl ruby and chrysolite."

Ubayd ibn 'Umayr said, "The lowest person in rank in Paradise will have a home of one single pearl with its apartments and gates."

Ibn Abbas reported that the Messenger of Allah, blessing and peace of Allah be upon him, said, "There are apartments in Paradise if their residents are inside them, things outside will not be hidden from them; and if they are behind them, things inside them will not be hidden from them."

He was asked, "For whom they are, Messenger of Allah?"
He said, "For the one who speaks sweet words, fasts constantly, offers food to others, disseminates greeting, and performs prayer while the people are asleep."

Someone asked, "What is a sweet word?"
He replied, "(To say) 'glory be to Allah, praise be to Allah, there is no god but Allah, and Allah is great.' They have got angels before them and behind them."

He was asked, "What is constant fasting?"
He said, "When someone fasts the month of Ramadan, and fasts the following Ramadan."

205. Tabarani, al-Bazzar (2346)
206. Tirmidhi (3688), Ahmad (12046)

He was further asked, "What is offering food?"
He said, "To provide food for the family."

"What is dissemination of greeting?" He was asked.
He said, "Shaking hands with your brother and greeting him."

"What is praying when the people are asleep?" He was asked.
He said, "The Isha' prayer."[207]

Although this report is weak, there are many others to support it.

Jabir ibn Abdullah narrated the Prophet ﷺ saying, "Shall I not tell you about the apartments of Paradise?"
"Surely, Messenger of Allah, tell us. May our fathers and mothers be ransom for you."
He said, "There are apartments in Paradise from all kinds of gems. Their outer parts will be seen from inside and their inner side will be seen from outside. They have the pleasure and enjoyments which no eye has ever seen, and no ear has heard of."

We said, "For who are these apartments, Messenger of Allah?"
He replied, "For the one who disseminates greeting, offers food, fasts constantly, and prays in the night when the people are asleep."

We asked, "Who has strength to do that?"
He said, "My Community can do it. I tell you how. When a person meets his brother, he greets him. In this way he disseminated greeting. When a person offers food to his family and children to their fill, he has offered food. Whoever fasts the Month of Ramadan and three days from every month, he has constantly fasted. Anyone who performed the last prayer of Isha' in congregation he has prayed while the people i.e. the Jews, the Christians and the Magians are asleep."[208]

The chain of this report is not trustworthy but it has support from other reports.

207. Al-Bayhaqi in al-Ba'th (254)
208. Ibid (253)

CHAPTER 37
THE PEOPLE OF PARADISE WILL KNOW THEIR HOMES WHEN THEY ENTER IT THOUGH THEY HAVE NOT SEEN THEM BEFORE

Allah, the Most Beneficent, said:
"He will not let the deeds of those who are killed for His cause come to nothing; He will guide them and put their hearts at rest. He will admit them into the Garden He has already made known to them." *(47: 4-6)*

Mujahid explained it saying, "The people of paradise will head for their homes and dwellings without missing them as though they have lived in them since their birth. They do not need to be guided."

Ibn Abbas said, "They are more familiar of their homes than the people who attended Friday prayer and returned to their homes."
Muhammad ibn Ka'b said, "They recognize their residences as you know your homes in the world when you come back from Friday prayer."

This is how the majority of commentators have explained the above verses. Abu 'Ubaydah put it in short saying that Allah has described them and they knew them without being guided.

Muqatil ibn Hayyan said, "We are told that the angel entrusted with the care of the children of Adam will walk in Paradise and the son of Adam will follow him. He will reach the last dwelling and he will tell the person about everything he was given in Paradise. When he enters his home and his wives, the angel will go away."

Hasan said, "Allah has described Paradise to them in the world and when they enter it they will know by its description."

According to this statement description was done in the world and the meaning of the verse will be that Allah will admit them in Paradise, which He has made known to them. But according to the first interpretation it will be done in the Hereafter, if the word 'ta'rif' is given the meaning of introducing. However there is another interpretation that the word is from 'arf' meaning pleasant fragrance. This is the choice of al-Zajjaj who said that Allah has made their home full of pleasant fragrance.

However, the first interpretation is better that Allah, the Glorious, has told them and described in a way that everyone will know his abode and dwelling and will not miss it.

Abu Sa'id al-Khudri reported that the Prophet ﷺ said, "When the believers are saved from the Fire, they will be halted on a bridge between Paradise and Hell settling their matters of the world. When they are cleared and cleansed permission will be granted to them to enter Paradise. By the One in whose Hand is my soul one of them will be more certain about his home than his home in the world."[209]

In another report Abu Hurayrah narrated the Prophet ﷺ saying, "By the One who sent me with truth, you are not more familiar with your dwellings and affairs than the people of the Garden are with their dwellings and wives when they enter Paradise." [210]

209. Bukhari (2440, 6535)
210. Abu Nu'aym in Sifat al-jannah (287)

CHAPTER 38
HOW WILL THE PEOPLE OF PARADISE ENTER IT AND HOW WILL THEY BE RECEIVED WHEN THEY ENTER

Allah, the Exalted, said, **"Those who were conscious of their Lord will be led in throngs to the Garden."** *(39: 73)*

"On the Day We gather the righteous as a delegation before the Lord of mercy." *(19: 85)*

Ali Narrated that he asked the Messenger of Allah, blessing and peace of Allah be upon him, about the above verse and said, "Messenger of Allah, the delegation is a travelling party."

The Prophet ﷺ said, "By the One in whose hand is my soul when these people come out of their graves, they will be received with white she-camels with wings and gold saddles. The laces of their hoofs will be brilliantly shining. Every step of them will be range of vision. They will reach the gate of the Garden on which will be a chain of red ruby over plates of gold. There will be a tree at the gate of the Garden from beneath it two streams will be gushing. When they drink from one of them the radiance of bliss will appear on their faces. When they performed ablution from the second stream, their hair will never be dishevelled. They will shake the chain with plate, if you could hear the ringing of the chain. Every beautiful dark-eyed woman will know that her husband has arrived and she will hurry to welcome him. Her guardian will open the gate for him. Had not Allah, the Owner of majesty and honour, told him about him, he would have bowed down to him for the light and radiance he would see.

He (the guardian) will say: 'I am your caretaker who is given the task of taking care of your affairs.' He will advance and the person will follow him until he reaches his wife. She will hurry to him from the tent and hug him saying: 'you are my love and I am your love. I am pleased and will never be displeased. I am fresh not to be dried ever. I will stay with you forever and will never depart from you.' He will then enter a lofty house the distance between its ground and the roof will be a hundred cubits. It is built on the waterfall of the pearl and ruby having red, green and yellow paths, none of these paths will be the same as the other. He will approach the couch, which will have a bed. On the bed will be seventy mattresses on which will be seventy wives. Each one will have seventy robes, yet the marrow of their legs will be seen from the inner of the skin. He will pass the night in intercourse with all of them.

There will be rivers constantly flowing beneath them: rivers of pure water not bitter or muddy. There will be streams of pure honey not extracted from the belly of the bees.

There will be other rivers of wine very tasty for the drinkers, which have not been squeezed out by the feet of men. Also there will be rivers of milk whose taste has not been spoiled and which has not been taken from the bellies of the animals. When they desire food white birds will come to them and raise their wings and they will eat any type of food they wish. Then they will fly away. There will be fruits hanging, when they desire them, the branch will come low and they will be able to eat any type of fruits they wish reclining or standing. This is what is described as 'the fruits of the two Gardens are close.' They will have attendants like pearls in their service."[211]

Ali said, "Those who are mindful of their Lord will be led in throng to the Garden. When they arrive at a gate of it, they find a tree from the root of it two streams are flowing. They approach one of them as though they have been commanded and drink from it. All the dirt, filth and foul matters are washed away. They drink from the other and performed ablution from its water, which causes the radiance of bliss to appear on them. After that their skin will never change or crack and their hair will not be dishevelled as if they have been lubricated. Then they will reach the keepers of Paradise who will say to them: 'Peace be upon you, you have become pure. Enter it to abide in it forever.' (39: 74)

Then they will be met by the children who will surround them as the children of the world surround when a close intimate comes back after absence. They say to them: Get good tiding of the honour which Allah has prepared for you. One of

---

211. Ibn Abi al-Dunya

those children will go to some of the beautiful wives of the person and announce to her that so and so has come. He will call him by the same name he was known in the world. She will ask him, 'Did you see him?'

He will say: 'Yes, I saw him and he is here behind me.' She will be thrilled by joy and will stand on the doorstep of her apartment. When he arrives at his home he will look at its foundation and realise that it was erected on the rock of pearl above which will be green, yellow and red lofty edifice of every colour. When he raises his eye to the roof it is like the lightening. Had Allah not decreed, it would have taken his eyesight. Then he lowers his gaze and looks at his wives, goblets set out, cushions in rows, and carpets spread; He looks at all these materials of pleasure and reclining says, 'Praise is to Allah Who guided us to this. We would have never been guided if Allah had not guided us.' Then a caller will call: 'you will live and never die; you will stay here and will not depart and enjoy health and will not fall sick.'"[212]

Humayd ibn Hilal said, "We are told that when a man enters Paradise, he is given the form of the people of Paradise, dressed up with their dress and adorned with their jewellery, shown his wives, servants, he is excited by such delight that if it was possible, he would have died of delight. It will be said to him: 'See your happiness, it is for you forever.'" [213]

Abu Abd al-Rahman al-Hubali said, "When the believer enters the Heaven first, he is received by seventy thousand servants as if they are pearl."[214]

Abu Abd al-Rahman said, "For a man of the people of Paradise two rows of young servants will be arranged the two sides of them are not seen. When he walks they walk behind him."[215]

Al-Dahhak said, "When the believer enters the Garden, an angel will lead him to its lanes and ask him, 'Look, what do you see?' He will reply, 'I see palaces of gold and silver.' The angel will say, 'All these are for you.' When he reaches there, servants will welcome him from every gate and every place saying, 'We are for you.'

---

212. Al-Bayhaqi al-Ba'th (272)
213. Ibn al-Mubarak in al-Zuhd (429)
214. Ibid (427)
215. Ibid (415)

Then the angel will tell him to walk and ask him, 'What do you see?'
He will say, 'I see many tents and friends.'

It will be said to him that all these belong to you. When he reaches there, they will be received by them who will say to him, 'We are for you.'"[216]

Sahl ibn Sa'd narrated that the Messenger ﷺ said, "Seventy thousand or seven hundred thousand of my Community will enter Paradise holding one another. The first one of them will not enter until the last person enters. Their face will be shining like the moon on a full moon night." [217]

216. Abu Nu'aym
217. Bukhari (3247), Muslim (iman: 219)

CHAPTER 39
DESCRIPTION OF THE STRUCTURE AND MANNERS OF THE PEOPLE OF THE HEAVEN

Abu Hurayrah narrated that the Prophet ﷺ said, "Allah created Adam on His image, his length being sixty cubits. When He created him, He asked him to go and greet a group of the angels who were sitting. He told him to listen to what they say and that will be your and your progeny's greeting. Adam went and said: 'Peace be on you.' They replied: 'Peace be on you and the mercy of Allah.' They added 'and the mercy of Allah.'

Anyone who enters Paradise will be in the form of Adam being sixty cubits tall. After that the people continued decreasing till now." [218]

Abu Hurayrah reported that the Messenger of Allah, blessing and peace of Allah be upon him, said, "The people of Paradise will enter it being free of hair on their bodies, white, with curly hair and eyes smeared with kohl. They will be of thirty three years old and will have the feature of Adam sixty cubits tall and seven cubits wide." [219]

Anas ibn Malik reported the Messenger of Allah ﷺ saying, "The people of Paradise will be raised in the form of Adam thirty three years of age, free of body hair with eyes smeared with kohl. They will be taken to a tree in Paradise and dressed from it with clothes that will never wear out and their youth will not end." [220]

Abu Sa'id al-Khudri narrated that the Messenger ﷺ said, "Whoever of the people of Paradise dies whether old or young, he will be turned of thirty years old. He will not grow older. The same will be the case of the people of the Fire." [221]

----

218. Bukhari (3326), Muslim (Jannah: 2841), Ahmad (8177)
219. Ahmad (7938) see also Tirmidhi (2545)
220. Siafat al-Jannah (255)
221. Tirmidhi (2562, Abu Ya'la (1405)

If this report is correct, it is not in contradiction of earlier ones because when the Arabs mention a figure that has a surplus, they use two ways:
Either they mention the surplus or drop it. It is well known in their system.

Anas ibn Malik reported that the Prophet ﷺ said, "The people of Paradise will enter it tall like Adam sixty cubits, being handsome like Yusuf, and at the age of Isa thirty years and free from hair and with eyes smeared with kohl."[222]

The above reports are about their physical feature. As for their character Allah said, "We will remove whatever is in their breasts of resentment, and (they will be like) brothers, on couches face to face." (15: 47)

Almighty told us that their hearts will be clean and their faces will be similar.

In a report of Bukhari and Muslim the Prophet ﷺ is reported to say, "Their feature will be like one man and on the form of their father Adam, sixty cubits tall."

Their character has been mentioned in the Hadith cited earlier, which has the following saying, "There will be no disagreement or hatred among them. Their hearts will be like one man's heart and they will be engaged in glorifying Allah morning and evening." [223]

Allah mentioned their wives that they will be of the same age not being old or young. In this age, length and width there is great wisdom, which is not hidden. With the combination of the two will be perfect joy and strength to the extent that a man will have intercourse with a hundred virgins in one day. There is complete equilibrium in their forms as for the length and width are concerned, there being no imbalance in them. Allah knows better.

222. Ibn Abi al-Dunya
223. Bukhari (3245, 3254), Muslim (al-jannah: 2834)

CHAPTER 40

THE HIGHEST AND THE LOWEST PERSON IN RANK IN PARADISE - THE HIGHEST BEING THE CHIEF OF THE CHILDREN OF ADAM, ALLAH'S BLESSING AND PEACE UPON HIM

Allah, the Exalted, said, **"We favoured some of these messengers above others. Allah spoke to some; others He raised in rank; We gave Jesus, son of Mary, the clear signs and strengthened him with the Holy Spirit."** *(2: 253)*

Mujahid and others said, "The one to whom Allah spoke was Moses, and the one who was raised in rank was Muhammad."

In the authentic report of the nocturnal journey when the Prophet ﷺ walked past Moses, he said, "My Lord, I never thought that You will raise anyone above me." Then the Prophet went as high as known only to Allah till he passed the Lot tree of the utmost boundary.[224]

'Amr ibn al-As narrated that he heard the Prophet ﷺ say, "When you hear the mu'adhdhin (caller for the prayer) say as he says, then send blessing to me. If a person sends blessing for me once, Allah will bless him ten times. After that ask Allah to grant me al-wasilah, which is a status in Paradise which only one servant of Allah will get. I hope to be that person. Whoever asks al-Wasilah for me, my intercession will be due for him."[225]

Al-Mughirah ibn Shu'bah reported that the Prophet ﷺ said, "Moses asked his Lord, 'Who was the lowest in rank among the people of Paradise?'
Allah replied, 'It will be a man who will come after the people of Paradise have

---
224. See the full account in Bukhari (6517)
225. Muslim (salah: 11)

entered it. He will be told to enter it. He will say, 'My Lord, how can I go in when the people have taken their places and grasped their shares?'

It will be said to him: 'Will you agree to have like a king of the world has?'

He will say: 'I agree, my Lord.' Allah will tell him, 'You have that and like it, like it, like It, like it, like it, in the fifth time he will say, I agree my Lord."

Moses then asked, 'And who is the highest in rank, my Lord?' Allah will reply, 'They are the one I planted their honour by My Hand and sealed it, and it is something which no eye has ever seen, no ear has ever heard and the thought of it has not passed in any heart.'[226]

Ibn 'Umar reported that the Messenger of Allah ﷺ said, "The lowest in rank among the people of Paradise will be a man who will look at his wives, his favour and his servants from a distance of one thousand years. The most honourable one will be the one who will look at the face of Almighty morning and evening."

Then the Messenger ﷺ recited: **"On that Day there will be radiant faces looking at their Lord."** *(75: 22-23)* [227]

Abu Hurayrah reported that the Messenger of Allah ﷺ said, "The lowest in rank among the people of Paradise will be a man who will have seven levels in it. He will be in the sixth and will have three hundred servants. Every day he will be served in the morning and the evening with three hundred plates of gold, each one of them will have a type of food which is not in the other one and he will find its beginning and end the same in taste. He will be served three hundred utensils of water each one of them being very tasty. He will say: 'My Lord' if You allow me, I will provide all the people of Paradise with food and drink without decreasing my supply.' He will have seventy-two wives in addition to his wives of the world. One of them will occupy her seat a mile of the land." [228]

This Hadith is unacceptable and contrary to what has been reported the authentic ones, which say that the first group to enter Paradise every one of them will have two wives from the beautiful maidens of Paradise. Being sixty cubits tall does not require a mile of land for seat. The other details given in the report are illogical, make no sense and are contrary to the authentic reports cited earlier.

226. Muslim (iman: 189)
227. Tirmidhi (2553), and he said that it was reported as the saying of Ibn Umar
228. Ahmad (10932)

CHAPTER 41
THE GIFT THE PEOPLE OF PARADISE WILL RECEIVE WHEN THEY ENTER IT

Thawban reported:
"I was standing with the Messenger of Allah ﷺ when a Jewish Rabbi came and said, 'Peace be on you, Muhammad.' I pushed him so strongly that he was about to fall to the ground. He said, 'Why do you push me?' I said, 'Can't you say *Messenger of Allah*?' He said, 'We call him by the name given to him by his family.' The Messenger of Allah, blessing and peace of Allah be upon him, said, 'My name Muhammad was given by my family.'

The Jew then said, 'I came to ask you some questions.'
'If I tell you something, is it going to benefit you?' The Prophet asked.
the Jew said, 'I will hear by ears.'

The Prophet ﷺ scratched up the ground by a wood that he held, and said, 'Ask.'
The Jew said, 'Where will the people be when the earth will be turned to another earth?'
The Prophet ﷺ said, 'In dark near the bridge.'
The Jew asked, 'Who will be the first person to cross it?'
The Prophet ﷺ replied, 'The poor emigrants.'
'What gift will they receive when they enter Paradise?'
'The caudate lobe of fish liver', he said.
'What will be their meal after that?'
'The ox of Paradise which grazed in its corners will be slaughtered for them.'
'What will be their drink?'
'From a spring called Salsabil.'

The Jew then said, 'You are right. I came to ask you about something which only a prophet or one or two men on earth know.'
The Prophet ﷺ said, 'Is it going to help you if I tell you?'
The Jew said, 'I will hear by my ear. I came to ask you about the child.'

The Prophet said, 'The sperm of the man is white and the sperm of the woman is yellow. When they meet and the sperm of the man prevails over the sperm of the woman, it results in a male by the leave of Allah. If the sperm of the woman dominates that of the man it is a female by the leave of Allah.'

The Jew said, 'You told truth and you are surely a Prophet.'
Then he left. The Prophet ﷺ said, 'This man asked those questions and I had no knowledge of any of them till Allah, the All-Knowing, told me.'"[229]

Anas gave the following account:
'Abdullah ibn Salam heard about the arrival of the Messenger of Allah ﷺ in Madinah while he was plucking the fruit of his farm. He came to the Messenger ﷺ and said, "I am going to ask you about three things, which only a prophet can know: What is the first sign of the Hour? What is the first meal of the people of Paradise? How a child is extracted to his father or mother?"
The Prophet ﷺ said, "Gabriel told me about these things just now."
He said, "Yes. He is the enemy of the Jews."
Then the Prophet ﷺ recited: "If anyone is an enemy of Gabriel, then it is he who brought down the Qur'an by the leave of Allah to your heart.

"The first sign of the Hour will be a fire, which will break out and gather the people from the east to the west. The first meal eaten by the people of Paradise will be liver of fish. When the sperm of man goes ahead of the sperm of woman, a male is born, and if the sperm of woman goes ahead a female is born."

Abdullah said, "I bear witness that there is no god but Allah, and I bear witness that you are the Messenger of Allah. Messenger of Allah, the Jews are confused people. If they know about my confession of Islam before you ask them, they will accuse me."

Then the Jews came and the Prophet asked them, "What kind of a person is Abdullah among you?"
They replied, "He is our best man and the son of our best man, and our chief and the son of our chief."
He ﷺ said, "What would you think if he becomes Muslim?"
They said, "May Allah protect him from this!"

---

229. Muslim (hayd: 315)

Then Abdullah came out and declared that "I bear witness that there is no god but Allah, and I bear witness that Muhammad is the Messenger of Allah."

They said, "He is the worst person among us and the son of the worst one." They disparaged him.

He said, "This is what I was sacred of, Messenger of Allah."

Abu Sa'id al-Khudri narrated that the Prophet ﷺ said, "The land will become like bread on the Day of Judgment, the Compeller (Allah) will turn it over in His hand as one of you does when on journey, a welcoming feast for the people of Paradise."

Afterwards a Jew came and said, "The Most Merciful bless you Abu al-Qasim! Shall I not tell you about the meal of the people of Paradise?

He said: "Yes."

He said: "The land will be like bread," as the Prophet has told us. He looked at us and smiled till his molar teeth were seen.

Then he said, "Shall I not tell you about their soup?"

He said, "Yes."

He said, "Their soup will be of oxtail and fish."

He asked, "What is that?"

He said, "An ox and fish seventy thousand people will eat from the caudate lobe of their liver." [230]

230. Bukhari (6520)Muslim (munafiqin (2792)

CHAPTER 42
THE FRAGRANCE OF PARADISE

Abdullah ibn 'Amr reported that the Messenger of Allah, blessing and peace of Allah be upon him, said, "Whoever kills a man from the people of *dhimmi* will not receive the smell of Paradise while its smell is received from the distance of a hundred years."[231]

In another report it is said, "Its smell is received from a distance of forty years."[232]

Abu Hurayrah related from the Prophet ﷺ saying, "Behold! Anyone who kills a man who has the pledge of Allah and His Messenger he has violated the pledge of Allah and will not receive the fragrance of Paradise. The fragrance of Paradise is received from a distance of seventy years."[233]

In another report the Prophet ﷺ said, "Whoever kills a man, who was given protection, unjustly will not get the smell of Paradise. The smell of Paradise is received from a distance of a hundred years."[234]

There is no contradiction in these reports as for as the period is mentioned.

Anas reported:
"My uncle could not take part with the Messenger of Allah, blessing and peace of Allah be upon him, in the battle of Badr. He was distressed and said, 'This was the first incident which the Messenger of Allah, blessing and peace of Allah be upon him, faced and I was not with him. If Allah Almighty brings another event after that with the Messenger ﷺ Allah will see what I can do.' He was scared of saying something more. It so happened that he participated in the battle of Uhud with the Messenger of Allah, ﷺ. He met Sa'd ibn Mu'adh who asked him, 'Where are you heading to?'

231. Nisa'i (4764)
232. Bukhari (3166)
233. Tirmidhi (1403)
234. Tabarani (433) A similar statement is also reported. See majma' (10756)

He said, 'How wonderful is the smell of Paradise! I can smell it from the side of Uhud.'

He fought and was killed. More than eighty wounds of cut, pierce and arrow were found in his body. His sister Al-Rubayyi' bint al-Nadr said, 'I could not recognize my brother except by his fingers.' The following verse was revealed:
"There are men among the believers who honoured their pledge to Allah."
(33: 23)

The people thought that it was revealed about him and his colleagues."[235]

The fragrance of Paradise is of two types: a smell which is felt sometimes by the souls and not found by people; and a smell which is noticed by the sense of smelling like that of the flowers. The people of Paradise in the Hereafter share this one, from near and far. In the world it is noticed by those who Allah wills from among His Prophets and Messengers. What Anas ibn al-Nadr sensed may be from this type or it may be from the first one.

Abu Hurayrah reported that the Prophet ﷺ said, "The smell of Paradise is noticed from a distance of five hundred years."[236]

Jabir narrated the Prophet ﷺ saying, "The smell of Paradise is found from a distance of one thousand years. By Allah the one who is disobedient to his parent and the one who severs the blood ties will not sense it."[237]

Abdullah ibn 'Amr reported that the Messenger of Allah ﷺ said, "Whoever claims to belong to other than his father will not get the smell of Paradise while its smell is noticed from a distance of five hundred years." [238]

Allah, the Glorious, has exhibited to His devoted slaves in this world sample of Paradise and examples of pleasant smell, delicious matters, attractive scenes, tasty fruits, pleasure and delight.

Jabir reported that the Prophet ﷺ said, "Allah, the Mighty, says to Paradise: 'be

235. Bukhari (2805), Muslim (imarah: 1903)
236. Abu Nu'aym in Sifat (194) and al-Hilyah (3: 307)
237. Tabarani (in al-awsat, see majma' (8533)
238. Ibn Majah (2611) see al-Sahihah of al-Albani (5988)

pleasant for your people and it becomes pleasant. This is the cold you notice in the morning." [239]

Allah, the Glorious, has made the fire of the world and its grief, worries and sorrows a reminder of the Fire of the Hereafter. Allah said about this fire: **"We made it a reminder."** *(56: 73)*

The Prophet ﷺ told us that the intense cold and heat is from the breath of Hell.[240] His slaves then must feel the breath of Paradise, which is a reminder for them. Allah's help is sought.

239. *Tabarani in al-saghir (75) It is a weak report.*
240. *See Bukhai (3260), Muslim (masajid: 617)*

CHAPTER 43
THE ANNOUNCEMENT MADE IN PARADISE

Abu Sa'id al-Khudri reported that the Messenger of Allah ﷺ said, "A caller will call to the people of Paradise: 'You are going to remain healthy and not falling ill ever. You will remain alive and will never die; you will remain young and will never be old; you will enjoy the pleasure and will never feel distressed.'"

This is how Allah will announce:
"A voice will call out to them, 'this is the Garden you have been given for what you used to do." *(7: 43)*[241]

Abu Hurayrah and Abu Sa'id reported the Prophet ﷺ, saying, "A caller will announce to them: 'This Garden you have been given for what you used to do.' The announcement will be: 'You remain healthy without suffering illness, abide there forever without facing death, and enjoy the pleasure without being in distress.'"[242]

Suhayb narrated that the Prophet ﷺ said, "When the people of Paradise enter it and the people of the Fire enter it a caller will call: 'People of Paradise, you have an appointment with Allah'. They will ask, 'What is it? Didn't He make our scales heavy, whiten our faces, admit us in Paradise and save us from Hell?' Then the veil will be lifted and they will see Allah. By Allah, Allah did not give them anything more pleasant to them than looking at Him."[243]

Abu Musa al-Ash'ari said in his sermon on the pulpit of Basra, "Allah, the Exalted, will send an angel on the Day of Judgement, and he will announce: 'People of Paradise, had Allah fulfilled His promise to you?' They will look and see ornaments, garments, streams and pure wives and say, 'Yes, He has fulfilled what He had

241. Muslim (al-jannah: 2837), Tirmidhi (3246)
242. Sifat al-jannah (290)
243. Muslim (iman: 181)

promised us.'They will say it three times and look and do not see anything missing from what they were promised. Then they will be told, 'Yes, one thing remained.' Allah says: **"Those who did well will have the best reward and more besides."** *(10: 2)* The best reward is Paradise and the more is looking at the Face of Allah."[244]

Abu Sa'id al-Khudri reported that the Messenger of Allah ﷺ said, "Allah Almighty will say to the people of Paradise: 'People of Paradise!' They will answer: 'Here we are, our Lord.' He will ask them: 'Are you pleased?' They will reply, 'Why shouldn't we be pleased when You have given us what You have not given to anyone of Your creation.' The Almighty will say, 'I am going to give you better than that.' They will ask, 'What is better than this, our Lord?' He will say, 'I will cover you by My pleasure and will never be angry with you.'" [245]

Ibn 'Umar reported that the Messenger of Allah ﷺ said, "The people of Paradise will enter it and the People of Hell will enter it, then a caller will announce, 'People of Paradise, there Is no death; the people of Hell, there is no death. Everyone will remain forever where he is." [246]

This call though will be made between Paradise and Hell - it will reach all the people of Paradise and Hell. There will be another call when the People of Paradise will be called to visit their Lord. They will hurry after the call as the believers hurry to the call on Friday.

244. Ibn al-Mubarak in al-Zuhd (127)
245. Bukhari (6549, 7518), Muslim (2829)
246. Bukhari (6544), Muslim (2850)

CHAPTER 44
THE TREES, GARDENS AND SHADES

Allah, the Magnificent, says:
"The people on the right, what are the people on the right? They will dwell amid thornless lote trees, banana clustered with spreading shade, constantly flowing water, abundant fruits, unfailing, unforbidden." *(56: 27-33)*

Allah, the Exalted, also described the two Gardens as:
"Having spreading branches." *(55: 48)*

He, the Glorious said:
"In both of them are fruits and palm trees and pomegranates." *(55: 68)*

In the above verse, the word "makhdud" was explained by Ibn Abbas, Mujahid, Qatadah, and Muqatil and others, as the tree whose thorns have been cut off, leaving no thorn on it.

'Uqbah ibn 'Abd al-Sulami reported:
"I was sitting with the Messenger of Allah, blessing and peace of Allah be upon him, when a Bedouin came and said, 'Messenger of Allah, I hear you mentioning a tree in Paradise. I do not know any tree with more thorns than it.'
The Prophet, peace be upon him, said, 'Allah has made in place of every thorn a fruit having seventy types of taste unmatched.'" [247]

Sulaym ibn 'Amir reported:
"The Companions of the Messenger of Allah, peace and blessing of Allah be upon him, said: 'Allah brings benefit to us by the Bedouins and their questions.' One day a Bedouin came and said, 'Messenger of Allah, Allah mentioned in Paradise a harmful tree and I do not think that there is a tree in Paradise which cause more harm to its people than it.'
The Prophet ﷺ asked, 'Which one is that?'
He said, 'It is the lote tree.'

---

247. *Tabarani (17: 130), Abu Nu'aym in Sifat al-jannah (347) and al-hilyah (6: 103)*

The Prophet said, 'Doesn't Allah say, *Thornless lote tree?* Allah has cut off its thorns and replaced every thorn with a fruit.'"[248]

A group of other commentators said that 'makhdud' means a tree that is burdened with load. This explanation was rejected on the ground that the dictionary did not support it. But this rejection is not right; it is a right statement. The people who said it held that when Allah, glory be to Him, cut off and removed its thorns and replaced them with fruits, the tree became burdened with loads. The above-cited two traditions combine both statements.

The same can be said about the explanation that 'makhdud' is the tree, which does not injure the hand and does not stop a person from it by its thorns. Here the meaning is given with the result, which is done many times by the commentators of the Qur'an.

The word 'talh' is interpreted by majority of the commentators as the banana tree. Mujahid said that the banana and its beauty fascinated them, so they were told that there will be banana trees with layers of fruits. It is the opinion of Ali ibn Abi Talib, Ibn Abbas, Abu Hurayrah and Abu Sa'id al-Khudri.

Another group interpreted it by big huge tree with many thorns, which is found in the deserts. It has beauty, smell and extended shade. Its thorns are removed and it will be loaded with fruits.

Ibn Qutaybah said, "It is loaded with fruits and leaves from the top to the bottom so that its trunk is not visible."

Al-Layth said, "Talh is the tree of Umm Gahylan, which has no crooked thorn. It is one of the trees, which have large thorns, strong stalk and best gum."

Abu Ishaq said, "That tree may have been intended because it has very sweet smell. The people are promised what they love; however, it will be superior to its kind in the world like the other things of Paradise compared with the like of them in the world. They carry the same names but are different in other qualities."

It is obvious that the people who explained *talh* by banana, they looked at its

---

248. *Ibn al-Mubarak in al-Zuhd (263)*

beauty of being in arranged in layers. Otherwise *talh* in the dictionary is the large huge tree of the desert.

As for the extended shade, Abu Hurayrah reported that the Messenger of Allah ﷺ said, "There is a tree in Paradise under its shade a rider will travel for a hundred years and will not cross it. Read if you want, ***And an extended shade.***" *(56: 30)*[249]

Sahl ibn Sa'd narrated that the Prophet, Allah's peace and blessing be upon him, said, "There is a tree in Paradise that a rider may go under it for a hundred years without crossing it."[250]

There is another report by Abu Sa'id al-Khudri to the same effect.[251]

Abu Hurayrah reported the Prophet, Allah's peace and blessing be upon him, saying, "There is a tree in Paradise a rider may go under its shade for seventy or a hundred years. It is the tree of the Garden of Eternity."[252]

Abu Hurayrah said, "There is a tree in Paradise under whose shade a rider will go a hundred years. Read if you like: ***'And an extended shade.'***"

This statement reached Ka'b and he said, "He spoke truth. By the One who revealed the Torah on Moses and the Criterion (i.e. Qur'an) on Muhammad ﷺ, if a man rides a sturdy mount and goes around its root a hundred years, he will not be able to cross it until he falls being old. Allah has planted it by His hand and blew in it. Its root is behind the wall of the Heaven. There is no stream in Paradise but it starts from the root of this tree."[253]

Ibn Abbas said, "The extended shade is a tree in Paradise on a huge trunk which a fast rider can go under its shade for a hundred years all around it. The residents of the apartments of Paradise gather under it and talk. Some of them would wish and remember the enjoyment of the world, so Allah will send a wind from Paradise which will move the tree and bring all the amusements of the world."[254]

249. Bukhari (3252), Muslim (al-jannah: (2826)
250. Bukhari 96552), Muslim (2827)
251. Bukhari (6553), Muslim (2828), Tirmidhi (2524)
252. Ahmad (9877)
253. Al-zuhd (267)
254. Ibn abi al-Dunya

Abu Hurayrah reported that the Messenger 舞, said, "There is no tree in Paradise but its trunk is of gold."[255]

Abu Hurayrah narrated that the Messenger of Allah, blessing and peace be upon him, said, "Allah, the Exalted, says:
'I have prepared for My righteous servants things which no eye has ever seen, no ear has ever heard and its thought has not passed in any heart. Read if you like: No soul knows what has been hidden for them of comfort of eyes as reward for what they used to do.' (32: 17)

And there is a tree in Paradise a rider will go under its shade but will not be able to cross it. Read if you want: *And an extended shade.* (56: 30)" [256]

And a place of a lash in Paradise is better than the world and what it contains. Read if you wish: He who is drawn away from the Fire and admitted to Paradise has attained success. (3: 185)"[257]

Abu Sa'id al-Khudri said, "A man asked, 'Messenger of Allah, what is Tuba?'
The Prophet replied, 'A huge tree in Paradise the distance of one hundred years, the dress of the people of Paradise comes from it.'"[258]

Abu Sa'id also reported that a man said to the Messenger of Allah, blessing and peace of Allah be upon him, "Messenger of Allah, state of joy is for the one who saw you and believed in you."
The Prophet said, "State of joy is for the one who saw me and believed in me, but state of joy then state of joy is for the one who believed in me and did not see me."

A man asked, "What is Tuba, Messenger of Allah?"
the Prophet replied: "A tree in Paradise the length of one hundred years journey, the dress of the people of Paradise comes from it."

This Hadith is cited in Musnad of Imam Ahmad and its wording is, "Tuba for the one who saw me and believed In me and Tuba for the one who did not see me

255. Tirmidhi (2525)
256. Tirmidhi (2525)
257. This is the full text of it in Tirmidhi (3292), Ibn Majah (4328) Its beginning part is in Bukhari (4779) and Muslim (2824)
258. Ahmad (11673) see al-Sahihah (3918)

and believed in me" He repeated it seven times.

Ibn Abba said, "The palm tree's roots in Paradise are from green emerald, its branch is red gold and its leaves are the dress of the people of Paradise. Its fruit is like huge jars and buckets whiter than milk, sweeter than honey and softer than butter. It has no stone in it."[259]

'Utbah ibn 'Abd al-Sulami said, "A Bedouin came to the Prophet, peace be upon him, and asked him about the pool and whether there are fruits in Paradise?'
The Prophet ﷺ replied, 'Yes and there is a tree in it called Tuba?'
He said something that I did not know what it was. The Bedouin asked: 'Is there a tree in our land similar to it?'
He said, 'No, it does not resemble any tree of your land.
Then he asked, 'Have you been in Syria?'
He replied, 'No. It resembles a tree of Syria called walnut, which grows on one trunk and spreads above."
Then the Bedouin asked: 'How big is its root?'
The Prophet ﷺ said, 'If a young camel goes around its root, it will not be able to cover it and will lose its strength out of weakness.'
The Bedouin asked, 'Is there grape in it?'
He said, "Yes."
'How big is the bunch of it?'
'The distance of a month for a crow, which does not feel exhausted and does not fall down.'
'How big is the grain?'
The Prophet ﷺ said, 'Has your father ever slaughtered a huge Billy goat from his herd?'
He said, 'Yes.'
The Prophet said, 'He then removed its skin and gave it to your mother and told her to make a bucket of it?'
He said, 'Yes.'
Then he said, 'This grain will be enough to satisfy me and my family.'
The Prophet said, 'Yes, and to your entire relatives.'"

Asma' bint Abu Bakr narrated, "I heard the Messenger of Allah ﷺ mention the lote tree of utmost bounty and he said, 'A rider will travel in the shade of its branch for

---

259. Sifat al-jannah (354)

a hundred years.' Or he said: 'In the shade of its branch a hundred travellers can rest. There is the spread of gold and its fruit is like huge jars.'"[260]

Mujahid said, "The ground of Paradise is of silver, its dust is musk and the roots of its trees are gold and silver, their branches are pearl and emerald under which are fruit and leaves. If someone eats them standing, it will not hurt him; and if someone eats sitting, it will not be harmful; and if someone eats lying, it will not harm him. Their fruits will be lowered to be within the reach."[261]

Jarir ibn Abdullah gave the following account:
"We halted at al-Safah and saw a man sleeping under a tree; the sun was about to reach him. I said to the slave, 'Take this blanket and put it over him.' He did as I said. When he woke up, we realized that he was Salman. I went to him and greeted him. He said: 'Jarir, do you know what darkness is on the Day of Resurrection?' I said: 'I do not know.' He said: 'It is the injustice of people among them.' Then he took a small twig between his fingers, which I hardly could see and said, 'Jarir, if you look for something similar to this, you will not find.' I said: Slave of Allah, where are the palm trees and other trees?' He replied: 'Their roots will be pearl and gold and above them will be fruits.'"[262]

260. Tirmidhi (2541)
261. Ibn al-Mubarak in al-Zuhd (229)
262. Al-Bayhaqi al-Ba'th (288)

CHAPTER 45
THE VARIETY OF THE FRUITS OF PARADISE AND THEIR QUALITIES AND SMELL

Allah, glory be to Him, says:
"Give those who believe and do good deeds the news that they will have Gardens graced with flowing streams. Whenever they are given sustenance from the fruits of these Gardens, they will say, 'We have been given this before,' because they were provided with something like it. They will have pure spouses." *(2: 25)*

Their saying that "We have been given this before" means that something similar to this not exactly the same one. What is the meaning of this sentence? Is it that we were given fruits similar to this in the world or we were given like this here in Paradise?

Ibn Mas'ud related from some of the companions of the Prophet, peace be upon him, that they said, "When the people of Paradise are provided with fruits, they will look at them and say, 'We have been given this before in the world." Others also said that they will be provided similar to what they had in the world. But some other commentators said that they will say, "This is what we have been given before in Paradise" because they will resemble greatly in the colour and the taste.

They support their view by the following arguments:
First, the likeness of the fruits of Paradise one to the other is greater than the likeness of them with the fruits of the world. Since they will be so similar, they will say it.

Secondly, Ibn Jarir al-Tabari said that they will say that because when the fruits of Paradise are consumed another exactly similar to them is brought. It is reported that Abu Ubaydah said when the fruits of Paradise were mentioned that when a fruit is consumed, it would be replaced by another like it.

Thirdly, the statement "They will be provided with something like it" is like the reason of their saying "This is what we have been given before."

Fourthly, it is known that not all the fruits of Paradise they were provided in the world, many people do not know some of the fruits of the world and they have never seen them.

Another group including Ibn Jarir al-Tabari prefer the opinion that the reference is to the fruits of the world. Al-Tabari said, "The opinion that they will refer to the fruits of the world is correct because Allah said: 'Whenever they are given sustenance from its fruits, they will say: 'This is what we were provided before.' The verse did not say that they will comment like it concerning some fruits and not others. Allah Almighty tells us that whenever they will be given the provision of fruit they will say. Definitely they will say it about the first fruit provided to them after entering Paradise. It is impossible that they say about the first provision given to them from the fruits of Paradise that this is what they have been given before. It is clear that the meaning of the verse is that whenever they are given the provision of the fruits, they will say that this is what we were given in the world."

Here it is to be noted that the people of the first opinion exempt the first provision from it and it is not strange in the style of the Qur'an. You have to specify it in some ways. Below are some suggestions:

1. Many of the fruits of Paradise have no similarity with the fruits of the world. In that case the statement that they will be provided with something like it does not fit in the context.

2. Many of the people had not been able to have all the fruits of the world, which are similar to those of Paradise.

3. It is known that they will not say this every time when they eat a fruit. They will not continue saying it forever. The Holy Qur'an did not mean it and it is not a part of their enjoyment. They will say it to express their amazement. The meaning is that the fruits of Paradise will resemble one another, its first not being better than the last one. They will not be affected by changes, which occur to the fruits of the world. Their trees will not grow old and will not suffer from shortage of production or reduction of the size. They will all be good resembling one another.

Hasan has explained the statement of Allah Almighty, "And they will be provided with something like this" in the following way:

"All the fruits of Paradise will be good without there being a bad one. Look at the fruits of the world a man rejects some of them because they are detestable. The fruits of Paradise will all be tasty and excellent."

Qatadah said, "The fruits of Paradise are all good, not detestable like the fruits of the world, which you select taking some and rejecting some."

Ibn Jurayj and others give the same interpretation.

Some other commentators including Ibn Mas'ud and Ibn Abbas and other Companions of the Messenger of Allah, peace be upon him, said that these fruits will be similar in colour and shape but different in taste.

Yahaya ibn Abi Kathir said, "The grass of Paradise is saffron and its dune is musk; the attending children will go round them with fruits which they will eat. Then they will bring another bunch of similar fruits; they will say, this is what you brought us just now. The servants will say, eat, because the colour is one and taste is different. This is what the following verse means:
'**Whenever they are provided with sustenance from its fruits, the will say, 'We have been given this before,' because they are given something like it.**'*(2: 25)*"

Another group said, "The meaning of the verse is that the fruits of Paradise will resemble the fruits of the world except that the fruits of Paradise are better and tastier."

Abd al-Rahman ibn Zayd said, "They will know the names as they were familiar in the world like apple, pomegranate. When they see the fruits of Paradise they will say, 'This is what we have had before.' The shape will be the same and they will recognize it, but the taste will be different.

This interpretation is preferred by Ibn Jarir al-Tabari.

Allah, the Great, said, "**Gardens of lasting bliss with gates wide open. They will be comfortably seated and will call for abundant fruit and drink.**" *(38: 50-51)*

"Secure and contended, they will call for every kind of fruit." *(44: 55)*

This indicates that they will be secure from its expiring and causing harm. Almighty also said, **"This is the Garden you are given as your own, because of what you used to do, and there is abundant fruit in it for you to eat."** *(43: 72-73)*

"And abundant fruit neither limited nor forbidden" *(56: 32-33)*

That means that it will not be limited to season and will not be forbidden for anyone who wants it.
Allah, the Glorious, also said, **"He will be in pleasant life - in the elevated Garden, its fruit will be hanging near."** *(69: 21-23)*

It means that its fruits will be close from the person and he will be able to take them as he wishes.

Al-Bara' ibn 'Azib said, "He will pluck the fruit while sleeping."

The Almighty further said, **"With shades over them, and its fruit hanging close to be picked."** *(76: 14)*

Ibn Abbas said, "Whenever he wished to have a fruit of it, it would come near him, and he would take what he wished.'"

Another Commentator said, "It will be lowered for them and they will take them standing, sitting or reclining."

Thawban reported that the Messenger of Allah, Blessing and peace of Allah be upon him, said, "When a man in paradise picks a fruit, another will be replaced."[263]

Abu Musa narrated that the Messenger of Allah, peace be upon him, said, "When Allah brought Adam down to earth, He taught him everything and provided him with the fruits of Paradise. So, these fruits you have are from the fruits of Paradise, but these change and those do not."
Jabir reported that the Prophet, peace be upon him, said, "Paradise was presented to me till if I wanted to pick a bunch, I would have done it."

---

263. *Tabarani (2: 102)*

In another version, "I tried to pick a bunch by my hand, but failed to reach it." [264]

Jabir reported, "While we were in the noon prayer the Messenger of Allah, blessing and peace of Allah be upon him, he advanced and we also advanced. He then tried to pick something but he withdrew. When the prayer was completed Ubayy ibn Ka'b asked him, 'Messenger of Allah, you did today something in your prayer which you did not do earlier.'
The Prophet replied, 'Paradise was brought before me with its flowers and beauty and I tried to pick a bunch of grapes to bring to you, but I was prevented from it. If I had succeeded and brought it to you, all those in the heavens and the earth would have eaten from it, and it would not have finished.'"

Usamah ibn Zayd reported that the Messenger of Allah, peace be upon him, said, "Is there anyone who is ready for Paradise? Paradise is not forbidden. It is, by the Lord of the Ka'bah, shining light, moving basil, lofty palace, constantly flowing stream, ripe fruit and beautiful attractive wives together with plenty of dresses, all to be available in a lasting secure house, with fruit, green, ornament, and pleasure in a lofty splendid place."
They said, "Messenger of Allah, We are ready for it."
He said, "Say: If Allah wills"
So the people said, "If Allah wills."

Laqit ibn Sabirah reported that he asked the Messenger of Allah, peace be upon him, "What will the people of Paradise get?"
He replied, "Streams of pure honey, cups of wine which will not result in headache or regret, rivers of milk the taste of which never changes, and unpolluted water: They will have fruit, by Allah, of that which they know and better than that."

---

264. Muslim (kusuf: 904)

CHAPTER 46
FARMING IN PARADISE

Allah Almighty said, "In it there is all that that souls desire and the eyes delight in." *(43: 71)*

Abu Hurayrah reported that while the Prophet, peace be upon him, was talking one day, and a Bedouin was present. The Prophet said, "A man from the people of Paradise will request his Lord Almighty permission to cultivate the land. Allah will ask him: 'Didn't you get all that you desired?' He replied: 'Yes, but I like to cultivate the land. (Allah will grant him permission), he will sow the seeds, and within seconds the plants will grow and ripen and the yield will be harvested and piled in heaps like mountains. Allah will say to him: 'Take, here you are, son of Adam, for nothing satisfies you.'"
On that the Bedouin said, "Messenger of Allah, such person must be either from Quraysh or from the Helpers, for they are farmers while we are not."
On that Allah's Messenger smiled. [265]

This shows that there will be farming in Paradise.

Now it could be asked, *how will the man ask his Lord the permission for farming when Allah has told him that there was no need for it?* The answer is that he asked the permission because he wanted to grow something by his own hand though he had no need.

'Ikrimah said, "A man in Paradise said in his mind: 'If Allah gives me permission, I will cultivate.' All of a sudden he noticed the angels at his door saying, 'Peace be in you. Your Lord is saying that you had a desire in your heart, and He knew it. He has sent with us the seeds.' He will tell the angels to sow them. They will do and the plants will grow like mountains. The Lord will say to him from His Throne, 'Eat, son of Adam, because the son of Adam is never satisfied.'

Allah knows better.

---

265. Bukhari (2348, 7519)

CHAPTER 47
THE RIVERS, SPRINGS OF PARADISE AND THEIR COURSE OF FLOWING

In many places in the Qur'an, Allah has said, **"Gardens beneath which will be flowing streams."** *(3: 195; 9: 89; 47: 12; 64: 9 and many other places.)*

In some places He said, **"Streams will be flowing beneath them"** *(10: 9; 18: 31)*

These verses indicate the following matters:
1. The existence of streams in Paradise is a fact.
2. These streams are flowing and are not stagnant.
3. They are beneath their apartments, palaces and gardens, as it is well known in the streams of the world.

Some commentators assumed that these streams will be flowing under the command of the people of Paradise and they will control them the way they like. What prompted them to say it was that they heard that the streams of Paradise flow without channels. They thought that 'flowing beneath their gardens' means that they will flow under their order. They missed the point because even when the streams of paradise flow without channels, they will be flowing underneath the palaces, dwellings, apartments and beneath the trees. Almighty did not say, 'beneath their land.' The Lord has spoken about streams below the people in the world.

He said, **"Have they not seen how many generations We destroyed before them which We had established upon the earth as We have not established you? And We sent (rain from) the sky upon them in showers and made rivers flow beneath them."** *(6: 6)*

This is what is known and that is what Allah cited the statement of Pharaoh: **"These rivers flow at my feet."** *(43: 51)*

The Almighty also said, **"In them is a pair of gushing streams."** (55: 66)

Sa'id interpreted it as 'gushing with water and fruit.'

Anas said, "They will be gushing with musk and ambergris over the houses of the people of Paradise as the rain pours on the homes of the people of the world."

Allah Almighty said, **"The description of the Garden promised to the righteous is that there will be rivers of water forever pure, rivers of milk the taste of which never changes, rivers of wine, a delight for those who drink, rivers of honey clarified and pure, (all flow in it). There they will find fruit of every kind as well as forgiveness from their Lord."** (47: 15)

Allah the Glorious spoke about these four categories and dismissed from them the damage that occurs to them in the world. The detriment of water is to be brackish and change its taste after remaining for a long time. The spoilage of milk is to be sour. The damage of wine is to change its taste to be distasteful in drink and the corruption of honey is impurity.

It is the sign of the Lord Almighty that in Paradise there are rivers which are not like the rivers of the world. They flow without channels and are removed from the damage, which spoils their perfect taste. The wine of Paradise does not have the bad effect of the wine of the world. It will not cause headaches, bad effects, nonsense talk, intoxication and lack of taste. These are five bad qualities of the wine of the world: it takes away reason, plenty of nonsense talks are made at the time of its drinking, its drinking is not complete without futile talks, it is exhausted and consumes wealth, it causes headaches and has a bad taste. It is defilement from the work of Satan, which creates enmity and hatred among the people and prevents from the remembrance of Allah and performing prayer. It stimulates to committing adultery, sometimes with one's own daughter, sister and other prohibited women from the blood relation. It takes away the sense of honour, produces disgrace, regret and shame and puts its drinker with the lowest type of human being, i.e. mad people. It snatches the good names and qualities and replaces them with ignominious names and characters. It drags to murder of the soul and disclosure of the secret, which may cause him harm or destruction. It leads to brotherhood with Satan in squandering wealth, which Allah has made the means of sustenance. It drags to the revelation of veil, disclosure of secrets, points out the defects, and facilitates committing of crime and evil deeds. It removes from the heart the respect of the forbidden and its addict is like the worshipper of idols.

How many wars it has roused and how many wealthy people it has made penniless? It renders an honourable person to despicable and a noble one to lowly status. It deprives from the favour and causes misfortune. It destroys friendships and brings enmity. How many relations it has spoiled? It separates husband and wife, which caused the loss of the reason for him. It produces regret and makes a person cry. It closes in the face of its drinker many doors of good and opens the doors of evil. It causes misfortune and enhances death. It brings humiliation and causes tribulation to its drinker and makes base people to insult him. It is the vessel of the sin, key of evil, snatcher of favour and cause of misfortune. If it were not enough for its bad quality that it and the wine of Paradise will not come together in the belly of a man, it would have been enough.

Allah's Messenger ﷺ said, "The one, who drinks wine in the world, will not get it in the Hereafter."

The bad qualities of wine are much more than we have cited and they all are removed from the wine of Paradise.

If it is asked, *Allah, the Most High, has described the rivers of Paradise to be flowing, and it is known that flowing water does not get spoiled. Then what is the use of adding "unaltered"?* The answer is that although flowing water does not get spoiled, but if some of it is taken and kept for long time, it will change. The water of Paradise is not affected no matter how long it is kept.

Pay attention to the putting of these four rivers together, which contain the best drink for the people. One is for their drink and their purification, the other for their nourishment and strength and the other for their pleasure and delight and the last one for their cure and benefit.

Allah knows the best.

The rivers of Paradise flow from the top and goes down to the lowest part. It is confirmed by the report of Abu Hurayrah from the Prophet ﷺ who said, "There are a hundred levels in Paradise Allah has prepared for the one who strives in His cause. Between every two levels the distance is like the distance between the sky and the earth. When you ask Allah, ask Him for Firdaws because it is the middle of Paradise, and the highest of it. Above it is the Throne of the Merciful, and from it the rivers of paradise flow." [266]

'Ubadah ibn al-Samit narrated that the Messenger of Allah, blessing and peace of Allah be upon him, said, "Paradise is a hundred levels between every two levels is the distance of a hundred years travelling. Firdaws is the highest of them, from it gush the four rivers and the Throne is above it. When you ask Allah, ask him for *Firdaws*." [267]

A similar Hadith is reported by Mu'adh ibn Jabal as well. [268]

Al-Hasan reported that the Messenger of Allah, peace be upon him, said, "*Firdaws* is at the high ground, the highest and middle of Paradise and from it flow the rivers of Paradise." [269]

Anas reported that Allah's Messenger, (peace be upon him), said, "I was taken to the lote tree of the utmost boundary in the seventh sky, its fruits were like the huge jars of Hajar, its leaves like the ears of elephants, from its roots flow two visible rivers and two hidden rivers. I asked Gabriel: 'What is this?'
He replied: 'the hidden rivers are in Paradise and the visible rivers are the Nile and Euphrates." [270]

Anas also reported the Messenger ﷺ saying, "While I was walking in Paradise I came across a stream the banks of which were of the domes of hollow pearl. I asked: 'What is this, Gabriel?' He replied: 'this is Kawthar, which Allah has given you. Then the angel hit it by his hand and its mud was of pleasant smelling musk." [271]

Anas also reported that the Prophet ﷺ said, "*Kawthar* is a stream in Paradise which

266. Bukhari (2790, 7423)
267. Tirmidhi (2531)
268. Ibid (2530)
269. Tabarni (7: 213), al-Bazzar (3513) see Majma' (18648)
270. Bukhari (3207)
271. Ibid (6581)

Allah has promised me."[272]

Anas reported that the Messenger of Allah, peace be upon him, said, "I entered Paradise and came across a flowing stream the banks of which had tents of pearl. I put my hand to the flowing water and it was good smelling musk. I asked Gabriel, 'For whom it is?' He replied, 'this is *Kawthar* which Allah has given you.'"[273]

Abdullah ibn 'Umar narrated the Prophet ﷺ saying, "*Kawthar* is a stream in Paradise the banks of which are of gold and it flows on pearl and ruby. Its base is musk and its water is sweeter than honey and whiter than the snow."[274]

Mujahid interpreted the word 'kawthar' as abundant good. Anas said, 'It is a stream in Paradise.' 'A'ishah said, 'It is a stream in Paradise, no one puts his fingers in his ears but will hear the ripple of the stream.'

Hakim ibn Mu'awiyah reported his father saying that the Messenger of Allah, peace be upon him, said, "There is in Paradise a sea of water, a sea of honey, a sea of milk and a sea of wine. The streams burst from them."[275]

Abu Hurayrah narrated that the Messenger of Allah, peace be upon him, said, "Whoever desires that Allah gives him the wine of the Hereafter he should shun it in the world. Whoever likes that Allah provides him with dress of silk in the Hereafter he should abandon it in the world. The streams of Paradise flow from beneath of the hills of musk. If the person with lowest ornament is to be compared with the entire ornaments of the world, his ornament will be superior to the ornaments of the entire world."[276]

Abdullah ibn Qays reported that the Prophet ﷺ said, "These streams originate from a pit in the Garden of Eden then burst in streams."[277]

Anas ibn Malik reported that the Messenger of Allah, peace be upon him said, "I feel that you think that the streams of Paradise are channels in the earth. No,

---

272. Muslim (salat: 400)
273. Bukhari
274. Tirmidhi (3361), Ibn Majah 94334)
275. Tirmidhi (2571), Ahmad (20072)
276. Al-Bayhaqi in al-Ba'th (266)
277. Tabarani in Kabir, and Ahamd (11253) see al-Da'ifah (2635)

by Allah, they flow on the surface of the earth one bank of them is pearl and the other ruby, its mud is pure musk." [278]

Anas read, "We gave you Kawthar". He then said that the Messenger ﷺ said, "I have been given Kawthar and it was flowing and was not split. Its banks are the domes of pearl and I touched its base and found it pure musk and its gravel was pearl." [279]

Abu Hurayrah reported that the Messenger of Allah, blessing and peace of Allah be upon him, said, "Sayhan, Jayhan, Euphrates and the Nile are from the rivers of Paradise." [280]

Ibn Abbas said, "There is a stream in Paradise called al-Baydaj. It has domes of ruby and under it are girls. The people of Paradise say: 'let us go to al-Baydaj, and they look at the girls. When one of them likes a girl he touches her wrist and she will follow him." [281]

Allah, the Supreme, said, **"The righteous will be in gardens and springs."** (15: 45; 51: 15)

"The righteous will drink from a cup mixed with kafur, a spring from which the righteous servants of Allah will drink; they will make it gush forth in force." (76: 5-6)

"They will be given a drink infused with ginger from a spring called Salsabil." (76: 17-18)

Almighty told us about the spring from which those brought near to Allah will drink that it will be pure and the drink of the righteous ones will be mixed. This will be because the former made all their deeds purely for the sake of Allah, so their drink will be pure and the latter's deeds were mixed, so they will have mixed drink.

Similar to this is the following statement of Allah, **"The truly good will live in bliss, seated on couches, gazing around. You will recognize on their faces the**

278. Al-Hilyah (6: 205)
279. Al-Bazzar (3488)
280. Muslim (jannah: 2839)
281. Sifat al-jannah (324)

radiance of bliss. They will be served sealed nectar, its seal (perfumed with) musk - let those who strive, strive for this - mixed with the water of Tasnim, a spring from which those brought near will drink." *(83: 22-28)*

The Lord Almighty informed that their drink will be mixed with two things, with kafur in the beginning of the chapter and ginger at the end of it. Kafur has cold and pleasant smell, and ginger has heat and good fragrance. When these two are mixed and one is taken after the other a new pleasant and delicious taste is produced which is not available in one of them alone. The quality of one of them is adjusted by the other. It is elegant expression to mention Kafur in the beginning and ginger at the end. It means that their drink is mixed first with Kafur, which has cold followed by ginger, which has heat to adjust it. It is clear that the second cup is different from the first one and they are two different delicious drinks, one mixed by Kafur and the other with ginger.

The Lord informed about mixing their drink with Kafur (camphor) and its coolness against what He mentioned about the heat of the fear, preference of others, patience and fulfilling of all the obligations which they took upon themselves. Besides, they strove to fulfil the duties that Allah put upon them. For that He said, **"He rewarded them, for their steadfastness, with Garden and silk (robes)."** *976: 12)*

Patience is hard and requires controlling the soul from its desires, so it was proper that its reward be opposite of it in the form of spacious Garden and smooth silk. Almighty combined radiance of bliss and happiness. It shows the beauty of their outside and beauty of their inner side as reward of their following the obligations of the Shari'ah physically and adorning their inner by the realities of faith.

It is similar to what is said at the end of the chapter:
"They will wear the garments of green silk and brocade; they will be adorned with silver bracelets." *(76: 21)*

This is the adornment of the outward; then He said:
"He will give them a pure drink." *(76: 21)*
This refers to the adornment of the internal, which is cleansed from every filth and impurity.

Similar to it are the words of Allah Almighty to their father Adam:

"In the Garden you will never go hungry, feel naked, be thirsty, or suffer the heat of the sun." *(20: 118-119)*

He, the Merciful, guaranteed for him not to be affected by the disgrace of the inner side with hunger, or the shame of outward by being naked. He is not going to suffer the heat of inside by thirst or the heat of outside by sun.

The other example is what the Merciful has enumerated His favours on His slaves that He provided them with garment to cover their nakedness and adornment for their outside. He gave another garment to adorn them, in and out, that is the garment of consciousness of Allah and He declared that it was the best of both garments. Similar to this is His saying that He adorned the lower sky with stars and a means of safeguard against every rebellious devil. He thus adorned the open side by stars and inner side with safeguard. Another example is that He ordered the person who intended to perform pilgrimage to take material provision and told him that the best provision is that of interior, which is consciousness of Allah. Another illustration is the statement of the wife of Aziz (the governor of Egypt) about Joseph:
"This is the one you blamed me for." *(12: 32)*

She showed them his beauty and charm then said:
"I tried to seduce him but he remained chaste."
She told them about the beauty of his inner and the adornment of his chastity.
There are many examples in the Qur'an for anyone who reflects.

CHAPTER 48
THE FOOD AND DRINK OF THE PEOPLE OF PARADISE

Allah, the Glorious, said, "The righteous will enjoy cool shades and springs, and any fruit of their desire; (they will be told): 'Eat and drink to your hearts' content as a reward for your deeds." *(77: 41-43)*

"Anyone who is given his record in his right hand will say, 'Here is my record, read it. I knew I would meet my Reckoning,' and so he will have a pleasant life in a lofty garden, with clustered fruit within his reach. It will be said, 'Eat and drink to your heart's content as reward for what you have done in days gone by." *(69: 19-24)*

"This is the Garden you are given as your own, because of what you used to do. There is abundant fruit in it for you to eat." *(43: 72-73)*

"The description of the Garden the righteous have been promised, is that beneath it rivers flow. Its fruit is lasting, and its shade." *(13: 35)*

"We provide them with any fruit or meat they desire. They pass around a cup which does not lead to any idle talk or sin." *(52: 22-23)*

"They will be served with a sealed nectar, its seal (perfumed with) musk, so for this let the competitors compete." *(83: 25-26)*

Jabir reported that the Messenger of Allah, blessing and peace be upon him, said, "The people of Paradise will eat and drink; they will not blow their noses, relieve nature or urinate. Their food is burp like the smell of musk. They will be inspired glorification and exaltation as you are inspired taking breath."

In another report, the Companions asked the Prophet ﷺ, "What will happen to the food?"

He replied, "They will have belch and sweat like the smell of musk. They will be inspired glorification and laudation of Allah."[282]

Zayd ibn Arqam narrated that a man from the community of the people of the Book came to the Prophet, peace be upon him, and said, "Abu al-Qasim, you claim that the people of Paradise will eat and drink?"

He said, "Yes, by the One in whose hand is Muhammad's soul, one of them will be given the potency of a hundred men in eating, drinking, intercourse and sexual appetite."

The man asked, "Anyone who eats and drinks will need to relieve, but there is no dirt in Paradise?"
The Prophet replied, "One of them will relieve by sweating which will appear on their skins and will smell like musk, which will contract his belly."[283]

Abdullah ibn Mas'ud reported that the Messenger of Allah, blessing and peace be upon him, said, "You will look at a bird in Paradise and desire it; it will immediately fall before you, roasted."[284]

The report of Anas concerning the case of Abdullah ibn Salam, and the narration of Abu Sa'id al-Khudri about the earth being a loaf of bread have already been cited.

Hudhayfah reported that the Prophet 鷺 said, "There are in Paradise birds huge like camels."
Abu Bakr asked, "Are they smooth, Messenger of Allah?"
He said, "Those who eat them are smoother than them. You are one of those who will eat them, Abu Bakr."[285]

Qatadah commented on the verse, **"The meat of any bird they like."** (56: 21)
He said, "We are told that Abu Bakr said, 'Messenger of Allah, I see that the birds of Paradise are tender as the people of Paradise are tender.'

282. Muslim (Jannah: 2835, 18, 20)
283. Ahmad (19289), Tabarani in Kabir (5004) and awsat (1743), al-Bazzar (3522).
284. Al-Bazzar (3532)
285. Al-Bayhaqi in al-Ba'th (319)

He said, 'The one who will eat them is more tender than them. They are huge like camels. I expect from Allah that you will be one to eat from them, Abu Bakr.'" [286]

Abdullah ibn 'Amrah explained the following verse:
"Dishes and goblets of gold will be passed around them." *(43: 71)*

He explained it, saying, "Seventy dishes of gold will be passed around them, each dish will have a type of food which is not in the other."[287]

Anas reported that the messenger of Allah, blessing and peace be upon him, said about *Kawthar*, "It is a stream which Allah has given me, whiter than milk and sweeter than honey. There are birds the necks of which are like the camels."
'Umar said, "They are tender, Messenger of Allah."
The Messenger said, "The one who eats them will be more tender." [288]

Masruq said, "Nectar is a wine which will be sealed, after drinking it the taste of musk will be noticed."

Abdullah said, "Mixed with the water of Tasnim, that will be mixed for the people on the right. Those brought near will drink it pure."

Ibn Abbas said the same thing as well.

'Ata' said, "Tasnim is the name of the spring from which the wine will be mixed."

Abu al-Darada' said about the verse **"Its seal will be musk"** that it is a drink white like silver; they will end their drink by it. If a man of the world puts his hand in it then takes it out, no man will remain without getting its fragrance.

These texts tell that in Paradise there will be bread, meat, fruit, sweet and variety if drink - water, milk and wine. The names of these materials are taken from what is available in the world otherwise they are totally different from them in taste.

It could be asked, *how will the meat be roasted when there is no fire in Paradise?'* Some people have answered this question by saying that it will be cooked by

---

286. Ibid (320)
287. Ibid (321)
288. Tirmidhi (2542)

order of Allah, "Be," and it will be done. Others say that it will be roasted outside Paradise then brought in it.

The right answer is that it will be cooked inside Paradise by the means which Allah, the Mighty, the Wise, will provide for cooking and preparing as He has arranged means for making fruits ripe. It is also possible that there will be a fire in Paradise which does not cause destruction. It is reported through authentic sources that the incense burners of the people of Paradise will be aloe wood, which will be burned for getting a good smell.

Allah, the Beneficent, said that there will be shades in Paradise. Shades must move from their position. Allah said,
"They and their spouses seated on couches in the shades. *(36: 56)*

"The righteous ones will enjoy shades and spring." *(77: 41)*

"We will admit them into cool refreshing shade." *(4: 57)*

The food and sweet and burning incense require means for preparation. Allah the Almighty is the Creator of the cause and effect. He is the Lord and Controller of everything, there is no being worthy of worship except Him. As He created cause and effect He also designed means of digestion of the food through burping and sweating. This is the means of getting the material out and that is the means of preparing it. He, glory be to Him, arranged for heat in their stomach to cook, make it mild and prepare it to get out in the form of belch and sweat. In the same way He creates heat for the trees and fruits to make them ripe, and He made the leaves of the tree shade. The Lord of the world and the Hereafter is one, and He is the Creator of causes and wisdom for what He creates. The servant is surprised when he notices things appearing without the known causes. It leads some people to reject and disbelieve, which is mere ignorance and injustice. His power is not incapable of creating other causes and effects, as His power is not limited to this visible world.

Perhaps when a sensible person looks at the first creation of the Lord Almighty, which is seen and witnessed, he becomes more surprised than the second one, which He has promised. He may find the production of these fruits from the hard ground with water and suitable air more amazing than their production from the ground, water and air of Paradise. He is surprised to see the generating of these drinks, which are nourishment, medicine, drink and delight from waste matter and blood, and from the emitting of a fly. He finds these things more amazing than seeing the rivers of them in Paradise. He also notices the extraction of gold and silver from the mountains and thinks it more surprising than their production from other sources. He finds origin of silk from the insect, which makes a solid white, red, and yellow edifice very strange compared to its production from the blossom of the trees in the Heaven. To him the flowing of rivers and seas between the sky and the earth on the backs of the clouds is more amazing than its flowing in Paradise without having a course.

In short, contemplating of the signs of Allah which He called His servants to think about and made them indications of His perfect power, knowledge, will, wisdom, and control, and being the sole being worthy of worship can open the minds of people to recognize Him. Look at what He has said about the Hereafter, Paradise and Hell and you will find that all these are perfect signs. You will also notice that all these originate from one niche, one Lord, one Creator and one Master. So away with the people who do not believe!

CHAPTER 49
DESCRIPTION OF THE VESSELS OF THE PEOPLE OF PARADISE THEY WILL USE FOR EATING AND DRINKING

Allah, the Exalted, said, **"Plates and goblets of gold will be circulated among them."** *(43: 71)*

The word "Sihaf" has been translated as round bowels without handles.

The Almighty also said, **"Endless youths will go round among them with glasses, flagons, and cups of pure drink from flowing spring."** *(56: 17-18)*

The word "Abariq" (translated here as flagons) is said to be vessels, which have handles. It is derived from "bariq" meaning clarity. These vessels will be shining from their clarity. The vessels of Paradise will be of silver like glass in clearness; its content will be seen from outside.

Allah Almighty said, **"They will be served with silver plates and gleaming silver goblets according to their fancy."** *(76: 15-16)*

Here Allah, the Glorious, told that these vessels will be of silver in the clarity of glass. He also said that these vessels are measured and made according to their satisfaction, no less and no more. This will increase the joy of the drinker because if they were less than what they needed, their joy will be reduced, and if they were bigger, they may feel weariness, and get bored.

The word "ka's" means a vessel with wine. Some commentators explained the word as wine. As a matter of fact it is a word which denotes the container and the content together.

Abu Musa al-Ash'ari reported that the Messenger of Allah, peace and blessing be upon him, said, "There will be two Gardens of gold with their vessels and all that they contain; and two Gardens of silver with their vessels and what there is. There is no barrier between the people and looking at their Lord except the veil of majesty on His Face in the Garden of Eden."[289]

Abu Hurayrah narrated that the Prophet ﷺ said, "The first group to enter Paradise will be in the shape of the moon on a full-moon night, the one following them will be like the brilliant shining stars. They will not urinate, or relieve nature, or blow nose or spit. Their combs will be of gold and their sweat will smell like musk. Their burning incense will be aloe wood. They will have spouses from among the beautiful dark-eyed maidens. Their structure will be the same as one man in the form of their father Adam sixty cubits tall."[290]

Hudhayfah ibn al-Yaman reported that the Prophet ﷺ said, "Do not drink in the vessels of gold and silver and do not eat in their plates; it is for them (i.e. unbelievers) in the world and for you in the Hereafter."[291]

Anas narrated that the Prophet, peace and blessing be upon him, liked the dreams. Sometimes a man saw a dream and he would ask the Prophet if he did not know and if it was good, he liked it. Once a woman came and said, "Messenger of Allah, I saw as if I was taken from Madinah and admitted into Paradise. I heard a noise and Paradise was opened, and I saw so and so, and so and so." She counted twelve people that the Messenger, peace be upon him, had earlier sent in an expedition. "They were brought having clothes of fine silk, their wounds running forth blood. It was said, "take them to the stream of Baydakh or Baydah." They were given a dip in it and came out with their faces shining like the moon on the full-moon night. They were served with a plate of gold with dates in it; they ate from it as much as they wanted. I also joined them in eating."

Soon after, a messenger from that contingent arrived and said, "So and so have been killed." He counted twelve people. The Prophet, peace be upon him, sent for the woman and told her to relate her dream. She did and said "So and so was brought as the Messenger said."[292]

289. Bukhari (4878, 4880, 7444), Muslim (iman: 180)
290. Bukhari
291. Bukhari (5426), Muslim (libas: 2067)
292. Ahmad (12388, 13699)

CHAPTER 50
THE DRESS OF THE PEOPLE OF PARADISE AND THEIR FURNITURE, ETC.

(Many repeated explanations of the words used in the Qur'an and linguistic interpretations in this chapter have been dropped)

Allah, the Exalted, said, **"Those conscious of Allah will be in safe place amid Gardens and springs, clothed in silk and fine brocade, facing one another."** *(44: 51-53)*

"Those who have believed and done righteous deeds, We do not let the reward of any who does a good deed go to waste. They will have Gardens of lasting bliss, beneath them rivers will flow. There they will be adorned with bracelets of gold and will wear green garments of fine silk and brocade, reclining there on adorned couches. Excellent is the reward, and good is the resting place." *(18: 30-31)*

"Their garment will be silk." *(22: 23)*

There is an issue here. Allah Almighty informed that the garment of the people of Paradise will be silk, and the Prophet, peace be upon him, said, "Whoever wears silk in the world will not wear it in the Hereafter."[293]

The scholars are in disagreement concerning the meaning of this Hadith. A group of early and later scholars said that the people of Paradise will not wear silk, but will wear other types of garments. The above verse is particularized. The warning in Hadith is from the category that indicates that the act requires that result but it may be altered for some reason. It is proved by the text and consensus that repentance will prevent application of the warning. The good deeds, calamities which remove the sins, supplication of the Muslims and the intercession of those who are allowed by Allah to intercede as well as Allah's mercy- all are a barrier to

---

293. *Bukhari (5832), Muslim (Libas: 2073)*

the promised punishment. So the Hadith is similar to the Hadith which says: "Whoever drinks wine in the world will not drink it in the Hereafter."

Allah further said about the garments of the people of Paradise:

"He will reward them, for their steadfastness, with a Garden and silk (robes)." *(76:12)*

"Upon them will be green garments of fine silk and brocade." *(76:21)*

Pay attention to the expression "upon them". It shows that their garment will be an adornment for their body. It is not to adorn the inner side but to be worn above the garments for decoration and beauty.

Consider how Allah, the Great, combined for them both the beauty of outside with garments and ornaments and the beauty of inside with by pure wine. He adorned their inside by pure drink, their hands with bracelets, and their bodies with silk.

Allah, the Most High, also said, **"Allah will admit those who believe and do good deeds to Gardens beneath which streams flow; there they will be adorned with golden bracelets and pearls; there they will have silken garments."** *(22:23)*

Their bracelets will be of gold studded with pearls.

Ka'b said, "Allah, the Owner of honour and glory, has created an angel who is assigned with the duty of shaping the ornaments of the People of Paradise till the Day of Resurrection. If one bangle of the ornaments of the people of Paradise is brought out, it will diminish the light of the sun. Do not ask after that about the ornaments of the people of Paradise."

Al-Hasan said, "The ornaments on the men are more charming than on women." He meant in Paradise.

Sa'd ibn Abi Waqqas reported that the Prophet ﷺ said, "If a man from the people of Paradise looks down and his bracelet appears, it will blot out the light of the sun as the sun blots out the light of stars." [294]

Abu Umamah narrated that the Messenger of Allah, peace and blessing be upon him, mentioned the ornaments of the people of Paradise and said, "They will have bracelets of gold and silver, garlands of pearl and ruby. They will have crowns like the crowns of kings. They will be young, without hair on their bodies, smeared with kohl." [295]

Abu Hazim narrated, "I was behind Abu Hurayrah when he was performing ablution. He used to extend his hand to reach his armpit. I said, 'What type of ablution is this, Abu Hurayrah?'
He said, 'The children of Farrukh, you are here! If I had known that you were around, I would have not performed this ablution. I heard my friend 쀻 say that the ornament of a believer will reach the part where water of ablution reaches.'" [296]

Some people argued on the basis of this Hadith that washing of the arm to the end is recommended. The right view is that it is not. The Hadith does not show the lengthening of washing. The bracelet is an ornament of the wrist and not for the arm and shoulder.

The addition of the statement of Abu Hurayrah "Whoever wishes to prolong his whiteness, he should do it", is not the statement of the Prophet; it is added by Abu Hurayrah. Many scholars have confirmed it.

Our Shaykh (i.e. Ibn Taymiyyah) used to say, "It is impossible that the Messenger of Allah, blessing and peace be upon him, had spoken these words. The *ghurrsh* (whiteness) is not in the hand, it is exclusively in the face, the prolonging of which is not possible."

Abu Hurayrah reported the Prophet 쀻 saying, "Anyone who enters Paradise will enjoy and will not feel miserable; his clothes will not be worn out, and his youth will not come to an end. There are in Paradise things which no eye has ever seen, no ear has ever heard of and the thought of it has not passed in the imagination of any man." [297]

294. Tirmidhi (2538)
295. Abu Nu'aym in Sifat al-jannah (267)
296. Bukhari (136), Muslim (taharah: 250)
297. Muslim (jannah: 2836), Ahmad (8835)

It means that he will always have new clothes like the food which he eats when finished, he will have a new one. Allah knows better.

Abdullah ibn 'Umar related that a bold Bedouin came to the Prophet, peace be upon him, and asked him, "Tell us about migration, Messenger of Allah. It is for a person wherever he is or to a particular land and when you die it will be suspended?"
He asked three times, and then sat down. The Messenger of Allah, peace be upon him, kept quiet for a while, then he asked, "Where is the person who asked the question?"
The Bedouin said, "Here he is, Messenger of Allah."

The Prophet said, "Migration is that you stay away from obscenities, open or secret, perform prayer regularly, and pay zakat. This will make you emigrant even though you die in your town."
Another person stood up and asked, "Messenger of Allah, tell me about the dress of the People of Paradise, will it be created or woven?"
Some people laughed at his question, and the Messenger of Allah, blessing and peace be upon him, said, "You are laughing at an ignorant person who is asking a learned one?"
He kept silent for a while then asked, "Where is the person who asked about the dress of the People of Paradise?"
The man said, "I am here Messenger of Allah."
He said, "It will come out of the fruits of Paradise."[298]

Abdullah ibn Mas'ud narrated that the Prophet 𐤀 said, "The Faces of the first group to enter Paradise will be shining like the moon on a full-moon night. The second one will be like a brilliant star in the sky. Each one of them will have two wives from the dark-eyed maidens, each one of them will have seventy robes on them, yet the marrow of their legs will be seen behind their flesh and robes as red drink is seen in a white glass." [299]

Abu Hurayrah reported that the Messenger of Allah, peace be upon him, said, "The space of the lash of one of you in Paradise is better than the world and more, the distance of the bow of one of you in Paradise is better than the world and its

298. Ahmad (7117)
299. Tabarani in Kabir (10: 198)

like. The veil of a woman in Paradise is better than the world and its like." [300]

Abu Sa'id al-Khudri reported that the Messenger of Allah, peace be upon him, said, "A man will recline in Paradise for seventy years then will change his side. His wife will come to him and pat on his shoulders; he will see his face In her cheek which is clearer than mirror. One single pearl on her will illuminate what is between the east and the west. She will greet him; he will answer the greeting and ask: 'Who are you?' She will reply: 'I am the addition.' She will have seventy garments on her the lowest of them is like Nu'man of Tuba. He will look at her and see the marrow of her leg beyond them. She will have crown on her; the smallest pearl of it will lighten what is between the east and the west." [301]

Abu Umamah reported that the Messenger of Allah, peace be upon him, said, "No one of you enters Paradise but will be taken to Tuba which will open its blossoms and he will select whichever he likes, white, red, green, yellow and black, like anemones, but finer and more beautiful."

Ibn Abbas was asked, "What is the robes of Paradise?"
He said, "There is a tree in Paradise which has a fruit like pomegranate. When one of Allah's friends wishes to have a dress, it lowers its branch and it bursts with seventy types of dress, then it closes as it was."

Abu Sa'id reported that a man said to the prophet ﷺ, "Messenger of Allah, blessed is the one who saw you and believed in you."
The Prophet ﷺ said, "Tuba i.e. blessed is he who saw me and believed in me. Blessed, and blessed and blessed is he who believed in me and did not see me"
A man asked, "What is Tuba?"
He replied, "It is a tree in Paradise a distance of hundred years. The dresses of the people of Paradise come from its blossom."

Abu Hurayrah said, "The house of the believer in Paradise is a pearl which has a tree which produces robes. A man can take by his two fingers seventy robes studded with pearl and corals."

Anas reported that Ukayder Dumah gave a robe of silk brocade to the Prophet,

---
300. Ahmad (10274)
301.Tirmidhi (25620, Ahmad (11715)

peace be upon him. Its beauty surprised the people. The Messenger, peace be upon him, said, "The handkerchiefs of Sa'd in Paradise are more beautiful than this."[302]

He mentioned Sa'd specially because he was among the Helpers like Abu Bakr al-Siddiq among the Emigrants. The Throne of Allah was shaken for his death, and he was not afraid of the blame of anyone in Allah's cause. His end was by martyrdom and he preferred the pleasure of Allah and His Messenger over the pleasure of his people, his family and his allies. Allah endorsed his judgment about the Jews above the seven skies. Gabriel lamented his death to the Prophet, peace be upon him. Such a noble person deserves to have his handkerchiefs to wipe his hands better than the robes of the kings.

They will have crowns on their heads

Abu Hurayrah reported that the Prophet ﷺ said, "Whoever reads the Qur'an and does his duty towards it day and night, making its permissible as permissible and taking its prohibited as prohibited, Allah will blend it with his flesh and blood and make him the companion of the noble and virtuous angels. On the Day of Resurrection, the Qur'an will be his defender. It will say, 'My Lord, every worker in the world used to charge for his work in the world, but so and so used to recite me day and night and follow my instruction concerning the permissible and prohibited. My Lord, grant him the reward.' Allah will put the crown of the kings on his head and dress him with the robe of honour. Allah then will ask, 'Are you pleased?' It will say, 'My Lord, I wish to have better that that.' Then Allah will give him sovereignty in his right hand and eternity in his left hand and ask, 'Have you agreed?' He will say: 'Yes, my Lord.'"[303]

Abu Buraydah narrated the following statement of the Prophet, peace be upon him, on the authority of his father, "Learn chapter of the Cow (Ch.2), its learning is blessing and abandoning it is regret, and the sorcerers are not able to learn it." He kept quiet for a while then said, "Learn the chapters of the Cow and the Family of 'Imran (Ch.3); they are brilliant and will provide shade to their reader on the Day of Judgement as though they are clouds or herd of lined birds. The Qur'an will meet its reader on the Day of Resurrection when his grave will split with pale

302. Bukhari (2616), Muslim (fada'il: 2469)
303. Al-Bayhaqi in Shu'ab al-iman (1991) with a weak chain.

face and ask him, 'Do you recognize me?' He will answer, 'No, I do not know you.' It will say, 'I am the Qur'an which kept you thirsty at noon and kept you awake in the night, every trader is after his trade and you are today above all traders.' He then will be given sovereignty in his right hand and eternity in his left hand, and will have the crown of dignity on his head. His parents will be dressed with two robes, which will be invaluable in the world. They will ask, 'Why are we given this?' it will be said to them, 'Because of your child's learning of the Qur'an.' Then it will be said to the reader of the Qur'an, 'Read and go up in the levels of Paradise and its apartments.' He will be climbing as long as he reads slowly." [304]

304. Ahmad (23011)

CHAPTER 51
THE PAVILIONS, BEDS, AND SOFAS OF PARADISE

Beds of the people of Paradise

Allah Almighty said, **"Reclining on beds of which the lining is from brocade."** *(55: 54)*

"On bed raised high." *(56: 34)*

The Almighty described the beds being upholstered with brocade. This indicates two things:
First, their outside is higher and more beautiful than the inner. Their inner is for the ground and their outer is for beauty and adornment.

Second, it shows that they are elevated beds with thick fillings between inside and outside.

Abu Sa'id al-Khudri reported that the Prophet ﷺ said, "Their height is as much as between the sky and the earth which can be covered in five hundred years."

It is a strange report; one of its narrators is not reliable. It may be referring to the levels with the beds.

In another version the Prophet, peace be upon him, is reported to have said, "Elevated beds" that is there is distance between two beds as the distance between the sky and the earth.

In another report the distance is to be forty years.

Abu Umamah reported that the Messenger ﷺ was asked about "elevated beds" and he said, "If a bed is dropped from its height, it will reach the bottom in a hundred years."

It is doubtful that this statement is from the Prophet, peace be upon him.

In a report it is attributed to Abu Umamah who said, "If its higher is dropped it will reach the bottom in forty years."

Cushions and Carpets

Allah, the Glorious, said, **"Reclining on green cushions and fine beautiful carpets"** *(55:76)*

"There are in it raised couches, cups put in plates, cushions lined up, and carpets spread around." *(88: 13-16)*

Al-Kalbi said, "The cushions lined together."[305]
Muqatil said, "Cushions spread on fine carpets."

The word "Rafraf" has been explained as green carpets, which are spread.
It is also explained additionally as cloth used by kings in beds and other things.
It is supported by the Hadith which says, "Then the drape was removed and we saw his face as if it was the page of Mushaf."

Ibn Mas'ud interpreted the verse "He saw some of the greatest signs of his Lord." *(53: 18)* that he saw green drapes that blocked up the horizon. [306]

The word "'Abqari" is said to be materials for decoration.

'Abqar originally is said to be a land inhabited by Jinn, then it was used for anything fine and lofty. The Arabs believed that the Jinn have many wonderful characteristics, and since 'Abqar was the place they lived; anything that was considered to be fantastic was attributed to it. They thought that it was made by them. In this sense the word is used in Arabic poetry and their sayings.

305. Bukhari (680)
306. Bukhari (3233), Muslim (iman: 174)

The description of the cushions and carpets being lined up and spread shows that they are always available for reclining and sitting; and they are not hidden or kept to be used from time to time.

Pavilions

Allah, the Exalted, said, **"Dark-eyed sheltered in pavilions."** *(55: 72)*

Abu Musa al-Ash'ari reported that the Messenger of Allah, peace be upon him, said, "The believer will have in Paradise a pavilion made up of one hollow pearl sixty miles long. There will be his family in it. He will go around them without being seen by one another."

In another version it says, "There is a pavilion of one hollow pearl in Paradise sixty mile wide; in each corner there will be some of his family who will not see the others. The believer will go around them." [307]

These pavilions are different from the apartments and palaces. They are pavilions in the gardens and on the beaches of the rivers.

Abu Sulayman said, "Allah Almighty created the virgin beautiful women. When their creation was completed, the angels pitched pavilions over them."

Some others said, "Since they were virgins and the custom about virgins is that they are kept in their private rooms until her husband takes her, Allah Almighty created the dark-eyed maidens and kept them in the rooms of pavilions until He will join them with their partners in Paradise."

Abdullah ibn Mas'ud said, "Every Muslim will have a pavilion which will have four doors. Every day will come from each door to him new gifts, present and favour which did not come before. There will be no ill disposition, moaning or craving. They will be dark-eyed maidens like the protected eggs."

Ibn Abbas said, "The pavilion will be of a gem of a hollow pearl one *farsakh*[308]

---

307. Bukhari (3243), Muslim (jannah: 2838)
308. A measurement of length

200

long and one *farsakh* wide. It will have one thousand doors of gold surrounded by canopy. An angel will enter from each door with a gift from Allah, the Majestic."

This is how Allah has described:
"The angels will enter on them from every door." *(13: 23)*

Allah knows better.

Allah, the Exalted, said, **"Reclining on beds lined up and We marry them with fair ladies of large eyes."** *(52: 20)*

"Many from the past and a few from later generations, on couches of well-woven cloth they will sit facing each other." *(56: 13-16)*

"There are couches raised high." *(88: 13)*

The Almighty told us that there will be couches arranged in row beautifully in line not one behind the other or far from it. He also informed that these couches were made of gold fabrics studded with pearl, ruby and chrysolite.

Ibn Abbas said, "The couches will be of gold studded with chrysolite, pearl, and ruby. The couch will be as high as the distance between Makkah and Allah."

Al-Kalbi said, "The length of the couch will be hundred cubits high. When a man wants to sit on it will come down, and when he is seated will go high to its place."

The word "Ara'ik", which is the plural of 'Arikah' has been explained as the beds with curtained canopy, which is prepared for brides.

So here are three things: a) Couch; b) the curtain that is hung over it; c) and the spreads. With the combination of these three items the *arikah* is made.

CHAPTER 52
THE SERVANTS AND ATTENDANTS

Allah, the Most High, said, "**Endless youths will go round among them with glasses, flagons, and cups of a pure drink.**" *(56: 17-18)*

"**Endless youths will attend them - if you could see them, you would think they were scattered pearls**" *(76: 19)*

Allah compared them with scattered pearls for their beauty and charm. The Almighty says that they are like scattered pearls. It means that they will not be idle but engaged in the service of the believers. Also when pearls are scattered on a carpet of gold or silk they will look more beautiful and attractive than if they are in one place.

Who are these youths? Are they from the world or will Allah create them in Paradise? There are two views regarding this. Ali ibn Abi Talib and Hasan al-Basri said that they are the children of the Muslims who died without having good or bad deeds in their accounts. They will be made the servants of the People of Paradise. Some of these people said that they will be the children of the unbelievers, whom Allah will make the servants of the people of Paradise. They support their view by the following report of Anas that the Prophet ﷺ said, "I asked my Lord to make neglectful children of mankind not to punish them. So, He granted my request and they will be the attendants of the people of Paradise."

This report is not authentic, all its chains have problems.

The other group said that Allah will create them in Paradise as He created the beautiful women. The children of the Muslims of the world will be of thirty-three years old. It is supported by the report of Abu Sa'id that the Messenger of Allah, peace be upon him, said, "Anyone old or young of the people of Paradise dies, he will be turned to thirty years in Paradise and will not grow further, the same will be the case of the people of the Fire." [309]

---

309. Tirmidhi

202

The most plausible view is that these servants will be created like the dark-eyed maidens in Paradise, to serve the believers. They are different from their children because Allah will do them the favour of being served, not to serve. Anas has reported that the Prophet ﷺ said, "I will be the first man to be raised."

It also says, "A thousand servants will go round me as though they are hidden pearls."

"Hidden" means that these youths are protected and not used or polluted.

CHAPTER 53
WOMEN OF PARADISE, THEIR PHYSICAL AND MORAL BEAUTY AS ALLAH DESCRIBED IN HIS BOOK

Allah, the Exalted, said, **"Give good tidings to those who believe and do righteous deeds that they will have Gardens beneath which rivers flow. Whenever they are provided with a provision of fruit from it, they say: 'this is what we were provided with before." And it is given to them in likeness. And they will have in it purified spouses, and they will abide in it eternally."** *(2: 25)*

Reflect on the glory of the One who gives this good tiding, and consider His status and truthfulness and greatness of the one who was chosen to pass this news to you. Also pay attention to the value of what He has promised and guaranteed for you in exchange of easy and light deeds. He, the Glorious, has combined in this good tiding the joy of the body with Gardens and their streams and fruits, and the pleasure of the soul with pure spouses, comfort of the heart and delight of the eye through asserting that this pleasant life will remain forever with no end.

Allah described the spouse to be purified - that means that they will be pure from menses, urine, faeces, confinement, mucus, spit and every filthy and dirty thing which affect women in the world. With this external purity Almighty purified them from evil characters and abominable qualities. He cleansed their tongue from obscenity and indecency, and restrained their eyes from gazing to anyone else besides their husbands. He protected their clothes from being polluted by dirt or filth.

Abu Sa'id reported from the Prophet ﷺ that he said, "They will have purified spouses', means that they will be pure from menses, faeces, phlegm, and spittle."

Abdullah ibn Mas'ud and Ibn Abbas give similar statements.

Mujahi said, "They will not urinate, relieve nature, discharge madhy or sperm, have menses, spit, blow their noses or give birth."

Qatadh said, "They will be pure from sin and filth. Allah, the Glorious has purified them from urine, faeces, filth and sin."

Allah, the Magnificent, said, **"The mindful of Allah will be in a safe place amid Gardens and springs, clothed in silk and fine brocade, facing one another: so it will be. We shall marry them with maidens with beautiful eyes. Secure and contented, they will call for every kind of fruit. After one death they will taste death no more. Allah will guard them from the torment of Hell."** *(44: 51-56)*

Here Allah, the Exalted, combined for them the beauty of residence and safety from every trouble. He also will provide them with fruits, springs, beautiful dress and perfect company sitting face to face. Almighty will complete their joy by beautiful dark-eyed maidens and the opportunity of ordering all types of fruits, which they will enjoy in safety not having the fear of their suspension or causing harm. At the end He told them that there will be no more death.

The word "HUR" (is plural of "Hawra" which means the young beautiful attractive fair woman with dark eyes.

Mujahid said, "Hawra' is a woman about whom the eye is puzzled because of her smooth skin and clarity of colour. The marrow of their legs will be seen behind their dresses. A person can see his face in the lever of one of them like mirror due to its fineness and clarity of skin."

The word 'IN' is plural of 'aina', which means the woman with big eyes. The correct meaning is that it denotes women whose eyes have the qualities of beauty and elegance. Among the beauty of the woman is to have wide eye; the narrowness of eye is considered a defect in her. The narrowness is desirable in certain parts of a woman such as her mouth, the hole of the ear and nose. Four parts are desired to be wide: face, breast, part between her shoulders and forehead. Four other parts are considered beautiful if they are white: skin, parting of the hair, teeth and the white piece of the eye. Blackness is desired in four parts: eye, eyebrow, eyelashes and hair. Four parts are regarded beautiful if they are long: posture, neck, hair and finger. Shortness, meaning figuratively, is appreciated in four parts:

tongue, hand, leg and eye. She controls her eye, restricts her leg from going out, prevents her tongue from speaking much and keeps her hand away from taking what her husband does not like. Four parts are to be appreciated for their thinness: waist, parting of the hair, eyebrow and nose.

Allah, the Glorious, said, **"We paired them with beautiful-eyed maidens."** *(52: 20)*

Abu 'Ubaydah said, "The meaning is that We made them in pairs like the shoes are paired. It does not mean marriage."

The Almighty also said, **"There will be maidens restraining their glances, untouched before by man or jinn. Which, then, of your Lord's blessings do you both deny? Like rubies and brilliant pearls."** *(55: 56-58)*

The Almighty described them for restraining their glances in two places:
1. In Chapter (37) **"With them will be women restraining their glances, with large beautiful eyes."** *(37: 48)*

2. In Chapter 38: **"They will have well-matched women restraining their gaze."** *(38: 52)*

All the commentators agree that the meaning is that these women restrain their gaze to their spouses and do not desire anyone else.

Another meaning is given that they restrain their spouses' gaze to themselves, and their beauty and charm does not let them to look at others.

Mujahid said, "They restrain their gaze and hearts to their spouses and do not desire anyone else."

The word "atrab", which is the plural of *tirb*, means that they will be of same age thirty-three years old. There will be no old one whose beauty has faded or the one because of given birth is unable for intercourse.

The Lord Supreme said, **"Untouched before by man or jinn."** *(55: 56)*

The commentators are unanimous that they are not subjected to sexual intercourse before. Then they differed among themselves. Some said that they are the ones who were created in Paradise. Others said that they will be the women of the world who were created anew virgin as they are described.

Ibn Abbas said: "They are women from human being who died as virgin."

I say that the obvious statement of the Qur'an indicates that they are not from the women of the world; they are beautiful maidens of Paradise, because the women of the world have had intercourse. It is supported by the fact that Allah Almighty mentioned them together with the materials He prepared in Paradise like fruits, rivers, dresses, etc.

Imam Ahmad said, "The beautiful dark-eyed maidens will not die at the blowing of the horn because they are created to remain forever."

The above verse indicates that the believing jinn will be in Paradise. Imam Bukhari has set a chapter: "The reward and punishment of Jinn."

Allah said, **"As though they are ruby and a beautiful pearl."**

They are described to be clear like ruby and fair like pearl. Abdullah ibn Mas'ud said: "A woman from Paradise will wear seventy robes of silk, yet the whiteness of her legs will be seen behind them. Ruby is a stone that if you put in it a string, you will be able to see it behind the stone.'

Allah, the Most High, said about the maidens of Paradise:
"Dark-eyed maidens sheltered in the pavilions." (55: 72)

It means that they are reserved in the pavilions. Another meaning is that they are confined to their spouses and do not look at others and they are not interested in them.

I say that this is the meaning of "restraining their glances" and here it is "reserved or confined". It means that they are confined in the pavilions and do not leave them to apartments and gardens. The other meaning is that Allah, the Exalted described them to be secured and protected and this is more appealing. It does not necessarily mean that they do not leave their pavilions to go to the apartments and gardens like the women of the kings and notables who are protected but they go on trip and to the park and gardens, etc. They are restrained in the house but go out with servants to the places of enjoyment.

Mujahid said, "They restrict their hearts to their spouses in the pavilions of pearl. The first women are described to restrain their glances. Both are the qualities of perfectness. One describes them to keep their glances to their spouses and not having any desire for others, and the second one mentions that they will adorn themselves for their spouses only."

Allah also said about them:
"There are good-natured beautiful maidens." *(55: 70)*

They are said to be of good characters and noble behaviour and have attractive and charming faces.

The Almighty also said about them:
"We have specially created them and made them virgin, loving, of matching age, for those on the right." *(56: 35-38)*

It means that We created them in a new creation. Ibn Abbas said, "Allah means the women of human being."

Others said, "The Almighty refers to the women of the world saying that We created them after they were old in the world in a new creation."

It is supported by a Prophetic statement that they are your old women, decrepit and bleary-eyed.

Another report to support is what came from 'A'ishah that the Messenger of Allah ﷺ entered her apartment and there was an old lady with her. He asked who she was. 'A'ishah said, "She is one of my aunts."
The Prophet ﷺ said, "Old women will not go to Paradise."
This upset the woman, and then the Prophet ﷺ read:*"We created them a new creation.* The people will be raised on the Day of Judgement barefooted, naked and uncircumcised. The first man to be provided with dress will be Ibrahim, the friend of Allah."

There are other statements from the Prophet to assert that old women of the world will be given a new form of young ones.

'A'ishah reported that an old woman from the Helpers came to the Prophet, peace be upon him, and asked him to pray to Allah to admit her into Paradise. The Prophet ﷺ said:
"Old women will not go to Paradise."

After that the Prophet ﷺ went and after performing prayer came back. 'A'ishah told him that the woman was worried and distressed by his statement. The Messenger ﷺ, said, "It is like that. When Allah Almighty admits them in Paradise, He will convert them to virgins."

Muqatil and al-Zajjaj said that the reference was to the beautiful maidens. Allah created them for His devoted servants and they did not experience giving birth, but they were created especially for the people of Paradise. The following points support this view:

1. Allah, the Exalted, said about the forerunners that they will be served by everlasting youths and He mentioned their couches, utensils, drinks, food, fruit and their spouses of the virgin maidens. Then He spoke about the people on the right and their food, drink, couches and spouses. It is obvious that the spouses will be like the ones mentioned before and they were created in Paradise.

2. Allah, the Glorious, said, **"We created them a new creation."**
It means that it is the first creation because anywhere Allah referred to the second creation He qualified it like His statement
"He will undertake the second creation," *(53: 47)*, and **"You have learned how the first creation was."** *(56: 62)*

3. He, the Most High, addressed the people saying, **"You will be sorted out into three classes."** *(56: 7)*

This is for both male and female, but He specially singled the female out for the new creation. The above report does not indicate that the old women will have this quality. It indicates that they will share the beautiful virgin maidens in these qualities.

The word 'urub', plural of 'arub' means women who are affectionate to their husbands. Another meaning is that she is amiable and friendly in intercourse. Another meaning given by the commentators is that they are the ones who are loving, affectionate, coquettish, flirting, warm-hearted, seized by sexual desire and having coquettish behaviour.

I say that Allah the Exalted has put together their attractive form and nice companionship in them. It is what is desired in a woman and it makes the enjoyment of a man perfect in her. In His statement "untouched before by a man or jinn" is information of full enjoyment in them. It indicates the enjoyment of the man by a woman who has not been taken for intercourse by anyone else. It will give extra pleasure and she also will be pleased.

The word "kawa'ib" plural of 'ka'ib' means that these women have full swelling breasts like pomegranates not hanging down.

Anas reported that the Messenger of Allah ﷺ said, "Marching in the morning or evening is better than the world and that which it contains. The measure of the bow of one of you or his lash in Paradise is better than the world and what is in it. If a woman of Paradise looks down to earth, she will fill what is between the earth and sky with fragrance and will illuminate what is between the earth and sky. The head-cover on her head is better than the world and what is in it."

Abu Hurayrah reported that the Prophet ﷺ said, "The first group to enter Paradise will be like the moon on the full-moon night, and the one following them will be like the most brilliant star in the sky. Every one of them will have two wives; the marrow of their legs will be seen behind their dress."

Umm Salmah reported, "I asked the Messenger of Allah ﷺ about the saying of Allah **"fair women with large beautiful eyes"**, and he said, 'They are fair, dark-eyed women with large eyes, and white like the wing of the eagle.'
I then asked about **"As though they are hidden pearls"**, and he said, 'Their purity will be like the purity of the pearl in the shell which is not touched by hands.'
I said, 'Tell me about **"There are in them beautiful good women"**, and he said, 'They will be of good characters and with attractive faces.'
I further asked him to explain, **"As if they are well-protected eggs"**, and he told me that their skin will be soft like the layer you see inside an egg behind the shell.

I said, 'Tell me about **"Devoted to their husbands and of equal age"**, and he said, 'They are those who passed away in the world as old, bleary-eyed and ugly, Allah will create them fresh as virgins, affectionate, loving devoted and of the same age.' I asked: 'Messenger of Allah, are the women of the world better or the beautiful maidens of Paradise?'

He replied, 'The women of the world are better than the beautiful maidens like the superiority of outer side of a bed over the lining.'

I asked: 'By what is it?'

He replied, 'By their prayers, fasting and engaging in worship of Allah Almighty. Allah will put light on their faces and silk on their bodies; they will be fair colour, have green dresses and yellow ornaments. Their censers will be of pearls and their combs of gold. They will say, 'We are immortal and will not die, we are delicate and will not fade, we are staying and will not go away, and we are pleased and will not be unhappy ever. Blessed is he for whom we are and he was for us."

I asked, 'Messenger of Allah, a woman from among us marries two, three or four husbands and she dies and goes to Paradise and her husbands also enter it, for whom she will be joined?'

He replied, 'Umm Salmah, she will be given an option and she will choose the one who was of the best character. She will say, 'My Lord, he treated me nicely in the world and was of good character, give him to me.' Umm Salmah, the good character took the good of the world and the Hereafter.'"

Abu Hurayrah narrated that the Prophet ﷺ said, "By the One who sent me with truth you are not in the world more familiar to your spouses and house than the people of Paradise are with their spouses and houses. One of them will enter to seventy-two wives whom Allah has created in addition to two from the children of Adam. These two will have superiority over the others because they worshipped Allah in the world. The man will enter on one of them in a chamber of ruby on a bed of gold studded with pearls. It will have seventy types of green silk and brocade. He will put his hand between her palms and then look at his hand from her breast and beyond her dress and her flesh and skin. He can see marrow of her shank as one of you sees a wire in the pipe of ruby. Her lever will be his mirror and his lever will be her mirror. With her neither of them will feel bored. Anytime he goes to her he will find her virgin; his penis will not weaken and her vulva will not feel tired. While he is there in that situation it will be announced that we know that you do not feel tired nor she is exhausted. He will have other spouses and go to them one by one. Whenever he goes to one of them she will say: 'By Allah, there is no one in Paradise more attractive than you, and there is nothing here more beloved to me than you.'"

Abu Sa'id reported that the Messenger of Allah, blessing and peace of Allah be upon him), said, "The person lowest in grade in Paradise will have eighty thousand attendants and seventy two wives. A pavilion of pearl and ruby will be set for him as wide as the distance between Jabiyah and Sana'a."

Abu Umamah reported the Prophet, Allah's blessing and peace be upon, saying, "Every slave will be given seventy two wives, two from the beautiful maidens and seventy from his stock in the world. Each woman will have lustful vagina and he will have a penis which will not bend."

Anas reported that the Messenger of Allah, blessing and peace be upon him, said, "A believer in Paradise will have seventy three wives."
We said, "Messenger of Allah, will he have power to deal with them?"
He said, "He will be given the power of a hundred men."

Abu Hurayrah narrated that the Prophet ﷺ was asked, "Messenger of Allah, will we have sexual contact with our women in Paradise?"
He replied, "A man will have sexual intercourse with a hundred virgins in a day."

Ibn Abbas reported that the people asked the Messenger of Allah, peace be upon him, "Will we go to our women in Paradise as we do here in the world?"
He said, "By the One in whose hand is Muhammad's soul, a man will have sexual intercourse with a hundred virgins in one day."

These are exaggerated figures. The authentic reports mentioned only two wives for every person in Paradise. There is no mention of more than that in them. If these figures are true and the reports are correct then either they mean that everyone will have concubines besides two wives and the numbers will be according to their status like attendants and serving youths, or they will have the power of having intercourse with this number. In this case some narrators understood that they will have so many wives.

Anas reported that the Prophet, blessing and peace of Allah be upon him said, "The believer in Paradise will be given so and so men's power of intercourse."

It is an authentic report, perhaps the one who reported that he will have intercourse with hundred virgins reported by meaning. It may mean that the number of women for the people will be in accordance with their status. Certainly a believer will have more than two wives in Paradise as reported by Abu Musa that the Messenger of Allah, blessing and peace be upon him, said, "A believing servant will have in Paradise a pavilion of a hollow pearl sixty mile long. He will have his family in it and go round them, and one of them will not see the other."

CHAPTER 54
THE SUBSTANCE FROM WHICH THE VIRGINS OF PARADISE ARE CREATED.

Anas ibn Malik reported that the Messenger of Allah, blessing and peace be upon him, said, "The beautiful virgins are created from saffron."[310]

There is a similar report by Ibn Abbas and Anas. However, theses women are created in Paradise and not born by parents. Allah knows better about their origin.

Anas reported from the Prophet ﷺ:
"If a virgin of Paradise spits in seven seas, their water will become sweet due to the sweetness of her mouth. The beautiful virgins are created from saffron."[311]

If a human being who is the most beautiful and charming is created from mud and had this attractive form, what do you think about the shape of a person created from saffron of Paradise?

Abdullah ibn Mas'ud narrated that the Messenger of Allah, blessing and peace be upon him, said, "A light shines in Paradise and the people raise their heads and find out that it was from the front tooth of a virgin of Paradise who smiled in the face of her husband."[312]

There are other reports concerning the substance of their creation.

Ibn Abbas said, "There is a stream in Paradise called al-Baydakh, over it are pavilions of ruby and below it are virgins who are created. The People of Paradise will say; 'Let's go to al-Baydakh. They will go and look at those beautiful women; when a person likes one of them, he will touch her wrist and she will follow him." [313]

---

310. Abu Nu'aym in Sifat al-jannah (384) Its chain is weak. A similar Hadith has been reported also by Tabarani (7813) on the authority of Abu Uamamah, which is also weak. See Da'if al- jami' al-saghir (2803, 2840)
311. Abu Nu'aym (386)
312. Ibid (381)
313. Ibid (324)

Al-Walid ibn 'Abdah reported that the Messenger of Allah, blessing and peace be upon him, said to Gabriel, "Take me to the beautiful virgins of Paradise." He took him and the Prophet asked them, "Who are you?"
They said, "We are beautiful virgins of noble people who stay and do not travel, are youthful and do not become old and are cleansed and do not get dirty."

Abu 'Ayyash said, "We were sitting one day with Ka'b and he said, 'If a hand of a virgin's of Paradise hangs from the sky, it will illuminate the earth as the sun illuminates it for the people of the world.' Then he added: 'I said her hand, what would happen with her face with its fair colour, beauty and charm?'"

Mu'adh ibn Jabal reported the Prophet 襲 saying, "No woman in the world misbehaves with her husband but his wife from among the virgin of Paradise says, 'Don't hurt him, may Allah destroy you! He is only for short time with you and will leave you to us.'" [314]

'Ikrimah reported the Prophet 襲 saying to the women, "The beautiful virgins of Paradise are more in number than you. They pray for their husbands, 'O Allah, help him on his religion, make his heart bend on Your obedience, and make him reach us by Your might, O the most Merciful.'"

Ibn Mas'ud said, "There is a beautiful virgin in Paradise called 'al-Lu'bah' (the amusement). All the virgins of the Gardens are fascinated with her; they pat their hands on her shoulder and say, 'Blessing is to you, O Lu'abh! If your seekers know you, they will strive more earnestly for you.' It is written between her eyes: 'Whoever desires someone like me he has to work for the pleasure of my Lord.'"

'Ata' al-Sulami said to Malik ibn Dinar, "Abu Yahya, arouse our desires."
He said, "'Ata', there is a beautiful virgin in Paradise, the people of Paradise boast of her beauty. If Allah, the Exalted, had not written for them no to die, they would have died from her beauty."
After that 'Ata' remained in distress from the words of Malik.

Ja'far ibn Muhammad said, "A wise man met another wise man and asked him, 'Do you long for the beautiful virgins of Paradise?'
He replied, 'No.'

314. Ahmad (22162)

He said to him, 'Long for them, because the light of their faces is from the light of Allah.'
He fainted and was taken to his house and we used to visit him for a month."

Zayd al-Raqashi said, "I was informed that a light shone in Paradise, and no place was left but it reached it. It was asked: 'What is that?'
They said: 'It was a virgin of Paradise who smiled in the face of her husband.'[315]
Hearing this, a man burst in moaning and remained like that until he died."

Ibn Abbas said, "If a virgin of Paradise brings her wrist out between the earth and the sky, the whole creation would be infatuated by her beauty. If she exposes her head cover, the sun will be before its radiance like a wick and lose its light. If she exposes her face, its beauty will illuminate what is between the earth and the sky."

Yahya ibn Kathir said, "The beautiful virgins will receive their husbands at the gate of Paradise and say, 'For long we were waiting for you, we are pleased and will not be angry, we are staying and will not move, and we are immortal and will not die.' They will sing it in the most beautiful voice. They will also say, 'You are my love, and I am your love. There is no restriction on you or turning away from you.'"

---

315. This is reported by al-Khatib from the statement of the Prophet, but is forged. (see Da'if al- Jami' (3266)

CHAPTER 55

THE ENJOYMENT OF THE PEOPLE OF PARADISE BY THEIR SEXUAL INTERCOURSE, AND ITS BEING PURE FROM IMPURITY

The report of Abu Hurayrah has already been cited which says that it was said to the Messenger of Allah, "Are we going to have sexual contact with our women?" He replied, "A man will contact in one day a hundred virgins."

The report of Abu Musa also has been mentioned which says, "The believer will have a pavilion made up of one hollow pearl sixty mile long; his family will be in it and he will visit them."

Also the Hadith of Anas has passed that a believer will be given in Paradise the strength of copulation with so many women.

Laqit ibn 'Amir asked the Messenger of Allah, blessing and peace be upon him, "What is to be seen in Paradise?"
He replied, "Rivers of pure honey, streams of wine which will cause no headache or regret, streams of milk the taste of which will not change and springs of unaltered water. Besides, there will be fruit, by your Lord, of the kind you know and other better than it, and pure spouses."
He then asked, "Are we going to have righteous women there?"
The Prophet ﷺ replied, "The righteous women will be for righteous men. You will enjoy them as you enjoy in the world except that there will be no production of children."[316]

Abu Hurayrah reported that the Messenger of Allah, blessing and peace be upon

---

316. Abdullah ibn Ahmad, Tabarani

him, was asked, "Are we going to have sexual intercourse in Paradise?"
He replied, "Yes, by the One in whose hand is my soul, with full energy, and when the man gets up from her she will return virgin again."[317]

Abu Sa'id al-Khudri narrated that the Prophet ﷺ said, "When the men of Paradise have intercourse with their wives, they will turn virgin again."[318]

Abu Umamah reported that the Messenger of Allah, blessing and peace be upon him, was asked, "Will the people of Paradise have copulation?"
He said, "Yes, with an untiring penis and unending lust, with force. Without discharging sperm or fearing death."[319]

Abu Hurayrah reported that the Prophet ﷺ was asked, "Will the people of Paradise copulate with their wives?"
He replied, "Yes, with an untiring penis, an insatiable pudendum and unending lust."[320]

Abdullah ibn Mas'ud explained the statement of Allah Almighty:
"The people of Paradise are today happily occupied." *(36: 55)*

He said, "They are occupied in deflowering the virgins."[321]

Muqatil said, "They are occupied in deflowering the virgins from the people of the Fire and do not remember them not pay attention to them."

Sa'id in Jubayr said, "The sexual desire of the man in Paradise will go on for seventy years, he will feel the joy and will not be polluted to be in need of purification, nor will they feel weakness or impotence. Their intercourse will be all joy and pleasure without any fault."

The most perfect among them will be the one who protected himself from illicit acts in this world. It is as the one who drinks wine in the world will not drink it in the Hereafter, and the one who wears silk in the world will not get it in the

317. Abu Nu'aym (393)
318. Al-Bazzar (3527), Tabarani in Saghir (249) It is an unsound report.
319. Tabarani in Kabir (7674, 7721)
320. Al-Bazzar (3524)
321. Sifat al-Jannah (375)

Hereafter, and the one who used the utensils of gold and silver in the world will be deprived of them in the Hereafter. The Prophet ﷺ said, "These things are for them in the world and for you in the Hereafter."

So anyone who has fully enjoyed the pleasure and joy of this world, Allah will forbid him from them in the world to come. Allah has condemned those who took fill of the pleasure of the world and enjoyed the finery of it. For this reason the Companions were very much scared of it.

Jabir narrated that Umar saw him and he had bought meat for a dirham for his family. He said to him, "Every time one of you desires something he buys it. Didn't you hear Allah, the Exalted, say, 'You exhausted your pleasures during your worldly life and enjoyed them in full?'" (46: 20) [322]

Hasan said, "The delegation of Basra went with Abu Musa to 'Umar. He said that we used to visit him daily and he had three pieces of bread sometimes enriched with butter, sometimes with olive oil, sometimes with milk and sometimes we found dry meat cut into stripes and boiled and sometimes we got tender meat, which was very rare. He said one day, 'I see that you do not like my food. By Allah, if I wished, I would have been the best of you in food and fine in living, but I heard the Messenger of Allah, blessing and of Allah be upon him, reproached some people for something they did and said, 'You squandered the good things you were given in your earthly life and you took your fill of pleasure there.'" (46: 20) [323]

The people who avoided the prohibited joy in the world will get it in most perfect form on the Day of Resurrection. On the other hand whoever gets indulged in the joy of the worldly materials will be deprived there or will be given in imperfect form. Allah will not put the joy of a person who was active in His disobedience like the joy of the person who shunned his lust for the sake of Allah.

Allah knows the best.

322. Ahmad in Zuhd (153)
323. Ibid (143)

CHAPTER 56
THE ARGUMENT WHETHER THERE WILL BE PREGNANCY AND DELIVERY IN PARADISE

Abu Sa'id al-Khudri reported that the Messenger of Allah, blessing and peace be upon him, said, "If the believer wishes to have a child in Paradise, his pregnancy, delivery and growth will be in a moment as he wished."[324]

After citing this report Tirmidhi said, 'It is a Hasan Gharib Hadith. This issue is disputed between the scholars: some said that there will be copulation in Paradise but no children. It is the view of Tawus, Mujahid, and Ibrahim al-Nakhi'i.

Bukhari said that 'Ishaq ibn Ibrahim reported the Prophet ﷺ as saying, "If a believer desires to have a child in Paradise, it will be done in one hour as he wished, but he will not wish."'

Bukhari further said that Abu Razin al-Uqayli reported that the Prophet ﷺ said, "The people of Paradise will not have children in it."

Abu Sa'id al-Khudri narrated that the Prophet ﷺ was asked, "Will the people of Paradise have children, as the children are the whole happiness?"
He replied, "Yes by the One who holds my soul in His hand. It will be according to his desire. His pregnancy, suckling and youth will be in no time."[325]

The report of Abu Sa'id is authentic and its reporters are reliable, but it is very strange. (The author cited this very Hadith from different sources).

I am going to quote at the length the report of Abu Razin pointed out by Bukhari to adorn our book as it has the greatness, dignity and the light of the prophethood, which proclaims its authenticity.

---

324. Tirmidhi (2563)
325. Sifat al-jannah (275)

'Asim ibn Laqit related that his father Laqit left to see the Messenger of Allah, blessing and Peace be upon him, in the company of Nahik ibn 'Asim ibn Malik, ibn al-Muntafiq. Laqit related, "My companion and I reached the Messenger of Allah ﷺ when he had completed the Morning Prayer. He stood to deliver a sermon, and said, 'People, I had kept my voice for four days from you, but now I am going to speak to you. Maybe someone has been sent by his people to learn what the Messenger of Allah, peace be upon him, says. He was afterward distracted by his thought or by his companion's talk or by misguidance. Behold! I am responsible. Behold! Have I conveyed? Listen, you will benefit. Sit down, sit down.'

The people sat down but my companion and I kept standing until the Messenger's heart and eye were free. I asked, 'Messenger of Allah, how much knowledge of unseen do you have?'
He laughed and shook his head and realised that I was after his error. He said, 'Your Lord has kept the keys of five matters of unseen with Him, and only He knows them.' He made gesture by his hand.

I asked, 'What are they?'
He said, 'It is the knowledge of death - He knows the time of the death of you and you do not know. He is aware of the sperm in the womb but you are not. He has the knowledge of what is going to come tomorrow and you do not have. He knows the time of rain, which comes to you while you are desperate and scared. He laughs and knows that it is coming soon.'
I said, 'We are not going to miss goodness from the Lord who laughs.'

The Prophet went on, 'He has the knowledge of the Hour.'
I said, 'Messenger of Allah, tell us about the things which people know and you know. We belong to a tribe who do not believe us. These are the tribes of Mizhaj who are more in number, Khath'am who is our neighbour and then our own clan to which we belong.'
He said, 'You will remain as long as it is decreed, then your Prophet will pass away. After him you will stay for a while, then the blast will be sent and, by your Lord, nothing will remain but destroyed. The angels will remain with your Lord. Your Lord will go round the earth when the towns have been deserted. He then will send rain from the Throne, and by your Lord, it will not leave anyone on the face of earth who was killed or buried but his grave will split and He will create him anew. Your Lord will ask him: 'What is the news?' He will say, 'My Lord, You caused

me to die today.' He will feel that he has been with his family recently.

I said, 'Messenger of Allah, how will Allah bring us together after we had been torn to pieces by wind, decomposition and beasts?'
The Prophet said, 'I tell you from the signs of Allah. You come across a land which is decayed, and you said, 'it will never come back to life.' Then your Lord sends rain and it is only few days that you see it fully alive. By your Lord, He is more capable of gathering them from water than the plants of earth. They will come out to light and from their graves and you will look at Him and He will look at you.'

I said, 'How is it possible when we are fill of earth and He is One being that He will look at us and we will look at Him?'
He said, 'I give you an example from the favours of Allah. The sun and the moon are small signs of Allah you see them and they see you in the same time. You have no doubt in seeing them. By your Lord, He is more capable of seeing you and you will see Him better than the sun and the moon.'

I asked, 'Messenger of Allah, what is our Lord going to do to us when we meet Him?'
He replied, You will be presented to Him, your accounts being open to Him. Nothing will be hidden, and then Your Lord, glory be to Him, will take a handful of water and spray your heart with it. By your Lord, the drop will not miss the face of anyone of you. It will leave the face of the Muslim like white garment and will stamp the face of the unbeliever like black ashes. Behold! Then your Prophet, peace be upon him, will turn and with him will go the righteous people and will pass a bridge of fire, One of you will step on a flame and say 'hiss'. Your Lord will say: 'This is the time.' Then they will reach the pool of the Messenger, peace be upon him, being thirsty and will drink from it. By your Lord, none of you extends his hand but a pure cup will be given to him, which will be clean from urine and filth. The sun and the moon will be detained and you will not see them.'

I said, 'How will we be able to see then?'
He said, 'You will see like you see at this moment with the rising of the sun which will shine the earth facing the mountains.'

I said, 'How are we going to be rewarded for our good and bad deeds?'
He said, 'Good deed is rewarded ten times more and bad deed will be rewarded

with similar punishment, unless Allah forgives.'

I said, 'What are Paradise and Hell?'
He said, 'By your Lord, Hell has seven gates; a rider will travel between every two gates for seventy years.'

I said, 'What are we going to see in Paradise, Messenger of Allah?'
He said, 'You will see rivers of pure honey, rivers of wine which will not cause headache or regret, rivers of milk the taste of which never changes, and streams of unaltered water. Besides, there will be variety of fruits, the one you know and better than that, and pure wives.'

I said, 'Messenger of Allah, will we have righteous wives?'
He said, 'The righteous women will be for righteous men. You will enjoy them as you enjoy in the world, and they will also enjoy with you except that there will be no birth.'

I said, 'This is the utmost we are going to achieve?'
The Prophet ﷺ did not reply.

I said, 'On what am I to pledge, Messenger of Allah?'
The Prophet ﷺ extended his hand and said, 'On performing prayer regularly, paying zakat and not to associate anyone with Allah.'

I said, 'We will have what is between the east and the west?'
The prophet withdrew his hand and spread out his fingers. He thought I was going to make some condition, which he will not accept.

I said, 'We will land anywhere we like and no one will commit an offence but to himself.'
He extended his hand and said, 'You will land anywhere you wish and you will not commit a crime but on yourself.'

Then we turned away. Then the Prophet said, 'These two, by your Lord, if you talk about them are the most righteous of the people in the world and the Hereafter.'
Ka'b ibn al-Jadariyya from Banu Bakr ibn Kilab asked, 'Who are they, Messenger of Allah?'

He replied, 'Banu al-Muntafiq are qualified for that.'

We turned away, and I went to him and said, 'Messenger of Allah, was there any good in those who passed in pre-Islamic period?'
A man amid the crowd of Quraysh said, "By Allah, your father al-Muntafiq is in the Fire."

His statement made me feel as though part of my skin, my face and flesh has fallen for what he said about my father in public. I intended to say, 'And you father, Messenger of Allah?' However something better occurred to my mind and I said, 'Messenger of Allah, what about your family?'
He said, 'As for my family, by Allah, when you pass by the grave of any polytheist Amiri or Qurashi say: Muhammad, peace be upon him, has sent me to tell you what you would not like. You will be dragged on your face and belly in the Fire.'

I asked, 'What did Allah do to them, Messenger of Allah? They did deeds which they could do and thought they were doing right things.'
He said, "Allah, the Glorious, sent at the end every seven nations a prophet, whosoever disobeyed him was among those who went astray and the one who obeyed His prophet was among the rightly guided ones.'"

It is a famous and great Hadith recorded by the big scholars of Hadith in their collections like Abdullah ibn Imam Ahmad, Abu Bakr ibn Abu 'Asim, Abu al-Qasim al-Tabarani, Abu al-Shaykh, Abu Abdullah ibn Mandah, Abu bakr ibn Mardawayh and Abu Nu'aym, considering it correct and accepting it. It was read in Iraq in the presence of a group of scholars and nobody had any objection about it nor did anyone speak against its chain. Abu al-Khayr ibn Hamdan said, "It is a great, popular and established tradition." I asked our Shaykh Abu al-Hajjaj al-Mizzi about it and he said, "It has the nobility of prophethood."

The people who reject the idea of reproduction in Paradise say that this Tradition is clear that there will be no reproduction in Paradise.

They say that it is proved by the following evidences:

1. This report of Abu Razin.

2. The words of Allah Almighty:
"They will have pure spouses."

It means that they will be pure from menstruation, excrement, urine and any filth. Mujahid said, "They will be pure from menstruation, excrement, urine, phlegm, spittle, sperm and giving birth."

3. The Hadith saying that there will be no sperm or death has already been cited. The semen of the man conceives the child, but if there is no semen or inflation in the vulva, there will not be conception.

4. It is established by authentic report from the Prophet ﷺ that, "There will remain some space in Paradise and Allah will create some people and lodge them in it."[326] If there were reproduction in Paradise the children of this reproduction would have been more deserving than others.

5. Allah, the Most High, has set pregnancy and birth with menstruation and sperm. If the women of Paradise were to conceive, menstruation and discharge of semen would not end.

6. Allah, the Mighty and Wise, decreed reproduction in the world because He has decreed death. So, He brought people to this world generation after generation and fixed a period for everyone. If there had been no reproduction, the human race would have expired. For this reason the angels do not reproduce because they do not die like Jinn and mankind. On the Day of Resurrection Allah Almighty will raise them from the ground and will recreate them to remain not to die. As such they do not need to reproduce to protect the human race. In the Hereafter the people will remain forever, so neither the people of Paradise nor the people of Hell will reproduce.

7. Allah, the Exalted, said, **"Those who believed and their offspring followed them in faith; We will join them with them."** (52: 21)

In this verse Allah told us that He will honour the believers by bringing their offspring to join them in order to provide them with the comfort of their eyes as the people of the world delight with their children.

---

326. Muslim (jannah: 2848)

8. If there is reproduction, then it is either to continue to no end or to a period after which it will end. Both propositions are impossible. The first option means that there will be unlimited people, and the second the end of a type of enjoyment of the people of Paradise. It is not possible to say that a generation will succeed another by the death of the previous one because there is no death in the Hereafter.

9. Human beings will not grow in Paradise as they grow in the world. Neither the children of Paradise will grow nor the men. The youth will remain as they are and the men will remain at the age of thirty-three as has been said earlier. If we suppose that there will be birth in Paradise, then the newly born child will grow until he becomes man. It is known that the Muslim children who died will be raised thirty-three years old, and will not go further.

10. Allah, the Glorious, will raise the people of Paradise like the angels or even better than them because they will not urinate, release nature or sleep. They will be inspired glorification of Allah and will not get old by the passage of time; their bodies will not grow bigger but remain as Allah fixed them. Allah knows better.

This is the truth in this case. Some people, however, said that the ability is available and everything is possible. Others said that Paradise is the abode, which the believers deserved by their deeds. These arguments are cheap and dealt with in the books of these people. Allah's help is sought.

Abu Sahl said, 'The deviated people reject this report i.e. the report of birth in Paradise whereas it has been reported through various chains. The Prophet ﷺ was asked about it and he replied that it will happen. Allah, the Exalted, said, **"It will have all that the souls desire and the eyes delight in."** *(43: 71)*

It is not impossible that a believer who is in control of his desire and has power on his joys desires the delight of his eyes and fruit of his heart from among those who have been favoured by Allah with pure wives.

It could be asked that the Hadith tells us that the women will not experience menstruation or confinement in childbed, yet how will a child be born?

I will answer that menstruation is the cause of pregnancy, the period of which differs. All the countries of the world differ in their food, drink and dress and each of these cause the bad consequences, which are feared. Look at the wine of the world, which is forbidden, and which is the cause of many calamities, but Allah will provide it to the people of Paradise cleansed from all these problems and full of delight. Why is it not possible that a child is given in the same way?

I say, that the people who deny the case of birth in Paradise did not do it because their hearts were deviated, but because of the report of Abu Razin which clearly stated that 'there will be no reproduction.'

We also have cited the statements of 'Ata' and others that the women of Paradise will be pure from menstruation and childbirth. Tirmidhi has cited two views from the scholars of past in this regard and mentioned the denial of Abu Ishaq of it. Abu Umamah said in his report: "Except that there will be no discharge of sperm and death."

Paradise is not a place for procreation but an abode of everlasting and eternity. No one will die so that his offspring can take his place. The report of Abu Sa'id cited in the beginning of the chapter is reported through various chains the best of which is Tirmidhi's chain, yet he judged it as strange. Allah knows better.

If the Messenger of Allah, blessing and peace be upon him, has said it, then it is true beyond any doubt and there is no contradiction between different wordings. The Report of Abu Razin clearly denies the childbirth as it is seen in the world. It does not reject the happening of pregnancy, delivery, growing and reaching the age of youth in one hour. This is where our limited knowledge has reached on this issue; we have discussed it in a manner you may not find in any book besides it. Allah knows better.

CHAPTER 57
MUSIC AND SINGING OF THE BEAUTIFUL VIRGINS IN PARADISE AND THE ENJOYMENT OF THE PEOPLE OF IT

Allah, glory be to Him, said:
"When the Hour arrives, on that Day people will be separated: those who believed and did good deeds will delight in a Garden." *(30: 14-15)*

Yahya ibn Kathir explained delight with joy and listening. It is not in contradiction with Ibn Abbas's interpretation by 'being honoured' or the explanation of Mujahid and Qatadah with 'enjoying', because the joy of the ear by listening is honour and pleasure.

Ali narrated that the Messenger of Allah, blessing and peace of Allah be upon him, said, "There will be a gathering of the beautiful women of large eyes in Paradise in which they will sing with beautiful voice not heard anything similar to that by the people. They will say: 'We are eternal and will never perish; we are tender and will not fade ever; we are pleased and will not be displeased.' Blessed is he who is for us and we are for him."

Tirmidhi cited it and passed the judgement of being strange. He said there are reports from Abu Hurayrah, Abu Sa'id and Anas on this issue.

I say that there are other reports from Abdullah ibn Abi Awfa, Abu Umamah, and Abdullah ibn 'Umar in this regard.

The report of Abu Hurayrah is as follows. He said, "There is a stream in Paradise on both sides of which will be virgins standing and singing with a voice which when the people hear, they will feel unprecedented joy." He was asked, "What will they be singing, Abu Hurayrah?"
He replied, "It will be glorification, praise, sanctification and glory of Allah

Almighty."

It is the statement of Abu Hurayrah, but he reported the Messenger of Allah, blessing and peace be upon him, as saying, "There is a tree in Paradise the roots of which are from gold and branches from chrysolite and pearl. When the wind blows the virgins of Paradise sing, and the people will not hear a sound more delicious than theirs."[327]

Anas narrated that the Messenger of Allah, peace be upon him, said, "The beautiful virgins of Paradise will sing in it saying: 'We are beautiful dark-eyed women created for noble partners.'"

The report of Abdullah ibn Abi awfa is that the Prophet ﷺ said, "Every man in Paradise will be married with four thousand virgins and eight thousand widows and one hundred beautiful virgins of Paradise. They gather together every seven days and sing with beautiful voices, which mankind has never heard. They sing, 'We are immortal and will never die, we are fresh and will not decay, we are pleased and will never be unhappy, and we are staying and will not leave. Blessed is he who is for us and we are for him.'"[328]

Abu Umamah reported that the Messenger of Allah, blessing and peace be upon him, said, "No believing man enters Paradise but will sit at his head and feet two virgins singing with the most beautiful voice a man or Jinn has ever heard, and it is not the single-pipes of Satan."[329]

Ibn 'Umar reported that the Messenger of Allah, peace be upon him, said, "The wives of the people of Paradise will sing for their husbands with the most beautiful voices ever heard by anyone. They will say in their song, 'We are beautiful nice ladies, the wives of noble men who look at us with comfort of eyes.' They also say, 'We are immortal and will not die, we are safe and not to be scared, and we are staying and will not depart.'"[330]

A man from Quraysh said to Ibn Shihab, "Will there be singing in Paradise, because I love songs?"

327. Sifat al-Jannah (433)
328. Ibid (431)
329. Ibid (434). Tabarani in Kabir (7478)
330. Tabarani in Saghir (734)

He said, "Yes, by the One in whose hand is Ibn Shihab's soul. There is a tree in Paradise full of pearls and chrysolite, and below it will be girls with round breasts singing variety of songs. They say, 'We are tender and fresh and we will not be miserable, and we are immortal and will not die.' When the tree listens to it, it claps and we do not know whether the sounds of the girls are more attractive or the sounds of the tree."

Khalid ibn Yazid said, "The beautiful dark-eyed virgins will sing for their husbands saying, 'We are beautiful maidens the wives of noble youths, we are immortal and will not die, we are fresh and will not dry, we are staying and will not leave and we are pleased and will not be unhappy.' On the breast of one of them will be written, 'You are my love, and I am your love. My soul ended with you. My eyes did not see like you.'"

They will listen to other songs higher than that, which will come from the angels.

Al-Awza'i said, "I learned that there is no one who has a more beautiful voice among the creation of Allah than Israfil. Allah, the Exalted, will command him to sing, and there will remain no angel in the skies but will suspend his prayer to listen to him. It will continue as long as Allah wishes, then Allah Almighty will say, 'If the people knew My greatness, they would not worship anyone beside Me.'"

Muhammad ibn al-Munkadir said, 'On the Day of Judgement a caller will call, 'Where are those who protected their ears and themselves from the meetings of amusement and the single-pipes of Satan? Put them up in the meadows of musk.' Then He will command the angels, 'Make them hear My glorification and My praise.'"

Malik ibn Dinar explained the statement of Allah, **"For him (i.e. Dawud) is nearness to Us and a good place to return to."** (38: 25) saying, "When the Day of resurrection comes, a high pulpit will be put in Paradise and it will be called, 'David, glorify Me with that beautiful and melodious voice with which you glorified Me in the world.' The voice of David will subsume the pleasure of the people of the Gardens. This is what Allah referred to by saying, **'He has in reward nearness to Us and a good place to return to.'"**

Shahr ibn Hawshab said, "Allah, the Sublime, will say to the angels, 'My devoted slaves loved beautiful voices in the world, but abandoned it for My sake. Make them hear good voices. So the angels will start glorification, exaltation and praise in a way they never heard before."

Ibn Abbas said, "There is a tree in Paradise standing on a trunk which a rider can travel in its shade for a hundred years. The people of Paradise will gather in its shade and some of them will desire the amusement of the world. So, Allah will send a breeze from Paradise which will shake that tree with all the amusement of the world."

Sa'id ibn Sa'id al-Harithi said, "I am told that there are forests of bamboos of gold in Paradise loaded with pearls. When the people of Paradise desire to hear a beautiful voice Allah will send on these forests wind and they will bring all the sound they desire. They will listen to a higher voice beyond all listening, and that will be when they hear the words of Allah, the Exalted, and His greeting and speech. He will recite His words to them. When they hear, they will feel as though they did not hear it before."

There are many good and authentic reports giving good tiding of listening to the most beautiful sounds, sweet to your ears and delight of your eyes. There is nothing more delightful in Paradise than to look at the Face of your Lord Almighty and listen to His words. The people of Paradise will not have anything more pleasant than it.

Abdullah ibn Buraydah said, "The people of Paradise will visit Allah, the Compeller, every day twice. He will recite the Qur'an to them while everyone will be sitting on the cushions of pearls, rubies, gold and emerald. They will find the delight of their eyes, as they never did before, and will listen to what is greater and more beautiful than anything. Then they will return to their places with comfort of eyes to visit Him the following day."

CHAPTER 58
THE MOUNTS AND HORSES OF THE PEOPLE OF PARADISE

Buraydah reported that a man asked the Prophet, ﷺ, "Messenger of Allah, are there horses in Paradise?"
He replied, "If Allah admits you in Paradise you will not desire to sit on a horse of red ruby which will take you anywhere you like in Paradise but you will have it."

Another person asked, "Are there camels in paradise, Messenger of Allah?"
He did not say what he said to his colleague, but said, "If Allah admits you in Paradise, you will have all that your soul wishes and your eye is delighted with."[331]

Abu Ayyub reported, "A Bedouin came to the Prophet ﷺ and said, 'Messenger of Allah, I love horses. Are there horses in Paradise?'
The Messenger of Allah ﷺ replied, "If you enter Paradise, you will be offered a horse of ruby with two wings and it will fly you anywhere you wish."[332]

Abu Hurayrah reported that the Messenger of Allah, blessing and peace be upon him, mentioned Paradise and said, "Firdaws is the highest one and most spacious one. From it flow the rivers of Paradise and on it will be placed the Throne of Allah on the day of Judgement."

A man from the audience stood up and said, "Messenger of Allah, horses have been endeared to me, are there horses in Paradise?"
He replied, "Yes, by the One who holds my soul in His hand, there are in Paradise flashing horses and camels which will run fast between the leaves of Paradise. The people will visit on them one another wherever they want."

Another man said, "Messenger of Allah, I like camels."
He cited the rest of the Hadith.[333]

----
331. Tirmidhi (2543)
332. Ibid (2544) It is not a strong report.
333. Sifat al-Jannah (427)

Abu Ayyub reported the Prophet ﷺ saying, "The people of Paradise will visit one another on white camels of noble breed as if they are rubies. There are no animals in Paradise except horses and camels."[334]

Jabir ibn Abdullah reported that the Prophet ﷺ said, "When the people of Paradise enter it, they will be brought horses of red rubies with wings. They do not urinate, and release nature. They will ride them and they will fly with them in Paradise. Then Allah Almighty will appear to them and they will fall prostrate. He will say, 'Raise your heads; it is not the day of act but the day of pleasure and honour.' They will raise their heads and Allah will shower over them fragrance. They will pass with the heaps of musk and Allah will send wind on those heaps which will stir them over them till when they return to their families, they are dust-covered and dishevelled."[335]

Abdullah ibn 'Amr said, "In Paradise there are horses and camels of noble breed."

334. Ibid (428)
335. Ibid (429)

CHAPTER 59
VISIT OF THE PEOPLE OF PARADISE TO ONE ANOTHER AND DISCUSSION OF WHAT WAS BETWEEN THEM IN THE WORLD

Allah, the Exalted, said, "They will turn to one another enquiring. A speaker among them will say, 'I had a close companion on earth who used to ask me, 'Do you really believe that after we die and become dust and bone, we shall be brought for judgement?' Then he will say, 'Shall we look for him?' He will look down and see him in the midst of the Fire, and say to him, 'By Allah, you almost brought me to ruin! Had it not been for the grace of my Lord, I too would have been taken to Hell." *(37: 50-57)*

In these verses Allah, the Glorious, tells that the people of paradise will turn to one another talking and asking about some incidents, which took place in the world. Their talks and discussions led one of them to remember and say that he had a close companion in the world who denied the resurrection and the Hereafter. He used to say as Allah Almighty has related, "Do you really believe that we will be brought for recompense of our deeds after we had decayed and become dust and bones?"

Then the believer will ask his colleagues in Paradise, "Would you look in the Fire so that we find the place and fate of my companion?"

This is the obvious meaning of these verses. However, there are two other interpretations:

One is that it will be the angels who will say to those involved in talk, 'Would you look down to find out?'

The other is that it will be Allah, the Honourable, who will ask them to look down in Hell.

The correct one is the first meaning that the believer will say to his companions to look. The context indicates that it is information about him and the condition of his companion.

Ka'b said, "Between Paradise and Hell there are peepholes, when a believer wants to look at his opponent of the world, he will peep through one of these holes."

Muqatil said, "When the believer said to his colleagues, 'Would you look down?' they said to him, 'You recognize him better, so look yourself. He looked and saw his companion in the midst of the Fire. Had not Allah made him recognize him, he would have not been able because his face and colour had changed and the torment had altered his shape. At this point he said, 'By Allah, you had almost ruined me. Had it not been for the favour of my Lord I would have been of those brought to Hell.'
That is you almost ruined me, and had it not been the favour of Allah to me I would have been brought with you for torment."

Allah, the Exalted, also said, **"They turn to one another and say, 'When we were still with our families (on earth) we used to live in fear but Allah has been gracious to us and saved us from the torment of intense heat. We used to pray to Him. He is the Beneficent and the Merciful."** (52: 25-28)

Abu Umamah reported that the Messenger of Allah, blessing and peace be upon him, was asked, "Will the people of Paradise visit one another?"
He said, "Those on the high level will visit those on the lower, and those of lower level will not visit the higher level ones except those who love each other for the sake of Allah. They will go anywhere they wish on she-camels decorated with pillows." [336]

Abu Ayyub reported from the Prophet ﷺ that he said, "The people of Paradise will visit one another on the camels of noble breed." [337]

---

336. Tabarani in Kabir (7936), Abu Nu'aym in Sifat al-jannah (421)
337. Sifat al-jannah (428)

So, the people of Paradise will visit one another and in this way their joy and happiness will be complete.

The Prophet ﷺ asked Harithah, "How did you enter upon morning?"

He replied, "By being a true believer."

He said, "Every truth has an essence, so what is the essence of your belief?"

He said, "My soul turned away from the world and as a result I passed the night awake and remained thirsty in daytime, and I feel as though I look at the Throne of my Lord openly and at the people of Paradise visiting one another and at the people of the Fire being punished in it."

The Prophet ﷺ said, "He is a slave whose heart Allah has illuminated." [338]

Anas reported that the Messenger of Allah, blessing and peace be upon him, said, "When the people of paradise enter it, the friends will long for one another. Then the couch of one will move to the couch of the other and they will come close together and meet. One of them will say to his friend, 'Do you know when Allah forgave us?' His friend will reply, 'On such and such day and in such and such place we called upon Allah and He forgave us.'"[339]

Shufayy ibn Mati' reported that the Messenger ﷺ said, "Among he delight of the people of Paradise will be that they will visit one another on the mounts and camels. They will be supplied with horses with saddle and bridle, which do not drop dung and do not urinate. They will ride them and go wherever Allah Almighty wishes. A cloud type thing will come to them, which will have that which no eye has ever seen and no ear has ever heard of. They will say, 'Bring rain to us.' The cloud will continue showering on them until it reaches above their desires. Then Allah will send a harmless wind and it will blow the heaps of musk on their right and their left. It will settle that musk in the foreheads and parting of hairs and heads of their horses. Every one of them will have long hair as he wishes and that musk will stick their hair and their dresses. Then they will go where Allah Almighty wishes, they come across some women who will call some of them saying, 'Slave of Allah, don't you need us?'

He will ask, 'What are you, and who are you?'

She will say, 'I am your wife and your love.'

He will say, 'I was unaware of your being.'

338. Al-Bazzar (32)
339. Ibid (3553)

She will say, 'Didn't you know that Allah Almighty has said, '**No soul knows what has been hidden for them of comfort for the eyes as reward for what they used to do.'** *(32: 17)*"

He will say, 'Yes indeed.' He may turn away from her for forty years and will not come back because of being engaged in pleasure and bliss."[340]

Abu Hurayrah said, "The people of Paradise will visit one another on white camels with solid saddles, their feet will blow musk and their rein will be better than the world and what it contains."

Abu Hurayrah reported that the Prophet, blessing and peace be upon him, asked Gabriel about the following verse:
"**And the Horn will be blown, and whoever is in the heavens and whoever is on the earth will fall dead except whom Allah wills.**" *39: 68)*

He asked, "Who are these people?"
He replied that they were the martyrs Allah will raise them while they will have their swords around their necks near the Throne. The angels will bring them camels of ruby their rein being white pearl and their saddle of gold, their necks will be green silk and brocade and their saddle pads will be softer than the silk, and they will travel as far as eyes can reach. The men will move in Paradise on horses and will say at the end of their walk, 'Let us go to see how Allah judges between His creations.' Allah will laugh to them and when Allah laughs to any slave in that place, he will be free from accounting."

'Ali said, "I heard the Messenger of Allah, blessing and peace be upon him, say, 'There is a tree in Paradise from the top of it come robes and below it are horses of gold saddled and reined from pearl and ruby. They do not drop dung and do not urinate. They have wings and their stride is as far as the eye can reach. The people of Paradise will mount them and they will fly with them wherever they wish. Those who are below them in level will say, 'Our Lord, how did You give this honour to these slaves of Yours?

It will be said to them, 'They used to pray in night when you were sleeping, they used to fast and you were eating, they used to spend while you were hoarding

340. Ibn al-Mubarak in al-zuhd (239)

and they used to fight while you showed cowardice.'"

Beside this they will have a higher and nobler visit when they visit their Lord Almighty. He will show His Face to them and make them listen to His speech, and will announce His pleasure with them. This visit will be discussed later.

CHAPTER 60
THE MARKETS OF PARADISE AND WHAT ALLAH HAS PREPARED FOR ITS PEOPLE THERE

Anas reported that the Messenger of Allah, blessing and peace be upon him, said, "There is a market in Paradise which the people will visit every Friday. The north wind will blow and fill their faces and dresses and they will increase in beauty and charm. They return with this additional beauty to their families who say to them, 'By Allah, you have increased in beauty and charm after leaving us.' They will respond: 'You as well have increased in beauty and charm after us.'" [341]

Sa'id ibn al-Musayyib said that he met Abu Hurayrah who said to him, "Pray to Allah to bring us together in the market of Paradise."

Sa'id said, "Is there a market in Paradise?"
Abu Hurayrah said, "Yes, the Messenger of Allah, blessing and peace be upon him, told me, 'When the people of Paradise enter it, they will be placed according to their deeds, and they will have permission on Friday of the days of the world. They will visit Allah, the Blessed and Exalted, who will appear on His Throne and come out in a meadow of Paradise. Pulpits of light, pearl, chrysolite, ruby, gold and silver will be put for them. The lowest of them will sit on the heaps of musk and camphor, the people on the chairs will not see them to be higher than themselves.'"

Abu Hurayrah said he then asked the Prophet ﷺ, "Are we going to see our Lord Almighty?"
The Prophet ﷺ replied, "Yes. Do you have any doubt in seeing the sun and the moon on full-moon night?"
He said: "No."
He then said, "In the same way you will not have doubt in seeing your Lord. No

---

341. Muslim (jannah; 2833)

one will be there but Allah will speak to him. He will say to someone, 'Do you remember what you did on such and such day?' And He will mention some of his shortcomings. The person will say, 'Yes, but haven't You forgiven me?' He will reply, 'Yes, and by My forgiveness you reached this status.'

While they are there a cloud will come over them and shower fragrance upon them they never witnessed like it before. Then Our Lord Almighty will say, 'Get up to see what I have prepared for you of honour and take what you wish.'"

He ﷺ further said, "They then will come to a market surrounded by the angels. In it will be things like of which no eye has ever seen, no ear has ever heard of and thought of it has not passed in any mind.

Allah will allow us to take what we wish without selling and buying. In that market the people of Paradise will meet one another. A man of high attire will approach someone lower than him, and there will be no one lower. However, he will be impressed by the dress and appearance of the person in front of him, but before he finishes his thought he finds himself in a better form. This is because not one body is to feel distressed in Paradise."

He then said, "Then we return to our homes and meet by our spouses who welcome us and say, 'Welcome to our love. You came with superior beauty and smell than you had when you left us.' He will answer that we had sat today with our Lord, the Compeller, the Owner of honour and dignity, and it was appropriate that we return in a better form than we had."[342]

Ali ibn Abi Talib reported that the Messenger of Allah, blessing and peace be upon him, said, "There is a market in Paradise where there is no selling or buying except the images of men and women. When a person craves an image, he will enter it."[343]

Anas said, "There are in Paradise heaps of musk the people of it will go to them and meet one another, Allah will send a wind which will enter their houses and when they return to their families, they will say that your beauty has increased since you left us. They will say to them, 'You as well have increased in charm after

342. Tirmidhi (2549), Ibn Majah (4336), Its chain is weak. It is also recorded by Ibn Abi al-Dunya and Ibn Abi 'Asim
343. Tirmidhi

you left us.'"

Jabir ibn Abdullah reported, "The Messenger of Allah, blessing and peace be upon him, came out to us while we were sitting together and said, 'The assembly of Muslims, there is a market in Paradise with no selling or buying except for images. If a person desires the image of a man or woman he will enter it.'"[344]

Allah knows better.

---

344. Ahmad, see Majma' (8533)

CHAPTER 61

THE VISIT OF THE PEOPLE OF PARADISE TO THEIR LORD, THE BLESSED

Anas ibn Malik reported that Gabriel brought a white mirror to the Prophet ﷺ which had a spot in it. The Prophet ﷺ asked him, "What is this?"
Gabriel replied, "It is Friday - you and your Community have been preferred by it. Other people, the Jews and the Christians, are behind you. It contains good for you, and there is a period in it no believer asks Allah for any good but He will grant him that. It is the day of more with us."

The Prophet asked, "Gabriel, what is the 'day of more?'"
He said, "Your Lord has taken an extensive valley in Firdaws which has heaps of musk. When the Day of Resurrection comes Almighty will send down as many angels as He wishes and around that valley will be platforms of light for the seats of the prophets. These platforms will be surrounded by the platforms of gold studded with rubies and precious stones for the martyrs and faithful devotees. They will sit on these platforms and Allah, the Exalted, will say, 'I am your Lord, you fulfilled My promise, so ask Me I will grant you.' They will say, 'Our Lord, we ask for Your pleasure.' He will say, 'I am pleased with you, and you will have all that you desire, and I have more.' They like Friday because Allah will grant them good things. That is the day on which your Lord will establish Himself on the Throne. On that day Adam was created and on that day the Hour will come."[345]

Abu Barzah al-Aslami reported that the Prophet ﷺ said, "The people of Paradise will wear one gown in the morning and another in the evening. As you go to see a king of the kings of the world, they will go in the same manner to visit their Lord at a fixed time they know." [346]

Ali reported that the Messenger of Allah, blessing and peace be upon you, said,

---
345. *Musnad al-Shafi'i (374)*
346. *Sifat al-jannah (394)*

"When the people of Paradise enter and settle in it an angel will come to them and tell them that Allah, Blessed be He, orders them to visit Him. They will gather and Allah Almighty will command David who will raise his voice with glorification and exaltation of Allah and then the table of eternity will be put."

The people asked, "What is the table of eternity, Messenger of Allah?"

He replied, "A huge table, one corner of which is wider than the distance between the east and the west. They will be served with food and drink and will be given dresses. They will say: 'Nothing remains but to look at the Face of our Lord almighty.'

Allah then will reveal Himself to them and they will fall in prostration and they will be told: 'You are not in the world of action but in the abode of recompense.'"[347]

Muhammad ibn Ali ibn al-Husayn reported that the Messenger of Allah, (peace be upon him), said, "There is a tree in Paradise called 'Tuba', if a rider goes on a fast horse in its shade, he will travel for a hundred years. Its leaves are green sheets, its flowers are yellow meadows, its courtyards are of fine silk and brocade, its fruits are robes and its gum is ginger and honey. Its ground is of red ruby and green emerald, its dust is musk, and its grass is saffron. Its flame is lighted without fuel. From its root gush the rivers, Salsabil, spring and nectar. Its shade is the meeting place of the People of Paradise; they love it and sit together to talk.

While they are sitting in its shade talking, the angels come to them with camels of noble breed created from ruby and then breeze was blown in them. They will be bridled with the chains of gold. Their faces will shine like lamps in beauty and brightness. Their fur will be mixed of red silk and white smooth velvet; no one had seen anything like that. They will have saddles of pearls and rubies studded with pearl and chrysolite lined with red gold and having the covers of purple fine rugs. They will make these camels sit and say to the people, 'Your Lord, the Blessed and High, extends His greeting to you and asks you to pay visit to Him, so that you can see Him and He can see you. He would like to greet you and you greet Him, to speak to you and you speak to Him and grant you more of His favour and grace; He is indeed of the vast mercy and great grace.' Then everyone will turn to his mount and will march in one harmonious row, nothing causing disorder. The ear of one camel will not surpass the other and none of them will halt. They will not pass by any tree of Paradise but it will present to them its fruits and move from their way in order not to break their rows or separate a person from his colleague.

---

347. Ibid (397)

When they reach to Almighty, the Blessed and High, he will uncover His noble Face and reveal to them in His great grandeur. They will say, 'Our Lord, You are peace and from You emerges peace and You deserve the majesty and honour.' Their Lord, the Glorious and Supreme will say, 'I am peace and from Me comes peace and I deserve majesty and honour. Welcome to My slaves who took care of My commands, honoured My pledge, feared Me without seeing Me and stood in awe in every situation.'

They will say, 'By Your might, majesty and greatness of Your status, we were not able to appreciate You as it was due, and failed to fulfil all Your dues, give us permission to bow down in prostration to You.'

Allah, the Most High and Sublime, will say, 'I have relieved you from the burden of worship and put your bodies at rest. You exhausted your bodies for Me very often, now you have reached My bliss, My mercy and My honour, ask Me anything you wish and bring your wishes I will grant you all your wishes. Today I will not reward you according to your deeds but according to My mercy, honour, greatness, height of My status and sublimity of My affair.'

They will remain in their desires, gifts and presents. The person who will have smallest wish will wish like the whole of the world since Allah, the Exalted, has created it to the day He destroyed it.

Their Lord, the Majestic and Supreme, will say, 'You fell short in your desires and agreed with less than you deserve. I have granted you all that you asked for and wished. Moreover, I joined your families with you, and completed what you missed in your desires.'"

The attribution of the above to the Prophet ﷺ is not correct, it may be the statement of Muhammad ibn Ali and some of the weak reporters made it from the statement of the Prophet, peace be upon him. Some of its reporters are rejected and some are unknown. Allah knows better.

CHAPTER 62
THE CLOUDS AND RAIN, WHICH WILL BE SEEN IN PARADISE

It has already been cited in the section of the market of Paradise that on the day of the visit of the people, a cloud will cover them and shower beautiful fragrance never experienced by them.

Kathir ibn Murrah said, "The 'more' is that a cloud will pass by the people of Paradise and ask them, 'What do you want to be showered over you?' They will not wish anything but it will shower on them."

Abd al-'Aziz ibn Marwan asked Safiyy al-Yamani about the delegation of the people of Paradise and he said, 'They will visit Allah, the Glorious and Exalted, every Thursday and seats will be put for them. Everyone will know his seat better than you know this seat of yours. When they take their seats and the people sit down, Allah Almighty will order, 'Serve food to My slaves, My creation and My neighbours and My visitors.' They will be served, then He will order to serve them with drinks and they will be brought different types of drinks all sealed and they will drink from them.

Then Allah will say, 'My slaves, My creations, My neighbours and My delegations have eaten and drank, now amuse them.'

The fruits of a tree will be brought near them and they will eat as much as they wish. Then Almighty will say, 'My slaves, My creations, My neighbours, and My visitors have eaten, drank and been amused, now bring dresses for them.'

The fruits of a tree yellow, green, red and all kinds of colours will come; they do not grow but the robes. They will spread robes and shirts for them. Then the Lord will say, 'My slaves, creations, neighbours and visitors have been provided with food, drink, amusement and dresses, now put on them fragrance.' Musk will fall on them like the drizzles.

Then Allah, the Exalted will say, 'My slaves, creations, neighbours and visitors have been given food, drink, amusement, dresses and perfumes; I should reveal Myself to them so that they can see Me.' Then the Lord will reveal Himself to them and they see Him, and their faces will be brightened.

It will then be said to them, 'Go to your homes. When they reach there, their wives say to them, 'You left us in a form and returned in a different shape.'

They will say to their wives, 'Allah, the Most Glorious, revealed Himself to us and we looked at Him and our faces became fresh and beautiful.'"

Shufayy ibn Mati' said that the Messenger of Allah, peace be upon him, said, "One of the pleasures of the people of Paradise will be that they will move on mounts and noble camels. Horses with saddles will be brought to them, which do not drop the dung or urinate. They will mount them and go wherever Allah wishes. A cloud will come over them having that which no eye has ever seen and no ear has ever heard of. They will say to it, 'Rain upon us'. It will rain until their wishes are fulfilled. Then Allah Almighty will send a harmless wind, which will spread heaps of musk on their right and their left. That musk will reach the foreheads and partings of the hairs of their horses, and their heads. Everyone will have long hair according to his desire. The musk will stick to their hair, their horses and their dresses. Then they will proceed until they reach where Allah wishes. A woman will call some of them, 'Slave of Abdullah, do you not need us?'
He will ask: 'What is you, and who are you?'
She will reply, 'I am your wife and you love.'
He will say, 'I did not know your existence.'
The woman will say, "Didn't you know that Allah, the Exalted has said 'No soul knows what has been hidden for them of the comfort of their eyes as reward of what they used to do." (32: 17)
He will say, 'Yes, by my Lord. He may get busy from her for forty years. Nothing will turn from her but the pleasure he will be in.'" [348]

It is to be noted that Allah, the Glorious and Mighty, has made the cloud and rain it brings cause of mercy and life in this world. He will make it the cause of recreating the people from their graves. It will rain on the earth for forty years consistently from below the Throne, and the people will grow from the earth like

348. Ibn al-Mubarak (239)

the plants, and on the Day of Resurrection it will rain and only Allah knows the impact of that great rain. As it is in the world He will spread clouds in Paradise, which will shower fragrance and anything they wish. In the same way He will raise up clouds, which will pour on the criminals torment over their torment. He did it for the people of Hud and Shu'ayb; He sent clouds which poured on them torment which destroyed them. He, glory be to Him, raises clouds for mercy as well as for punishment.

CHAPTER 63
THE SOVEREIGNTY IN PARADISE BELONGS TO ITS PEOPLE

Allah, the Exalted, said, **"If you look there, you will see pleasure and great dominion."** *(76: 20)*

Mujahid explained 'great dominion' as authority, and said it referred to seeking permission by the angels to visit them.

Ka'b said, "It means that their Lord will send angels to them; they will come and seek permission from them."

Abu Sulayman said, "The great dominion is that the messenger from Allah will come with gifts and souvenirs and will not be allowed to enter until permission is granted to him. He will say to the gatekeeper, 'Ask permission for me to see the friend of Allah because I cannot reach him.' He will inform another chamberlain and many chamberlains one after the other. From his home to the Home of safety there is a door through which he can enter to His Lord anytime he wishes without any restriction. So the great dominion is that the messenger of Allah, the Owner of Might, cannot enter to him without permission, and he will enter to his Lord without permission."

Anas ibn Malik related the Prophet ﷺ saying, "The lowest man in rank in Paradise will be a person who will have ten thousand attendants waiting on him."[349]

Abu Hurayrah reported the Messenger of Allah, blessing and peace be upon him, said, "The lowest person in rank in Paradise, and there is no one low there, is the one who will be attended by fifteen thousand servants in the morning and the evening. Every servant has a duty which anyone else does not have."

Abu Abd al-Rahman al-Hubli said, "When the believing person enters Paradise, he

---

349. Ibn al-Mubarak (1530)

is received by seventy thousand attendants as they are pearl."

Abu Abd al-Rahman al-Ma'afiri said, "For a person in Paradise two tables of meal will be arranged the two corners of them will not be seen because of his attendants. When he moves, they walk behind him."

Abu Sa'id reported that the Prophet ﷺ said, "The lowest person in rank in Paradise will be the one who will have eighty thousand attendants and seventy two wives. A huge dome of pearl, ruby and chrysolite will be built for him, the length of which will be like the distance between Jabiyah and Sana'a."

Abu Umamah said, "The believer will be reclining in Paradise after entering it and he will have two rows of attendants. At the end of them will be a gate, and an angel from the angels of Allah Almighty will approach him and ask for permission. The lowest attendant will go to the gate and find an angel asking for permission. He will say to the next one that there was an angel asking permission. He in his turn will tell the next one until it reaches the believer. He will say, 'Let him in,' the message will reach through these attendants to the angel and the gate will be opened. He will enter, greet the believer and then leave."

Al-Dahhak ibn Muzahim said, "While the friend of Allah will be in his residence in Paradise, a messenger from Allah, the Exalted and Sublime, will visit him and will say to the doorkeeper, 'Seek permission for the messenger of Allah to the friend of Allah.' He will go in and say, 'Friend of Allah, here is the messenger of Allah asking permission to see you.'

He will permit him and the messenger will enter and put before him the gifts, and he will say to him, 'Friend of Allah, your Lord sends His greeting to you and orders you to eat from it.' He will find the food similar to what he has eaten before. He will say: 'I have just eaten it now.'

He will say: 'Your Lord has commanded you to eat from it.'
He will eat and find in it the taste of every fruit of Paradise."

This is what Allah said:
"And they have been this before." *(2: 25)*

Al-Mughirah ibn Sh'bah reported that the Prophet ﷺ said, "Moses asked his Lord, 'What will be the lowest person in Paradise?'

Allah replied, 'He will be a man who will arrive after the people of Paradise have entered it. He will be told to go in. He will say: 'My Lord, how can I enter when the people have entered and taken their places?'
He will be told: 'Would you like to have, like a king of the kings of the world?'
He will reply: 'Yes, my Lord, I agree.'
The Almighty will say to him, 'You have that and similar and similar and similar and similar to that.' In the fifth time he will say, 'I agree, my Lord.'

He will tell him, 'You have all that and ten times more, and you have all that your soul desires and you eye is comfortable with.'
He will say: 'My Lord, I agreed.'" [350]

Abu Sa'id said, "Allah created Paradise from one brick of gold and another of silver. He planted it by His hand, and said, 'Speak.'
It said, 'The believers have achieved success.'
The angels entered it and said, 'Blessed are you, a residence of the kings!' [351]

This report has come from the statement of the Prophet, but its chain is not sound.

350. Muslim
351. Al-Bazzar (3507, 3508)

CHAPTER 64
PARADISE HAS THINGS BEYOND THE IMAGINATION AND A PLACE OF A LASH IN IT IS BETTER THAN THE WORLD AND WHAT IS IN IT

Allah, the Exalted, said, **"Their sides shun their beds in order to pray to their Lord in fear and hope; they give to others some of what We have given them. No soul knows what joy is kept hidden In store for them as a reward for what they have done."** *(32: 16-17)*

They hid of their prayer in the night, so Allah Almighty kept the reward hidden for them, which nobody knows. Allah compared their restlessness, fear and anxiety in their beds in order to stand up for prayer of the night with the comfort of eyes in Paradise.

Abu Hurayrah reported that Allah's Messenger ﷺ said, "Allah, the Exalted, says: 'I have prepared for My righteous slaves that which no eye has seen, no ear has heard of and no heart has ever imagined.'

It is confirmed in the Book of Allah:
"No soul knows what joy is kept hidden in store for them as a reward for what they have done." *(32: 17)*

In another version, Allah's Messenger ﷺ said, "Allah, the Exalted, says: 'I have prepared for My righteous servants what no eye has seen, no ear has heard of and no heart has imagined, except what I have told you.'"

Then the Prophet read, "No soul knows what has been hidden for them of comfort of eyes as reward for what they used to do."

Sahl ibn Sa'd narrated, 'I attended a meeting with the Prophet ﷺ in which he described Paradise and said at the end, 'There are things which no eye has seen, no ear has heard of and no heart has imagined.'

Then he read, '**Their sides shun their beds and they call upon their Lord in fear and hope; they give to others some of what We have given them. No soul knows what has been hidden for them of comfort of eyes as reward for what they used to do.**' *(32: 16-17)*"[352]

Abu Hurayrah reported that the Messenger of Allah, blessing and peace be upon him, said, "The length of the bow of one of you in Paradise is better than what the sun rises or sets on."[353]

The report of Abu Umamah has already been cited in which the Prophet ﷺ said, "Is there anyone who is ready for Paradise? Paradise is very important. It is, by the Lord of the Ka'bah, shining light, moving sweet basil, lofty palace, flowing stream, ripe fruit, beautiful and charming wife and many robes. It is a place of lasting staying in safe home, with fruit, green, joy, pleasure and high and brilliant station."

Had it not been that nothing else is sought by the Face of Allah except Paradise, it would have been enough for its merit and excellence. Jabir reported that the Prophet ﷺ said, "Nothing should be asked by the Face of Allah except Paradise."

Sahl ibn Sa'd said, 'I heard the Messenger of Allah, peace be upon him, say, "The place of a lash in Paradise is better than the world and what is in it."[354]

Abu Hurayrah reported that the Messenger of Allah, blessing and peace be upon him, said, "The space of the lash of one of you in Paradise is better than what is between the heavens and the earth."[355]

Sa'd ibn Abi Waqqas reported that the Prophet ﷺ said, "If less than a fingernail of what is in Paradise appears, what is between the sky and the earth will be embellished, and if a man of the people of Paradise shows up and his bracelets appear, they will efface the light of the sun as the sun effaces the light of the

352. Muslim (jannah: 2825)
353. Bukhari (2793), Muslim (imarah: 1881)
354. Bukhari (2792)
355. Ahmad (8173)

stars."[356]

Tirmidhi declared this report as weak but said it was supported by another report.

There are reports on this issue from Anas ibn Malik, Abu Sa'id al-Khudri, and Abdullah ibn 'Amr ibn al-'As.

How can a house, which Allah Almighty has set by His hand, fully be appreciated? He, the Exalted, fixed it and made it resting place for His beloved servants, and filled it with His mercy, honour and pleasure. He described its comfort as the great success and its dominion as the big dominion. He deposited in it all the good materials and cleansed it from every fault, deficiency and defect. If you ask about its land and ground, it is musk and saffron. If you ask about its roof, it is the Throne of the Merciful. If you ask about its floor tiles, it is strong smelling musk. If you ask about its pebbles, they are pearls and gems. If you ask about its structure, it is built by one brick of silver and one of gold. If you want to know about its tress, then there is no tree but its trunk is of gold and silver and not of wood and timber. Its fruits are like big jars but softer than butter and sweeter than honey. If you ask about their leaves, they are the best of what is possible of fine robes. If you want to know about its streams, then there are rivers of milk the taste of which does not change, and rivers of wine delight of the drinkers, and rivers of pure honey.

If you want to know about their food, it is fruit of their choice and the meat of the birds they desire. As for their drink it is Tasnim, ginger and camphor. Their utensils will be of gold and silver clear like glass

If you want to know about the wideness of the gates of Paradise, it is the distance of forty-year journey between its two parts. However, a day will come when the crowds will overfill it. If you ask about the wind moving its trees, it will be moving with ecstasy anyone who listens to it. As for its shade it has one tree in the shade of which a fast rider will travel a hundred years without crossing it. If you want to know its spaciousness, its lowest person will walk in his dominion, couches, palaces and gardens two thousand years. If you ask about its pavilions and domes, one pavilion is made of a hollow pearl sixty mile long. If you ask about its upper rooms and villas, they are chambers above chambers beneath which rive will be flowing. If you want to know their height, then look at the rising or setting

356. Tirmidhi (2538)

star in the horizon, which eyes cannot reach.

If you ask about the dress of the people in it, it is silk and gold. If you want to know their beds, their interior is brocade lined in the upper side. If you ask about their couches, they are decorated with buttons of gold without having any hole or peg. If you want to know the faces of the people and their beauty, they will be on the form of the moon. If you ask about their age, they will be of thirty-three years on the image of their father Adam. If you want to know their listening to the song, it will be singing of their wives from the beautiful dark-eyed women. Above it they will listen to the voices of the angels and the prophets, and more than that they will listen to the address of the Lord of the Universe.

If you ask about their mounts on which they will move to visit one another, they are camels of good breed, which will take them anywhere they wish to go. If you want to know their jewellery and distinguishing marks, they are bracelets of gold and pearl and crowns on their heads. As for their servants, they will be everlasting children as though they are hidden pearls. If you ask about their brides and wives, they are maidens of matching age and full breasts. The freshness of youth running in their limbs; their cheeks will have the colour of rose and apple, their breast like pomegranates, their teeth like arranged pearls, and their waists will have fineness and delicateness.

The brightness will appear from their faces when they show up, and lightening will shine from their middle incisors when they smile. When one of them meets her beloved, say what you like in meeting of the sun and the moon! When she talks to him, just imagine the talking of two lovers. If he embraces her, it is like the hugging of two twigs. He will see his face in the surface of her cheek as it is seen in a mirror, which has been cleaned. The marrow of her leg will be seen from behind the flesh and her skin, bone and jewellery will not cover it. If she looks down to the world all that is between the sky and the earth will be filled with fragrance, and the mouths of the creations will engage in glorification, extolling and praise of Allah. It will adore all that is between the earth and the sky, and it will turn all the eyes to her away from anything else.

Her beauty will efface the light of the sun as the sun blocks the light of the stars, and all those on earth will believe in Allah, the Living and the Sustainer. Her head-cover on her head is better than the world and what is in it. Her communion with him is more desirable to him than anything else. With the passage of time she will increase her beauty and charm, and he will increase in her love and union. She is free from pregnancy, childbirth, menstruation, and postnatal bleeding. She is also free from phlegm, spittle, urine release of nature and all types of filth. Her youth is not going to fade, her garment will not wear out, her dress will not hide her beauty and the joy of her union will never end. She has fixed her gaze on her husband and has no interest in anyone else, and he as well focuses his eye on her because she is his utmost desire and love. If he looks at her, she pleases him, if he asks her to do anything, she obeys him, and if he is away from her, she protects herself. He is in this way in the best security for her and receives the fulfilment of his desires. Moreover she has not been touched by any human or Jinn before him. Whenever he looks at her, she fills his heart with happiness, whenever she talks to him she fills his ears with arranged pearls, and when she appears she fills the palace and the chamber with brightness.

If you ask about their age, they are of the same age in the middle of the age of youth. If you ask about their beauty, they are like the sun and the moon. If you ask about their eyes, they are the beautiful black in clear whiteness and darkness. If you ask about their stature, they are like the best of the branches. If you ask about their breasts, they are full round like the fine pomegranate. If you ask about the colour, it is like ruby and emerald.

If you want to know their characters, they are the best who have combined the beauty and good character. They have been given the beauty of inner and outside. They thus are the delight of the souls and comfort of the eyes. If you ask about the conjugal companionship and its Joy, they are loving and affectionate to their husbands with delicate union that is blended with the souls. What do you think about a woman who when she smiles in the face of her husband, Paradise is illuminated by her smile? When she moves from one palace to another, you say that it is the sun moving in its constellations. When she talks to her husband, it is the most beautiful talk. If he puts his hand around her waist, the joy of that embracing and hugging is unimaginable.

A poet says, "Her talk is permissible magic, which is not going to kill a cautious Muslim. Even if is long, does not cause boredom, and when she speaks the listening person wishes that she does not make her talk brief."

If she sings, her song is the joy of eyes and ears? If she entertains and amuses, do not ask the delight of that entertainment and amusement. If she kisses, nothing is more delicious to him than that kiss, and if she copulates, there is nothing more enjoyable and delightful that that union.

If you ask about the day of more and the visit of the Lord Almighty and Praiseworthy and seeing His Face in real sense, it is like you see the sun in midday and the moon on the night of full moon. It has been so reported from the Prophet, the truthful and trustworthy through many narrations in authentic sources of Hadith. There are reports from the following Companions: Jarir, Suhayb, Anas, Abu Hurayrah, Abu Musa and Abu Sa'īd.

Listen when a caller will call, "People of Paradise, your Lord, the Most Blessed and High, is inviting you to visit Him, so proceed to His visit." They will respond, "We heard and we obey."

They will hurry up to the visit and find the camel waiting for them. They will mount on their backs and march quickly till they reach the spacious valley, which was made their meeting place. They all gather there and the caller will not miss a single person. The Lord Almighty will order His Chair to be put, and the platforms of light, pearl, chrysolite, gold and silver will be set for them. The lowest of them will be seated on them - and there is no low among them - on the heaps of musk; they will not feel that those sitting on the chairs are above them in favour. When they take their seats and settle in their places, the caller will call, "People of Paradise, you have an appointment with Allah which He wants to fulfil." They will say, "What is that? Didn't He brighten our faces and make our scales heavy, and admit us in Paradise and keep us away from the Hellfire?"

While they are there a light will appear which will shine Paradise. They will raise their heads and see that the Most Powerful, the Glorious, has looked down on them from the above. He will greet them, "People of Paradise, peace be upon you!" They will reply, "O Allah! You are Peace, from You emerges peace, blessed are you, the owner of Majesty and Honour." The Lord, the Most Exalted, will reveal Himself to them smiling, and call, "People of Paradise!" The first thing they will hear will be, "Where are those who believed in Me being unseen, this is the day of more." They will all speak together with one word, "We are pleased, so You be pleased with us."

He will say, "People of Paradise, had I not been pleased with you, I would have not admitted you to My Paradise. This is the day of more, so ask Me." They will all say, "Show us Your Face; we would like to look at it." The Lord will remove the veils and reveal Himself to them; His light will overwhelm them. Had He not decreed for them not to be burnt they would have been burnt down. No one in that gathering will remain but Allah will address him till He will say to one of them, 'So and so, do you remember you did such and such on that day?'

He will remind him of some of his shortcomings.

The man will say, "My Lord, haven't You forgiven me?"

He will reply, "Yes, and by My forgiveness you reached this status."

What a pleasant listening to that speech and what the delight of the eyes of the righteous ones by looking at the Noble Face in the Hereafter! What a humiliation for those who had losing bargain!

"Some faces on that Day will be radiant looking at their Lord; on that Day there will be sad and despairing faces and realize that a great calamity is about to befall them." *(75: 22-25)*

"Come to the Paradise of Eden, it is your first abode and there is the pavilion. But we are captives of the enemy, I wonder whether we will return to our homelands and submit!"

CHAPTER 65
SEEING ALLAH, THE BLESSED AND THE GLORIOUS, BY NAKED EYES AS THE MOON IS SEEN, AND ALLAH'S SMILING AND TALKING TO THEM

This chapter is the noblest, the most valuable and the highest in importance. It is a source of the comfort for the followers of the Sunnah and the hardest for the people of innovation and misguidance. It is the goal to which the enthusiastic people race, the competitors compete and the contesters contest. The workers should strive to achieve it. When the people of Paradise achieve it, they forget all the pleasure they have. To be kept away from it is harder and more severe to the people of Hell than the torment they suffer. This is an issue on which all the prophets and messengers as well as the Companions, their followers and the leading figures of Islam have agreed. On the other side the renegade innovators, arrogant Jahmiyyah, the Pharaonic type deniers of the Attributes of Allah and Batiniyyah who are out of all the religions deny it (i.e. Allah being seen). With these are the Rafidah who are deceived by the tricks of Satan, deserting the rope of Allah and bent on the abuse of the Companions of the Messenger of Allah. They declare war against the Sunnah and its followers, and make every enemy of Allah, His Messenger and His religion as their friends. All these people will be barred from their Lord and driven away from His door. They are the party of misguidance and disciples of the cursed Satan. They are enemies of the Messenger and his party.

Here are the proofs for the fact that Allah will be seen:

1. First proof:
Allah informed about the most knowledgeable person of his time (i.e. Moses), who was His chosen person from the people of the earth, and to whom He spoke

and who asked his Lord to see Him. The Almighty said to him:
"You will not see Me, but look at the mountain: if it remains standing firm, you will see Me,' and when his lord revealed Himself to the mountain, He made it crumble." *(7: 143)*

This statement indicates that Allah will be seen by many ways:
1. It is unthinkable that the noble Messenger of the Merciful to whom Allah spoke will ask his Lord something which was impossible for Him. It is false and inconceivable. It is to the chicks of the Greeks, Sabi'ah and Pharaonic people who compare it like asking Him to eat, drink, sleep, etc., which He is free from. It is surprising how the followers of the Sabi'ah, Magians, and the polytheists, the worshippers of idols and the protégés of Jahmiyyah and Pharaonic people became more knowledgeable about Allah, the Exalted, than Moses son of Imran concerning what is possible and what is absurd for Him!

2. Allah, the Glorious, did not object to the question of Moses. If it were impossible, He would have rejected and denied it. In the same way when Ibrahim, the friend of Allah, asked his Lord Almighty to show him how He brings the dead to life, He did not reject it. When Jesus son of Mary asked Him to send down a table from the heaven, He did not object to his request. But when Noah asked his Lord to save his son, He disapproved his request and said, "I am warning you not to be foolish." He said, "My Lord, I take refuge with You from asking for things I know nothing about. If You do not forgive me, and have mercy on me, I shall be one of the losers." *(11: 46-47)*

3. Allah responded to the request of Moses by saying: 'You will not see Me.' He did not say that you cannot see Me, and I am not an object of seeing or seeing Me is not possible. The difference between these statements is clear for anyone who looks attentively to them. The verse indicates that Allah, the Exalted and the Glorious, can be seen, but Moses' powers cannot bear seeing Him in this world because the power of mankind is weak to bear it.

4. His statement, "But look at the mountain, if it stands firm in its place, you will see Me", indicated to Moses that the mountain despite its strength and hardness cannot stand firm for the exposure of Allah in this world, so how can a weak human who is created weak?

5. Allah, the Exalted, had power to make the mountain stand in its place. It was not out of His power, but possible for Him, and He conditioned the seeing to it. If it were impossible in itself, He would not have attached it to a possible matter. If the seeing was impossible, His statement would be like saying: 'If the mountain stands in its place, I will eat, drink and sleep', as both matters are the same to you.

6. The statement of Allah, the Glorious, "When his Lord revealed Himself, he made it crumble", is clear evidence that Allah, the Exalted, can be seen. If he can reveal Himself to the mountain, which is an inanimate body and has no reward or punishment, how then it could be impossible for Him to reveal Himself for His Prophets, His messengers and his devoted servants in the house of His honour. In the above verse Allah, the Exalted, declared that the mountain did not remain standing to see Him in this world, how then can man who is weaker than the mountain see Him?

7. Allah, the Glorious, spoke to Moses, addressed him, talked to him and called him. When someone can talk and make his addressee hear his words without any intermediary, he could be seen more so. The seeing cannot be denied without denying speaking. The opponents have combined the denial of both matters: they denied that He can speak to anyone or anyone can see Him. Moses asked the Lord to see Him after He made him hear His words; he knew from His speech that He can be seen. Almighty did not tell him that it was impossible, but rather showed that what he had asked, he had no strength to stand it as the mountain could not stand for His manifestation. He statement "You will not see Me" indicates negation of seeing in future not forever.

2. The second proof:

Allah, the Exalted said, **"Be mindful of Allah, and remember that you will meet Him."** *(2: 223)*

"Their greeting on the Day they meet Him will be 'peace'. *(33: 44)*

"Anyone who hopes meeting his Lord should do good deeds". *(18: 110)*

"Those who knew that they were going to meet their Lord said: "how often a small force has defeated a large army with Allah's permission." *(2: 249)*

The scholars of the language have unanimously agreed that when meeting is attributed to a living being and free from blindness and other barriers indicates seeing and looking. This is not to be contested by the words of Allah Almighty: **"He made hypocrisy settle in their hearts until the day they meet Him."** *(9: 77)*

The authentic traditions stated clearly that the hypocrites will see Allah, the Exalted, in the plain of the Resurrection; even the unbelievers will see Him. The reports in this regard will be cited soon, if Allah wills.

On this issue there are three opinions for the followers of the Sunnah:
First, that only the believers will see Allah Almighty.
Second, that all those who are gathered in the station, whether believer or unbeliever will see Him, then He will disappear from their sight and they will not see Him again.
Third, hypocrites will see Him, but not the unbelievers.

The followers of Imam Ahmad hold all three opinions. The same opinions are expressed concerning His speaking to them. Our Shaykh (i.e. Ibn Taymiyyah) has a book in which he cited the three statements and their arguments.

The statement of Allah, the Exalted :
"O mankind, you are labouring towards your Lord with exertion and will meet Him." *(84: 6)*

If the pronoun refers to the deed then it means that he will see it written in the book; and if it refers to the Lord Almighty, then it means meeting Him, which He has promised.

3. The third proof
Allah, the Exalted, said, **"Allah invites to the Home of Peace, and guides whoever He will to a straight path. Those who did well will have the best reward and more besides. Neither darkness nor shame will cover their faces; these are the companions of Paradise, and there they will abide forever."** *(10: 25-26)*

'The best reward' is Paradise and 'more' is looking at the Face of the Honourable Lord. This is how the Messenger of Allah, blessing and peace be upon him, on whom the Qur'an was revealed, has explained, and His Companions after him also said the same.

Suhayb reported that the Messenger of Allah, blessing and peace be upon him, read, "Those who did well will have the best reward and more" and said, "When the people of Paradise will enter it and the people of the Fire will go to it, a caller will call, 'People of Paradise, You have a promise with Allah and He wants to fulfil it.' They will say, 'What is that? Didn't He make our scale heavy, whiten our faces, and admit us in Paradise and save us from the Fire?' Then the veil will be removed and they will look at Him. There was nothing more beloved to them than seeing Him. This is what 'more' is."[357]

Anas said, "The messenger of Allah, blessing and peace of be upon him, was asked about the verse, 'For those who did well is best reward and more.' He said that those who did good deeds in the world will be given best reward that is Paradise, and more which is looking at the Face of Allah."

Ka'b ibn 'Ujrah reported that the Prophet ﷺ, said, "More is looking at the Face of the Merciful, glory be to Him."

Ubayy ibn Ka'b said, "I asked the Messenger of Allah, peace be upon him, about 'more' in the Book of Allah and he said, 'The best reward is Paradise and more to look at the Face of Allah, the Glorious.'"[358]

Abu Musa narrated that he heard the Messenger of Allah, peace be upon him, saying, "Allah will send on the Day of Judgment a caller who will call, 'People of Paradise' - his voice will be heard from the first and the last person - 'Allah promised you the best reward and more.' The best reward is Paradise and more is looking at the Face of the Merciful."[359]

Many Companions also interpreted the above verse in the same way. Abu Bakr al-Siddiq said that 'the more' is looking at the noble Face of Allah Almighty. Hudhayfah also said this. [360]

Abu Tamimah narrated, "I heard Abu Musa al-Ash'ari delivering a sermon in the Mosque of Basra. He said, 'Allah, the Exalted, will send an angel who will say, 'People of Paradise, did Allah fulfil what He promised you?' They will look at the

357. Muslim
358. Darqutni in al-Ru'yah (183)
359. Ibid (44)
360. Ibid (201)

jewellery, robes, streams and pure wives and say, 'Yes, Allah Almighty has fulfilled His promise to us.'

The angel will repeat his question three times and the people of Paradise will look around and do not find anything missing, and answer, 'Yes.'
The angel will say, 'There is something remaining. Allah has said, 'For those who did good deeds is the best reward and more.' The best reward is Paradise and more is looking at the Face of Allah, the Exalted.'"

Ibn Abbas and Ibn Mas'ud also said, "The best reward is Paradise and more is looking at the Face of Allah Almighty."

Among the later generation are Abd al-Rahman ibn Abi Layla, 'Amir ibn Sa'd, Isma'il ibn Abd al-Rahman, as-Suddi, al-Dahhak ibn Muzahim, Abd al-Rahman ibn Sabit, Abu Ishaq al-Sabi'i, Qatadah, Sa'id ibn al-Musayyib, al-Hasan al-Basri, 'Ikrimah and Mujahid - all of them said, "The best reward is Paradise and more is looking at the Face of Allah, the Glorious."

Many early scholars said about the verse, "No darkness or humiliation will cover their faces", that it is after they have seen Allah.

All the reports in this regard are authentic. Besides, Allah Almighty linked al-husna (the best reward), which is Paradise with ziyadah (more) by the letter of conjugation, which requires that more should be something beyond Paradise. Those who interpreted more with forgiveness and pleasure, it is among the accessories of the looking at the Lord, the Exalted.

4. The Fourth proof
Allah, the Exalted, said, **"No! On that Day they will be screened off from their Lord."** *(83: 15)*

The point of argument here is that Allah Almighty made the gravest punishment of the unbelievers their being screened off from seeing Him and listening to His words. If the believers are also kept away from seeing Him and listening to His speech, they are also screened off. Imam al-Shafi'i and other Imams forwarded this argument. Al-Muzani said, "I heard al-Shafi'i saying about the following statement of Allah Almighty, 'No! On that Day they will be screened off from their Lord,' that it is proof that the devotees of Allah will see Him on the Day of Judgement.'"

Al-Rabi' ibn Sulayman said, "I was with Muhammad ibn Idris al-Shafi'i when a slip came to him from Sa'id (upper Egypt) which asked, 'What do you say about the saying of Allah, the Blessed, 'No! They will be screened off from their Lord on that Day?'"

Al-Shafi'i replied, 'Since they (i.e. the unbelievers) were kept away from their Lord because of His anger, it is clear that His devoted friends will see Him in His pleasure.'

I asked, 'Abu Abdullah, do you hold this view?'

He replied, 'Yes, and I believe in it. If Muhammad ibn Idris was not sure that he is going to see Allah, he would not worship Him, glory be to Him.'"

A similar statement is reported from Muhammad ibn Abdullah ibn al-Hakam.

5. The fifth Proof
Allah, the Supreme, said, **"They will have all that they wish in it, and We have more for them."** (50: 35)

Ali ibn Abi Talib and Anas ibn Malik said, "'More' is looking at the Face of Allah, the Glorious."

Zayd ibn Wahab and others said the same from among the Followers.

6. The Sixth Proof
Allah, the Mighty and Honourable, said, **"No vision can perceive Him, but He perceives all vision."** (6: 103)

To argue on the basis of this verse is amazing because it is one of the proofs of those who deny seeing Allah. Our Shaykh (i.e. Ibn Taymiyyah) explained the argument in the best and most convincing way. He said to me, "I believe that no one who rejects seeing Allah argues on the basis of a verse or authentic Tradition to his claim, but it contains proof against his claim. One of them is this verse, which is an evidence for the possibility of Him being seen rather than impossibility. Allah, the Glorious, cited it in the context of praise. It is known that praise is by the positive qualities. The mere nonexistence is not perfection and a matter of praise. The Lord Almighty is praised with Non-existence when it implies the perfection of life, rejection of tiredness and fatigue, which indicate the perfect power. In the same way the denial of associates, wife and child, and the rejection of supporter contain His perfect Lordship, worthy of being worshipped and His power. Similarly, the rejection of eating and drinking shows His Everlasting and Self-sufficiency. It is the same in the following negations: Negation of intercession with Him without His permission is a proof of His perfect Oneness and self-sufficiency, negation of injustice shows His perfect justice and knowledge, negation of forgetting or anything being beyond His knowledge indicates His perfect knowledge and encompassing. The denial of like of Him indicates Him being perfect in essence and attributes. For this reason He was not praised with mere negation which does not include a positive side. A non-existent joins the object in that nonexistence, and a perfect object cannot be described with a matter shared with a non-existent."

Now if the meaning of "vision can perceive Him" is that He cannot be seen at all, it is not praise, and there is no perfection in it as the non-existent share this matter with Him. The total non-existent is not seen; eyes cannot perceive it. The Lord, the Great, is above being praised with what is common with the mere non-existent. The meaning then is that He will be seen, but not understood and grasped thoroughly. It is like the verse **"Not even the weight of speck of dust in the earth or sky escapes your Lord."** (10:61)

It means that He knows everything. His statement, "There touched Us no weariness." (50:38) means that He has perfect power. His saying, "Your Lord does not do injustice to anyone" (18:49) means that He is perfect in justice. His saying,"Neither slumber nor sleep overtakes Him." (2:255) means that He is perfect in His watchfulness.

So, His saying: "vision cannot perceive Him," means that He is great beyond imagination, and as such He cannot be grasped thoroughly. Comprehending completely is to know something thoroughly from every side, which is beyond seeing. It is as Allah, the Exalted, said, "When the two sides came within the sight of one another, the companions of Moses said, 'Indeed, we are to be overtaken.'" *(26 61)*

Moses did not deny seeing, and his followers did not mean by saying 'We are to be overtaken' that they were seen. Moses, may Allah's peace be upon him, rejected the idea of being overtaken by saying, 'Never'. Allah, the Glorious, told Moses that he should not fear being caught. He said, "We revealed to Moses, 'Go out at night with My servants and strike a dry path for them across the sea. Have no fear of being overtaken and do not be dismayed.'" *(20: 77)*

Seeing and comprehending are found together and separately. The Lord Almighty will be seen but not comprehended as He is known but not comprehended fully. This is what the Companions and leading scholars understood from the verse.

Ibn Abbas said, "The meaning of 'visions cannot perceive Him' is that visions cannot comprehend Him."

Qatadah said, "He is greater than being comprehended by visions."

'Atiyyah said, "They will look at Allah but their visions will not be able to comprehend Him because of His greatness, while he encompasses them. This is what His statement, 'Vision cannot perceive Him, but He perceives the visions,' means. The believers will see their Lord, the Blessed and Exalted, by their eyes openly but their visions will not comprehend Him in the sense that they will not be able to encompass Him. He encompasses everything. In the same way He makes whoever He wishes to hear His words but they cannot comprehend His speech; He knows what His creatures know, but they cannot grasp His knowledge."

Similar to this is the argument of those who deny Divine Attributes by the saying of Allah, "There is nothing like Him". *(42: 11)*

It is as a matter of fact the strongest proof of the multitude of His perfect Attributes and manifestation of His supremacy. It indicates that because of the multiplicity and greatness of His Attributes there is no match to Him in them. If the negation of the Attributes were meant, the total nonexistence would have been more deserving of this praise than Him. It is well known that all the people of reason understand when someone says: So and so has no match or similar or equal, that the person in question is distinguished from all other people by those qualities and characters and no one shares them with him. As the qualities and distinguishing features increase, he tops his colleagues and goes higher than his matches.

Now His statement that there is nothing like Him is the clearest evidence that He has many attributes and qualities. His saying that visions cannot perceive Him indicates that He can be seen but not comprehended thoroughly.

He says, **"It is He who has created the heavens and earth in six Days and then established Himself on the Throne. He knows what enters the earth and what comes out of it; what descends from the sky and what ascends to it. He is with you wherever you are; He sees all that you do."** (57: 4)

It is the profound evidence that the Lord is separate from His creation; He did not create them in His essence but created them out of His essence; then parted from them by establishing Himself on His Throne. He knows what they are doing and His vision encompasses them, and He embraces them by His knowledge, power, will, looking and hearing. This is the meaning of Him, glory be to Him, being with them wherever they are.

Consider the beauty of comparison in word and meaning in His saying, "No vision can perceive Him, but He perceives all visions."

He, the Exalted, because of His sublimity is above being perceived and comprehended by visions, but by His kindness and knowledge perceives visions. They are not hidden from Him; He is superb in His delicate grace, Benevolent in His sublimity, High in His nearness and near in His highness. There is nothing similar to Him, and He is the Hearing and Seeing. Visions cannot perceive Him but He perceives all the visions and He is the All Subtle, the All Aware.

7. The Seventh Proof
Allah, the Exalted, says, **"Some faces that day will be radiant, looking at their**

Lord." *(75: 22-23)*

If you keep this verse away from distorting its meaning and telling lie about the One who spoke it in order to distract it from what He intended, you will see that it is saying unequivocally that Allah, the Glorious, will be seen openly by eyes on the Day of Judgment. However, if you are bent on distorting its meaning, which is called by the miscreants 'interpretation', then the interpretation of the texts dealing with the resurrection, Paradise, Hell and accounting is easier for them than this particular verse. No evil person on earth who wishes to distort the texts from their proper meaning but he will find a way to it. This is what has corrupted the world and the religion.

In the above verse connecting the sight of the Face and joining it with the preposition 'ila' is a clear indication that seeing by eye is meant. There is no indication showing that seeing here is to be taken against its real meaning. It is obvious that Allah, the Exalted, meant seeing of the eye to the Face of the Lord Almighty.

The word 'nazr' (seeing) has been used in the Qur'an in different meanings according to its links or when it is used independently. When it is used independently it gives the meaning of halting and waiting. The example is Allah's saying that the hypocrites will say to the believers on the Day of Judgment, **"Wait for us; let us have some of your light."** *(57: 13)*

When it is used in connection with preposition 'fi', it means to contemplate and ponder. Allah said,
"Have they not contemplated the realm of the heavens and earth?" *(7: 185)*

When it used in connection with 'ila', it gives the meaning of seeing by eyes. Allah said, **"Look at its fruit when it yields."** *(6: 99)*

Its meaning will be clearer when it is connected with the face which is the object of seeing by the eye.

Al-Hasn said, "The eyes of the believers will look at their Lord; they will see by His light."

Listen now O follower of the Sunnah to the interpretation of this verse by the Prophet ﷺ his Companions, their followers and the leading scholars of Islam.

Abdullah ibn 'Amr reported that the Messenger of Allah, blessing and peace be upon him, said, "Some faces will be radiant, with splendour and beauty, looking at their Lord, they will look at the Face of their Lord, the Glorious."

This is how Ibn Abbas and 'Ikrimah also commented. It is the interpretation of every commentator from the followers of the Sunnah and Hadith.

The reports from the Prophet, peace be upon him, and the Companions indicating the seeing of Allah are in succession. They are reported by Abu Bakr al-Siddiq, Abu Hurayrah, Abu Sa'id al-Khudri, Jarir ibn Abdullah al-Bajali, Suhayb ibn Sinan al-Rumi, Abdullah ibn Mas'ud, 'Ali ibn Abi Talib, Abu Musa al-Ash'ari, 'Adi ibn Abi Hatim al Ta'i, Anas ibn Malik, Buraydah ibn al-Husayb al-Aslami, Abu Razin al-'Uqayli, Jabir ibn Abdullah al-Ansari, Abu Umamah al-Bahili, Zayd ibn Thabit, 'Ammar ibn Yasir, 'A'ishah, Abdullah ibn 'Umar, 'Umarah ibn Ruwaybah, Salman al-Farsi, Hudhayfah ibn al-Yaman, Abdullah ibn Abbas, Abdullah ibn 'Amr ibn al-'As, Ubayy ibn Ka'b, Ka'b ibn 'Ujrah, Fudalah ibn 'Ubayd, and an unnamed person from the Companions of the Prophet, peace be upon him.

We are going to cite their reports from authentic, Musnad and Sunan collections of the Hadith. They have been received with agreement, and open hearts not with distortion, changing, and parochialism. You should not reject them because the one who rejects them will not be among the people who will look at the Face of the Lord, and will be screened off on the Day of Judgement.

The reports of the Companions from the Messenger

1. Abu Bakr al-Siddiq's report:
One day the Messenger of Allah, peace be upon him, performed the Morning Prayer, then sat until the forenoon and he smiled. He sat in his place and performed the noon, afternoon and sunset prayers without saying anything. He performed the night prayer and then went to his family room. The people said to Abu Bakr, "Why do you not ask the Messenger of Allah, blessing and peace be upon him, what is the matter with him? He did something which he never did before."

Abu Bakr asked, and the Messenger said, "Yes, to me was presented what is going to happen from the affairs of the world and the Hereafter. All the people from the beginning to the end were gathered in one ground, and they were worried and walked to Adam while sweat was pouring on them. They said, 'Adam, you are the father of mankind. Allah has chosen you, so intercede for us to your Lord.'

He replied, 'I suffer from what you suffer. Go to your father after your first father, Noah because 'Allah chose Adam and Noah and the family of Abraham and the family of Imran over the world.' (3; 33)

They will go to Noah and say to him, 'Make intercession for us to your Lord; Allah chose you and granted your prayer and did not leave a single disbeliever on earth.'

He will answer. 'I am not the person to do it. Go to Abraham because Allah selected him as a friend.'

They will go to Abraham and will speak to him. He will say, 'I am not able to do it, go to Moses. Allah spoke to him.'

Moses will say to them, 'I am unable to do it. Go to Jesus, son of Mary. He healed the blind person and the leper and brought the dead back to life.'

Jesus will say to them, 'I am not the person to do it. Go to the master of the children of Adam. Go to Muhammad ﷺ and he can intercede for you to your Lord, the Glorious.'

The Prophet will walk and Gabriel will ask the Lord, the Blessed and High, for permission. Allah will say, 'Grant him permission and give him good tiding of Paradise.'

Gabriel will take him and he (the Prophet) will fall down in prostration about the period of a week. Then Allah, the Exalted, will say, 'Raise your head and speak, you will be heard and make intercession, your intercession will be granted.'

He will raise his head, but when he looks at the Face of his lord, he will fall down again in prostration for the period of another week. Allah, the Exalted, will say to him, 'Raise your head and speak, you will be heard, and intercede, your intercession will be accepted.'

He will move to fall down in prostration again but Gabriel will hold him by his armpits. Allah will open to him the supplication, which He did not open to any human being before.

He will say, 'My Lord! You created me the master of the children of Adam. I say it without boasting. You made me the first person to come out of the earth, and there is no boasting for it.'

Then the people will come to the Pool more than to fill the distance between Sana'a and Allah. It will be announced, 'Call the true devoted ones.' They will come and make intercession. Then the prophets will be called. One of them will come having with him a group; another will come having five and six people and another with no follower with him. Then martyrs will be called and they will intercede for whom they wish. When the martyrs complete, Allah, the Glorious, will say, 'I am the Most Merciful of all, admit My Paradise anyone who had not associated anything with Me'. They will be admitted.

Then Allah Almighty will say, 'Look in the Fire, do you see anyone who had done some good deed at all.'

They will find a man in the Fire and ask him, 'Did you do any good deed at all?'

He will reply, 'No, except that I used to deal with the people in transactions with leniency.'

Allah, the Blessed, will say, 'Show leniency to My servant for being lenient to My servants.'

Then they will bring out a man from the Fire and ask him, 'Did you do any good deed?' He will reply, 'No, except that I asked my children when I die burn me in fire then grind me until I become like antimony powder, then take Me to the sea and spread me in the air. By Allah, in this way the Lord of the universe will not be able to find me.'

Allah will ask him, 'Why did you do this?'
He will answer, 'Because of the fear of You.'

Allah will say to him, 'Look at the greatest kingdom and you will have like it and ten times like it.'

He will say, 'Are you laughing at me and You are the King?'"

The Prophet ﷺ then said, "This was the occasion I laughed in the morning."[361]

2. The reports of Abu Hurayrah and Abu Sa'id are cited below:
Abu Hurayrah said, "Some people asked the Messenger of Allah, 'Are we going to see our Lord on the Day of Resurrection?'

The Messenger ﷺ replied, 'Do you have any doubt in seeing the moon on the full-moon night?'

They said, 'No, Messenger of Allah.'

He asked further, 'Do you have doubt in seeing the sun which is not behind the cloud?'

They said, 'No.'

He said, 'You will see Him in the same way. Allah will gather the people on the Day of Judgment and say: 'Anyone who worshipped something should follow it. The one who worshipped the sun should follow the sun, the one who worshipped the moon should follow it, and the one who worshipped the idols should follow them. After that this community will remain with the hypocrites among them. Allah will appear in a form other than they know and He will say: 'I am your Lord.' They will say, 'We seek refuge with Allah from you; we stay here till our Lord comes. When He appears we will recognize Him.' Then Allah will come in the form they know and say, 'I am your Lord.'

---

361. Ahmad (15), Abu Ya'la (56), al-Bazzar (3465). It is a weak report. See Majma' al-zawa'id (18507) Parts of it have been recorded in the authentic collections of Bukhari and Muslim

They will say, 'You are our Lord, and they will follow Him; and the bridge will be set. The slogan of the messengers on that Day will be, 'O Allah, save, save.' In Hell there will be hooks like the thorns of Sa'dan. Have you seen Sa'dan?'

They replied, 'Yes, O Messenger of Allah.'

He said, 'They will be like the thorns of Sa'dan except that only Allah Almighty knows their largeness. They will snatch the people according to their deeds - some of them will be destroyed because of their deeds and others will be recompensed till he is saved. When Allah completes the judgement between the servants, and wishes to get whom He wants out of Hell by His mercy, He will ask the angels to bring out from Hell anyone who did not associate anything with Allah and confessed that there is no being worthy of worship but Allah. They will recognize them by the mark of the prostration. The Fire will burn children of Adam except the mark of the prostration. Allah has forbidden for Hell to consume the mark of prostration. They will be brought out from the Fire while they have been charred, the water of life will be poured upon them and they will grow as the seed comes out in the torrent of the flood.

Then Allah will finish judgement among the people only a man will remain facing the Fire. He will be the last one to enter Paradise. He will say: 'My Lord, turn my face away from the Fire; its smell has hurt me and its flame has scorched me. He will call upon Him as long as He wishes, then Allah, the Exalted, will say to him: 'But could it be that when I do it, you would not ask something else?' He will say, 'I will not ask for anything beside that.' He will give his pledge and promise as Allah wishes. Allah will turn his face from the Fire. When he faces Paradise and sees it, he keeps quiet as long as he wishes, then he will say, 'Bring me closer to Paradise.' Allah will say, 'Didn't you give your pledge and vows that you will not ask more than I have given you? Woe to you, son of Adam! How deceitful you are!' He will continue calling Allah. Then He will say, 'Would it not be that if I give it to you, you will ask something else beside it?'

He will say, No, by Your majesty.' He will give his Lord his pledges and vows. Allah will bring him near to the gate of Paradise. When he stands at the gate of Paradise and sees the pleasure and joys of it, he keeps silent for a while as Allah wills, then will say, 'My Lord, admit me into Paradise.' Allah will say, 'Didn't you give your pledges and vows that you will not ask Me anything else? Woe to you, son of

Adam, how faithless you are!'

He will say, 'My Lord, I do not want to be the most unfortunate of Your creature.'
He will continue begging Allah till Allah will laugh. When Allah laughs, He allows
him to enter Paradise. When He enters, Allah tells him to put his desires. He puts
his wishes and asks his Lord. Allah reminds him and tells him to wish this and that
until his wishes expire. Allah will say, You have all that you wished and similar to
that."

Abu Sa'id added that he Prophet said that Allah will say, "And ten times more of
them."

'Ata' ibn Yazid said, "When Abu Hurayrah was reporting the above Hadith Abu Sa'id
was there and did not refuse anything till when Abu Hurayrah said that Allah, the
Glorious, would say to the man, 'you will get that and similar to that.' Abu Sa'id
said, 'And ten time more, Abu Hurayrah.' Abu Hurayrah said, 'I remembered from
the Messenger of Allah, blessing and peace be upon him, 'You will have that and
similar to that.'

Abu Sa'id said, 'I bear witness that I remember Allah's Messenger saying, 'You will
have that and ten times more of it.'

Abu Hurayrah said, 'That man will be the last man to enter Paradise.'"[362]

3. Abu Sa'id reported:
"Some people in the time of the Messenger of Allah, blessing and peace be upon
him, said, 'Messenger of Allah, will we see our Lord on the Day of Resurrection?'

The Messenger replied, 'Do you doubt in seeing the sun at noon when there is
no cloud? Do you doubt in seeing the moon on the full-moon night when there
is no cloud?'

They said, 'No, Messenger of Allah.'

The Prophet ﷺ said, "You will not have any doubt in seeing Allah, the Glorious,

---

362. Bukhari (106, 6573, 7437), Muslim (iman (112)

on the Day of Resurrection as you have no doubt in seeing any of these two. When the Day of Judgement comes a Caller will call, 'Every community should follow what it used to worship. No one from those who worshipped objects like idols and stone images other than Allah will remain but will fall in Hellfire. When there will remain those who worshipped Allah of the righteous or wicked or the members of the Jews, the Jews will be called and asked, 'What were you worshipping?'

They will reply, We worshipped 'Uzayr son of Allah.'

It will be said to them, 'You are liars. Allah has no partner or son. What do you want?' They will say, 'Our Lord, we feel thirsty, so give us drink.'

They will be told, 'Why do you not go to the water sources?'

They will be pushed to the Fire as though it is mirage, smashing one another, and will fall in the Fire. When only those who worshipped Allah, whether righteous or evil remain, Allah, the Lord of the universe, will come to them in an inferior form than they had seen Him. He will ask, 'What are you waiting for? Every community has followed what it worshipped.'

They will say, 'Our Lord we departed from the world when we were in greater need of them, but we did not accompany them.'

He will say, 'I am your Lord'

They will say, 'We seek refuge with Allah from you; we do not associate anything with Allah. They say it two or three times. Then some of them will be on the verge of failing the test. He will say, 'Is there any sign between Him and you by which you will recognize Him?' They will say, 'Yes.' Then the Shin will be laid bare and there will be no one who prostrated to Allah of his own accord but Allah will grant him permission to prostrate, and there will be no one who prostrated out of fear of the people and to show off, but Allah will make his back unyielding, and every time he tries to prostrate, he will fall on his back. Then they will raise their heads and He will have changed into the appearance they knew before. He will say, 'I am your Lord.'

Then the bridge will be set up over Hell, and intercession will be permitted. They will say, 'O Allah, grant safety, grant safety.'

They asked, 'Messenger of Allah, what is the bridge?'

He replied, 'A slippery place, on which there are hooks and spikes and thorns. There are thorns like that called Sa'dan. The believers will cross the bridge like the blink of an eye, like lightening, like the wind, like birds and like the swiftest horses and camels. Some will cross safe and sound, some will be scratched then let go, and some will be piled up in the Fire of Hell, until the believers have been saved from the Fire. By the One in Whose Hand is my soul, none of you is more eager to claim a right than the believers will be on the Day of Resurrection when they seek help for their brethren who are in the Fire. They will say, 'Our Lord, they used to observe fasting, prayer and perform pilgrimage.'

It will be said to them, 'Bring out whomever you recognize' -for their faces will be forbidden to the Fire to burn - and they will bring out many people whom the Fire had consumed halfway up their shanks or up to their knees. Then they will say, 'Our Lord, there is no one left of those whom You commanded us to bring out.'

He will say, 'Go back and whoever you find with a Dinar weight of goodness in his heart, bring him out.'

They will bring many people out, then they will say, 'Our Lord, we have not left therein any of those whom You commanded us to bring out.'

Then He will say, 'Go back, and whomever you find with half a Dinar's weight of goodness in his heart, bring him out.' They will bring out many people, then they will say, 'Our Lord we have not left therein any of those whom You commanded us to bring out.'

He will say, 'Go back and whomever you find with a speck of goodness in his heart, bring him out.' They will bring out many people, and then they will say, 'Our Lord, we have not left any goodness there in.'"

Abu Sa'id al-Khudri said, "If you do not believe me in this Hadith then recite if you wish, 'Surely Allah wrongs not even of the weight of an atom, and if there is any good done, He doubles it, and gives from Him a great reward.'" (4, 40)

The Prophet ﷺ said, "Allah will say, 'The angels have interceded and the believers have interceded, the Prophets have interceded and there is no one left to intercede except the Most Merciful of those who show mercy.'

Then He will take a handful from Hell, and will bring out people who never did any good and who will have turned into charcoal. He will throw them into a river on the outskirt of Paradise that is called the River of Life, and they will emerge like seeds from that which is carried by a flood. Do you not see when they are near a stone or a tree, that which in the sun grows yellow and green and that which is in the shade turns white?"

They said, "O Messenger of Allah, it is as you used to tend flocks in the desert."

He said, "They will emerge like pearls with jewels around their necks, and the people of Paradise will recognize them. These are the ones ransomed by Allah, whom Allah admitted to Paradise with no good deed that they did or sent on ahead. Then He will say, 'Enter Paradise and whatever you see is yours.' They will say, 'Our Lord, You have given us what You have never given to anyone else in all the world.'

He will say, 'You will have something better than that with Me.' They will say 'Our Lord, what could be better than this?'

He will say, 'My good pleasure, for I will never be angry with you again.'"[363]

4. The report of Jarir ibn Abdullah is as follows:

"While we were sitting with the Prophet ﷺ he looked at the moon on the fourteenth night and said, 'You will see your Lord openly as you see it without being in doubt in its seeing. So, if you are able not to miss prayer before the sunrise and sunset, do it.' Then he recited, 'Exalt your Lord with praise before the rising of the sun and before its setting.'" (50, 39)[364]

363. Bukhari (7439), Muslim (iman (183)
364. Bukhari (7434), Muslim (masajid (633)

This Hadith is reported by Isma'il ibn Abi Khalid from Qays ibn Hazim who got it from Jarir. From Isma'il more than a hundred people have reported. (The author gave the full list of those who reported it from Isma'il.)

Isma'il was followed by five other reporters in reporting it from Qays ibn Abi Hazim. All these people bear witness that Jarir narrated this and Jarir bore witness that the Messenger of Allah, peace be upon him, said it as though you hear the Messenger as he is speaking and passing the information to his community. There was nothing more joyful to them than this statement. But the Jahmiyyah, Pharaohic people, Qaramitah, Batiniyyah and the kids of Sabi'ah and Magians and Greek declare those who believe in it as disbeliever and consider them among the people of anthropomorphism and embodiment. They were followed by all the enemies of the Sunnah and its people, and Allah is the helper of His Book and His Messenger's Sunnah although the disbelievers dislike it.

5. The report of Suhayb came through Hammad ibn Salmah, from Tahbit from Abd al-Rahman ibn Abi Layala from Suhayb. It is as follows:
"The Messenger of Allah, blessing and peace be upon him, said, 'When the people of Paradise enter it, Allah, the Exalted, will say, 'Do you want anything more?'

They will say, 'Didn't You brighten our faces, admit us in Paradise and save us from the Fire?'

Then the veil will be lifted and they will not have been given anything more beloved than looking at their Lord. Then the Prophet read, **'Those who have done good deeds will have good and more.'** (10, 26)" [365]

This report is narrated by many scholars from Hammad and accepted as true and authentic.

6. The report of Abdullah ibn Mas'ud:
He related that the Messenger of Allah, peace be upon him, said, "Allah will gather the earliest and the latest generations on a fixed day, they will be standing for forty years, their eyes staring at the sky waiting for the judgement. Allah will descend

---

365. Muslim

in the shadow of the clouds from the Thorne to the Chair and a caller will call, 'People, were you not pleased with your Lord Who created you, provided you and ordered you to worship Him and not associate any partner with Him, that He assigned every community to the one who they worshipped in the world? Is it not a fair deal from your Lord?'

They will say, 'Yes.'

Then every community will go to what they were befriending and worshipping in the world. The objects of their worship will be presented to them. Some of them will go to the sun, some to the moon or idols of stones and similar things. For those who worshipped Jesus, the devil of Jesus will be presented to them, for those who worshipped Uzayr, the Satan of Uzayr will be presented to them. Only Muhammad and his followers will remain; the Lord, the Exalted, will come to them and ask, 'Why do you not move like other people?'

They will say, 'We have a God, we have not seen him yet.'

He will say, 'Will you recognize him if you see him?'

They will say, 'Yes, there is a sign between us and him, when we see it we will recognize him.'

He will ask what it was.

They will say, 'He will uncover His shin. At that point the Shin will be uncovered and they will fall in prostration and some people will remain their backs being hard like cows; they will want to prostrate but could not do it. They were called to prostrate when they were safe. He will tell them to raise their heads, and they will do so. He will grant them His light in accordance with their deeds. Some of them will be given their light like big mountains running in front them. Some will be given smaller than that. Some will be given like the palm tree, and others will be given smaller than it. The last person will be a man who will be given the size of the toe of his foot, which will illuminate some time and turn off sometime. When it illuminates he advances and walks, and when it is extinguishes, he stops. The Lord Almighty will be before them until they reach the Hellfire and on it will be bridge like the edge of the sword. Almighty will ask them to cross it; they will cross according to their light. Some will pass in the twinkling of eye, others like lightening, others like cloud, and others like swooping stars. Some will cross like wind, others like the gallop of the horse and some like running of a man. The person who was given the size of the toe of his feet will crawl on his face, his hands and legs. He will drag one hand and the other will stick; drag one leg and the other will stick, and the Fire will touch is sides. In this way he will be away from it; when he gets away from it, he will stand around it and say, 'Praise is to Allah Who gave me what He did not give to anyone as He rescued me from the Fire after I witnessed it.'

Then he will be taken to a pool at the gate of Paradise; he will be bathed in it. He will feel the fragrance of Paradise and see its colours. He will look through the gate and say, 'My Lord, admit me into Paradise.'

Allah, the Exalted, will say, 'Now are you asking for Paradise when I have rescued you from Hell?'

He will say, 'My Lord, make a curtain between me and it so that I do not hear its noise.'

He then will be admitted into Paradise. A place will be shown to him ahead of it which will make him feel as though he is dreaming and will desire to enter it. He will ask, 'My Lord, grant me that status.'

Allah will say, 'Perhaps if I grant you that rank, you will ask for another.'
He will say, 'By Your might I will not ask for anything else; and what rank could be better than it?'

He will be given that and will settle there. Then another site will be shown to him and he will say, 'My Lord, take me to that place.'

Allah will say, 'Perhaps if I give you that, you will ask for another.'
He will say, 'By Your might I will not ask for anything else and what will better than that?'

He will be given that. Then another station will be shown to him ahead of it, and he will feel that it is a dream concerning the one he is in. He will say, 'My Lord, take me to that station.'

Allah will say, 'Perhaps if I take you there, you will ask for something else.'
He will say, 'By Your might, I will not ask for anything beside it and what can be better than that?'

He will be granted that, and then he will be silent. Allah, the Exalted, will say, 'What happened to you? Why do you not ask for something more?'

He will say, 'I asked till I became ashamed of You, and I swore until I felt ashamed of You.'

Allah will say, 'Don't you like if I give you like the world since I created it till I destroyed it and ten times more of it?'
He will say, 'Do You mock me when You are the Owner of might?'

Allah will laugh at his statement."

Abdullah ibn Mas'ud laughed when he reached this place. He was asked why you laughed anytime you came to this point. He said, "I saw the Messenger of Allah, peace be upon him, he narrated this story many times and when he reached this point laughed till his molar teeth were seen."

The Prophet ﷺ went on, "The Lord, the Glorious and Blessed, will say, 'No, I have power to that, so ask.'
He will say, 'Put me together with other people.'

He will be told to join them. He will walk proudly in Paradise till when he comes close to the people, a palace of pearl will be raised to him and he will fall in prostration. He will be told to raise his head and be asked, 'What is wrong with you?'

He will say, 'I saw my Lord, or He appeared to me.'

He will be told that that it was one of your homes. He will meet there an angel and he will prepare to prostrate and he will be asked what happened to you?

He will say, 'I thought that you are an angel.'

He will say, 'I am one of the keepers of your belongings and one of your servants. Under me there are a thousand stewards responsible for similar duties, which I am responsible for. He will walk in front of him till they reach the palace which will be opened for him. It is in a hollow pearl its roofs, doors and locks and their keys are all of pearl. There he will see a green jewel studded with red ones; every jewel will lead to another one different in colour from the first one. In each of them will be couches and wives and maids the lowest of them will be a beautiful, large and dark-eyed lady with seventy robes, the marrow of her leg will be seen behind her robes. Her liver will be his mirror and his liver her mirror. When he turns away for a while, she looks seventy times more beautiful in his eyes than earlier. He will say, 'By Allah, you have become seventy times more beautiful in my eye.' She will say, 'By Allah, you have become seventy times more beautiful in my eye.'

He will be told look around. He will, and will be told, 'Your domain is the distance of a hundred years walk.'"

At this point 'Umar said, 'Ka'b, Look what Ibn Umm 'Ubayd is saying about the man of the lowest rank, what will be the person at the highest rank?'

Ka'b said, 'Commander of the faithful, in it there are things which no eye has ever seen and no ear has heard of. Allah, the Glorious, has made a house and put what He wanted of spouses, fruits and drinks then closed it and none of His creature saw it neither Gabriel nor any other angel. Then Ka'b recited, **"No soul knows what has been hidden for them of the comfort of their eye as reward of what they used to do."** (32, 17)

The Almighty created beside it two other Gardens and decorated it whatever He wanted and showed them to whomever He wished of His creature."

Ka'b went on, "Anyone whose book was in Illiyyin will be accommodated in that house. He will come out and walk in his domain and no pavilion of Paradise will remain but the light of his face will enter it and the people of it will rejoice from his fragrance and say, 'How wonderful is this fragrance! It is a man from the people of Illiyyin who has come out to walk in his domain."

'Umar said, "Well, Ka'b these hearts are relaxed so restrain them."

Ka'b said, "Hell has a moaning no close angel, or messenger listens to it but will fall down on his knees, even Ibrahim, the friend of Allah will say, 'My Lord, my soul, my soul! Even if you add the deeds of seventy prophets, you will still feel that you are not going to be saved.'"

It is a big and good report many scholars of the Sunnah have recorded it like Abdullah ibn Ahmad, al-Tabarani,[366] al-Darqutni[367] and Ibn Sa'id through various chains.

7. The report of Ali ibn Abi Talib is as follows:
He said that the Messenger of Allah, peace be upon him, said, "The people of Paradise will visit the Lord Almighty every Friday".

Then he mentioned what they are going to receive then he said, "Then Allah, the Exalted, will say, 'Remove a curtain'. Then a curtain will be removed and Allah, the Most Blessed will unveil His Face, and they will feel as though they had not seen any favour before that. This is what Allah says, 'We have more.'"(50, 35)

8. Abu Musa narrated that the Messenger of Allah, peace be upon him, said, "There are two Gardens of silver with their utensils and everything in them, and two Gardens of gold with their utensils and everything in them. There will be no barrier between the people and seeing their Lord, the Exalted, except the veil of majesty over His Face in the Garden of Eden."[368]

In another version Abu Musa said that the Messenger of Allah, peace be upon him, said, "Allah will gather the people on the Day of Resurrection on one ground. When He decides to judge among His creatures, He will bring the images of those which were worshipped by every community. They will follow them till they throw them in the Fire. Then Our Lord will come to us and we will be on a high place. He will ask, 'Who are you?'

We will answer, 'We are Muslims.'

366. See al-kabir (9763, 9764)
367. Al-Ru'yah (160-161)
368. Bukhari (4878), Muslim (iman: 180)

He will ask, 'What are you waiting for?'

We will say, 'We are waiting for our Lord, the Glorious.'

He will say, 'Will you be able to recognize if you see Him?'

We will say, 'Yes, He has no match for Him.'

Then Allah will reveal Himself to us smiling, and say, 'Be happy, the assembly of the Muslims. There was no one of you but I placed a Jew or Christian in his place in the Fire.'" [369]

In another version Abu Musa related the Prophet ﷺ saying, "Allah will send a caller on the Day of Judgement who will call in a voice which every- one from the first to the last will hear, 'Allah, the Most High, had promised you the best reward and more; the best reward is Paradise, and more is to see the Face of Allah Almighty." [370]

9. As for the report of 'Adi ibn Hatim it is recorded by Bukhari. It goes as follows: 'While we were with the Prophet ﷺ a man came to him and complained about poverty. Then another person came and complained about robbery. The Prophet, peace be upon him, said, 'Adi have you seen Hirah?'

I said, 'I have not seen it but I am informed about it.'

The Prophet ﷺ said, 'If you should live long, you will certainly see a woman in a sedan chair travel from Hirah till she goes round the Ka'bah, and will have no fear of anyone except Allah.'

I said in my mind, *where will be the bands of Tayy who had spread evil throughout the countryside?*

The Prophet ﷺ went on, 'If you should live long, you will conquer the treasures of Khosrau son of Hurmuz.'

---

369. Ahmad (19674)
370. Darqutni in al-Ru'yah

I asked, 'You mean Khosrau son of Hurmuz?'

He replied, 'Yes, Khosrau son of Hurmuz. If you should live longer, you will see a man coming out with handful of gold or silver searching for someone to take it, but he will not find anyone. Each of you will surely meet Allah on the Day he meets Him without there being a cover between Him and him or any interpreter. He will ask, 'Didn't I send a messenger to you to convey the message?' He will say, 'Yes, my Lord'

He will further ask, 'Didn't I give you wealth and showed My favour to you?' He will say, 'Yes.'

Then he will look to his right and see nothing but Hellfire, and look at his left, and there also he will see Fire.'
Adi sai, "I heard the Prophet ﷺ, saying, 'Protect yourself from the Fire even by a piece of a date, if someone does not get a piece of date, then by a sweet word.'"

Adi later said, "I have seen the woman travelling from Hirah and going round the Ka'bah fearing none but Allah, and I was among those who conquered the treasures of Kisra ibn Hurmuz. If your life is long you will see what else the Prophet has said."[371]

10. The report of Anas is as follows:

"Allah's Messenger ﷺ said, 'Allah will gather the people on the Day of Judgement, and they will be worried about that. They will say, 'Why don't we seek intercession with our Lord, the Mighty and the Sublime, so that we might be relived of our predicament?'

They will go to Adam and say to him, 'You are Adam, the father of mankind. Allah created you with His own Hand and breathed into you a spirit from Him, and He commanded the angels to prostrate to you. Intercede for us with our Lord so that we might be relieved of the predicament we are in.'

He will say, 'I am not capable of that.'

------
371. Bukhari (3595)

He will mention the mistake that he made, and he will feel shy before his Lord because of it. He will tell them to go to Noah, the first messenger whom Allah, the Most High sent. They will go to him and he will say, 'I am not capable of that.' He will mention the mistake that he made, and feel shy before his Lord because of it.

'But go to Abraham, whom Allah as a close friend', he will say.

They will go to Abraham and he will say, 'I am not capable of that.' He will mention the mistake that he made and will feel shy before his Lord because of that. He will ask them to go to Moses to whom Allah spoke and gave the Torah. They will go to Moses, and he will say, 'I am not capable of that. He will mention the mistake that he made and feel shy before his Lord for that. 'Go to Jesus, the spirit from Allah and His word', he will say. They will go to Jesus and he will say, 'I am not capable of that, but go to Muhammad, a slave whose past and future sins were forgiven.'"

The Messenger ﷺ, continued, "They will come to me, and I will ask for permission to speak to my Lord, the Most High, and permission will be given to me. When I see Him, I will fall down in prostration and He will leave me in that state for as long as He wills. Then it will be said, 'Muhammad, raise your head, and speak, you will be heard; ask, you will be given; intercede, your intercession will be accepted.' I will raise my head and praise my Lord, the Most High, with words of praise that my Lord, the Mighty and Sublime, will teach me. Then I will intercede, and a limit will be set for me. I will bring them out of the Fire and admit them into Paradise. Then I will go back and fall prostrate, and He will leave me as long as He wills. Then it will be said, "Muhammad, raise your head, and speak, you will be heard; ask, you will be given; intercede, your intercession will be accepted.' I will raise my head and praise my Lord with words of praise that my Lord will teach me. Then I will intercede, and a limit will be set for me. I will bring them out of Hell and admit them into Paradise."

Anas said, "I do not know whether it was the third or fourth time that the Prophet said, 'Then I will say, 'My Lord, there is no one left in the Fire but those who have been detained by the Qur'an.' That is those are bound to abide in it forever." [372]

Ibn Khuzaymah reported similar narration from Anas as follows, "The people will face detention as long as Allah wills then they will say, 'Let's go to Adam who will

---

372. Bukhari (4476), Muslim (iman: 193)

intercede for us to our Lord.'"

He cited the Hadith till he said, "They will go to Muhammad. I will say, I am for it. I will go and ask the door of Paradise to be opened; it will be opened and I will enter and see my Lord on His Throne. I will fall in prostration."

In some version it is as follows, "I will walk to my Lord Who is on His Chair and I will fall in prostration."

In another, "I will ask the door to be opened and when I look at the Most Merciful, I will fall in prostration."

Ibn Khuzaymah reported in a long narration.

The seeing of the Prophet ﷺ of his Lord in this place is certainly proved beyond any doubt. The scholars of the Hadith and the Sunnah confirm it.
Abu Hurayrah has reported the Prophet, peace be upon him, saying, "I will be the first person to come out from the earth on the Day of Resurrection; I am saying it without basting. I am the chief of the children of Adam, without boasting. I am the carrier of the banner of the praise, without boasting. I will be the first to enter Paradise, without boasting. I will hold the chain of the gate of Paradise, and permission will be granted to me. The Face of Almighty, Powerful and Honourable, will be in front of me and I will fall in prostration to Him."

Anas ibn Malik reported, "I heard the Messenger of Allah, peace be upon him, say, 'Gabriel came to me and in his hand was like the white mirror which has a black spot in it. I asked, 'What is this in your hand, Gabriel?'

He replied, 'It is Friday.'
'What is Friday? I asked.

He said, 'There is a great deal of benefit for you in it.'

I asked, 'What is there for us in it?'

He said, 'It is a day of celebration for you and your community after you. The Jews and the Christians will follow you.'

'What is there for us on that day?' I asked.

He said, 'There is a period in it for you; no one will ask Allah for anything which he is to be given but Almighty will give it to him. If it is not his share in this world, He will store in the Hereafter something greater than that.'

I asked,
'What is the spot in it?' He replied, It is the Hour, and we call it the Day of More.'

'What is that, Gabriel?'

He said, 'Your Lord has singled out a valley in Paradise, which has hills of white musk. When Friday comes He descends from Illiyyin on His Chair, and His Chair is surrounded by chairs of light. The prophets come and sit on those chairs. These chairs will be surrounded with pulpits of light and gold studded with gems. The most truthful and martyrs will sit on those pulpits. Then the people of apartments will come down and sit on those hills. After that Allah, the Exalted, will reveal Himself to them and say,

'I have fulfilled My promise and completed My grace upon you. It is the place of My honour. Ask Me. They will ask until their desire is exhausted and He will open for them what no eye has ever seen, no ear has ever heard of and no heart has ever thought of it. This will be done in the period of your return from Friday. Then His Chair will ascend and the prophets and most truthful ones will leave and the people of the apartments will go to their apartments. These apartments and their gates are of white pearls, green chrysolite and red ruby. Their streams will flow constantly and their wives and servants will be with them, and the fruits will be within their reach.

They will not be more eager for anything than the day of Friday so that they can look more at their Lord and receive further honour and gifts.

It is a Hadith of great significance reported by the Imams of the Sunnah and accepted by them.[373] Imam al-Shafi'i has beautified his Musand by it, and narrated it through various chains.[374]

---

373. See Darqutni in al-Ru'yah (59)
374. See his Musnad (374)

In another citation of Anas the story includes the following, "Then their Lord, the Most Exalted and the Most High, will reveal Himself to them; they will look at Him and He will say, 'I am the One who fulfilled His promise and completed My favour upon you and this is the place of My honour, so ask Me.'

They will ask for His pleasure. He will say, 'My pleasure is that I have made My house safe for you and shown My honour to you. Ask Me.'

They will ask for pleasure and He will be pleased with them. They will ask until their desires are exhausted." [375]

In another context Anas narrated, "While we were around the Messenger of Allah, blessing and peace be upon him, he said, 'Gabriel came to me holding like a white mirror in his hand in the middle of which there was a black spot. I asked, 'What is this Gabriel?'

He said, 'This the day of Friday your Lord presents to you to be a day of celebration for you and for your community after you.'

I asked, 'What is that black spot, Gabriel?' He said, 'It the Hour which will come on Friday. Friday is the master of the days of the world and we call it in Paradise the Day of More.'

I asked, Why do you call it the Day of More?' He replied, 'Allah, the Most High, has chosen a vast valley of white musk. When Friday comes, our Lord Almighty comes down on His Chair to that valley, which is surrounded with pulpits of god studded with gems and chairs of light. Then the people of the apartments will be called; they will come and walk in the piles of musk till their knees, having bracelets of gold and silver and dress of silk brocade. When they reach the valley and sat comfortably, Allah will send on them a breeze called 'stimulant', which will spray white musk on their faces and their dresses. They will be hairless, beardless with eyes decorated with kohl; they will be the thirty-three years old on the form of their father Adam when Allah created him.

Allah, the Most Blessed and High, will call Ridwan, the keeper of Paradise and say to him, 'Ridwan, remove the veil between Me and My devotees and visitors. When

375. Al-Ru'yah (60-63)

the veil is lifted and they see His beauty and light, they intend to prostrate to Him. The Lord Almighty will speak to them in His voice, 'Raise your heads, the worship was in the world; today you are in the abode of recompense, ask Me whatever you wish. I am your Lord Who fulfilled His promise to you and completed His favour upon you. This is the place of My honour, so ask Me whatever you wish.'

They will say, 'Our Lord what good remains which You did not give us? Didn't You help us on the difficulties of death, give us company in loneliness of the darkness of the graves and remove our fear at the time of the blowing of the horn? Didn't You remove our mistakes and cover our evil deeds and keep our feet firm on the bridge of Hell? Didn't You bring us near You and make us hear the beautiful speech of Yours and reveal Yourself to us with Your light? So, what good remains that You did not do to us?'

Allah, the Exalted, will call them again and say,'I am your Lord Who has fulfilled His promise to you and completed His favour to you. So, ask Me.'

They will say, 'We ask for Your pleasure.'

He will say, With My pleasure I cancelled your shortcomings and covered your bad deeds, brought you near Me, made you enjoy My beautiful speech and revealed Myself to you with My light. So ask Me.'

They will ask till their desires will come to an end. Still Allah Almighty will ask them to ask.

They will say, 'Our Lord, we are satisfied and agreed.'

Then Allah, the Exalted, will give them from His grace and honour what no eyes has ever seen, no ear has ever heard and no heart has ever imagined. All this will be done in the period of their dispersing from Friday."

Anas said, "May my father and mother be ransom to you, Messenger of Allah! What is the period of their dispersing?"

He replied, "Like Friday to the next Friday."
Then he further said, "The angels will lift the Throne of our Lord, the Most Blessed

and High, and with them will be the prophets. Then the people of the apartments will be allowed to move to their chambers. There are two chambers of green emerald but they will not be more interested in anything than Friday in order to see their Lord Almighty Who will grant them more of His bounties and favours."

Anas said, "I heard all this from the Messenger of Allah, blessing and peace be upon him, and nobody was there between me and him."[376]

11. The report of Buraydah ibn al-Husayb is recorded by Ibn Khuzaymah who narrated that the Messenger of Allah, blessing and peace be upon him, said, "There is no one of you but Allah will see him alone on the Day of Judgement without there being any barrier between him and Him or any interpreter." [377]

12. The report of Abu Razin al-Uqayli is cited by Imam Ahmad in which Abu Razin said, "We said, 'Messenger of Allah, will every one of us see his Lord, the Most High?'"

He replied, "Yes."

I said, "What is its proof in His creature?"

He said, "Does not every one of you see the moon on the night of full-moon?"

We said, "Yes."

He said, "Allah is greater and more Magnificent."[378]

13. As for the report of Jabir ibn Abdullah it is recorded in the Musnad of Imam Ahmad as follows:
He said that the Prophet 鸞, was asked about *wurud* (approaching) and he said, "We will be on the Day of Judgement above the people, and the nations will be

---

376. *Ibid (64) It is also by Ibn Abi Shaybah, Ibn Khuzaymah and Ibn Battah with various chains. Ibn Abi Dawud has collected all the chains.*
377. *Darqutni in al-Ru'yah (184), al-Bazzar (3440)*
378. *Ahmad (16186) It is also reported by Abu Dawud.*

called with their idols and the objects they used to worship in sequence, the first then the next. Then our Lord will come to us and asked, 'Whom are you waiting for?'

They will say, 'We are waiting our Lord.'
He will say, 'I am your Lord.'

They will say, 'We will not believe until we see you.'
Then Allah, the Most High and Blessed, will reveal Himself to them smiling.

The Prophet ﷺ, went on, "Allah Almighty will walk with them after Him. Every man of them whether believer or hypocrite, will be given light. Then they will follow Him to the Bridge of Hell, which has hooks and spikes that will catch whoever Allah wishes. Later the light of the hypocrite will go out and the believers will be saved. The first group to be rescued their faces will be like the moon on a full-moon night. There will be seventy thousand who will not be subjected to accounting. Then the next will be like the brightest star in the sky, and so on. Then intercession will be allowed till anyone who said 'there is no god but Allah' and has good deeds in his heart less than the weight of barley will be taken out of Hell. They will be gathered in the open space of Paradise, and the people of Paradise will sprinkle on them water till they sprout like the plant in flood and their burn will go away. One of them will ask till Allah grants him the world and ten times more like it." [379]

In another version the Messenger of Allah, peace be upon him, said, "The Lord, the Most High and Blessed, will appear to them and they will look at His Face and fall down in prostration. He will say, 'Raise your heads; it is not the day of worship.'" [380]

In another version the Messenger of Allah, blessing and peace be upon him, said, "When it is the Day of Judgment the nations will be gathered."

The rest of the account was cited and it has the following:
"Allah will ask them, 'would you be able to recognize Allah Almighty if you see Him?'

379. Ahmad (15117), Muslim (iman: 191)
380. Darqutni in al-Ru'yah (52)

They will answer, 'Yes.'

He will say, 'How can you recognize Him when you have not seen Him?'

They will say, 'We know that He has no match.' Then Allah, the Exalted, will appear to them and they will fall in prostration to Him."[381]

In another report from Jabir the Prophet ﷺ said, "While the people of Paradise are enjoying their pleasure a light appeared to them and they raise their heads and see that the Lord, the Most Majestic, has appeared to them from the above. He says, 'Peace be on you, people of Paradise!' This is what Allah, the Exalted has said, "Peace", a word from the Merciful Lord." *(36, 58)*

He will look at them and they will look at Him. They will not turn to anything of their pleasure as long as they look at Him till He disappears. His blessing and light will remain."[382]

In another report from Jabir the Messenger of Allah blessing and peace of Allah be upon him, said, "While the people of Paradise are sitting together a light will appear at the gate of Paradise. They will raise their heads and find that the Lord, the Most Blessed and High, has appeared and says, 'People of paradise, ask Me.' They will say, 'We ask You to be pleased with us.'

He will say, 'By My pleasure I put you in My home and granted you My honour. This is the time, so ask Me.'

They will say, 'We ask for more and more.'

They will be brought camels of red ruby their bridles will be green emerald and red ruby. They will ride them and they will put their hoofs at the end of their sight. Then Allah will order the trees with fruits, and the beautiful dark-eyed women will come and say, 'We are fresh and will not fade, and we are immortal and will not die. We are the wives of honourable believing people.' Allah will also order heaps of white musk, which will blow breeze over them. It is called 'stimulant.' Then they will end up at the Paradise of Eden, which is the centre of Paradise. The angels will

381. Darqutni (53-54)
382. Ibn Majah (184)

say, 'Our Lord, the people have arrived.'

He will say, 'Welcome to the truthful ones, welcome to the obedient ones!'

Then the veil will be removed and they will look at Allah, the Most Blessed and High. They will be engrossed in the light of the Merciful and will not see one another. Then Almighty will say, 'take them to the palaces with gifts.' They will return while they are seeing one another. The Messenger 雞, said, "This is what Allah, the Exalted said, "A welcoming gif from the Most Forgiving, Most Merciful One." *(41, 32)* [383]

In another report Jabir related the Prophet 雞 saying, "Allah, the Exalted will appear to the general people and to Abu Bakr specially." [384]

14. The report of Abu Umamah:

He said, "The Messenger of Allah, peace be upon him, delivered a sermon to us and most of his talk was about *Dajjal* (anti Christ), he warned us from him and spoke at length about him until the end of his sermon. He said in his sermon, "Allah, the Exalted, did not send a prophet but he warned his community of him. I am the last of the prophets and you are the last of the people. He is certainly going to appear among you. If he appears while I am among you, I will defend every Muslim. If he comes out after me, then it is the duty of every Muslim to defend himself, and Allah will be supporter of every Muslim after me. He will come out from the area between Iraq and Syria causing havoc to the right and the left. You, the worshippers of Allah, stand firm. He will start by saying, 'I am prophet', but there is no prophet after me. Then he will say, 'I am your Lord.' Remember you will not see your Lord until you die. It will be written 'kafir' between his two eyes, which every believer will read it. Whoever of you meets him should spit on his face and read the firs verses of Chapter of the Cave (18). He will be given power over one of the children of Adam; he will kill him then bring him back to life. He cannot do it to anyone else. One of his tricks is that he will have Paradise and Hell with him. His Fire is Paradise and his Paradise is Hell. If anyone of you faces his Fire, he should close his eyes and ask refuge with Allah, his Fire will become cool and safe for him as it became cool and safe for Ibrahim. His days will be forty days, one

383. *Bayhaqi in al-Ba'th 9448) al-Ru'yah 951)*
384. *Al-ruyah (48)*

day like a year, another like a month, another like a week and the rest of the days will be like normal days. The last of his days will be like a mirage. A person will be in the morning at the gate of the city and will get the evening before reaching the end of the other gate."

They asked, 'How are going to perform prayers in those days, Messenger of Allah?' "Estimate as you do in long days", he replied.[385]

15. The Hadith of Zayd ibn Thabit:

He said, "The Messenger of Allah, peace be upon him, taught him a supplication and ordered him to observe it with his family every day. He said, "Say when you reach morning, 'I am here, O Allah, I am here. I am here, all the good is in Your hand and from You and to You. O Allah, anything I said or any vow I made or any oath I took, it is under Your will. What You willed would happen and what You did not would not. There is no power nor strength but with You; You have surely power over everything. O Allah any blessing I made it was for those whom I blessed, and any curse I made it was for those whom I cursed. You are my supporter in the world and in the Hereafter. Cause me to die as Muslim and join me with the righteous ones. O Allah, I ask for satisfaction after the decree and coolness of life after death, and the joy of looking at Your Face and desire to meet You without affecting harm or misguiding trial. O Allah, I seek refuge with You from doing injustice or being subject of injustice, from being aggressive or subject of aggression, or committing a destructive sin which You will not forgive. O Allah, the Creator of the heavens and the earth, Knower of the unseen and present, the owner of majesty and honour, I commit to You in this worldly life and make You witness - and You are sufficient as witness - I bear witness that there is no god but You, alone with no partner with You. For You is sovereignty and for You is praise, and You have power over every thing. I also bear witness that Muhammad is Your servant and Your Messenger. I bear witness that Your promise is true, meeting with You is true, Paradise is true, the Hour is surely coming and You will raise those who are in the graves. I bear witness that if You surrender me to my self, You will surrender me to loss, deficiency, sin and mistake. I have no confidence except in Your mercy, forgive for me my sin, no one forgives sins except You, turn to me with mercy, You are surely the Most relenting and Most Merciful." [386]

---

385. It was reported by Darqutni
386. Ahmad (21724), Hakim (1: 516)

16. Hadith of Ammar ibn Yasir:

Abu Mijlaz said, "'Ammar led us in prayer, and made it short. The people did not like it. He said, 'Didn't I make the ruku' and sujud complete?'

They said, 'Yes.'

He said, 'I made in it supplication the Messenger of Allah, blessing and peace be upon him, used to make it. It is, "O Allah, by Your knowledge of unseen and Your power for creation, keep me alive as long as life is good for me, and cause me to die when You know that death is better for me. I ask for Your fear in hidden and open, telling truth in the situation of anger and happiness, moderation in poverty and affluence, the joy of looking at Your Face, and desire to meet You without any disturbing misguidance or misleading trial. O Allah, decorate us with belief and make us guiding and guided."[387]

17. The Hadith of 'A'ishah:

She said, "The Messenger of Allah, blessing and peace be upon him, said to Jabir, "Jabir, should I give you good news?"

He said, 'Yes, may Allah grant you good tiding.'
He said, "I learnt that Allah brought your father back to life and made him sit in front of Him, and said to him, 'Make whatsoever wishes you have, I will give you all that.'

He said, 'My Lord, I could not fulfil the dues of Your worship; I wish You send me back to the world so that I fight for Your Prophet and be killed another time. Allah said to him, 'The word has passed that you are not going back.'"[388]

Tirmidhi has cited it in a full text on the authority of Jabir who said, 'When Abdullah ibn 'Amr ibn Hizam i.e. the father of Jabir) was killed in the battle of Uhud, the Messenger of Allah, peace be upon him, said, "Should I tell you what Allah, the Exalted said to your father?"

He said, 'Yes.'

---

387. Ahmad (18353), Hakim (1: 524) Nisa'i (1304)
388. Hakim (3:203), It is also in Musnad of Ahmad (14881)

He said, "Allah, the Most High did not speak to anyone but from behind the veil, but He spoke to your father face to face and said to him, 'My slave, make wish, I will grant you your wishes.'

He said, 'My Lord, bring me back to life so that I may be killed second time in Your way.'

Allah said to him, 'It has been decreed that they will not be sent.'

He said, 'My Lord, then pass the message to those who are there of the reward You gave me.' Then Allah, the Exalted, revealed, "Do not consider those who were killed in the way of Allah martyrs." *(3, 169)* [389]

18. The Hadith of Abdullah ibn 'Umar:

He said that the Messenger of Allah, peace be upon him, said, "The lowest person in rank among the people of Paradise will look in his domain like the distance of two thousand years. He will see the farthest of it as he sees the closest. He will see his wives, his couches and his servants; and the highest in rank among them will see the Face of Allah, the Most High and Blessed, twice every day." [390]

In another narration Ibn 'Umar said, 'The Messenger of Allah, peace be upon him, then recited, "Some faces on that Day will be radiant looking at their Lord." **(75, 23)** On the Day of Resurrection the eye will see Allah, the Exalted, for the first time." [391]

In another version Ibn Umar said, "I heard the Messenger of Allah, blessing and peace be upon him, saying, "Should I tell you the person of lowest rank among the people of Paradise?"

They said, Yes, O Messenger of Allah.'

Then he cited the above report and said, "When the pleasure was complete and they thought there was no more, the Lord, the Exalted, will look down at them and they will see the Face of the Merciful, the Exalted and the Most High. He will

---

389. *Tirmidhi (3010), Hakim (3: 204)*
390. *Tirmidhi (255)*
391. *Darqutni (175)*

say, 'People of Paradise, extol Me, glorify Me and praise Me as you used to do in the world. They will echo with the glorification of the Merciful. Allah, the Exalted, then He will say to David, 'David, rise and glorify Me'.

David will stand up and glorify his Lord, the Exalted.[392]

19. The Hadith of Umarah ibn Ruwaybah:
He said, "The Prophet, peace be upon him, looked at the moon on the full-moon night and said, "You will see your Lord as you see this moon without any doubt in seeing it. So, if you are able not to miss a prayer before the sunrise and another before the sunset, then do it."

In another version the Prophet, peace be upon him, said, "If you are able not to miss two *rak'ah*s before sunrise and two *rak'ah*s after sunset, do them." [393]

20. Salman al-Farsi's report:
He reported the Hadith of intercession and said, 'The people will go to the Prophet ﷺ and say, 'Allah has opened by you and sealed the prophethood by you, and forgiven you. Rise up and intercede for us to your Lord.'

He will say, "Yes, I am the person to do it." He will go with the people until he reaches the gate of Paradise and holding the chain of it will knock at it. It will be said, 'Who is it?'

He will reply, 'Muhammad.'

The gate will be opened for him; he will proceed till he will stand in front of Allah Almighty and ask His permission for prostration, which will be granted.'

21. The report of Hudhayfah ibn al-Yaman:
He said that the Messenger of Allah, peace be upon him, said, "Gabriel came to me holding in his hand the like of the cleanest and most beautiful mirror, which

---

392. Ibid (176)
393. Ibn Battah in al-Ibanah

has a black spot in its middle. I asked, 'What is that, Gabriel?'

He replied, 'It is the world in its beauty and clarity.'

I asked, 'What is that spot in its middle?'

He said, 'It is Friday.'

I asked, 'what is Friday?'

He said, 'A great day from the days of your Lord, and I will tell you about its nobility and excellence and its name in the Hereafter. As for its nobility and excellence in the world Allah has gathered the creatures on it. What is hoped for in it is that there is a period in it no believing man or woman asks any good but Allah Almighty will grant him that. As for its nobility and excellence and its name in the Hereafter, when Allah, the Exalted will take the people of Paradise to it and the people of the Fire in it, and its days and hours continue. There is no day or night but Allah knows its length and hours.

When Friday comes and the people of Paradise go out for their Friday, a caller will call, 'People of Paradise, walk to the home of more, the length and width of which is known only to Allah, which will be on the hills of musk. The followers of the prophets will come out with pulpit of light and the servants from among the believers will come with chairs of ruby. When they are put and the people take their seats, Allah will send on them a breeze called stimulant, which will blow over them the fragrance of white musk, which will enter from below their dresses and pass their faces and hairs. The breeze knows what to do with that musk better than the wife of one of you who is given that perfume.

Then Allah Almighty will inspire the carriers of the Throne who will put it in the midst of Paradise. There will be veils between it and the people. The first thing they will listen will be that He says, 'Where are My servants who obeyed Me unseen without seeing Me, believed My messengers and followed My command?' Ask Me, it is the day of more.'
They will say one thing, 'Our Lord, we are pleased with You, so be pleased with us.'
Allah, the Exalted will say, 'People of Paradise, if I was not please with you, I would not have put you in My Paradise. Ask Me, this is the day of more.'

They will again say, 'We are pleased with You, so be pleased with us.'

Again He will say, 'People of Paradise, if I were not pleased with you, I would have not placed you in My Paradise. This is the day of more, so ask Me.'

They will all say, 'Our Lord, Your Face, Your Face, show us Your Face so that we can see it.'

Then Allah, the Exalted, will remove the veils and appear to them; His light will cover them. Had it not been decreed that they should not be burnt they would have been burnt. Then they will be ordered to return to their places. They will return and their wives had no idea of the light which covered them. When they return, their light increase and takes root. Their wives will say, 'You went out from here on a form and returned with another one.'

They will say, 'It is because Allah, the Most High appeared to us and we looked at Him.'

They will have every seven days double of what they had earlier. This is what Allah, the Exalted, said, "No soul knows what has been hidden for them of the comfort of the eyes as reward for what they used to do." *(32, 17)* [394]

22. The Hadith of Ibn Abbas:

Abu Nadrah said, "Ibn Abbas spoke to us and said that the Prophet ﷺ said, "Every prophet was granted a supplication which he made in the world, but I kept my supplication for the intercession of my community on the Day of Judgement. I will go to the gate of Paradise, hold its chain, and knock. It will be said, 'Who are you?'

I will say, 'Muhammad.'

Then I will approach my Lord who will be on His Chair or couch, He will appear to me and I will fall in prostration to Him." [395]

---

394. *Al-Bazzar (3518), he declared the report to be weak.*
395. *Ahmad (2546)*

In another report by Ibn Abbas the Prophet is reported to say, "The people of Paradise will see their Lord, the Most high, every Friday on the heaps of camphor. The nearest of them in sitting will be the one who is fast and reaches earlier."

23. The Hadith of Abdullah ibn 'Amr ibn al-'As:

'Amr ibn 'Uthman narrated, "I heard Abdullah ibn 'Amr ibn al-'As talking to Marwan ibn al-Hakam, the governor of Madinah. He said, 'Allah, the Most High, created the angels in different types for His worship, there are angels who are standing since they were created and will remain like that until the Day of Resurrection; there are those who are in bowing condition from the time they were created until the Day of Resurrection and there are those who are in the posture of prostration since they were created until the Day of Judgement. On the Day of Judgment Allah Almighty will appear to them; they will look at His Noble Face and say, 'Glory be to You, we could not worship You as it was due.'"

24. The Hadith of Ubayy ibn Ka'b:

He reported that the Prophet ﷺ said, "He explained the words of Allah, the Exalted, "For those who did good deeds is good reward and more."

He said, "More is to look at the Face of Allah, the Exalted." [396]

A similar report has come from Ka'b ibn 'Ujrah.

25. The report of Fudalah ibn 'Ubayd:

Abu al-Darda' said, 'Fudalah ibn 'Ubayd used to say, 'O Allah, I ask You for satisfaction after the decree, coolness of life after death, joy of looking at Your Face and desire to meet You without a disturbing harm or misleading trial.' [397]

26. The report of 'Ubadah ibn al-Samit:

He related the Prophet ﷺ saying, "I spoke to you about *Dajjal* , the anti-Christ to make sure that you may understand. He is a short with curly hair and blotted eye

396. Darqutni (183)
397. Ibid (207)

not bulging or hidden. If you are confused, remember your Lord is not one-eyed and you will not see your Lord till you die." [398]

27. The report of a man from the Companions of the Prophet, ﷺ:

Abbad ibn Mansur said, 'I heard 'Adi ibn Artat delivering a sermon on the pulpit of Mada'in. He spoke till he cried and made us cry and said, 'Be like a man who said to his son while advising him, 'My son, I command you not to perform a prayer but think that you will not do another after that till you die. Come my son, let us work like two people as though they stood at the Fire and asked for return. I heard a man -Abbad forgot his name- there was no one else between me and the Messenger of Allah, peace be upon him, saying that the Messenger of Allah, blessing and peace be upon him, said, "There are angels whose jugular veins tremble because of the fear of Allah. There is no angel from whose eye a drop of tear falls but it drops on an angel who is engaged in glorifying Allah. His angels are in prostration since Allah created the heavens and the earth; they have not raised their heads and will not raise them until the Day of Judgment. Others are in rows and did not break their rows and will no do so until the Day of the Judgment. When the Day of Judgment comes and their Lord appears to them, they will look at Him and say, 'Glory be to You, we did not worship You as it was suitable for You."

The Statements of the Companions of the Prophet and their Followers and the notable leaders of Islam

Here are the statements of the Companions of the Messenger of Allah, peace be upon him, their Followers and the leading scholars of Islam after them.

Abu Bakr Siddiq read, "For those who did good deeds there is good reward and more." *(10, 26)*

He was asked, 'What is more, the successor of the Messenger of Allah?'
He replied, 'To look at the Face of Allah, the Most High and Blessed.' [399]

---

398. Ahmad (22828)
399. Darqutni (192)

Ali ibn Abi Talib said, 'The completion of the favour is entering Paradise and looking at the Face of Allah, the Most Blessed and High in His Paradise.'

Hudhayfah ibn al-Yaman said, 'More is to look at the Face of Allah, the Exalted.'[400]

Abdullah ibn Mas'ud said in the mosque of Kufah, 'No one of you but his Lord will meet him in private as he sees the moon on the full-time night. Allah will say to him, 'What deceived you, O son of Adam? How did you respond to the messengers?' He will ask three times. 'How did you act in what you learnt?'
He also said, 'More is to look at the Face of Allah, the Most Glorious.'

Ibn Abbas was asked, 'Will everyone who goes to Paradise see Allah, the Exalted?' He said, 'Yes.'

Mu'adh ibn Jabal said, 'The people will be gathered in one ground, and it will be announced; 'Where are the righteous people?'

They will stand under the cover of the Merciful, He will not conceal or cover Himself from them.

Mu'adh was asked, 'Who are the righteous people?'
He replied, 'They are the people who kept away from the association and the worship of idols, and devoted themselves sincerely to the worship of Allah. They will be taken to Paradise.'

Abu Hurayrah said, 'You will not see your Lord until you die.'

Abdullah ibn 'Umar said, 'The man of the lowest rank in Paradise will look at his domain the distance of two thousand years; he will see the nearest of it as he see the farthest. The highest in rank will be the one who will see the Face of Allah twice every day.'

Fudalah ibn 'Ubayd used to pray, 'O Allah, I ask satisfaction after decree, coolness of eye after death and joy of looking at Your Face.'[401]

---

400. Ibid (202)
401. Darqutni (207)

Abu Musa al-Ash'ari said, 'More is to look at the Face of Allah.'

Once he was talking to the people and then they raised their eye toward the sky. He asked, 'What made you turn your eyes from me?'

They said, The new moon.
He said, 'What will you do when you see the Face of Allah openly?'

Anas ibn Malik interpreted the saying of Allah "And We have more" to mean that Allah the Most High will appear to them on the Day of Judgement.'

Jabir ibn Abdullah said, 'When the people of Paradise will enter it, horses of red ruby will be brought to them, which do not urinate or drop dung. They will sit on them and go to the Compeller. When He will appear to them they will fall in prostration to Him. He will say, 'People of Paradise raise your heads, I am pleased with you and there will be no displeasure after that.'

Al-Tabari said, 'Twenty three Companions have reported from the Messenger of Allah, peace be upon him, the Hadith of seeing including Ali, Abu Hurayrah, Abu Sa'id, Jarir, Abu Musa, Suhayb, Jabir, Ibn Abbas, Anas, Ammar ibn Yasir, Ubayy ibn Ka'b, Ibn Mas'ud, Zayd ibn Thabit, Hudhayfah ibn al-Yaman, 'Ubadah ibn al-Samit, Adi ibn Hatim, Abu Razin al-Uqayli, Ka'b ibn 'Ujrah, Fusalah ibn 'Ubayd, Buraydah ibn al-Husayb, and a man from the Companions.' [402]

Darqutni reported Yahya ibn Ma'in saying, 'I have seventeen Hadith concerning the seeing of Allah all of which are authentic.'

Al-Bayhaqi said, 'The reports about the seeing of Allah have come from Abu Bakr Siddiq, Hudhayfah ibn al-Yaman, Abdullah ibn Mas'ud, Abdullah ibn Abbas, Abu Musa and others. No rejection has been reported from any of them. If they had disputed, it would have been reported to us. Since the seeing of Allah by eye in the Hereafter has been reported from them without any dispute, we are sure they were all agreed on the question of His being seen in the Hereafter by eyes. As for the Followers of the Companions and leagues of faith among the scholars Hadith, *fiqh*, Tafisr and leaders of Sufism their statements in this regard are more than can be counted except by Allah, the Exalted.

---

402. As a matter of fact the number is 26 as cited above.

Sa'id ibn al-Musayyib said, 'More is to look at the Face of Allah Almighty.'

The same is said by al-Hasan, Abd al-Rahman ibn Abi Layla, Amir ibn Sa'd al-Bajali, Abd al-Rahman ibn Sabit, 'Ikrimah, Mujahid, Qatadah, al-Suddi, al-Dahhak and Ka'b.

'Umar ibn Abd al-Aziz wrote to some of his governors, 'I instruct you to have fear of Allah, abide by His obedience, follow His command and fulfil the duties which He has assigned to you and told you in His Book. It is because of the fear of Allah that His friends are rescued from His wrath and will be in company of His prophets. It is the cause of the brightness of their faces and looking at their Creator. It is a source of protection in the world from the trials and from the troubles of the Day of the Resurrection.'

Hasan said, 'If the worshippers were to know in the world that they would not see their Lord in the Hereafter, their souls would melt in the world.'

Al-A'mash and Sa'id ibn Jubayr said, 'The most eminent people of Paradise will be those who will see Allah, the Most Blessed and High, in the morning and evening.'

Ka'b said, 'Never did Allah, the Exalted, look at Paradise but said, 'Be pleasant to your people'; and it increases in beauty till its people go to it. There was no day of festival in the world but they will go out about its period to the meadows of Paradise, and Allah, the Exalted, will appear to them and they will look at Him. The wind will blow over them musk, and they will not ask the Lord Almighty for anything but Allah will grant them that till they return to their wives and they had increased in their beauty.'

Hisham ibn Hassan said, 'Allah, the Most Supreme and High, will appear to the people of Paradise; when they see Him, they forget their pleasure.'[403]

Tawus said, 'The followers of dispute and analogy will continue in their discussion till they deny seeing of Allah, and go against the followers of the Sunnah.'

Abd al-Rahman ibn Abi Layla said after reading the verse, "For those who did good deeds there is good reward and more."

---

403. Darqutni (298)

He said, 'When the people of Paradise enter it, they will be given anything they ask for and wish. Allah, the Exalted, will say to them, Something of your dues remains, which have not been given to you. Then He will appear to them, and what they had been given will be considered nothing compared to it.' The good reward' is Paradise and 'more' is to look at the Face of their Lord Almighty. "No darkness or humiliation will cover their faces after looking at their Lord Almighty.'

Ali ibn al-Madini said, 'I asked Abdullah ibn al-Mubarak about the words of Allah, the Exalted, "Anyone who hopes to meet his Lord should do good deeds." *(18, 110)*

He said, 'Anyone who wishes to look at the Face of his Creator should do good deeds and not associate anyone with Him.'

Nu'aym ibn Hammad said, 'I heard Abdullah ibn al-Mubarak say, 'Allah did not screen off anyone from Him but would punish him.' He then recited,

"No! On that Day they will be screened off from their Lord, then they will burn in Hell, and then they will be told, 'This is what you called a lie." *(83, 15-17)*

He said, '(Screened off) from seeing.'

Abbad ibn al-Awwam said, 'Sharik ibn Abdullah came to us fifty years ago, and I said to him, 'Abu Abdullah, there are some people of Mu'tazilah around us who reject the Traditions saying that Allah comes down to the lowest sky, and that the people of Paradise will see their Lord.'

He narrated about ten Hadith regarding this matter and said, 'We have taken our religion from the Followers from the Companions of the Messenger of Allah, peace be upon him, but from whom they took this information?'

'Uqbah ibn Qabisah said, 'We went to 'Abu Nu'aym one day and he came down from the staircase of his house and sat in its middle as though he was angry. He said, 'We were told by Sufyan ibn Sa'id, Mundhir al-Tawri, Zuhayr ibn Mu'awiyah, as well as from Hasan ibn Salih and Sharik ibn Abdullah al-Nakha'i -who are the children of the Emigrants - reporting to us from the Messenger of Allah, peace be upon him, that he said, "Allah, the Exalted and Blessed, will be seen in the Hereafter."

Then a son of a Jewish dyer came and claimed that Allah will not be seen.' He was referring to Bishr al-Mirrisi.

The opinions of the four Imams, their colleagues, their teachers and their followers.

Imam Malik ibn Anas said, 'People will see their Lord Almighty by their eyes on the Day of Resurrection.'

Malik was asked about the statement of Allah, "Some faces will be radiant, looking at their Lord." (75, 22-23)

'Are we going to see Allah, the Exalted? He replied, 'Yes.'

He was told that there are people who say that you will see what is with Him. He said, 'You will see Him directly. Moses said, "My Lord, show Yourself to me so that I can see You. He said, 'You cannot see Me." (7, 143)

Allah, the Most High said, "No! They will be screened off on that Day from their Lord." (83, 15)

Al-Tabari and others said that it was said to Malik that there are people who claim that Allah will not be seen. He said, They deserve sword (i.e. to be killed).

Ibn al-Majishun was asked about the Jahmiyyah's view that Allah will not be seen, and he said, 'Satan continued dictating to them until they rejected Allah's saying, "Some faces will be radiant on that Day looking at their Lord."

They said, 'No one will see Him on the Day of Judgment. They denied the best honour Allah will bestow upon His friends on the Day of Judgement to look at His Face and making them radiant and secure in the presence of an all-powerful Sovereign. By the Lord of the heaven and the earth He will make seeing Him on the Day of Judgement purely for His devoted servants as reward to make their faces radiant with exclusion of the evildoers. Their arguments will dominate over the deniers who will be screened off from their Lord. They will not see Him as they claimed and He will not talk to them or look at them and for them will be painful torment.

Al-Awza'i said, 'I hope that Allah, the Exalted, will keep away Jahm and his colleagues from His best reward, which He has promised His friends in His statement, "Some faces will be radiant on that Day looking at their Lord."

Jahm and his followers have denied the best reward which Allah Almighty has promised His friends.'

Al-Walid ibn Muslim said, 'I asked al-Awza'i, Sufyan al-Thawri, Malik ibn Anas and a-Layth ibn Sa'd about the reports which mention seeing of Allah. They said, 'It should be taken as they are.'

Sufyan ibn Uyaynah said, 'Whoever did not believe that the Qur'an is the speech of Allah, and Allah will not be seen in Paradise is a Jahmi. Prayer should not be performed behind a Jahmi who says Allah will not be seen on the Day of Judgement.'

A man from the followers of Jahm said to Abdullah ibn al-Mubarak, 'How will Allah be seen on the Day of Judgement?' He replied, 'By eyes.'

Waki' ibn al-Jarrah said, the believers will see Allah, the Exalted and the Most Blessed, in Paradise. Only believers will see Him.'

Qutaybah ibn Sa'id said, 'The opinion of the leading scholars in Islam is to believe that Allah will be seen, and to accept the Traditions which have come down from the Messenger of Allah, peace be upon him, in this regard.

The reports concerning seeing Allah were mentioned to Abu 'Ubayd al-Qasim ibn Sallam and he said, 'they are true passed through reliable narrators to us and we are not to interpret them but we pass them as they are.'

Aswad ibn Salim the teacher of Imam Ahmad was asked about these reports and he said, 'I swear by divorce that they are true.'

Muhammad ibn Idris al-Shafi'i said concerning the verse "No! They will be screened off from their Lord", the screening off these people is an indication that His friends will see Him.' He was asked, 'Abu Abdullah, do you believe in it?'

He replied, 'Yes, I yield to it. If Muhammad ibn Idris did not believe that he would see Allah, the Exalted, he would not worship Him.

Ishaq ibn Mansur said, 'I said to Ahmad ibn Hanbal, 'will the people of Paradise see Allah, the Most High? What do you say about these reports concerning it?' He said, 'They are authentic.'

Ishaq ibn Rahwayh said, These reports are genuine and only an innovator or someone of a week opinion will aband.

Al-Fadl ibn Ziyad said, 'I heard Abu Abdullah (i.e. Ahmad) and it was said to him, 'Do you say that seeing Allah is true? He said, 'Anyone who did not believe in seeing is Jahmi.

I le was told about a person who said that Allah will not be seen in the Hereafter, and he was enraged and said; 'Anyone who says that Allah will not be seen in the Hereafter has committed disbelief and upon him is the curse and wrath of Allah, no matter who he was. Doesn't Allah say, "Some faces on that Day will be radiant looking at their Lord",

And "No! They will surely be screened off on that Day from their Lord"?

Abu Bakr al-Marwazi said, 'It was said to Abu Abdullah, do you know the report of Yazid ibn Harun from Abu al-Atuf from Abu al-Zubayr from Jabir that if the mountain remained in its place you will see Me, and if it did not then you will not see Me neither in the word nor in the Hereafter?

He was enraged till it was seen in his face, and he was sitting around the people then he took his shoes and put them on and said, 'May Allah humiliate this person! This report should not be written.' He refused to accept that Yazid ibn Harun reported it. He further said, 'This person is a Jahmi, disbeliever, going against what Allah has said, "Some faces will be radiant on that Day looking at their Lord", and "No! They will be screened off from their Lord."

May Allah humiliate this wicked man!

He also said, 'Whoever claimed that Allah will not be seen in the Hereafter is an unbeliever.'

Abu Abdullah recited the following statements of Allah, the Exalted, "Are they waiting for Allah to come to them in the shadow of the clouds, together with the angels, and the matters are decided?" *(2, 210)*

"And your Lord will come with angels, rank upon rank." *(89, 22)*

He said, 'After these verses if someone says that Allah will not be seen, he committed disbelief.'

He also said, 'Anyone who does not believe in seeing Allah is a Jahmi, and Jahmi is disbeliever.'

He was asked, 'Will the people of Paradise see their Lord, the Exalted, speak to Him and He will speak to them?'

He replied, 'Yes, He will look at them and they will look at Him; He will speak to them and they will speak to Him as they wish and when they wish.'

He also said, 'The people tend to go to deny all Attributes. They deny seeing Allah and the reports cited in this regard. I did not believe until I heard their talk.'

He said, 'Anyone who claimed that Allah will not be seen in the Hereafter is a Jahmi and unbeliever. He has rejected the words of Allah and His Messenger. Anyone who said that Allah did not take Abraham as friend is unbeliever and refused to accept what Allah Has said. We believe in these Hadith and pass them as they are.'

He also said, 'We found people not denying any of the Hadith of seeing; they reported them and pass them as they were without having any doubt and denying them.

He said further, Allah, the Most High, said, "It is not for any human being that Allah should speak to him except by revelation or from behind a veil or that He sends a messenger to reveal by His command what He will." *(42, 51)*

The Almighty spoke to Moses from behind a veil; Moses said, "My Lord, show Yourself to me so that I can see You. He said, 'You cannot see Me, but look at the mountain; if it stays in its place, you will see Me." (7, 43)

Allah informed that Moses will see Him in the Hereafter. He, the Exalted said, "No! They on that Day will certainly be screened off from their Lord." (83, 15)

Screening off will be from seeing. Allah has confirmed that whomever He willed he will see Him and the disbelievers will not see Him.

Imam Ahmad said that the reports telling the seeing of Allah are all authentic. He said, 'Allah said, "Those who did well will have good reward and more besides."

We believe in it and know that reports concerning seeing are true. We believe that Allah will be seen. We will see Him on the Day of Judgement; we have no doubt or suspicion about it.'

He further said, 'Anyone who said that Allah will not be seen on the Day of Judgement has disbelieved, denied the Qur'an and rejected the statement of Allah. He will be asked to repent, if he refuses, he will be killed.'

He said, 'The reports concerning seeing are authentic, we accept them. If we reject them, we will be rejecting Allah's command as He said, "Accept whatever the Messenger gives you, and refrain from whatever he forbids you." (59, 7)

Abdullah ibn Tahir the governor of Khurasan asked Ishaq ibn Rahwayh, 'Abu Yaqub, what are these reports narrated about descending and seeing of Allah?'

He replied, 'These are reported by the people who reported Traditions about cleanliness, purification, prayer and other areas. If they are not reliable in these reports, then their rulings are dismissed and the Shari'ah is made null and void.' He said, 'May Allah satisfy you as you satisfied me.'

Ibn Khuzaymah said in his book, 'All the believers have no dispute concerning the issue that the believers will see their Lord on the Day of Resurrection; whoever denies it is not a believer according to them.'

Abu Dawud al-Misri said, 'We were sitting with Nu'aym ibn Hammad, and he asked al-Muzani, 'What do you say about the Qur'an?'

He said, 'It is the speech of Allah.'
He asked, 'uncreated?' He said, 'Yes, uncreated.'

He further asked, 'Do you say that Allah will be seen on the Day of Resurrection?' He replied, 'Yes.'

When the people dispersed al-Muzani stood up to him and said, 'Abu Abdullah, you exposed me in front of the people.

He said, 'The people spoke much about you so I wanted to exonerate you.'

Ahmad ibn Yahya Tha'lab said concerning the statement of Allah Almighty, "He is Merciful to the believers. Their greeting the Day they meet Him will be, Peace." (33,43-44)

He said, 'All the scholars of the Arabic language said, 'Meeting here is not but by seeing and looking with eyes.'

Meeting is established by the text of the Qur'an and by the continuous reports from the Prophet, ﷺ. These reports are established like the report of Anas in the story of the well of Ma'unah when the martyrs said, 'We have met our Lord and He was pleased with us and pleased us.' [404]

Also Abdullah ibn Mas'ud reported the Messenger ﷺ saying, "Whoever loves meeting Allah, Allah loves meeting him." [405]

Anas reported that that the Prophet ﷺ said, "You will face partiality after me, so be patience till you meet Allah and His Messenger." [406]

Abu Dharr narrated in a Divine Hadith, "If you meet Me with the sins full of the earth and meet Me without associating any partner with Me, I will meet you with

404. See the story in Bukhari (2801), Muslim (masajid: 677)
405. Bukhari (6507, 7504), Muslim (Dhikr: 2684) Nisa'i (1834), Tirmidhi (1065), Ibn Majah (4264), Ahmad (24227, 24338, 25889)
406. Bukhari (3147), Muslim (zakat: 1059)

similar amount of forgiveness." [407]

Abu Musa reported the prophet ﷺ saying, "Whoever meets Allah without associating a partner with Him, will enter Paradise." [408]

There are many Hadith in this regard with almost similar wordings.

Warning to those who deny seeing Allah the Exalted.

It has already been cited that Allah Almighty said, "No! On that Day they will certainly be screened off from their Lord." (83, 15)

It has also been mentioned that Abdullah ibn al-Mubarak said, 'Allah did not keep anyone away from Him but punished him. He recited, "Then they surely will enter Hellfire, then it will be said to them, this is what you had been denying." i.e. seeing of Allah. (83, 16-17)

Abu Hurayrah reported, 'They said, 'Messenger of Allah, will we see our Lord on the Day of Judgement?'

He replied, "Do you have any problem in seeing he sun at noon when there is no cloud?"

They said, 'No.'

He then asked, "Do you have any problem in seeing the moon on the full-moon night?"

They said, 'No.'

Then he said, "By the One Who holds Muhammad's soul in His hand you will not have trouble in seeing your Lord as you do not have trouble in seeing one of these two. Allah will meet a servant and say to him, 'O so and so, did I not honour you, make you master, give you a wife and provide you with horses and camels and leave you to be proud and high?'

407. Muslim (dhikr: 2687), Ahmad (21418)
408. Bukhari, Ahamd (12606)

He will say, 'Yes.'

Then He will ask, 'Did you believe that you were going to meet Me?'

He will reply, 'No.'

The Almighty will say, 'I will forget you as you forgot Me.'

He then will meet another person and ask him,

'So and so, did I not honour you, make you master, give you wife and provide you with horses and camels and leave you be proud and leader?'

He will say, 'Yes, my Lord.'

The Almighty will ask him, Did you believe that you were going to meet Me?'

He will answer, 'No.'

Allah will say to him, 'I will forget you as you forgot Me.'

Then He will meet a third person and ask him the same question. He will say, 'My Lord, I believed in You, in Your Books, in Your messengers, and I performed prayer, fasted and gave out in charity. He will mention other good deeds. Allah will say, 'We will raise a witness on you.'

The man will think who is going to witness against me? Then Allah will place seal on his mouth ad order his thigh to speak. It will speak as will his flesh, and his bones about his deeds. He is the hypocrite who wanted to exonerate himself and he will be the one with whom Allah will be angry."[409]

Now you look at the Prophet's saying "You will surely see your Lord", and the saying of Allah Almighty to the one who thought he was not going to meet Him "I will forget you as you forgot Me". Remember that the experts of Arabic language agreed that meeting means seeing with eyes. It will prove to you that the one who denies seeing of Allah deserves this warning more. That is why the Scholars of the followers of the Sunnah set the heading of a chapter, 'Warning

409. Muslim (zuhd; 2968)

to those who deny seeing Allah,' as it was done by Shaykh al-Islam and others. Support comes from Allah.

It has been proved by the Qur'an, the authentic numerous Sunnah, the consensus of the Companions, the leaders of Islam, the followers of Hadith and supporters of Islam that Allah will be seen with eyes on the Day of Judgement. As the Messenger of Allah, peace be upon him, said, "He will be seen openly as the moon is seen on a clear night and the sun is seen in noon."

What Allah and His Messenger said is a reality, and the believers will see Him above them; it is impossible that they see Him beneath them or behind them or before them or at the right or left of them. If what the Messenger had said was not reality as the children of Sabi'ah, Philosophers, Magians and Pharaonic people say, the Shari'ah and the Qur'an will be reduced to nothing. The one who spoke in these Hadith is the very one who brought the Qur'an and the Shari'ah. He is the one who conveyed the religion to mankind. It is, therefore, not reasonable to make the statements of Allah and His Messenger divided to believe in some and reject the other. It is not possible for a person who knew these Hadith and understood their meaning to combine in his heart their rejection and bearing witness that Muhammad is the Messenger of Allah.

Praise is for Allah Who guided us to this, we were unable to be guided if Allah had not guided us and the Messengers of our Lord brought us the truth. Those who deny the seeing of the Lord Almighty are two types, those who claim that He will be seen in the world and speak and chat; and those who claim that He will not be seen in the Hereafter and will not speak to His servants at all. What Allah and His Messenger have told and the Companions and the Muslim leaders have unanimously agreed denies the claim of both groups. Only from Allah comes help.

CHAPTER 66
ALLAH'S TALKING TO THE PEOPLE OF PARADISE, HIS ADDRESSING THEM AND HIS GREETING THEM

Allah, the Exalted said, "**Those who sell out Allah's covenant and their oaths for a small price will have no share in the life to come. Allah will neither speak to them nor look at them on the Day of Resurrection. He will not purify them and agonizing torment awaits them.**" *(3: 77)*

He, the Most High, said about those who hide the evidences and guidance, which Allah has revealed: "**Allah will not speak to them on the Day of Resurrection.**" *(2: 174)*

If Allah were no to speak to His believing servants, they will be equal with His enemy and there will be no sense in specifying His enemy that He will not speak to them. His speaking to His servants is to the Pharaonic groups and the deniers of the Attributes like eating and drinking with them, Allah is above what they say! The Almighty has said that He will greet the people of Paradise and that is a real greeting, which will be done by a Merciful Lord. The explanation of the Prophet ﷺ, of this verse is reported in the Hadith of Jabir concerning the seeing. It says that Allah Almighty will look at them from the above and say: 'Peace be on you, the people of Paradise.' They will see him clearly. It proves being seen, talking and being above, but the deniers of the Attributes reject these three qualities and declare anyone who says it as disbeliever.

Abu Hurayrah's report about the market has already been cited in which the Prophet ﷺ, said, "No one will remain in that meeting but Allah will address him and say: 'So and so, do you remember the day when you did such and such deed?"

The report of 'Adi ibn Hatim has also been mentioned which says, "No one of you but Allah will speak to him on the Day of Judgement."

Also the report of Abu Hurayrah has been mentioned in which Allah, the Exalted, will ask the person: 'Did I not honour you and give you power?'

Then there is the Hadith of Buraydah which says that every one of you Allah will meet alone without there being any interpreter or veil. The Hadith of Anas, which mentioned the day of more and addressing of Allah many times. Just pay attention to the reports of seeing, you will notice in most of them the mention of speaking.

Bukhari set a chapter in his Sahih under the heading of 'The speaking of the Lord, the Exalted and the Most High, to the people of Paradise', and cited a number of Hadith. The best blessing for the people of Paradise will be to look at the Face of the Lord, the Most Blessed and High, and His talking to them; to deny it is to deny the core of Paradise, its highest and the best blessing, which the people of Paradise were honoured by Him.

Allah's help is sought.

CHAPTER 67
THE INFINITE LASTING OF PARADISE AND THAT IT WILL NOT COME TO AN END

It is definitely known that the Messenger ﷺ informed about it, and Allah, the Most High, said, "As for those who have been blessed, they will be in Paradise, to remain there as long as the heavens and earth endure, unless your Lord wills otherwise; it is an unceasing gift." *(11: 108)*

The early scholars are not agreed regarding the exception 'unless'. Al-Dahhak said: 'It is about those who will be taken out of Hellfire and admitted in Paradise. Allah Almighty says: They will remain in Paradise as long as the heavens and earth endure except the period of their staying in Hell.'

I say: This implies two things: first that the information about those who were fortunate was about particular people; second, which is clearer, that the information is about all the fortunate people and exception be about those who are mentioned. Better than these two assumptions is to refer the will to all as they were not in Paradise when they were in station of the Judgement. In this case there will be no particularization.

Another group said: The exception here is what Allah made but He is not going to do it as you say: 'By Allah, I will beat you unless I see something different, and you do not see it and are determined on beating him.

Another group said: When the Arabs make large exception from its kind and more than it, it gives the meaning of save. The meaning of the verse in this case will be 'except what Allah wills to add the period of the remaining of the heavens and earth.

Another group said: The exception refers to the period of their detention from Paradise between the death and resurrection until they go to Paradise. Then it is eternal stay and they were not away from Paradise but the period of their staying in Barzakh.

Another group held that the decree of Allah for them was for permanent stay unless Allah wills otherwise. This is to tell them that their everlasting stay is subject to Divine will. This is as He said to His Prophet:

"If We willed, We could surely do away with what We revealed to you." (17: 86)
"If Allah so willed, He would seal your heart." (42: 24)
"Say, 'if Allah has so willed, I would have not recited it to you." (10: 16)

In these verses and many others Allah is telling His servants that all matters are by His will. What He willed was done and what He did not, did not occur.

Some other people said, "The endurance of the heavens and earth is meant in this world. Allah, the Exalted, tells us that they will remain in Paradise as long as the heavens and earth endure unless Allah wills to increase."

Another group said, "The word 'ma' (translated as 'as long') means in the verse 'man'(who), as it is used in the verse "Marry from women whom who see good." (4:3)

The meaning will be 'except those whom your Lord wills to be cast in Hellfire because of his sins.'

Another group said, "The heavens and the earth refer to the heavens and the earth of Paradise, which will remain forever. The phrase 'except as your Lord wills' will be if 'ma'is taken to mean ma will refer to those people who will be put in Hell then taken out of it. If the reference is to the period then the reference will be to the time passed in Barzakh and before the judgement."

Another group said that the exception refers to the period of their life in the world. All these statements are close to one another and it could be said that Allah, the Exalted, said that the righteous people will remain forever in Paradise except the time He wills. It includes their life in the world, in Barzakh, on the Day of Judgement, on the bridge or being for some time in Hell. This verse is ambiguous and the statement 'an unceasing gift' is clear. There are many other verses, which support it, such as:
"This is Our provision which will never end." (38: 54)
"Its food and shade will be perpetual." (13: 35)

"They are not to be taken out from it." *(15: 48)*

Allah, the Exalted, has affirmed in many places the eternal staying of the people of Paradise and said, "They will not taste death there except the first one." *(44: 54)*

The statement of the Prophet 鷺, has passed that the one who enters Paradise will remain in joy and will not be distressed; he will live forever and will not die.

He also said: "A caller will call: people of Paradise, you will remain healthy without falling ill, young without being old and alive without ever dying."

Abu Sa'id al-Khudri reported that the Prophet 鷺, said, "Death will be brought in the shape of beautiful sheep and stationed between Paradise and Hell and the people of Paradise will be called; they will look being afraid. Then the people of Hell will be called and they will come being happy. They will be asked: 'Do you know it?'
They will reply: 'Yes, it is death.'

Then it will be slaughtered between Paradise and Hell and it will be announced: 'People of Paradise, it is eternal stay without death; and the People of Hell, it is eternal stay without death."[410]

The issue of the eternity of Paradise and Hell has been disputed among the later Muslim groups. There are three opinions concerning it:

1. Both Paradise and Hell will come to an end and they are not eternal, but as they were created they will cease to exist.

2. They will remain forever and will never end.

3. Paradise will remain forever and Hell will come to and end.

We will discuss these opinions and the arguments of every group and we will reject what is against the Book of Allah and the Sunnah of His Messenger.

The statement that Paradise and Hell will be eliminated is the view of Jahm ibn

---

410. Bukhari (4730), Muslim (jannah: 2849)

Safawan, the leader of Jahmiyyah who deniers of the Divine Attributes. He has no predecessor in that from among the Companions or the Followers or any of the leaders of Islam. No follower of the Sunnah has ever said it. This view has been condemned by the scholars of Islam from every corner of the world and considered as disbelief. Abdullah Ibn Ahmad said in his book 'al-Sunnah' that Kharijah ibn Mus'ab said: 'Jahmiyyah rejected three verses of the Book of Allah, the Most High:

Allah said: **"Its food and shade will be perpetual."** *(13: 35)*

But they said that it will come to an end.

The Almighty said: **"This is Our provision which will not end."** *(38: 54)*

But these people say that it will be exhausted.

Allah said: **"What you have will finish and what Allah has will remain."** *(16: 96)*

Shaykh al-Islam Ibn Taymiyyah said that this statement of Jahm is based on a principle he believed that is the impossibility of the existence of unending matters. It is the basis of the people of Theology on which they based the idea of the incidence of the matters and recurrence of them. They argued on its basis for the possibility of the world. Jahm believed that what prevents occurrence of matters without past also will prevent occurrence of something without end in future. To him perpetuity of act in future is impossible for Allah, the Exalted and Most High, as it is impossible for Him in the past. Abu al-Hudhayl al-Allaf, the leader of the Mu'tazilah agreed with him on this principle but said this requires the end of the movements because they occur one after the other. He said that the movements of the people of Paradise and Hell will come to an end and they will be in permanent silence no one of them will be able to move.

A group of those who agreed with them said that though the existence of matters without end is in accordance with the reason, but since the revelation affirmed the perpetuity of Paradise and Hell we accept it. These people did not realize that what is impossible in reason, the Shari'ah will not affirm its occurrence. It will never speak about the existence of what is impossible in reason. The revelation informs about things that the reason is incapable of understanding and does not speak about the matters which are impossible with reason.

Most of those who joined Jahm and Abu al-Hudhayl in this principle made difference between the past and the future. They said that the past has come into existence unlike the future. What is impossible is the existence of perpetual matters not their existence bit by bit. It is like the words of a person 'I will not give you a dirham but give you another after that. This is possible. To these people existence of perpetual matter in the past is impossible and its existence in the future is obligatory. The others disputed with them and said that there was no difference between the two. Past and future are relative matters; what is in future becomes past and what was in the past will be future. So it is unimaginable the possibility of perpetuity on one side and its impossibility on the other.

The followers of the Hadith say that both are equally possible and found. The Lord, glory be to Him, has infinitely power of will and having the attributes of perfection and power. Someone who is capable of act every time is not like the one who is able to act only in particular times. The one who creates is not like the one who has no power to create, and the one who manages the affairs is not like the one who is unable to do that. What kind of perfection is it in saying that the Lord of the worlds is unable to work in a known period? It will mean that He has no power to act. If you do not like this statement and say that impossible cannot be described by being out of the power, then you combined two impossible matters: saying that act was possible without reason and the transformation of a matter from proper impossibility to proper possibility without there being a reason. You claim that this is the basis on which the existence of the Creator and the occurrence of the world are based. In this way you committed crime against the reason and the Shari'ah. The Lord Almighty remains powerful on acting and speaking and He is doing what He wishes and He remains a Benevolent Lord forever.

The point is that the opinion of the end of Paradise and Hell is a heretical statement no one from the Companions, their Followers or the Muslim leaders/ scholars had said it. It is based on a false analogy. Its foundation was dubious for many people and they thought that it was true, and based on it the idea of the creation of the Qur'an and the rejection of the attributes. The Qur'an, the Sunnah and the reason have proved that the words and acts of Allah are infinite and they do not have the beginning or the end. Allah, the Exalted, said, "Say, if the whole

ocean were ink for writing the words of my Lord, it would run dry before those words were exhausted- even if We were to bring another ocean to it." (18: 109)
"If all the tress on earth were pens and all the seas, with seven more seas besides, were ink, still Allah's words would not run out. Allah is Almighty, All Wise." *(31: 27)*

Almighty informed that His words will not be exhausted because of His power and wisdom. Our Lord is as He says and above what He says; no one can imagine His power, and praise Him as He has praised Himself. One has also to remember that all the pleasure of the world from the beginning to the end is like a mustard seed in comparison to the pleasure of the Hereafter.

As for the eternity and perpetuity of Hell is concerned Shaykh al-Islam said: There are two well-known statements from the early and later scholars and the dispute about it among the Followers is well known.

I say: There are seven statements in this respect:
1. Anyone who enters it will never come out. He will abide there forever by the decree of Allah. It is the opinion of the Kharijites and the Mu'tazilah.

2. The people of Hell will be punished in it for a certain period then it will change and their nature will become fiery. They will enjoy it because of its conformity with their nature. It is the opinion of the leader of Pantheists Ibn Arabi al-Ta'i. He said in his book "Fusus al-hikam":

'Praise is for the truthfulness of the promise not of the threat. The Divine Being wishes praise for good deeds, and as such He is praised for the fulfilment of the promise and not for the threat but for relinquishing it. He said, "Never think that Allah will fail in His promise to His messengers." *(14: 47)*

He did not say 'His threat', He said:
"We will overlook their misdeeds." *(46: 16)*

He will overlook though He has given warning against them.

His statement on one side and the statement of the Mu'tazilah who say that it is not possible that Allah breaks His warning, but is rather obligatory for Him to punish those whom He has warned of torment, is on the other side. To them no one who enters Hell will be rescued, and to the Pantheists He is not going to punish anyone. Both are opposing what the Messenger stated and Allah, the Exalted, has informed.

3. The opinion that the sinners will be punished in Hell for a limited period then will be taken out and another group will take their place. This is what the Jews said to the Prophet ﷺ, and he rejected their claim as Allah had rejected it in the Qur'an. He said, "They say, 'The fire will not touch us but for a numbered days.' Say to them, 'Have you taken covenant with Allah? For Allah never breaks His covenant, or are you saying things about Allah of which you have no knowledge?' Truly whoever does evil and his sin has surrounded him; they will be the inhabitants of the Fire, they will remain in it forever." *(2: 80-81)*

"Have you considered those who were given a share of the Scripture, they are invited to the Scripture of Allah so that it should arbitrate between them; then a party of them turn away and they are refusing? This is because they declare, 'The Fire will not touch us but for a limited number of days.' The lies they have invented have led them astray in their own religion." *(3: 23-24)*

It is the statement of the Jews, the enemies of Allah. The Qur'an, the Sunnah, and the consensus of the Companions and the Followers and the leaders of Islam have proved it to be wrong.

Allah said:
"They are not going to get out of the Fire." *(2: 167)*
"They are never to be expelled from it." *(15: 48)*
"Whenever, in their anguish, they try to escape, they will be pushed back." *(22: 22)*
"There (in the Fire) they will not be finished off by death, nor be relieved from Hell's torment." *(35: 36)*
"They will not enter the Garden till a thick rope was to pass through the eye of a needle." *(7: 40)*

4. The opinion of those who say that the people of Hell will come out of it, but it will remain as it is without there a person remaining to be punished. This was mentioned by Shaykh al-Islam. The Qur'an and the Sunnah reject this view.

5. It will finish by itself because it was created after it was not there. Things that are created cannot remain forever. This is the view of Jahm ibn Safwan and his followers; they do not make difference between Paradise and Hell in this regard.

6. The view that the life and the movements of the people of Paradise and Hell will come to an end; they will become like solid and not feel any pain. It is the view of Abu al-Hudhayl al-Allaf, the Imam of the Mu'tazilah. According to him it is impossible that created matter remains eternally. Paradise and Hell are the same in this respect.

7. Some people believe that Allah who has created Hell will exterminate it; He has fixed a period for it after that it will be eliminated and its torment will end. Shaykh al-Islam said that this opinion has been attributed to 'Umar, Ibn Mas'ud, Abu Hurayrah, Abu Sa'id and others. 'Umar is reported to say:
'If the people of Hell stay in Hell for a long period there will come a day in which they will come out of it.'

Abd ibn Humayd reported it in the commentary of the words of Allah "They will stay in it for long, long time." *(78: 23)*

Abd ibn Humayd is one of the expert scholars of the Sunnah, and he reported the above statement of 'Umar from two well known scholars, namely Sulayman ibn Hrb and Hajjaj ibn Minhal who reported it from Hammad ibn Salmah who in his turn reported from Thabit and Humayd from Hasan. This chain is excellent, and though Hasan has not met 'Umar he must have heard it from some Followers, otherwise he would not have been so sure.

The people who reported it from Umar understood it to include the general people of Hell. As for those who were to be punished for their sins these scholars knew that they were to be taken out and they were not to stay in it for ages. The word 'people of Hell' is not spoken only for the believing people, but is inclusive of others as well. It is borne out by the saying of the Prophet, 襟:
"The people of Hell who are its residents will not die or live in it."[411]

It is not in contradiction with the declaration of Allah that they will abide in it eternally, and that they will not be taken out. What Allah Almighty has said is true

---
411. Muslim (iman: 185)

and will be fulfilled, but when the period of Hell is completed it will come to an end and will remain no more Fire and there will be no punishment.

Ibn Abbas said in the interpretation of the words of Allah:
"He will say: The Fire is your residence, in which you will abide eternally, except for what Allah wills. Your Lord, surely, is Wise and Knowing." *(6: 128)*

He said, "No one has right to judge for Allah in His creation and put people in Paradise or Hell."

The holders of the above view said that the verse is not restricted to the followers of the Qiblah (Muslims) because Allah Almighty said, "On the Day He will gather everyone together (saying): 'Company of Jinn! You have seduced a great many humans,' their adherents among mankind will say, 'Lord, we have profited from one another, but now we have reached the appointed time You decreed for us.' He will say: 'Your home is the Fire, and there you shall remain unless Allah wills otherwise.' Your Lord is All Wise, All Knowing. In this way, We make some evildoers have power over others through their misdeeds." *(6: 128-129)*

The allies of the Jinn from among the mankind definitely include disbelievers; they are more fit to their friendship than the evildoing Muslims. Allah said, "We made the Devils allies of those who do not believe." *(7: 27)*

"He has no power over those who believe and trust in their Lord; his power is only over those who ally themselves with him and those who, because of him, join partners with Allah." *(16: 99-100)*

"Those who are aware of Allah think of Him when Satan prompts them to do some misdeeds and immediately they see (straight); the followers of devils are led relentlessly into error by them and cannot stop." *(7: 201-202)*

"Are you going to take him and his offspring as your allies instead of Me, even though they are your enemies?" *(18: 50)*

"Fight the allies of Satan." *(4: 76)*

"They are the allies of Satan; and Satan's allies are losers." *(58: 19)*

"The devils incite their followers to argue with you; if you listen to them, you too will become idolaters." *(6; 121)*

The exception occurred in the verse which mentioned the entrance of the allies of devils into the Fire; and for this reason Ibn Abbas said that no one has authority to dictate to Allah concerning His creation.

The advocate of the view that Hell will come to an end continued saying that the argument of the people that exception made in the case of the people of Hell was to exclude the period before their entrance into it like the period of Barzakh, waiting on the Day of Judgement and the period of the world does not fit in the context of the speech. It is an exception from the declarative sentence that when these people enter Hell, they will stay there the period of the remaining of the heavens and the earth except what Allah wills. The exception does not apply to the period before entrance. No one will understand this. Consider that Allah, the Exalted, addresses them while they are in Hell when they say:

"Lord, we have profited from one another, and now we have reached the appointed time You decreed for us."

The Almighty will say then to them:
"Your home is the Fire, and there you shall remain unless Allah wills otherwise." *(6: 128)*

In their saying: "Our Lord we profited from one another" is a kind of confession and regret. It means that Jinn profited from us and we profited from them. We participated in the association, its motives and causes, and preferred indulging in enjoyment from obeying You and Your messengers. Our life passed and we wasted it in disobedience, and did not try to gain Your pleasure; we were busy throughout our life in profiting from one another. Look how they admitted the reality of their misdeeds which appeared to them on that Day. It is like their saying:

"If only we had listened, or reasoned, we would not be with the inhabitants of the blazing fire', they will confess their sin" *(67: 10-11)*

And Allah said:
"They knew that truth belongs to Allah alone." *(28: 75)*

The point is that His saying, 'except Allah wills otherwise' refers to all those mentioned whether exclusively or to them and the sinner believers. To claim that it refers only to sinful Muslims is not correct.

They said that the correct meaning is that you will remain in Hell forever unless Allah wills to punish you with something different like biting cold. Allah said, "Hell lies in wait, a home for oppressors to stay in for long, long time." *(78: 21-23)*

Long time does not imply eternity. Ibn Mas'ud said concerning this verse: 'A time will come on Hell when there will remain no one, after they have stayed in it for long time.'

Similar statements are reported from Abu Hurayrah and Abdullah ibn 'Umar. Many other scholars said about the statement of Allah:
"They will abide in it as long as the heavens and the earth endure, except what your Lord wills." *(11: 107)* that it has eliminated all the threat of the Qur'an.

Al-Tabari has quoted many scholars of the past having this opinion.

Ibn Abbas said concerning the verse that the inhabitants of Hell will not die and they will not be taken out of it as long as the heavens and the earth endure except what Allah wills, Allah has made an exception. He also said that Allah has ordered the Fire not to burn them.

Al-Sha'bi said, "Hell is the quickest of the two abodes in flourishing and the quickest in being destroyed."

Some scholars said, "Allah, the Exalted, has told us about His will concerning the inhabitants of Paradise when He said: "An uninterrupted gift", that shows that it will go beyond the endurance of the heavens and the earth, but He did not tell us about His will concerning the inhabitants of Hell, it may be in increase or may be in reduction."

Jabir reported that the Messenger of Allah, peace be upon him, read the following verse:
"Those who are wretched will be in the Fire sighing and moaning, abiding in it as along as the heavens and the earth endure except what your Lord wills."

(11:106-107)

Then he said, "If Allah wills to take out some wretched people from Hell and admit them in Paradise, He will do it."

This Hadith shows two things:
First is that if Allah wills to take some of the wretched people from Hell, He will do it. Secondly it is clear that exception refers to people who had entered Hell no to those who had not entered. The meaning then will be that except those unfortunate ones who will remain in it. It means that the unfortunates will be of two types: one who will be taken out of Hell and the other who will remain there. They will be unfortunate first then will be made among the fortunate ones. They will taste misfortune and fortune at two periods. Allah has said, "Indeed, Hell is lying in wait for the transgressors, a place of return, in which they will remain for ages. They will not taste there coolness or drink except scalding water and foul purulence, an appropriate recompense. They were not expecting an account and denied our verses emphatic denial." *(78: 23- 28)*

These verses are clear in threatening the disbelievers that their stay is not calculated by long period. That is why Abdullah ibn Amr said, "There will come a day when the doors of Hell will be shut down and no one will remain in it, and this will happen after its inhabitants have stayed in it for long, long time."

The Arguments of the people who believe that Hell will remain forever.

The people who believe that Hell will remain eternally argue for their view in the following six ways:

1. Claim of consensus. Many people believe that it is an agreed matter between the Companions and the Followers, the dispute in it happened later.

2. The Qur'an has said clearly and Allah, the Exalted, has declared that the punishment was lasting and will not subside. He will increase their torment and they will remain in it forever and will not come out of it. He also declared that Paradise is forbidden on the disbelievers and they will not enter Paradise till a

thick rope enters the eye of the needle. It will not be decreed for them to die nor its torment will be lightened fro them; its torment will be continuous without break. All this shows that Hell will be permanent and eternal.

3. Exhaustive Sunnah has spoken about coming out of those who have an atom's weight of faith in their hearts from Hell but not those who were disbelievers. All the Hadith of intercession are connected with the sinful believers that they will be brought out of Hell. If the disbelievers were to be taken out it as well, they will be like the believers and there will remain no difference between the two.

4. The Messenger has told us about it and we learnt from him. We do not need any specific text as he has also told us about the eternity of Paradise.

5. The beliefs of the early generation and the followers of the Sunnah include that Paradise and Hell are created and will not be eliminated. It is the people of innovation who say that they will come to an end.

6. The reason requires permanent stay of the disbelievers in Hell. It is based on the question which is that whether life after death and reward of the obedient and punishment of the sinners can be known by reason or it is known only by tradition? There are two answers given by the Muslim thinkers. Many of them hold that it is known by both the reason and the tradition. The Qur'an has indicated it in many places. It rejected the claim of those who tried to make the righteous and sinful equal in life and after death. It also rejected the thought that Allah created people in vain and that they will not be brought back to Him, and He will leave them without rewarding or punishing. It is damaging His wisdom and perfection; it is to say about Him that which is not appropriate for Him.
They say that the human souls will remain and their beliefs and characters will be attached to them permanently. They will regret when they see the torment but it is not because they consider their acts bad; if they were to be rescued from the torment they will go back to their deeds as Allah, the Exalted, has described:

"If you could see, when they are made to stand before the Fire, how they will say: 'If only we could be sent back, we would not reject the revelation of our Lord, but be among the believers.' No! The truth they used to hide will become all too clear to them. Even if they were brought back, they would only return to the very thing that was forbidden to them. They are certainly liars." (6: 27-28)

These people tasted the torment and experienced it but its cause and reason remained with them, and their disbelief did not go away from them. Even if they were to be sent back, they would remain disbeliever. It shows that their permanent punishment is required by the reason as it is affirmed by the revelation.

The people who believe that Hell will come to an end replied to these arguments and refuted them in the following ways:

1. The first evidence that there is consensus on this matter is not known. Only those who are not aware of dispute in this matter can claim consensus. The case is disputed in the past and the later period. If the person who claims the consensus was asked to produce ten or even one Companion who said that Hell will never be eliminated, he will fail. The reality is that the Companions believed in the opposite view as we have reported. The Followers reported it from them. Then the recognized consensus is of three types: two agreed upon and a third disputed; none of them is available in this case:

1. Consensus on those matters which are known to be parts of the religion like the pillars of Islam and prohibition of clear forbidden matters.

2. The matters about which the people of ijtihad have passed their verdict.

3. Something which was said by some people and it spread among the community and no one rejected it.

Where are any of these types in this case? If one was to claim consensus on the opposite opinion and claim that the Companions held the view that Hell will come to an end and nobody disputed it, he would be in better position than you.

The second argument that the Qur'an indicated the perpetuity of Hell and that it is not going to finish is also incorrect. Where is single evidence in the Qur'an to support it? The Qur'an tells that the disbelievers will abide forever in Hell and will not get out of it, and that their torment will not be lightened, and that they will not die and their torment in it will be permanent. There is no dispute among the Companions, the Followers and the Muslim scholars about it. This is not the matter of dispute. Dispute is about whether Hell is eternal or it is going to terminate? As for the question of the disbelievers not coming out of it and their punishment not being lightened and that they will not die and will not enter Paradise until the thick rope goes through the eye of the needle, there is no dispute among the Companions or the Followers and the Muslim leaders. Jews, the Pantheists and some followers of innovations rejected it. The texts of the Qur'an and Hadith affirm their remaining in the abode of torment as long as it is there; they will not get out of it. It is the believers in the oneness of Allah who will be taken out of it while it is still there. The difference is between the one who will be released from the prison while it is there and the one who will be rescued because of the destruction of the prison.

3. The claim that widespread reports speak about the getting out of the believers who committed grave sins from Hell and not the polytheists, is true. It is a proof of what we have said that the believers will be taken out of Hell while it is there not terminated. The polytheist will remain in it as long as it there.

4. Your claim that the Messenger of Allah, peace be upon him, has informed us that the disbelievers will remain in Hell is true. But they will be in it as long as it is there. He did not say that Hell will not come to an end like Paradise, give us a single piece of evidence from the Qur'an or the Sunnah to support your claim.

5. Your argument that it is among the beliefs of the followers of the Sunnah that Paradise and Hell are created and they will not be terminated is not absolutely correct. It is the opinion of the Jahmiyyah and the Mu'tazilah. No one among the Companions or their Followers or the Muslim scholars has said it. The termination of Hell is said by the Companions and their Followers as we had shown you. There is difference between the two abodes. What has been proved by the Book and the Sunnah and the statements of the Companions must be accepted and anything against it must be rejected. Mu'adh ibn Jabal used to say:

'Allah is the Fair judge. May the doubtful people perish! After your period there will be trials; wealth will be plenty and the Qur'an will be available, and the believer, hypocrite, women, and children, black and red - everyone will read it. It is likely that a man says: 'I read the Qur'an and I do not see that you follow me. So I have to invent something else.' Be watchful of his innovation because every innovation is misguidance. Be also careful about the deviation of the wise man. Satan sometimes speaks on the tongue of the wise man the word of deviation. A hypocrite may speak true; you should accept the truth from anyone who brings it. Truth has light.

They asked him: 'What is the deviation of the wise person?'
He replied: it is something that Impresses you and you reject it, and say: What is it? Be careful from his deviation because he may turn around and say truth. Knowledge and faith will remain on their places until the Day of Judgement.'[412]

The belief of the followers of the Sunnah is based on what has been established in the Book and the Sunnah and on which the pious ancestors have agreed. It includes that Paradise and Hell are created and that the inhabitants of Hell are not going to get out of it, nor their punishment will be lightened and they will abide there forever. Anyone who said that Hell is not going to be terminated took it from the followers of innovation and was unaware of the reports concerning it.

The last point made by those who said that Hell is eternal is that it is determined by reason. It is a case that cannot be known but by the information of the truthful i.e. the Prophet, peace be upon him. The matter of reward and punishment whether it can be known by reason together with tradition or can be known only by tradition? There are two opinions among the Muslim scholars. The correct is that reason has indicated life after death and reward and punishment in general but the details can only be known by tradition. The eternity of reward and punishment is not known by reason alone; it is known by the tradition and it has indicated that the reward of the righteous people was eternal and the punishment of the sinful Muslims will come to an end. What will happen to the disbelievers is disputed and the one who has support from the tradition is luckiest. With Allah rests help.

Difference between the position of Paradise and Hell

Now we would like to explain the difference between the perpetuity of Paradise and Hell by reason and religion. It is by the following ways:

1. Allah, the Exalted has stated that the pleasure of the people of Paradise was permanent not to end and suspended. He, glory be to Him, did not tell us more than the inhabitants of Hell will remain in it forever and will not come out of it;

---

412. Abu Dawud (4611)

they will neither die or live, and it is closed on them whenever they want to get out they will be pushed back in it, and its torment is lasting and there will be no relief for them. The difference between two statements is clear.

2. Allah, the Glorious, has spoken of Hell in three verses, which indicate that it is not perpetual. First He said, **"Hell is your residence; you will abide in it forever except what Allah wills. Your Lord is Wise, Knowledgeable."** *(6: 128)*

Secondly He said:
"They will remain there forever as long as the heavens and the earth endure except what your Lord wills. Surely, your Lord carries out what He wills." *(11: 106)*

Thirdly, he said:
"They will stay in it for long, long time." *(78: 23)*

If it were not for the evidences of perpetuity of Paradise both exceptions would have been one, but there is difference between the two. He said in the case of the inhabitants of Hell: "Your Lord carries out what He wills." We learnt from His statement that the Almighty wants to do something, which He did not inform us. On the other hand, He said concerning the people of Paradise "It is an uninterrupted gift." We learnt that the gift and the pleasure of the residents of Paradise are not going to be cut off. The conclusion is that torment is temporary and limited and the pleasure is not.

3. It has been established that no one who has not done any good at all from those who will be taken by Allah from Hell will enter Paradise, and no one who has not committed any sin will not go to Hell because Allah does not subject to torment except those who have disobeyed Him.

4. It is also established that Allah, the Exalted, will create another people for Paradise on the Day of Judgment. He will put them in it, but He will not do this in the case of Hell. The report in Bukhari that Allah will create another people for Hell is a mistake by some reporters who turned the statement upside down. It is as Bukhari himself has recorded in the same chapter 'For Paradise Allah will create another people'. [413]

---

413. Bukhari (7448, 4850, 7384)

The purpose is to declare that Hell cannot be compared with Paradise in the case of eternity.

5. Paradise is the cause of the mercy and pleasure of Allah and Hell is the result of His anger and wrath, and the mercy of Almighty dominates and overwhelms His wrath as is reported in the following authentic Hadith:
"When Allah completed the creation He wrote in a book which is with Him, 'My mercy overwhelms My anger.'[414]

If it is as described, putting what is the cause of His mercy on the same level with the result of His anger is unacceptable.

6. What is for mercy and by mercy is meant for itself like the goals; and what is the cause of the wrath and anger is intended for other purposes like the means. It means that what is by mercy will be ahead and overwhelming that which is by anger.

7. Allah, the Glorious and Exalted, said to Paradise: 'You are My mercy, I show it to whoever I wish', and said to Hell: 'You are My wrath, I show it to whoever I will.'

His punishment is a separate matter produced by His anger, but His mercy here is Paradise itself. It is created from the mercy, which is among the attributes of the Merciful. Here there are four matters: mercy that is the attribute of Allah, the Merciful; the reward which a separate matter produced by His mercy; and anger which is attached to Him, and the punishment which the result of it. When the quality of mercy dominates the quality of anger, it is more appropriate that what is by mercy should dominate what is by wrath. Hell which is the result of anger cannot face Paradise, which is the outcome of mercy.

8. Hellfire is created to scare the believers and purify the sinners and guilty. It is, therefore, meant to cleanse the soul from the filth attached to it in this world. If it was purified here by sincere repentance, erasing good deeds and obliterating afflictions, there will be no need of purification there. It will be said to it with other pure people: 'Peace be upon you, enter it to remain there forever.' But if it was not cleansed in this world and passed to the other world with its filth, impurity and dirt, it will be put in Hell and will remain there to get purified from these filths,

---

414. Bukhari (7384)

which cannot be wiped out by water. When it is purified completely will be taken out of the Fire.

Allah, the Exalted, created His servants on upright way which is the natural disposition of Allah instilled in mankind. If they were left with their natural disposition, they would have grown on Tawhid, but many of them faced things which changed them. That is why the portion of Hell is more than that of Paradise. The change in the nature of mankind was of various levels known only to Allah. Then Allah sent His messengers and revealed His books to remind the people of their nature on which they were created. Those who were helped and Allah has decreed good for them realized that what the messengers brought was correct. The books guided them to the first natural disposition. They knew that Allah's religion which He has sent with His messengers agree with the natural disposition on which Allah created them. The revealed guidance and pure natural instinct kept them away from being polluted with filth and dirt. Whenever something of that touched them and Satan prompts them, they attack it by the religion and instinct and remove its impact. The Lord Almighty designs for them what they love and hate by which they remove those traces which confuses the instinct. Then the cause of mercy approaches and finds a place suitable and ready having nothing to thwart it. It says: 'This is where I am commanded to be.'

Allah, the Exalted, has no purpose in punishing His servants without reason. He has declared:
"What Allah will gain by making you suffer torment if you are thankful and believe in Him? Allah is Appreciative, All-Knowing." (4: 147)

However, the unfortunate ones continued in changing the upright nature and turning it from what it was created to its opposite till corruption took root and change was complete. They, therefore, needed another change which can undertake their purification because they recited verses of Allah, and the evidences of the world and His good and bad decrees did not bring them to the right path. He provided them with other signs, decrees and torments above what was in the world to remove the filth and dirt which can only be removed by the Fire. Once the cause of punishment was removed, the torment was taken off and remained only the reason of mercy without any resistance.

If it is said that what you said is true but the cause of punishment will not go away

unless it is temporary like the sins of the believers. If it is a permanent one like disbelief or association of partners, its effect will not go away. Allah, the Glorious, has indicated this fact in many places of His Book. He said for example:
"If they were returned, they would return to what they were forbidden." *(6: 28)*

It shows that their nature is willing to accept anything but the disbelief and association of partners; it is unable to believe. In another verse Allah, the Exalted, said, "Whoever is blind in this world will be blind in the Hereafter, even further of the path." *(17: 72)*

Here Allah Almighty says that their blindness from the guidance is permanent and will not go away even with witnessing the facts which the messengers brought. If it is so that their error and blindness will not depart them, so their result and effect will also remain with them.

In another verse Allah said, **"If Allah had known there was any good in them, He would have made them hear, but even if He had, they would still have turned away and taken no notice."** *(8:23)*

This verse tells that there is no good in them to make them deserve mercy. If there was any good in them, its impact would not have been lost. The following Hadith also indicates that there is no good in them:
"Get out from Hell anyone in whose heart there is an atom's weight of good."

If these people had smallest atom's weight of good, they would have been taken out from Hell with others.

It will be said in answer to the above question that by Allah it is the strongest point to be held on this issue. The matter is as you said that the punishment will remain with the cause. Undoubtedly, they are in the Hereafter in error and blindness as they were in the world; their inner sides are dirty as they were in the world. So the torment will continue as long as they remain like that. However, the point is that the disbelief, rejection and the wickedness are an innate quality in them, which cannot be removed, or they are accidental and temporary which can be removed? This is the core of the issue, and there is nothing to suggest that they are innate and cannot be removed. Allah, the Exalted, has said that He created His servants on the upright path, but Satan turned them away from it. It means that Almighty did not create them on disbelief and denial of truth, but created them on acknowledgement of their Creator and love of Him and confession of His oneness. If the truth, which they were born with, can be removed by disbelief and false association, the possibility of the removal of disbelief and association by their opposite is easier.

There is no doubt that if they were returned on that condition which they were, they would return to things they were forbidden. But how can you say that that condition will not change and replaced by another, which Allah Almighty will create after the Fire had cleansed them, and the wisdom of their torment was fulfilled? The torment was not in vain but for a desired wisdom. When that wisdom was achieved no purpose remained in their punishment. Allah, the Glorious, does not vent out His anger by punishing His servants as a wronged gets satisfaction from his oppressor. He, glory be to Him, dose not punish His servants for this purpose, but punishes to cleanse them and show His mercy to them. His punishment is in the interest of the servant even if it causes him pain as the prescribed punishments in the world are in the interest of the offender. Allah has called these legal punishments as torment. His wisdom requires fixing a suitable medicine for every disease, and the medicine of the serious disease always is the hardest. A kind doctor treats the patient by cauterization with fire again and again to take out the bad stuff, which occurs on straight nature. If he thinks that cutting off a part of the body is good for the patient, he cuts it and makes him experience severe pain. It is the decree of the Lord in removing the strange material, which appeared on the right nature of the servant without his choice. What will be the case if the bad materials appear on the right nature by the choice of the servant?

If an intelligent person considers the rules and decrees of the Lord in the world and His reward and punishment in the Hereafter, he will realize the balance and uniformity and the connection of one with the other. This is because the source of all that is the perfect knowledge, comprehensive mercy and encompassing wisdom of the Lord. He, the Glorious, is the Truth and Manifest; His kingdom is the kingdom of mercy, generosity and justice.

9. Allah, the Merciful, does not punish a person because He needs to do that. His punishment is not to gain any benefit or remove any harm or do away with pain. He is above all these matters as He is pure from all faults and imperfections,

which have no purpose or wisdom. His punishment is either a part of the grace of His allies and beloved ones, or in the interest of the unfortunate to cure them. It could be for this and that. In any case punishment is a matter which is meant as a tool and not as a goal. When the object of the tool is achieved it is abandoned. The pleasure of His obedient servants is not dependent on the continuity of the punishment of His enemies. The interest of the unlucky ones is not in perpetuity and continuity though there is interest in mere punishment of them.

10. The pleasure and mercy of the Lord Almighty are personal qualities of Him. There is no limit for His pleasure; it is as the most knowledgeable man of Him has said, "Glory be to Allah and praise is for Him the amount of His creation, pleasure of Him, the weight of His Throne and the ink of His words."[415]

If His mercy dominates His anger then His pleasure is greater and more superb. His pleasure, in reality, is more than the Gardens and their delights and all that is in them. He has told the residents of Paradise that He will show His pleasure to them and will never be angry with them. As for His anger and wrath are concerned, they are not personal qualities of Him, which cannot be separated from Him to make Him angry throughout. People have two opinions about the quality of anger:

1. That it is a practical attribute of Him like other acts;
2. it is a practical quality separate from Him and not attached to Him.

In either case it is not like the attributes of life, knowledge and power which can never be detached from Him. Punishment originates from His quality of anger; the Fire was started by His anger. It is reported in a Prophetic Tradition:
"Allah has created a people from His anger and lodged them in the east; He revenges by them those who disobey Him."

His creations are of two types one created by mercy and the other created by anger. He has absolute perfection from all sides and its opposite is not possible. He is pleased, gets angry, rewards and punishes, gives and withholds, grants honours and causes humiliation, takes revenge and forgives. This is the effect of His power which is joined with wisdom, mercy and praise. If His anger is changed by His pleasure, His punishment goes away, and it becomes mercy. In reality

---

415. Muslim (dhikr: 2726)

it has been mercy though its shape and quality were of different shape. The punishment of the sinful was mercy and their getting out of the Fire was mercy. They lived in His mercy in the world and in the Hereafter. One is in line with their wishes and they like it, and the other is not according to their liking and they dislike it and find it hard. It is like the mercy of the doctor who cuts off some of the flesh of a sick person and burns it to take out the bad and spoiled stuff from it.

It could be said that this is a wrong analogy. The doctor does it to the patient because he loves him; his action is not out of anger with him, and it is not considered punishment. The punishment of the sinners was due to the anger of Almighty; and that is pure punishment.

The answer is that what you said is true, but though it is punishment, it is mercy to them as well, and there is no contradiction between the two. It is like applying the legal punishment in the world, which is punishment and mercy as it is meant for removing the fault and purifying the person. These disbelievers caused Allah to be angry and deserved the severe anger and wrath of Him. They treated Him in a way which was not appropriate for Him, denied Him and rejecting His messengers.

Furthermore, they set the meanest of His creature as partner with Him, preferred his pleasure over the pleasure of their Lord and obeyed him in place of obedience of Allah Almighty while it was He who did favour to them; created them, provided them and He was their real Master. This shows the perfection of His Name and Attributes the effects of which cannot be missed. The rejection of His Attributes is to abandon their realities, which is impossible. The people who deny the Attributes of Allah are two types: those who deny His Attributes; and those who deny their rules and effects. For this reason their torment was punishment from this side and a remedy from the side of the mercy which preceded the anger. Here they two matters come together. When the anger disappears because of the removal of its cause, and the spoiled material is removed by the change of the nature through burning in Hell for a long period and the wisdom which required the punishment was completed, the mercy did its job and showed its effect without any hindrance.

11. Forgiving is a more desirable matter to Almighty than taking revenge, and mercy is dearer to Him than punishment. He also loves to be pleased more

than be angry, and do favour instead of exacting the justice. The traces of this love are noticed in His decrees and commands and they are very clear in the reward and punishment of His servants. Since He loves to show kindness and for this He created the creation, revealed the Books and set the religious rules and regulations, decreed to purify the sinful by subjecting them to torment. His power is absolute; there is no defect in it. The sinners were affected with these spoiled materials, which were a kind of disease and He holds cure for it. It is He who knows medicine for every disease, and He has absolute power, complete mercy and unlimited capability while the servant is in great need of someone who can treat his illness, which is causing him severe pain and harm. The servant is aware that he is ill and his cure is in the hand of the Praiseworthy who is above need. Knowing this he approaches Him, pleads with Him, shows humility, his heart is broken, he submits to His power and realizes that all praise belongs to Him and all the creatures are under His command. He also realizes that it is he who is ignorant and wrongdoing; his Lord treated him with full justice, and He deserves full praise for all what He has done. He also comes to understand that it was due to His praise that brought him to this position and gave him access to Him. He has no good by himself in any way; it is only the grace and favour of Allah, which rescued him. He had no way for release from his ordeal except by the acknowledging his shortcomings and begging for pardon. His soul is to be blamed for all defect, failing and disgrace while his Lord deserves every praise, perfection and glorification. If the residents of the Hellfire realize His grace, mercy, perfection and praise which brought them to this position, and they asked for His pleasure even by remaining in that condition and said:

'If it is Your pleasure to keep us in this condition, we have no objection. Our aim is to achieve Your pleasure. We reached this stage because we pursued what was undesirable to You. If it is makes You pleased, Your pleasure is what we seek. Any wound which makes You pleased is not painful to us. You are more kind to us than ourselves. You have better knowledge of our interests; praise is for You whether You punish us or forgive us.' If they plead in this way the fire will turn for them cool and safe.

Al-Aswad ibn Sari' reported that the Prophet ﷺ said, "Four people will come on the Day of Judgement; a deaf who could no hear anything; a stupid; an aged man and a person who died in the period of break of the messengers. The deaf will say, 'Lord, Islam came and I was unable to hear anything.' The stupid will say, Lord, 'Islam came and the children used to hit me by dung.' The aged person will say,

Lord, 'Islam came and I was unable to understand anything.' The person who died in the period of the break of messengers will say, 'Lord, no messenger came to me.' Allah will take their pledge that they will obey Him. Then He will order them to enter the Fire. By the One who holds Muhammad's soul in His hand, if they entered it, it would have become cool and safe for them."

A similar report by Abu Hurayrah has the following addition:
"Whoever enters it, it will be cool and safe for him, and the one who does not, will be dragged to it."[416]

These people when they agreed for their punishment and rushed to it knowing that it was the pleasure of their Lord and obeyed His command, the Fire turned for them as delight.

Abu Hurayrah also reported the Messenger of Allah, peace be upon him, saying, "Two people from among those who were put in the Fire started yelling and screaming. Allah, the Exalted ordered to bring them out. When they were presented before Him, He asked: 'Why were you yelling so loudly?' They replied: 'We did it so that You show mercy to us.' He said: My mercy for you is to go back and throw yourselves where you were in Hell.' One of them throws himself in the Fire and Allah, the Most High, makes it cool and safe for him. The other one stays and does not do as he was told. Allah will ask him: 'What made you not follow your companion and throw yourself in the Fire?' He will say: 'My Lord, I hope You will not return me to it after You had taken me out of it.' Allah Almighty will say, 'You got what you hoped for and both will enter Paradise by the mercy of Allah."
[417]

Bilal ibn Sa'd narrated, "Two people of Hell will be taken out of Hell. When they will stand before Allah, He will ask them; 'How did you find your stay and the result of your misdeeds? They will reply: 'The worst place and the worst result for people to gain.' Almighty will say to them: This is the result of what you did, I am not dealing unfairly with the people.' Then He will order them to be taken to the Fire. One of them will go in his chains and handcuffs and throw himself in Hell. The other will hesitate and they will be ordered to be brought back, and He will ask the one who threw himself to the Fire: 'What made you do it when you were

416. Ahmad (16300-16302)
417. Tirmidhi (2599)

taken out of it?' He replied: 'I have experienced the result of disobeying You and had no intention of doing it again.' He will ask the one who hesitated: 'Why did you do that?' He said: 'My good opinion about You was that once You brought me out, You will not return me back to it.'

Then Allah will show His mercy to both of them and order them to be taken to Paradise."

12. The reward and delight are the requisite of His mercy, pardon, kindness and generosity. That is why He attributes them to Himself. The punishment and castigation are His creations. He, therefore, is not called the punisher and castigator. He distinguishes between them even in one verse as He said, **"Tell My servants that I am the Forgiving, Merciful; and My torment is painful torment."** *(15: 49-50)*

"Know that Allah is severe in punishment and Allah is Forgiving, Merciful." *(5: 98)*

"Your Lord is quick in punishment and He is Forgiving, Merciful." *(7: 167)*

What is the requisite of His Names and Attributes will last like them mainly if it is among the matters He loves; and it is required by itself. The evil, which is torment, is not included in His Name and Attributes though it is among His acts for some wisdom. When it is achieved, the result disappears unlike the good; He is permanent in doing good; His good never ceases. He is eternally generous from the time immemorial. He has been and still is kind, but it is not so in the case of punishment. He is not eternally in punishing and is not always angry taking revenge. Consider this difference in the case of the Names and Attributes of Allah, the Exalted, it will open a door for you about His recognition and love.

13. The person who knew Him better and understood His Names and Attributes said "Evil is not to You."

The one who explained it that evil is not a means of coming close to You did not get to the intended meaning. Evil is in no way to be attributed to Him, glory be to Him, neither in His essence nor His attributes, nor His acts nor His Names. He has full perfection from every side. His Attributes are the qualities of perfection for which He is praised and lauded. His acts are all good, mercy, justice and wisdom there is no evil in them in any way. His Names are all beautiful. How then can evil be attributed to Him? Evil is among His works and creations which are separate from Him. The created matter has both good and evil in it. The Prophet did not say: 'You do not create evil' so that we need its explanation. He denied the attribution of evil to Him in His Names, acts and Attributes.

When it is known then evil is no more than sins and their causes. The good, on the other hand, is belief, righteous deeds ant their cause. Belief and good deeds are connected with Allah, the Glorious, and for them He created the creation and sent His messengers and revealed His books. They are acknowledgement of the sovereignty of Allah Almighty, His glorification, exaltation and praise. These acts have effects which continue as long they are found. Evils are not meant for themselves; they are not the aim for which He created His creation. They are designed for some desirable matters for which they are made as means. When their goal is achieved they are suppressed and vanish and the matter returns back to good.

14. Almighty has told that His mercy covers everything. There is nothing but His mercy is found in it. It is not in contradiction with the fact that He sometimes shows His mercy in a way which is painful and difficult for a person, and he does not like it. It is also part of His mercy as has been explained. We have cited the Hadith of Abu Hurayrah about two persons to whom He said:
"My mercy to you is that you go and throw yourselves where you were in the Fire."

It is said in some reports that when a person prays for someone severely afflicted and says, 'O Allah, show mercy to him', the Lord Almighty says: 'How can I show mercy for something which is mercy for him?' Affliction is mercy from Him for His servants.

In a Divine narration Allah, the Exalted, says, "Those who remember Me are the people of my company, those who carry out My commands are the people of My honour, and those who thank Me are the people who deserve more. Those who disobey Me I will not make them despair of My mercy. If they repent, I am their beloved, if they do not, I am their curer. I try them with disasters in order to cleanse them from defects."

The affliction and punishment are the means to remove the diseases that cannot be cured except by them. The Fire is the biggest remedy. If a person was cured in the world, he will be free from treatment in the Hereafter. Otherwise he must undergo the treatment according to his disease. Anyone who knows the Lord Almighty with His attributes of greatness and perfection, and acknowledges His wisdom, mercy, kindness, benevolence, generosity and love of His servants and that His mercy is ahead of His wrath, he will not deny it though he may not hurry to accept it.

15. The actions of Allah, the Exalted, are not out of wisdom and mercy, and interest and justice. He does not do anything in vain or unfairly or without reason. He is above all these as He is above all defects and faults. If it is so, then the punishment of the disobedient people is mercy for them to remove their dirt and complete their purification. If it is for wisdom so when it is achieved, the punishment ends. It is not part of the wisdom of the Lord Almighty to continuously punish the people. If it is in the interest of punishment of His friends, it does not require it to be eternal. The joy of His friends is not dependent on their parents, sons and spouses on remaining in permanent torment.

If you say that it is based only on the will of Allah and there is no wisdom involved in it, it will be answered in two ways:

First, it is impossible for the fairest of the judges and All- Knowing that His actions be empty from interests, wisdom and good aims. The Qur'an, the Sunnah and the evidences of the reasons and intellects and all present signs prove it.

Secondly, if it were so, to keep them in torment and remove it from them will be same to His will. To end it is not damaging His perfectness. He has not said that punishment is eternal and will never end. The only option in this case will be to say that it is among the possible matters and depends on the information of the true one. If you follow the way of justifying by the wisdom and mercy, it will not require permanency, and if you follow the way of wisdom not known, it does not require it either, and if it is based on mere narration, there in nothing in it to decide it.

16. The mercy of Allah, the Glorious, overwhelmed His anger concerning those who are punished. He created them by His mercy and took care of them by His

mercy. He provided them and granted them safety by His mercy. He sent to them the messengers out of His mercy. The causes of revenge and punishment are after the motives of the mercy and temporary. His mercy went ahead of His anger for them. He created them in a way that His mercy was closer to them than His anger and punishment. This is proved by the fact that He covered the children of the disbelievers with His mercy; whoever sees them, shows kindness to them. This is why He forbade killing them; here also His mercy dominates His wrath. In every condition they are under His mercy whether in trial or safety. When His mercy is dominant, its effect is not eliminated completely though because of their deeds the effect of anger and wrath may appear on it. The effect of mercy is from Almighty; He wants to show mercy to them, but they cause punishment for themselves. If His mercy overwhelms His anger, the impact of mercy should necessarily overwhelm the impact of anger.

17. The Lord Almighty tells us that the punishment is the punishment of a barren Day, the great Day and the punishment of painful Day, but He never said that the pleasure is of one day, not in a single place in His Book. In an authentic Hadith the Messenger of Allah, peace be upon him, said, "The day of the Judgement is estimated to be of fifty thousand years."

Those who are punished will be staying in torment in accordance with their misdeeds. Allah Almighty made punishment for what was done in the world, and what was done for the sake of the world and not for the sake of Allah. But what was done for the Hereafter and meant by it the pleasure of Allah, there will be no punishment for it. The world has a limited period after which it will come to an end; what a person sends from it to the Hereafter, which was not meant for Allah, will be the cause of his torment. But what he sent ahead and intended by it the pleasure of Allah and the Hereafter, he intended what is not going to end, and as such it remain forever because the aim he had in mind is not going to finish. It is so because if the desired aim is permanent, its effect will also be permanent, unlike the diminishing aim, which will come to an end. Whatever is done for the sake of Allah will remain forever. When the world comes to the end and its works stop, and what was done in it for the sake of other than Allah Almighty, it will turn into pain and torment unlike the pleasure, which will last forever.

18. It is not the part of the wisdom of the best of the Judges to create a creation to punish them forever, which will not end and cease. There are evidences of

revelation and reason and nature to prove that He, the Glorious, is Wise and is the best of the Judges. If He punishes His creation, He does it for some wisdom. In the same way all the pains and afflictions in the world, which Almighty decrees they come from the Wise who has wisdom and benefit for the servants, and they are meant to purify them and treat them by taking the rotten stuff out of them. They are to lead the purification and the remedy of the souls and to give them warning and tell them about their poverty and need to their Lord. There are many other benefits and good aims, which are known only to Allah Almighty. Paradise is pure and only pure people will enter it. This explains that those who will enter it will be stopped after crossing the Bridge on a place between Hell and Paradise and they will have to account for the wrongs they did to one another in the world. When they are cleansed and purified they will be allowed to enter Paradise. It is well known that if the wicked souls were returned to the world before punishment, they will return to those acts, which they were prohibited; these types of people are entitled to stay in the House of Peace in the neighbourhood of the Lord of the universe. When they are punished by fire, their souls will be cleansed from the filth and dirt, and this is also by the wisdom of the Most Powerful Judge. His mercy is not in contradiction with His wisdom. He created them with some dirt, which will be removed by lengthy affliction and burning in the Fire as the dirt and filth of gold and silver are removed. This is understood as wisdom and is required for the world, which is created on this quality. The creation of the souls the evil of which cannot be removed and their punishment will not end is not the part of wisdom and mercy. The scholars are not agreed about the existence of people who are evil from every side and have no good at all. If we consider their existence, the Lord Almighty, has power to change the nature and qualities of things. When the desired wisdom of their creation is found, Allah has power to recreate them on a different nature and show a different type of His mercy to them in that form.

19. It has been established that Allah, the Glorious, will create another people for Paradise and put them in it. They will be the people who had not done any good deeds to deserve to enter Paradise. For those people who were put in Hellfire when the torment reached its limit and achieved its objective, their souls would be humbled down, submit and subdue and acknowledge the praise of their Lord and that He had dealt fairly with them. They will realize that in that condition they were in lighter punishment; if He had wished, He would have made it much harder. He decreed punishment for them in order to bring

them to achieve His pleasure. He knew that punishment suited them and they deserved it. Once they experienced the punishment all their bad materials were cleansed and disappeared and were replaced by the humbleness and praise of the Lord, the Blessed and Exalted. It was not His wisdom to keep them in torment after that as their evil has changed into good; their association has turned into acknowledgement of the oneness and their arrogance into humility and submissiveness.

It is not in contradiction with the words of Allah Almighty, **"If they were brought back, they would have returned to what they were forbidden."** *(6: 28)*

It applies to the situation before the punishment, which removes all the filths. The verse describes the condition when they will see the Fire before they enter it. Allah said, **"If you could only see, when they are made to stand before the Fire, and they say: 'If only we could be sent back, we would not reject the revelations of our Lord, but be among believers.' No! The truth they used to hide will become completely clear to them. Even if they were returned back, they would return to the very things that were forbidden to them. They are such liars!"** *(6: 27-28)*

They will say it before the punishment will purge from them their filths. But when they stay in the punishment for a long period, it is impossible that the association, arrogance and filth will remain in them.

20. It is reported on the authority of Abu Sa'id al-Khudri in the Hadith of intercession that the Messenger of Allah, peace be upon him, said, "Then Allah, the Most High, will say: 'The angels have interceded as well as the prophets and the believers, now only the Greatest of the merciful remains. He will take one handful from Hell and will bring out of it people who had never done any good deed. They had become charred, He will put them in a river of Paradise called 'the River of Life', and they will come out of it as the seed grows in the flood. The people of Paradise will say: 'They are the freed people of Allah; He put them in Paradise without doing any good deed.'"[418]

The Fire has burnt these people and there was no part in their bodies, which was not burnt by it. The apparent citation shows that these will be people who had

---

418. Bukhari

not an atom's equal of faith. It is clear from the context of the report because it says that Allah will order the angels to go back to the Fire and get out of it anyone who had an atom's equal of faith in his heart, and they will bring out a large number of such people. Then Almighty will say that the angels have made intercession and so did the prophets and the believers, and remains only the Most Merciful of the merciful, and He will take a handful people out of the Fire.

It is clear from the text that these people did not have the tiniest part of faith in their hearts, but the mercy brought them out. An example of the mercy of the Merciful is the case of the person who instructed his family to burn him after his death and spread his ashes in the land and the sea thinking that he will escape Allah in this way. This man doubted in the return and power of Allah, and had never done any good deed. Despite that Allah will ask him: 'What made you to do that?' He will reply: 'Fear of You, and You know better.' Allah showed mercy to him. [419]

The Almighty had points of wisdom in His creation which the reasons of mankind cannot comprehend.

In another Hadith reported by Anas the Messenger of Allah, peace be upon him, said, "Allah, the Exalted will say: 'Bring out of the Fire anyone who had remembered Me only one day or feared Me in a situation.'"[420]

Who is there who has not remembered Allah once throughout his life from the beginning to the end or feared Him at all? When Allah's mercy will take out anyone who has remembered Him or feared Him once, it is not strange that Hell is destroyed.

21. The full acknowledgement of the servant of his shortcoming, which includes attribution of wrongdoing and failing to himself and attribution of justice, praise, mercy and perfection to his Lord from every side, will implore his Lord, the Glorious, and attract His mercy towards him. When Almighty wills to show His mercy to His servant, He puts it in his heart especially when it is accompanied by a firm intention of the servant that he will never go back to commit anything that will cause the anger of his Lord. When Allah knows that this feeling has taken root

419. Bukhari 97508)
420. Tirmidhi (2594)

in the heart of the servant, His mercy comes to him immediately. Abu Umamah reported that the Messenger of Allah, blessing and peace be upon him, said, "The Last person to enter Paradise will be a man who will be turning on the Bridge upside down like a boy whom his father beats and he runs away from him. This person's deeds are unable to make him run, so he says: 'My Lord, take me to Paradise and save me from Hell.' Allah will inspire to him: 'My servant, if I rescued you from the Fire and admit you into Paradise, you will confess your sins and faults?' He will reply: 'Yes my Lord, by Your might and power, if You rescue me from the Fire, I will surely admit my sins and faults.'

He will cross the Bridge, and say in his mind: 'If I confess my sins and faults, He will return me to the Fire.' Allah will inspire to him: 'My servant, confess your sins and mistakes, I will forgive you and admit you to Paradise.'

The servant will say: 'By Your might and power, I never committed any sin and did not make any mistake.'

Allah will say to him: 'My servant, I have a witness against you.'

The man will look right and left and see no one. He will say: 'My lord, show me your witness.' Then Allah will make his skin speak of his minor sins. When the servant sees it, he will say: 'My Lord, by Your might and power, I have great sins.'

Allah will say: 'My servant, I know them more than you. Confess them and I will forgive you, and admit you into Paradise.'

The servant will confess his sins and will enter Paradise.

The Messenger of Allah, peace be upon him, laughed at this point till his molar teeth were seen, then he said, "He is the lowest person in rank, how will be the one above him?"

The Lord Almighty wants the servant to admit his shortcoming, submit and subdue himself before Him, and make firm intention to follow what can bring His pleasure. As long as the people of Hell lack this spirit they are lacking the spirit of Paradise. When the Lord, the Exalted, wishes to show His mercy to them, He puts it in their minds and the mercy reaches them. Allah's power is not short of doing it, and there is nothing against the prerequisite of His Names and Attributes, and He had said that He is going to do what He wishes.

22. Allah, the Most Powerful, has told that He had fixed permanent staying in Hell on certain grave sins and enforced it with forever. But it does not mean that it will not end. He said, "Whoever kills a believer intentionally, his recompense is Hell, where he will abide eternally. Allah has become angry with him and has cursed him and has prepared for him a great punishment." (4: 93)

The Prophet ﷺ confirmed it by saying, "Whoever kills himself by a piece of iron, his piece will be with him and he will hurt himself with it in the Hell fire forever."[421]

In another Hadith he said, "Allah will say about a man who killed himself: 'My servant hurried to Me, I have forbidden Paradise for him.'"[422]

More precise than all that is the words of Allah, the Glorious, **"Whoever disobeys Allah and His Messenger, for him is the Fire of Hell in which they will abide forever."** (72: 23)

This is a warning fixed with permanency and eternity, yet it is to end with a cause of the servant that is acknowledgement of the oneness of Allah. In the same way the general warning of the people of Hell does not mean that it will not be suspended by the One who has decreed upon Himself mercy, and His mercy has dominated His wrath. The Messenger ﷺ, said, "Allah created mercy on the day He created hundred parts of mercy."

He said at the end of the Hadith, "If a disbeliever knows the amount of mercy which is with Allah, he would never despair of Paradise. And if a Muslim knows what kind of punishment He has in store, he will not feel safe from the Fire."[423]

23. If Allah, the Exalted, had said in clear words that the torment of Hell has no end and it is eternal, it would have been a promise from Him, and Allah does not break His promise. As for the threat the view of the followers of the Sunnah is that breaking it is kindness, pardon and relinquishment from Him for which He is praised and glorified. It is His right if He wishes, He can leave it, and if He

421. Bukhari (5778), Muslim (iman: 175), Tirmidhi (2044), Nisa'i (1963)
422. Bukhari (1364)
423. Bukhari (6469)

wishes, He can take it in full. However, a generous person does not take his dues in full; so imagine what the most generous of all generous beings would do. He, the Glorious, has stated in many places in His Book that He does not break His promise, but He never said in any place that He does not break His threat.

Anas reported that the Messenger of Allah, peace be upon him, said:

"Whoever Allah has promised a reward on a deed, He will fulfil it, but anyone whom He has threatened punishment on a deed, He has option in it."[424]

Amr ibn 'Ubayd came to Abu 'Amr ibn al-'Ala' and said, 'Abu 'Amr, does Allah break what He promises?'

He replied: 'No.'

Amr said, 'Tell me if Allah has threatened someone a punishment on a deed, will He break His threat?'

Abu 'Amr said, 'You made a mistake from the lack of the knowledge of Arabic. Promise is other than threat; the Arabs do not consider shame or disgrace if you promise to do an evil deed and fail to carry it out, rather they consider it kindness and generosity. Disgrace is that you promise to do something good and fail to carry it out.

He demanded a support from the saying of the Arabs, and Abu 'Amr recited the following lines:

'My cousin is not scared of my attack as long as I live, and I am not scared of the assault of menacing person. When I make a promise or threat, I am going to break my threat and fulfil my promise.'

Yahay ibn Mu'adh said, 'Promise and threat are true. Promise is the right of the servants on Allah; He has guaranteed that if they do such and such deeds, He will give them such and such reward. Who is more prompt in fulfilling his promise than Allah? Threat is the right of Allah on the servants. He said: 'Do not do this or that, otherwise I will punish you. Now if He wishes, He will forgive and if He

---

424. Abu Ya'la (3316)

wishes, He will punish because it is His right. However, the most appropriate act for our Lord, the Blessed and the Most High, is to pardon and show kindness. He is indeed Most Forgiving, the Most Merciful.'

Ka'b ibn Zuhayr said when he learnt that the Messenger of Allah, blessing and peace of Allah be upon him, has threatened him, 'I am told that the Messenger of Allah has threatened me, but forgiveness with the Messenger of Allah is expected.'

This is what is the case in general threat, now consider the threat joined with His statement "Your Lord is going to do what He wishes." *(11: 107)*

The companions understood this verse properly and said, 'This verse has demolished every threat in the Qur'an. This rejoinder is like His saying, "They will abide in it forever except what Allah wills. Your Lord is surely All Wise, All Knowing." *(6: 128)*

The Almighty told that their punishment at all times or its removal as He wills is the result of His perfect knowledge and wisdom not from a will free from wisdom, mercy and justice. His will is never free from these qualities.

24. The side of mercy in this soon vanishing home is dominant on the side of punishment and anger. If it were not so, this world would have not remained and existed. Allah said, "If Allah took the people to task for the evil they do, He would not leave one living creature on earth." *(16: 61)*

"If Allah were to punish people for wrong they have done, there would not be a single creature left on the surface of the earth." *(35: 45)*

If it were not for the great mercy, pardon and forgiveness of Allah, this world would not have survived. This in spite of the fact that mercy He showed in this world is one part of the hundred parts of mercy. If the side of mercy is dominant in this world and encompasses every good and bad, believer and disbeliever despite the causes of punishment and the anger of Almighty, how this side will not be dominant in a world where its ninety-nine parts are found? Once the disbelievers were put in Hell and the torment took its course their souls were humbled and the punishment exhausted them and their filth and evil were dissolved, there remains no barrier between them and the mercy. The mercy covered them in the world despite the causes of punishment. So, now when the causes of anger and punishment are gone and the side of mercy became stronger in the other world, and any dirt that was found was eliminated, the mercy will show its impact on them.

The secret of the matter is that the names implying mercy, generosity are more dominant than the qualities of revenge, and the act of mercy is more than the act of revenge, and the effects of mercy are more evident than the effects of revenge. Mercy is more beloved to the Merciful than revenge, and it was by His mercy that He created the creatures. He created them to show His mercy to them. It is the mercy that has taken lead over His anger. He decreed it for Himself and made it encompass everything. It is sought for its sake whereas punishment is discipline and purification. Mercy is kindness, generosity and favour while punishment is treatment; mercy is gift and offer.

25. It is necessary that Allah, the Exalted, shows to all His creatures on the Day of Judgement the truth of His message and His messengers, and prove that His enemies were wrong and liars. He will demonstrate to the creatures that His judgment is the fairest judgement concerning His enemies. He passed His judgement about them in the way that they should praise Him. His judgment about His allies, His angels and His messengers is so fantastic that the universe will say 'praise belongs to Allah, the Lord of the universe.' Allah said it in His Book:

"True judgement has been passed between them, and it will be said, 'Praise is to Allah, the Lord of the worlds." *(39: 75)*

The speaker is not mentioned to make the statement general and to show that it will be on the tongue and heart of everyone.

Al-Hasan said, 'They enter the Fire and their hearts will be full of His praise as much as they can.'

It is the reason for omission of the subject of the verb in His statement:
"It is said: 'Enter the gates of Hell to abide in it forever." *(39: 72)*

It is to show that the whole universe says that because it is the just judgement about them and it is the result of His wisdom and praise. As for the people of Paradise Allah said, "Its keepers will say to them: 'Peace be upon you, you have been good. Enter it to live forever." *(39: 73)*

They did not deserve it by their deeds, but rather by His pardon, mercy and favour. Allah has made His angels and all His creatures witness of His just judgement and clear wisdom. He put the punishment where the reasons and the creature feel that it was the suitable place. It is the sign of His perfect praise, which is the requirement of His Names and Attributes, and the unjust evil souls deserved that punishment. They themselves admitted that they were entitled for it. This is how the wisdom was completed for which the evil and its motives were found in this world and the one to come. It is not in the Divine wisdom that evils should remain forever without end and limit, and so they and good deeds become equal in this respect.

This is the conclusion of the arguments of both groups on this issue. You may not find It In any other book. Now if someone asks: 'What is your opinion in this important matter, which is greater many times than the world?'

The answer will be that we stop at the statement of the Lord, the Most Blessed:

"Certainly, your Lord is going to do what He wishes." *(11: 107)*

This is where Ali ibn Abu Talib also stopped when he described the entrance of the people of Paradise in it and the entrance of the people of Hell into it and what both of them will face, he said: 'Then Allah will do what He wishes.'

It is also the conclusion of all the people. What we have said on this issue, and rather in the entire book, if it is right, then it is from Allah, the Exalted, and He is the One Who graciously guided to it; anything wrong is from me and from Satan. Allah and His Messenger are free from it. He is aware of the tongue and heart and intention of very person. Allah knows better

CHAPTER 68
THE LAST PERSON TO ENTER PARADISE

Abdullah ibn Mas'ud reported that the Messenger of Allah blessing and peace be upon him, said, "I know the last person to get out of Hell and the last person to enter Paradise. A man will come out of the Fire crawling, and Allah will say to him: 'Go and enter Paradise.' He will approach it and it will seem to him that it is full. He will return to Allah and say to Him: 'My Lord, I found it full.' Allah will say to him again: 'Go and enter Paradise.' He will go and it will seem to him to be full. He will return to Allah and say to Him: 'My Lord, I found it full.' Allah will say to him: 'Go and enter Paradise, you will have similar to the world and ten times more.' He will say: Do You joke with me and laugh at me and You are the King?'

Ibn Mas'ud said: 'I saw the Messenger of Allah laughing till his teeth were seen.' He said: "This will be the person of the lowest rank in Paradise." [425]

Abu Dharr reported that Allah's Messenger ﷺ, said, "I know the last person to enter Paradise and the last one to get out of Hell. A man will be brought on the Day of Judgement and it will be said: 'Present to him his minor sins and keep away from him the major ones.' His minor sins will be shown to him and said to him: 'You did so and so on such and such day. You did so and so on such and such day.' He will admit and say: 'Yes.' He cannot deny, and in the meantime he is scared of his major sins to be presented to him. Then it will be said to him: 'You have a good deed in place of every bad deed. He will say: 'My Lord, I committed some other offences which I do not see here."

I saw the Messenger of Allah laughed till his teeth were seen.'[426]

Abu Umamah reported that the Prophet ﷺ said, "The last person to enter Paradise will be a man turning upside down on the Bridge like a boy whom his father is beating and he is trying to escape from him. His deeds are unable to let him run. He will say: 'My Lord, take me to Paradise and save me from Hell.' Allah will say to

425. Bukhari (6571), Muslim (iman: 186)
426. Muslim (iman: 190)

him: 'My servant, if I rescue you from Hell and admit you into Paradise, will you confess your sins and mistakes?' He will say: 'Yes, by Your honour and power, if You save me from Hell I will confess my sins and faults.' He will cross the Bridge, and will say in his mind: 'If I confess my sins and mistakes, He will send me back to Hell.' Allah will say to him: 'My servant, confess your sins and mistakes, I will forgive them for you and admit you into Paradise.'

He will say: 'By Your might and power, I never committed a sin or made any mistake.'

Allah will say to him: 'I have witness against you.'

The man will look right and left and will not see anyone. So, he will say: 'My Lord, show me your witness.' Allah will give power to speak to his skin and it will mention the minor sins. When he sees it, he will say: 'My Lord, by Your might, I have greater sins.' Allah will say: 'I know them better than you. Confess them I will forgive them and admit you into Paradise.' The servant will confess his sins and will enter Paradise."

Then the Messenger of Allah peace be upon him, laughed till his teeth were seen. He said, "This is the man of the lowest rank, so what do you think of the one above him?"[427]

Abdullah ibn Mas'ud reported that Messenger of Allah, blessing and peace be upon him, said, "The last person to enter Paradise will be a man who will walk once on the Bridge, stumble once and the Fire will burn him once. When he gets past it, he will turn to it and say: 'Blessed is He who rescued me from you. Allah granted me something which He has not given to anyone from the first and last men.' A tree will be raised up for him and he will say: 'My Lord, bring me closer to that tree so that I might find shelter under its shade and drink of its water.' Allah, the Mighty and Sublime, will say to him: 'Son of Adam, if I give you that, you may ask Me for something else.'

He will say: 'No, my Lord.' He will promise that he will not ask Him for anything else. His Lord will excuse him because he saw something which he has no patience at it. He will bring him closer to it, and he will enjoy its shade and drink of its water.

427. Tabarani in Kabir (7669)

Then another tree will be raised for him much more beautiful that the first one. He will say: 'My Lord, bring me closer to this tree so that I may take shelter in its shade and drink of its water. I will not ask You for anything else.' Allah will say: 'Son of Adam, did you not make a promise to Me that you will not ask Me for anything else. If I take you closer to it, you may ask Me for something else.' He will promise that he will not ask for anything else. Allah knowing that he has seen something he cannot control himself from it will accept his excuse and take him closer to that tree. Then another tree will be raised up for him near the gate of Paradise more beautiful than the firs two. He will say: 'My Lord, take me closer to that tree so that I can take shelter in its shade and drink of its water. I will not ask You for anything else.' Allah will say: 'Son of Adam, didn't you promise that you will not ask Me for anything else?' He will say: 'Yes, my Lord. Give it to me and I will not ask You for anything more.' Allah, the Most High, will excuse him because he has seen something he cannot control himself from it. So, He will take him near it. When he draws near it he will hear the voices of the people of Paradise and say: 'My Lord, put me inside it.' Allah will say: 'Son of Adam, what is going to satisfy you?

Will you be satisfied if I give the world and as much again?' He will say: 'Do You joke with me and You are the Lord of the worlds?'

Ibn Mas'ud laughed at this point and said: 'Don't you ask me why I laughed?' They asked him why he laughed. He said that the Messenger of Allah laughed and he was asked why he laughed and he replied:

"Because Allah laughed when the man said; are You making fun of me and You are the Lord of the worlds? Allah will say: 'I am not making fun of you, but I have power to do any thing I wish.'"[428]

There is a similar report by Abu Sa'id al-Khudri at the end of which the Prophet ﷺ said, "When the man will enter Paradise, Allah will ask him to make wishes. He will make wishes and Allah will remind him to ask for this and that. When his wishes will end, Allah will say: 'You have all that and ten times as much.'

Then he will go to his home and his two wives from the Hur al-'in will come to him and say: 'Praise be to Allah Who brought you back to life for us and gave us

---

428. Muslim (iman: 187)

life for you.' He will say: 'No one has been given similar to what I have got.'"[429]

Al-Mughirah ibn Shu'bah narrated that the Prophet ﷺ said, "Moses asked his Lord: 'Who is the lowest among the people of Paradise in rank?' He said: 'A man who will come after the people of Paradise have entered it; he will be told to enter Paradise. He will say: 'My Lord, how can I go in when the people have taken their places and have taken what they have taken?' It will be said to him: 'Would it please you if you are given the like of what one of the kings of the world had?' He will say: 'I would be pleased, my Lord.' He will say: 'You will have that, and as much again, and as much again, and as much again and as much again.' The fifth time he will say: 'I am pleased, my Lord.' He will say: 'You will have that and ten times as much, and you will have what your heart desires, and what will delight your eyes'

He will say: 'I am pleased, my Lord.'

Moses said: 'Who will be the highest of them in status, my Lord?' Almighty said: 'They will the ones whom I have chosen, and I have planted their honour with My own hand. I have set a seal over it so that no eye has seen, no ear has heard, nor has it entered the heart of a man.'

The Prophet ﷺ said: The confirmation of it is in the Book of Allah, the Mighty and Sublime:
"No person knows what is kept hidden for them of joy as reward for what they used to do." *(32: 17)*

---

429. Ibid (iman: 188)

CHAPTER 69
A GENERAL CHAPTER CONTAINING VARIOUS ISSUES, WHICH HAVE NOT BEEN MENTIONED IN PREVIOUS CHAPTERS

1. The language of the people of Paradise

Anas ibn Malik reported that the Messenger of Allah, peace be upon him, said, "The people of Paradise will enter Paradise their height being sixty cubic. They will have the beauty of Joseph and the age of Jesus i.e. thirty-three years. They will speak the language of Muhammad peace be upon him, and be hairless, beardless and with eyed darkened with kohl."[430]

Ibn Abbas said:
'The language of the people of Paradise will be Arabic.'

The same is said by al-Zuhri as well.

2. The argument of Paradise and Hell

Abu Hurayrah reported that the Prophet ﷺ said, "Paradise and Hell argued and Hell said: 'Only arrogant and powerful people enter me.' Paradise will say: 'Only weak and poor are my share.'

Allah, the Mighty and Sublime, will say to Hell: 'You are my punishment I use you to punish whoever I wish, and said to Paradise: You are my mercy I show it to those whom I wish. Both of you are going to get full quota.'"

In another report it is:
"Hell and Paradise argued among themselves and Hell said: 'I have been reserved for arrogant and tyrant, and Paradise said: Why only weak, worthless and powerless enter me?' Allah Almighty will say to Paradise: 'You are my mercy, I

---

430. Ibn Abi al-Dunya

show it to whom I wish of My servants, and said to Hell: You are My punishment I use you to punish whom I wish. Both of you are going to have its full. Hell will not be filled until Allah will put His foot in it and it will say: 'enough, enough.' Only then it will be filled and its parts will come close to one another. Allah will not do injustice to any one. For Paradise He will create other people for it."[431]

3. Allah will create additional people for Paradise

There will remain space in Paradise to fill it Allah will create people but it will no be the case with Hell.

Anas reported the Prophet, peace be upon him, saying, "The evil people will be cast in Hell and it will say: 'Is there any more?' until the Lord of Power puts His foot in it. It will squeeze and its parts will come close to one another and it will say: 'enough, enough by Your might and power.' There will be space in Paradise and Allah will create some people and lodge them in it."[432]

4. The people of Paradise will not sleep

Jabir reported that the Messenger of Allah, peace be upon him, said, "Sleep is like death and the people of Paradise will not sleep."[433]

In another report of Jabir he said, "The Prophet ﷺ was asked: 'Will the people of Paradise sleep?' He replied, 'Sleep is like death, and the people of Paradise will not sleep.'"[434]

5. Raising the rank of the people of Paradise

A man in Paradise will be taken to a higher rank than the previous one.

Abu Hurayrah reported that the Messenger of Allah, peace be upon him, said, "Allah will raise the rank of a righteous servant, and he will ask: 'Why I got it, my Lord?' Allah will tell him: 'It is because of your son's prayer and seeking forgiveness

431. Bukhari (4850), Muslim (Jannah: 2846)
432. Bukhari (7384), Muslim (Jannah: 2848)
433. Abu Nu'aym (90)
434. Tabarani in al-awsat (923), al-Bazzar (3517)

for you." [435]

6. Joining of the members of the family together

The descendants of righteous persons will be joined with him even though they have not done like his deeds. Allah, the Exalted said:

"Those who believed and their descendants followed them in faith We will unite them with their descendants. We will not deny them any of the reward for their deed. Each person is retained with what he has earned." *(52: 21)*

Ibn Abbas reported that the Messenger of Allah, peace be upon him, said, "Allah will raise the offspring of a believer to his rank even if they have not done deeds like him in order to cause the delight of his eye. He then recited:

"Those who believed and their descendants followed them in faith, We will join them with their descendants and We will not deprive them of any of their deed." *(52: 21)*

He said, "Allah says: 'We do not reduce the reward of the fathers because of what We gave to the descendants." [436]

Ibn Abbas reported the Prophet ﷺ saying, "When a person enters Paradise he will ask about his parents, wife and children. He will be told that they did not reach his status. He will say: 'My Lord, I worked for myself and for them.' Then his family will be joined with him."

Ibn Abbas then recited the verse: "Those who believed." to the end.

The commentators have disagreed on the meaning of the word "Dhurriyah" (offspring) in the above verse. Does it apply to the young children or the grown ups or both?

Some commentators said that it refers to grown up and the meaning is that those who believed and their offspring followed them in faith and have belief like them; We will join them with their fathers in ranks. Allah, the Exalted has used the word "Dhurriyah" for the grown up in many places of His Book as He said, **"And**

435. Ahmad (10615)
436. Al-Bazzar (2260)

from his offspring were David and Suleiman." *(6: 84)*
"The offspring of those whom We carried with Nuh." *(17: 3)*

And we were only descendants who came after them. Will You destroy us because of the deeds of those who invented falsehood?" *(7: 173)*

The grown up intelligent people will say this.

This interpretation is supported by a report of Ibn Abbas that the Prophet ﷺ said, "The offspring of the believer will be raised to his status even if they were below him in deeds so that they have delight of their eyes."

This shows that they entered Paradise because of their good deeds but their deeds were not able to take them to the status of their fathers, but Allah brought them to the rank of their fathers even if their deeds were short of it.

The advocate of this opinion said:
Faith consists of speech, deed and intention; and this can be achieved by the grown up. The meaning of the verse in this case will be that Allah, the Magnificent, will join the descendants of the believer with him if they have faith like him. This is the reality of following. Even if they are below his faith, Allah will raise them to his status in order to cause them to be with him in status though they did not reach it by their deeds.

Another group of scholars said that offspring in the verse refers to the young children. The meaning will be 'those who believed and We made their offspring follow them in the faith of their fathers.'

The offspring follow the fathers in faith even if they are minor. The religious rule of inheritance, blood money, funeral prayer and burial in the grave yards of the Muslims apply to them except those areas which are applicable only to the grown ups.

They say that the validity of this statement is supported by the fact that the children who reach maturity are independent in the matters of reward and punishment. They are not linked with the fathers in any of the rules of the world nor the matters of reward and punishment. If the meaning was the mature children, it will lead to say that the mature children of the Companions will be in the status of their fathers, the children of the Followers will be in the status of their fathers and so on so forth; and it will mean that the later people will be in the status of the forerunners.

They also said that Allah Almighty made them subordinate to their fathers in rank as He made them subordinate in faith. If they were mature, their faith would not be dependent but it would be independent.

They further said:
Allah, the Exalted, fixed the ranks in Paradise in accordance with deeds in the case of independent people, but He will raise dependents to the rank of their families even if their deeds were less. The beautiful dark-eyed women and servants will be in the ranks of their families despite being short of deeds unlike the mature people who will be placed according to their deeds.

Some other people including al-Wahidi said that the right view is that the offspring should include both minor and mature because the mature will follow the father by his faith and the minor will follow the father by the faith of the father.

These people said that the offspring is spoken on minor and mature, one or more, and the son and the father. The following statement of Allah supports it:

"And another sign for them is that We carried their dhurriyyah in laden ship."
(36: 41)

Faith includes dependent one as well as acquired by free will. The example of the dependent faith is in the statement of Allah Almighty:
"Freeing of a believing slave." *(4: 92)*

If someone frees a minor, it will be all right.

They said that the statements of the early scholars indicate it. Ibn Abbas said, "Allah will raise the offspring of the believer to his rank even if they were below him in deeds in order to provide him with the delight of his eye." Then he recited this verse.

Ibn Mas'ud said, "A man will have precedence and he has offspring; he will go to Paradise and his offspring will be raised to him to make him happy even if they have not reached that rank."

Abu Mijlaz said, "Allah will put then together as the man loved to be together with them in the world."

Al-Kalbi reported the following saying of Ibn Abbas:
"If the fathers were in higher rank than the sons, Allah will raise the sons to their status, and if the sons were higher in ranks, Allah will raise the fathers to the tank of the sons."

Ibrahim said, "The descendants will be given like the reward of their fathers without their reward being reduced."

I say: The meaning of dhurriyyah in the verse as minor is more appropriate so that the forerunner and latecomer are not put on the same level. This will not happen in the case of the minor because the children and offspring of everyone will be with him in his status.

Allah knows the best.

7. Paradise speaks

The statement of the Prophet ﷺ that Paradise and Hell argued with one another has already been cited.

He, peace be upon him, also said, "Paradise said: 'My Lord, my rivers have been full and my fruits have become ready, hurry up with my people to me'"

Sa'id al-Ta'i said, "I am told that when Allah, the Exalted, created Paradise, He told it to adorn itself, and it did; then He told it to speak and it said: 'Blessed is he whom You are pleased with.'" [437]

Qatadah said, "When Allah created Paradise, He told it to speak and it said: 'Good news is for the righteous ones.'"

---

437. Abu Nu'aym (19)

Ibn Abbas reported that the Messenger of Allah, peace be upon him, said, "When Allah, the Exalted, created Paradise, He created in it that which no eye had ever seen, no ear had ever heard of and no heart had ever imagined. Then he told it to speak and it said: 'The believers have succeeded.'"[438]

8. The beauty of Paradise is constantly in increase.

Ka'b said, "Never Allah looked at Paradise but said: 'Be pleasant for your people', but it increased in its beauty until its people enter it."[439]

9. The love and affection of the beautiful women of Paradise to their husbands

The beautiful dark-eyed women are more fond of their husbands than their husband are for them

Mu'adh ibn Jabal reported the Prophet peace be upon him, saying, "The dark-eyed beautiful woman of Paradise says to the wife of the man who is going to enter Paradise: 'Do not misbehave with him; he is very soon going to leave you and join us.'"

'Ikrimah reported the Messenger of Allah, peace be upon him, saying, "The beautiful dark-eyed women of Paradise say: 'O Allah, help him to keep on Your religion and make his heart move to Your obedience.'"

Abu Sulayman al-Darani said, "A youth from Iraq was devoted to worship; he went out with a colleague to Makkah. Whenever they halted he started praying. When they eat he is fasting. His colleague was patient with him in journey going and coming back. When they came to part, he said: My brother, tell me what made you to do what you were doing?

He said, 'I saw in dream a palace in Paradise, one brick of it was of silver and another of gold. When its construction was complete one of balcony was of chrysolite and other of ruby and between them there was a beautiful dark-eyed

438. Ibid (21)
439. Ibid (21)

damsel hanging her hair, she has a dress of silver, which bent whenever she bent. She said, 'Exert yourself to Allah in my search. I by Allah, put my strength in her search.' What you saw was that attempt."

Abu Sulayman said, "This is what he did in search of a beautiful dark-eyed damsel. What do you think of a person who is after what is more than that?"

10. The slaughter of death between Paradise and Hell

Allah, the Glorious, said, "Warn them of the Day of Remorse, when the matter will be concluded, for they are in the condition of heedlessness and they do not believe." (19: 39)

Abu Sa'id al-Khudri reported that the Messenger of Allah, peace be upon him, said, "Death will be brought as though it is a beautiful sheep, it will be placed between Paradise and Hell and it will be said: People of Paradise, do you recognize this? They will stretch their necks and see and say: 'Yes, it is death.' Then it will be said to the people of Hell: 'People of Hell, do you recognize this? They will stretch their necks to look and say: 'Yes, it is death.' Then it will be ordered and it will be slaughtered. Then it will be said: 'People of Paradise, there is eternity without death, and people of Hell, there is eternity without death.'"

Then the Prophet recited, "Warn them of the Day of Remorse, when the matter will be decided, for they are heedless and they do not believe."

Ibn 'Umar reported that the Messenger of Allah, peace be upon him, said, "The people of Paradise will enter Paradise and the people of Hell will enter Hell, then a caller will call: 'The people of Paradise eternity and no death, and people of Hell, eternity and no death. Every one will remain forever in what he is.'"

Ibn 'Umar also reported that the Messenger of Allah, peace be upon him, said, "When the people of Paradise will go to paradise and the people of Hell to Hell, death will be brought and placed between Hell and Paradise. Then a caller will call: 'People of Paradise, there is no death; and people of Hell, there is no death.' The people of Paradise will feel happier and the people of Hell's grief will increase."[440]

---

440. Bukhari (6548), Muslim (jannah: 2850)

Abu Hurayrah reported that the Messenger of Allah, peace be upon him, said, "When the people of Paradise will enter Paradise and the people of Hell into Hell, death will be brought and will be placed on the barrier between the people of Paradise and the people of Hell, then it will be said: 'People of Paradise! They will appear being scared. Then it will be said: 'People of Hell! They will show up being happy expecting intercession. Both, the people of Paradise and the people of Hell will be asked: 'Do you know this? Both will reply: 'We know it; it is death which was assigned to us.' Then it will be laid down and slaughtered on the barrier. Then it will be announced: 'People of Paradise, it is eternity and no death; people of Hell, it is eternity and no death.'"[441]

The description of death in the form of sheep, laying it down, slaughtering and watching of two parties is reality not imagination or illustration as some people considered it wrongly. They said: 'Death is accidental, and accidental matters cannot take a form let alone to be slaughtered.' It is a wrong statement. Allah Almighty will create death in the form of a sheep as He will create deeds in the forms being seen and to reward or punish on them. Allah, the Exalted, will change accidental matters into bodies and can change bodies into accident as He can make from accidents other accidents and from bodies other bodies. All these four categories are possible and under the power of Allah, the Glorious. It does not mean combining two opposite things or any impossibility. There is no need to say that the slaughtering is for the angel of death. These are all false assumptions about Allah and His Messenger, and are invalid explanation not required by reason or revelation. It is the result of lack of understanding the objective of the words of the Messenger, peace be upon him.

This person thought that the words of the Hadith imply that it will be accidental matter that will be slaughtered. Another mistaken person thought that the accidental matter will be annihilated and it will take the shape of a body which will be killed.

Both groups did not realize what we have said and that Allah Almighty creates from accidental matters bodies and makes them substance of them. It is reported in an authentic narration that al-Baqarah and Al-'Imran (Ch 2 & 3) will come on the Day of Judgement as though they are two clouds.[442]

441. Tirmidhi (2557)
442. Muslim (salat al-musafirin: 804)

The Prophet said in another Hadith, "What you say concerning the glorification of Allah and His praise and exaltation will come together around the Throne and they have reverberation like the humming of the bees. They remember their speakers."[443]

The same is the case in the Prophet's statement in the Hadith of the punishment of the grave and pleasure of it when he said that the person will see an image and ask: 'Who are you?' It will reply that I am your good or bad deed.' It is a reality not imagination. Allah Almighty will create from his deed a beautiful or ugly form. The light which He will distribute among the believers is nothing but their faith which Allah, the Exalted, will convert into light, which will be moving in front of them. This is an understandable matter even if there was no text to say it. When the statement came it is in agreement with reason.

Qatadah said, "We learnt that the Prophet ﷺ said, 'When a believer comes out of his grave, his deeds will be presented to him in a beautiful shape and good sign. He will ask it: 'Who are you? By Allah, I notice you to be a true person.' It will say: 'I am your deeds.' It will be a light to him and lead him to Paradise. On the other hand when a disbeliever comes out of his grave, his deeds will be presented to him in an ugly image and bad sign. He will ask: 'Who are you? I see you a bad person.' It will reply: 'I am your deeds', and it will take him to Hell.'"

Ibn Jurayj said, "His deeds will be put in a beautiful shape with pleasant fragrance; it will meet the person and give good tiding. He will ask: 'Who are you?' It will reply: 'I am your deed', and it will turn into a light before him and take him to Paradise. This is what Allah said, "Their Lord will guide them because of their faith." (10: 9) As for the disbeliever his deed will be presented to him in an ugly shape and bad smell, and will remain with the person till he ends up in the Hellfire."

Hasan recited the following verse, **"Are we never to die again after our earlier death and we will not be punished?"** (37: 58-59)

Then he said, "They knew that every pleasure which is followed by death will be suspended, so they said it. They will be told: No. Then they will say that it is the great success."

---

443. Ahmad (18390)

Yazid al-Raqashi said, "The people of Paradise were safe from death, so life became pleasant for them; they were safe from illnesses so it was delightful for them."

He used to speak and cry till his tears flow on his beard.

11. Suspension of the acts of worship in Paradise

Acts of worship will be suspended in Paradise except the remembrance of Allah, which will continue.

Jabir reported that the Prophet ﷺ said, "The people of Paradise will eat and drink, and they will not blow their noses, or relieve nature or urinate. Their food will be digested in the form of belching and sweating like the fragrance of musk. They will be inspired glorification and praise as you are given breaths."[444]

12. The talk of the people of Paradise among them

The people of Paradise will discuss what they had in the world.

Allah, the Exalted, said, **"They will turn to one another with questions: one will say, 'I had a close companion (on earth).'"** *(37: 50-51)*

"They turn to one another and say: 'When we were still with our families (on earth) we used to live in fear but Allah has been gracious to us and saved us from the torment of intense heat." *(52: 25-270)*

Anas reported the Prophet ﷺ saying, "When the people of Paradise settle in it, they will yearn for their friends one another. The couch of one will move to the other and vice versa till they meet and lean against their couches. One of them will say to the other: 'Do you remember when Allah forgave us?' He will say: 'Yes, on such and such day in such and such place, when we asked Allah to forgive us, and He forgave us.'"

When they discuss what was there in the world between them, they will also discuss the issues of knowledge, understanding of the Qur'an and the Sunnah

---

444. Muslim (jannah: 2835)

and its authenticity, which used to cause problems for them. This kind of discussion in the world was more delicious than food, drink and intercourse; now in Paradise it will be more delicious. This delight will be especially achieved only by the people of knowledge.

CHAPTER SEVENTY
WHO EXCLUSIVELY DESERVES THIS GOOD TIDING?

Allah, the Glorious, said, **"Give those who believe and do good deeds the news that they will have Gardens beneath which streams will flow. Whenever they are given sustenance from the fruits, they will say, 'We have been given this before."** *(2: 25)*

"For the allies of Allah there will be no fear nor shall they grieve; they are those who believe and are conscious of Allah. For them there is good news in this life and in the Hereafter. There is no changing of the word of Allah. That is truly the supreme triumph." *(10: 62-63)*

"Surely those who say, 'Our Lord is Allah', and take the straight path towards Him, the angels will come down to them and say, 'Have no fear or grief, but rejoice in the good news of Paradise, which you have been promised." *(41: 30)*

Give good news to My servants who listen to what is said and follow what is best in it. These are the ones Allah has guided; these are the people of understanding." *(39:17-18)*

"Those who believe, migrated and strove hard in Allah's way with their possessions and their persons are with Allah on a higher rank; it is they who will triumph. Their Lord gives them the good news of His mercy and pleasure, Gardens where they will have lasting bliss and where they will remain forever. Truly, there is a tremendous reward with Allah." *(9: 21-22)*

"Those who believe and do good deeds will be in the lush meadows of the Gardens. They will have whatever they wish from their Lord. This is the great bounty. It is that of which Allah gives good tidings to His servants who believe and do righteous deeds." *(42: 22-23)*

"You can warn only the one who follows the Remembrance and holds the

Merciful One in awe, though he cannot see Him. Give such people the glad news of forgiveness and a noble reward." *(36: 11)*

"O Prophet, We have sent you as a witness and a bearer of good tiding and a warner, and one who invites to Allah, by His permission, and an illuminating lamp. Give good tiding to the believers that they will have from Allah great bounty." *(33: 45-47)*

"Never think of those who have been killed in the cause of Allah as dead. They are alive with their Lord, receiving provision, rejoicing in what Allah has bestowed upon them of His bounty, and they receive good tidings about those after them, who have not yet joined them, that there will be no fear for them, nor will they grieve. They rejoice the blessing and favour from Allah and that Allah does not allow the reward of believers to be lost." *(3:169-171)*

"Allah has purchased the persons and possessions of the believers in return for the Garden. They fight in Allah's cause: they kill and are killed. This is a true promise given by Him in the Torah, the Gospel, and the Qur'an. Who could be more faithful to his promise than Allah? So be happy with the bargain you have made. That is the supreme triumph." *(9: 111)*

"We shall certainly test you with fear and hunger, and loss of property, lives, and crops. But give good tiding to those who are steadfast, those who say, when afflicted with a calamity, 'We belong to Allah and to Him we shall return.' These will be given blessings and mercy from their Lord and it is they who are rightly guided." *(2: 155-157)*

"And He will give other things that will please you: His help and an imminent conquest." *(61; 13)*

He, the Exalted, said about Paradise:
"It is prepared for the righteous ones." *(3: 133)*

"It is prepared for those who believe in Allah and His Messengers." *(57: 21)*

"Those who believe and do good deeds will be given the Gardens of Paradise as lodging." *(18: 107)*

He also said, "The faithful have succeeded" to His statement: "They are the inheritors who will inherit the highest part of Paradise to live there eternally." *(23: 1-11)*[445]

It is reported that the Prophet ﷺ said, "Ten verses have been revealed to me; whoever follows them will enter Paradise."

Then he recited: "The faithful have succeeded," until he completed the ten verses.
[446]

Allah, the Exalted, also said, **"For men and women who are devoted to Allah - believing men and women, obedient men and women, truthful men and women, steadfast men and women, humble men and women, charitable men and women, fasting men and women, chaste men and women who guard their private parts, and men and women who remember Allah often - Allah has prepared for them forgiveness and a rich reward."** *(33: 35)*

"This is the Garden We shall give as inheritance to those of Our servants who are devout." *(19: 63)*

"Hurry towards your Lord's forgiveness and a Garden as wide as the heavens and earth prepared for the righteous, who give, both in prosperity and adversity, who restrain their anger and pardon people - Allah loves those who do good -those who remember Allah and implore forgiveness for their sins if they do something shameful or wrong themselves - who forgives sins but Allah? And who never knowingly persist in doing wrong. The reward for such people is forgiveness from their Lord, the Gardens below which streams flow, where they will remain. How excellent is the reward of those who work rightly!" *(3:133-136)*

"You who believe, shall I show you a bargain that will save you from painful torment? Have faith in Allah and His Messenger and struggle for His cause

---

445. *The full text is as follows:*
"The faithful have succeeded: those who pray humbly, who shun frivolity, who pay the prescribed alms, who guard their chastity except with their spouses or their slaves – with these they are not to blame, but those who seek beyond this are exceeding the limits – those who are faithful to their trusts and pledges and who keep up their prayers; they are given Paradise as their own to remain there."

446. *Ahmad (223)*

with your possessions and your persons - that is better for you, if only you knew. He will forgive your sins; admit you into Gardens below which rivers flow, into pleasant dwellings in the Gardens of Eternity. This is the supreme triumph." *(61: 10-12)*

"For those who fear standing before their Lord there are two gardens." *(55: 46)*

"As for the one who feared standing before his Lord and prevented the soul from base desires, Paradise will be his home." *(79: 40-41)*

These types of statements are many in the Qur'an. They are based on three principles: faith, consciousness of Allah and deeds sincerely done for the sake of Allah in accordance with the Sunnah. Those who stick to these principles are the ones for whom this good tiding is given not others. On these principles revolve all the good news of the Qur'an and the Sunnah. They are found in two basic things: Sincerity in obedience of Allah and being kind to His creature. Their opposite is found in those who show off and withhold simple things. All the good qualities return to one and that is to follow the deeds which Allah loves and that could only be achieved by taking the Messenger of Allah, peace be upon him, as model openly and secretly.

The deeds are the details of this principle, and they include seventy plus branches the highest of them is saying 'there is no god but Allah', and the lowest one is to remove hurtful materials from the path. Between these two there are other branches all of which revolve on accepting what the Messenger has brought and following him in all that he has commanded. It is either obligatory or recommended, and it includes the belief in the Names and Attributes, as acts and sigs of Allah without giving a distorted meaning to them. They should not be rendered futile or given the meaning of description or illustration. Imam al-Shafi'i said: 'Praise belongs to Allah as He has described Himself and above what His creature describes Him.' He seems to have taken it from the following statement of the Prophet, peace be upon him, "O Allah, for you is praise as You say and better than we say."

We have cited in the beginning of the book the statements of the followers of the Sunnah and Hadith on which they have agreed and as al-Ash'ari recorded. Now we relate their consensus as reported by Harb, the colleague of Imam Ahmad in his own words. He said in his famous 'masa'il':

The beliefs of the people of the Sunnah

These are the views of the people of knowledge, scholars of tradition and the followers of the Sunnah who are followed from the generation of the Companions of the Prophet peace be upon him, to this day. I found the scholars of the Hejaz, Syria and others holding them. Anyone who goes against these views or criticises them or denounces those who pronounce them is an innovator, out of the group and away from the way of the Sunnah and right path.

He further said:
This is the opinion of Ahmad, Ishaq ibn Ibrahim, Abdullah ibn Makhlad, Abdullah ibn al-Zubayr al-Humaydi, Sa'id ibn Mansur and others with whom we sat and from whom we received the knowledge. They said:
Belief consists of statement, action, intention and following the Sunnah.

Faith increases and decreases. Exception is allowed in faith unless it is based on doubt. When a man was asked: 'Are you believer?' He would say: 'I am believer if Allah wills or I hope I am believer'

He says: I believed in Allah, His angels, His Books and His messengers. Anyone who claims that faith is without action, he is murji'i; anyone who says that faith is statement and the deeds are part of Shari'ah he is murji'i. Whoever says that faith increases but does not decrease, he is following the view of the Murji'ah. The one who does not accept exception in faith he is Murji'i. Anyone who says that his faith is like the faith of Gabriel and the angels, he is a Murji'i, the same is the man who says that knowledge is in the heart even if the person does not speak of it. The decree bad or good, small or big, open or secret, sweet or sour, loved or hated, good or bad, the first and the last - all come from Allah, the Most High, which He has decreed on His servants.

He has fixed His decree for them and no one can go beyond the will of Allah. His decree will not miss them; all of them are moving towards what He created them for, and are subject of what He has decreed for them. In all what He decreed, our Lord, the Glorious, is just. Adultery, theft, drinking wine, killing a person, eating the prohibited wealth, association of partners with Him and all kinds of sins are by the decree of Allah Almighty without there being any excuse before Allah for any creature. The conclusive argument against His creature belongs to Him; He will not be asked about what He does and they will be questioned.

The Knowledge of Allah covers His creature by His will. He, the Exalted, has knowledge of the Devil and all those who disobeyed Him from the time He created the world to the time of the coming of the Hour, and for it He created them. On the other hand He knew the obedience of those who obeyed Him and He created them for it. Every one works for what he has been created, and moving to what Allah has decreed for him, none of them can overstep His decree and will. Allah does what He wills. Anyone who claims that Allah willed for those of His servants who disobeyed Him and showed arrogance, good and obedience and it were the servants who willed for themselves evil and disobedience and acted upon it, he claims that the will of the servants overpowered the will of Allah. What a bigger falsity against Allah than this? Anyone who claims that adultery is not predestined, he will be asked: 'what do say about a woman who conceived by adultery and gave birth to a child, did Allah will to create this child? Was it in His previous knowledge?' If he says, 'no', then he is saying that there is another creator beside Allah, and this is open association of partner with Allah. Whoever says that theft, drinking wine, eating prohibited wealth is not because of decree and predestined, he is saying that a man has power to eat the provision of others; and it is the clear statement of Majians. As a matter of fact, he ate his provision which Allah decided for him to eat in that way. If someone says that killing a soul is not predestined by Allah Almighty, he is saying that the diseased died against his decreed time. Is there any disbelief clearer than this? It was by the decree of Allah, the Exalted, and it was His just act for His creature, and by His decision according to His previous knowledge. He is Just and True and does what He wills.

Anyone who acknowledges the knowledge has to acknowledge the decree and will on small and little things. We do not claim for any one of the people of the Qiblah (i.e. Muslim) that he will go to Hell for an offence he made or a major sin he committed unless there is a Hadith in this regard. In the same way we do not say about anyone that he is going to Paradise because of his righteous deeds unless there is a Hadith regarding it. Caliphate is the right of Quraysh as long as there are two members of that tribe. No one has right to contest them. We will not rebel against them and will not accept the authority of others till the Day of Judgement.

Jihad, struggle for the cause of Allah, will continue with the rulers whether they are righteous or evil; the injustice of an unjust or the justice of a just will not cancel it. Friday prayer as well as two 'Ids and pilgrimage will be performed with the rulers even if they are not pious, just and righteous. Payment of charity, land tax, tenth and booty is in the hands of the rulers whether they deal with it fairly or unjustly. The obedience is for the one whom Allah has appointed over you, no one has right to disobey him and use sword against him until Allah makes a way out for you. You are not allowed to rebel against the ruler but to listen and obey and not to break the pledge. Anyone who does it is an innovator and out of the community. However, if the ruler orders you to do something which involves the disobedience of Allah, you have right to disobey him. Even in this case you are no to rebel against him and refuse to pay his due. Keeping away during the sedition is a continuous way which should be respected. If you happen to be trapped then offer your soul and not your religion. Do not give support in civil strife by hand or by tongue, control your hand and tongue. Allah is the helper.

You should refrain from passing remarks on any Muslim. Do not declare anyone as disbeliever for a sin he committed and do not declare him out of Islam for any deed unless there is a Hadith concerning it. What is reported, you accept it and believe in it as is reported. For example a person who regards abandoning prayer and drinking wine or similar offences as lawful, or invents an act which is considered to be disbelief and renouncing Islam, you may declare him a disbeliever. Do not go beyond that.

The one-eyed anti Christ is going to appear, there is no doubt about it; he is the biggest liar. The Punishment of the grave is real; in it a person will be asked about his religion, his Lord, Paradise and Hell. Munkar and Nakir are valid; they are the tempters of the grave. We seek Allah to keep us firm. The pool of Muhammad, peace be upon him, is true, which his Community will come to it to drink its water with special vessels. The Bridge is true, which will be placed on Hell and people will cross it to Paradise after it. The balance is true in which the good and bad deeds will be weighed as Allah wishes. The horn is true; Israfil will blow it and all the people will die, then he will blow it again and they will stand before the Lord of the worlds for accounting. There the judgement will be passed, reward and punishment will be decided and consequently Paradise or Hell will be the resort. The deeds of the people will be noted from the Preserved Tablet as Allah had fixed the decree and fate. The pen is true; with it Allah has written and recorded the destiny of every thing. Intercession on the Day of Judgement is true. Some people will intercede for others and they will not go to Hell. Some other people will get out of Hell after they enter it and stayed for as long as Allah willed. There will be others who will remain in Hell forever; they are the people who committed association of partners with Allah, denied His message and disbelieved in Allah, the Glorious.

Death will be slaughtered on the Day of Resurrection between Paradise and Hell. Paradise and what is in it has been created and so has Hell and what is in it, they will not finish or things which are in them. Allah has created people for both of them. If an innovator or heretic argues that Allah said: "Every thing will perish except for His Face" or similar ambiguous verses of the Qur'an, it will be said to him: 'Everything for which Allah has written to perish will perish, He has created Paradise and Hell for existence not for annihilation. They are in the Hereafter not in the world. The beautiful dark-eyed women will not pass away at the time of the happening of the Hour even at the time of the blowing of the Horn because Allah has created them to remain not to perish. He has not written death for them. Any one who says against it is an innovator who has lost the right path.

Allah Almighty created seven skies one above the other, and seven earths one below the other. The distance between the highest earth and the lowest sky is the distance of five hundred years and between every sky and the next one is the distance of five hundred years. The water is above the seventh highest sky, the Throne of the Merciful is above the water and Allah, the Most High and Powerful, is on the Throne, and the Chair is under His feet. He has knowledge of what is in the heavens and the earth and what is between them and below the ground. He knows what is in the depth of the sea, and the root of every hair and tree, plant, the place of the falling leaf, the number of every word, sand, pebble dust, the weight of the mountains and the deeds of the people, their talks and breathes. He also knows every thing nothing is hidden from Him. He is on the Throne over the seventh sky before Him are curtains of fire, light darkness and what He only knows.

If an innovator argues on the basis of the statement of Allah Almighty: "We are closer to him than his jugular vein" and His saying: "There is no private conversation between three but He is the fourth of them, nor are there five but He is the sixth of them, and no less than that and no more than that but He is with them wherever they are." *(58: 7)*

or similar ambiguous verses tell him that Allah Almighty is on the Throne above the seventh sky but He knows every thing. He is separate from His creature; nothing is out of His knowledge. Allah has the Throne, which is borne by the angels. Allah is established on His Throne, which has no limit.

Allah, the Great and Sublime, is All-Hearing without doubt, All-Seeing without suspicion, All-Knowing without being unaware, Generous not being stingy, Clement without being in haste, Guarding who does not forget or be distracted, Close without being unmindful. He speaks, sees, laughs, is happy, loves, hates and dislikes, is pleased and gets angry, is displeased and shows mercy, pardons and forgives and gives and withholds. He descends every night to the lowest heaven the way He wishes. There is nothing similar to Him and He is All-Hearing, All-Seeing. The hearts of the people are between two fingers of the Merciful, He turns them the way He wishes and puts in them what He wants. He created Adam on His image by His hand. The heavens and the earth will be in His hand on the Day of Resurrection. He will put His foot in Hell and it will shrink. He will bring out some people from Hell by His hand. The People of Paradise will look at His Face. They will see Him and He will honour them and reveal Himself to them. The people will be presented to Him, and He will undertake their accounting by Himself, and will not give the responsibility to anyone else. The Qur'an is the speech of Allah spoken by Him, it is not created. Anyone who says the Qur'an is created is a Jahmi disbeliever. Whoever said that the Qur'an was the word of Allah then stopped and did not say that was not created he is worse than the first group. Anyone who says that our words and our recitation are created and the Qur'an is the speech of Allah he is Jahmi.

Allah spoke to Moses directly and handed him the Torah by His hand to his hand. Allah has always been speaker. Dream is from Allah and it is true. When a person saw a dream and was not confused and told it to a learned person exactly what he saw and the learned man interpreted it correctly without distorting, his interpretation is true. Dreams of the prophets were a kind of revelation. There is no bigger ignorant than the one who raises question about dreams and claims that they are nothing. I am told that the person who said it also said that taking bath after wet dream is not necessary. It is reported from the Prophet ﷺ that he said:

"The dream of a believer is speech through which the Lord speaks to His servant."[447]

He also said, "Dream is from Allah."[448]

It is required that the good deeds of the Companions of the Messenger of Allah, peace be upon him, be mentioned and the disputes which occurred among them are not to be discussed. Anyone who abuses the Companions of the Messenger of Allah, peace be upon him, or any one of them or shows prejudice against him, or criticises him, or exposes his fault or accuses him, is an innovator and wicked Rafidi. Allah will not accept any obligatory or voluntary act of him. To love the Companions is Sunnah, to pray for them is a good deed, to follow them is a means of coming close to Allah, and to learn their way is an excellence.

The best of the Community after the Prophet, peace be upon him, is Abu Bakr and after him is 'Umar and after 'Umar is 'Uthman and after him Ali. Some people stop at Ali. These four are the rightly guided caliphs. The rest of the Companions after them are the best of the people. Nobody is allowed to mention their faults or criticise them for any shortcoming. If someone does it, then the ruler has a duty to chastise him and punish him. He should not forgive him but punish him and ask him to repent; if he repents, it will be alright, but if he refuses, he should be punished again and put in prison until his death or until he repents.

We acknowledge their right, merit and superiority in the religion. We love them for the saying of the Messenger of Allah, peace be upon him:
"The love of the Companions is faith and hatred of them is hypocrisy."[449]

We do not follow the lowly anti Arab people who do not love the Arabs and do not acknowledge their excellence. Their view is innovation.

Anyone who prohibited earning, trading and acquiring wealth from its proper way is an ignorant and mistaken. Earning money from its right way is permissible; Allah and His Messenger have allowed it. A man is required to struggle to provide himself and his family from the bounty of Allah. If he abandons it saying that he does not consider earning right, he is going against the religious teaching.

447. *Tabarani (25: 338) Ahmad (5:325)*
448. *Bukhari (5747), Muslim (Ru'ya:2261)*
449. *Hakim (4: 87)*

The religion is based on the Book of Allah, the Sublime, and authentic reports and narrations through reliable channels, which support one another till it reaches the Messenger of Allah, peace be upon him. It is also accepted if it goes to the Companions, the Followers, their Followers and the leaders who came after them. They are to be followed if they adhere to the Sunnah and follow the reports, and are not known with any innovation or accused of telling lie or involved in any dispute.

These are the statements that are attributed to the followers of the Sunnah and Jama'ah, those who follow the reports and are involved in carrying the knowledge. We met them and learnt Hadith from them and acquired the Sunnah through them. They were well-known scholars, reliable, truthful and trustworthy to be followed and to be taken as teachers. They did not get involved in innovation or false dispute and creating confusion. They learnt these matters from their leaders and acquired them from scholars who were before them.

I say: Harb whose statement has been cited at length is a disciple of Ahmad and Ishaq. He has reported important statements from both of them. He also learnt from Sa'id ibn Mansur, Abdullah ibn al-Zubayr al-Humaydi and their colleagues. He affirmed that these opinions are agreed among them. Whoever looks carefully what has been said by the leaders of the Sunnah and Hadith, he will find it in full agreement to what Harb has reported. If we try to quote them, it will be more than this book. I have collected some of their statements especially about the exaltedness of Allah over His creature and His position on the Throne, and it came in a medium size book.

In short, what has been said is the view of those who deserve the good tiding by their statement, deeds and belief. Allah is the Helper.

CONCLUSION

We conclude the book with what we started it and it is the conclusion of the last part of the prayer of the people of Paradise. Allah, the Exalted, said, "Those who believe and do good deeds, their Lord will guide them because of their faith. Streams will flow at their feet in the Garden of Bliss. Their prayer in them will be, 'Glory be to You, O Allah!' and their greeting, 'Peace,' and the last part of their prayer, 'Praise be to Allah, the Lord of the Worlds.'" *(10: 9-10)*

Ibn Jurayj said regarding their saying: 'Glory be to You, O Allah!' that when a bird passes by them, which they would like to have, they will say, 'Glory be to You, O Allah', and the angel will bring to them what they desired. He will greet them and they will answer. This is what Allah said: 'Their greeting in them will be, 'Peace.' When they finish eating they praise their Lord and this is what Allah described, "The last part of their prayer is 'Praise be to Allah, the Lord of the World."

Sufyan al-Thawri said, "When they want something, they say: 'Glory be to You, O Allah!', and that thing will be given to them. The meaning of this phrase is to declare the glory, greatness and exaltation of the Lord from what is not suitable for Him."

Talhah ibn Ubaydullah reported:
"I asked the Messenger of Allah, blessing and peace of Allah be upon him, the meaning of 'glory be to Allah', and he said, 'It means to declare Allah to be above any defect.'"

A similar report has come down from Talhah ibn 'Ubaydullah.

Allah, the Glorious, told us about their first prayer; when they needed anything they said, 'Glory be to Allah', and their last prayer when they get that thing; which is 'Praise be to Allah, the Lord of the worlds.'

The meaning of the verse is more comprehensive than this prayer. Prayer Is used to praise and it is used for asking. In a Hadith it is said:
"The best prayer is 'praise be to Allah, the Lord of the worlds."

383

It is a prayer and praise that Allah Almighty will inspire the people of Paradise. He told us that the beginning is glorification and the end is praise, they will be inspired as they will be inspired breathing.

This shows that the duties will be removed in Paradise and no more worship will be required except this prayer. The word 'O Allah' indicates pure prayer. The phrase contains asking and praising and this is what was understood by the person who said 'when they wanted something they would say, 'glory be to You, O Allah.' They mentioned some meaning and did not tell the whole. Their statement gives impression that they will say it when they need something. The verse does not indicate that, but rather says that their first prayer will be glorification and the last will be praise. The Hadith has indicated that they will be inspired saying this as they are inspired breathing. So the prayer is not restricted with the need of something. It is not proper to the meaning of the verse as it is not proper to their situation.

Allah knows the right meaning.